UDDERLY ART 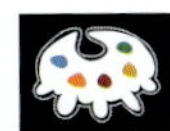 COLOURFUL COWS FOR CALGARY

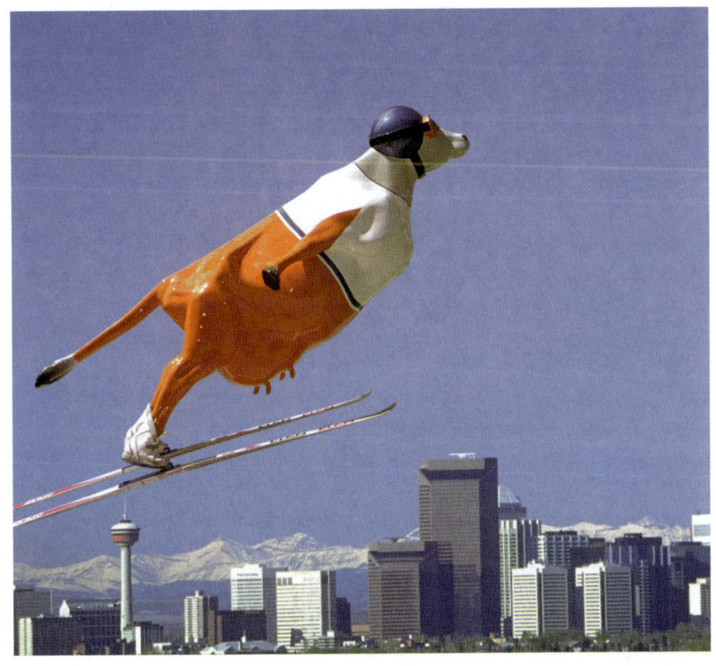

Tom Keyser

Photography by Clayton B. Kaplar

Johnson Gorman Publishers

THE PUBLISHERS
Johnson Gorman Publishers

CREDITS
Design by Boldface Technologies Inc.
Cover photo, background skyline of Calgary courtesy of Larry MacDougal Photography
Cover photo, foreground courtesy of Clayton B. Kaplar
Printed and bound in Canada by Friesens for Johnson Gorman Publishers

ACKNOWLEDGEMENTS
Financial support provided by the Alberta Foundation for the Arts,
a beneficiary of the Lottery Fund of the Government of Alberta.

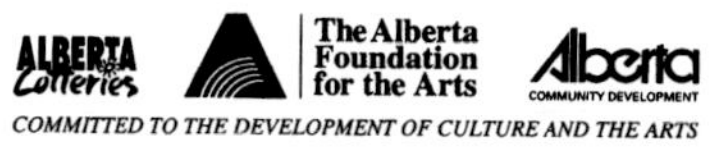

Canadian Cataloguing in Publication Data
Keyser, Tom, 1948–
Udderly art
ISBN 0-921835-55-8
1. Street art—Alberta—Calgary. I. Title.
ND2643.C3K49 2000   751.7'3'09712338   C00-911105-0

5 4 3 2 1

Contents

Introduction

The Herd Guide

* Denotes Maverick – first 20 buyers

The Herd Guide

* Denotes Maverick – first 20 buyers

Introduction

The friendly cow all red and white,
I love with all my heart;
She gives me cream with all her might,
To eat with apple tart.

Robert Louis Stevenson [1885]

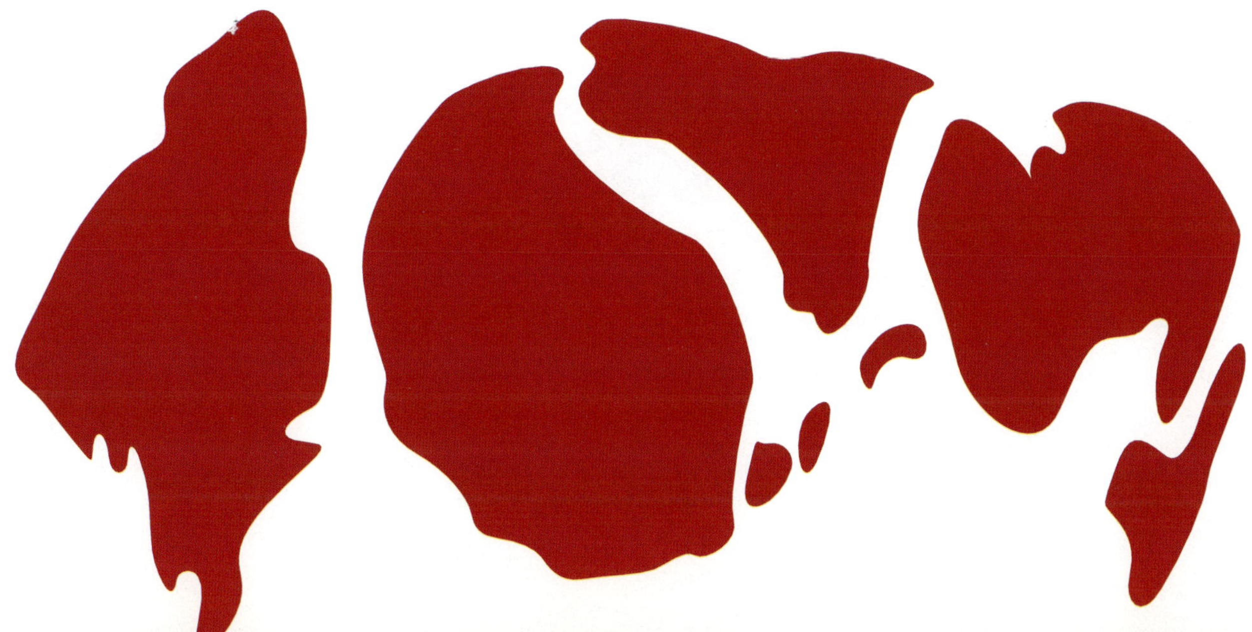

ARTISTS STAMPEDE HERD OF WILD COWS THROUGH CALGARY STREETS

Veterinarians Dumbfounded

CITIZENS AMAZED

Tourists Appreciative

Charities Thankful

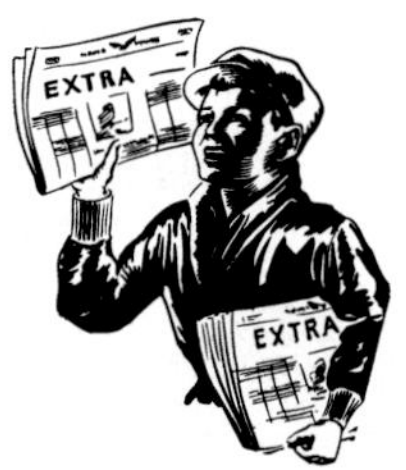

COWGARY, AB—The symbolism was poetic and potent. Perfection itself. This would be a matchmaker's dream: a dazzling technicolour harem of more than 120 bovine sirens to dress up a proud Canadian Cowtown.

Late in 1999 word began to slip out. A volunteer brigade of energetic, charity-minded, pun-loving art fanciers had sounded a cow . . . er . . . a call to arms.

Known collectively as Udderly Art Inc., this group of urban, public-art guerillas planned to create a diverse and strikingly decorated cattle herd to grace the parks, sidewalks, plazas and even lagoons of Calgary, long the undisputed buckle of the Beef Belt. From the concrete canyons to the rolling ranchlands west of Priddis, from the suburbs to the pastured hillocks near Cochrane, old hands and city slickers alike nodded with approval.

About time, they agreed. At last the noble bovine breeds of Southern Alberta were to receive their due and become immortalized in art. Udderly Art's posse of cultural wranglers was out to lasso the finest artists in Southern Alberta. The plan was to remove art from airless galleries, take art to the streets and demonstrate how much unpretentious fun it can be to soak up the pure pleasures induced by genuine works of art. And in this case, the medium really was the message. With fibreglass cows standing in as compliant canvases, any intimidation factor was neutralized.

Citizens at large would be free to roam the herd without feeling ever so slightly . . . well . . . cowed. Locals and tourists alike would learn for themselves that art can be both exceedingly fine and exhilaratingly fun. In the familiar, informal setting of city byways, strollers would be free to chat about it, smile at it, photograph it, even touch it.

Yet there were even more profound forces at work here. Behind the street-art philosophy was a far, far better thing—a scheme to spread around a concrete expression of goodwill. Cold, hard cash from the sponsorship and sale of the

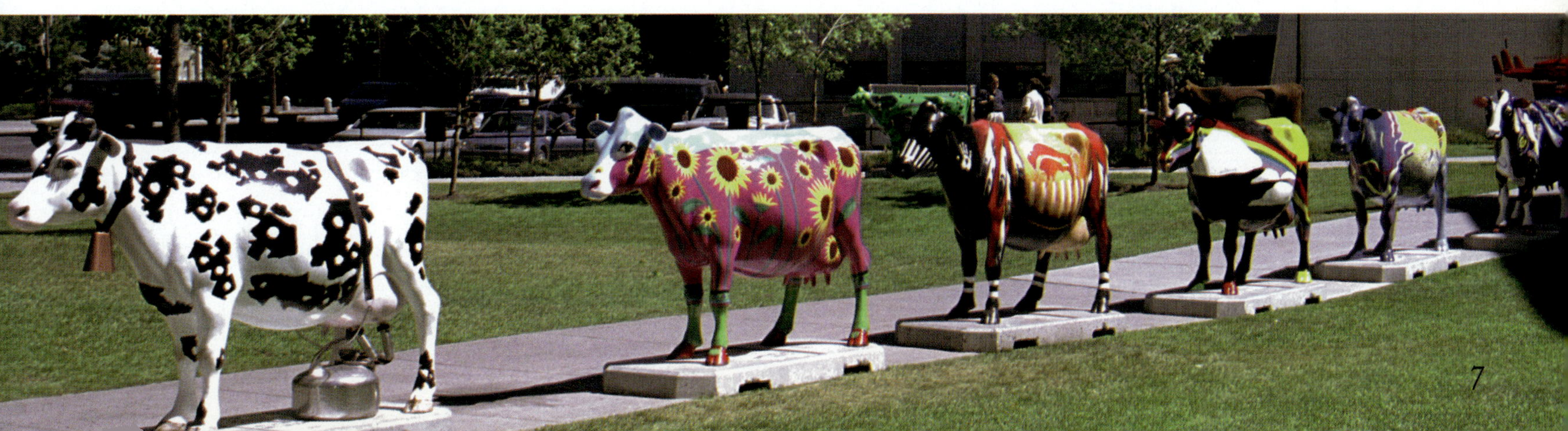

bovine beauties would be streamed into a variety of Southern Alberta charities and worthy causes.

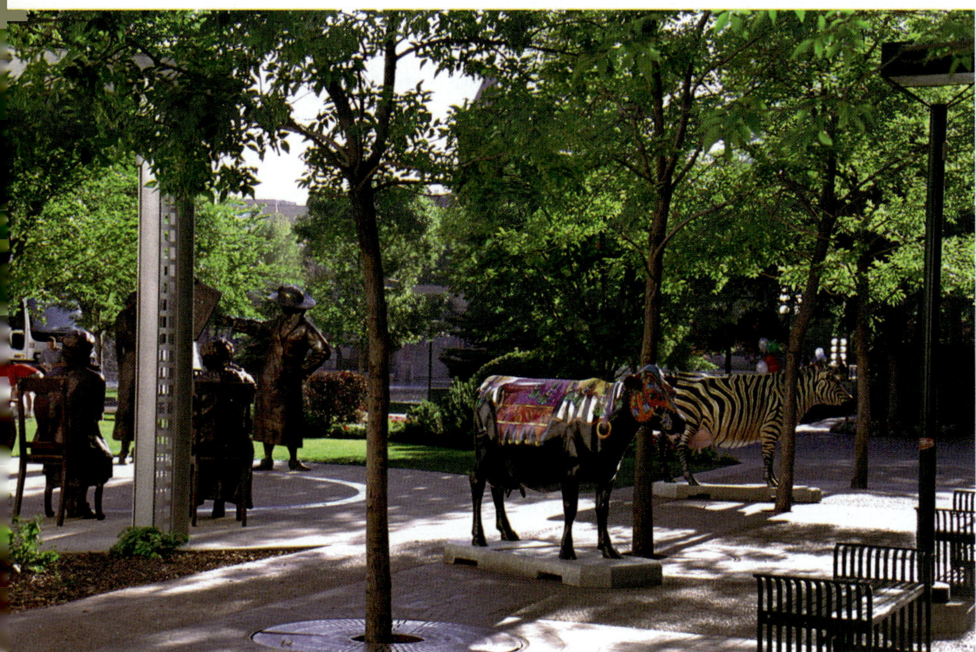

Here was a concept for an openhearted town to buy into. And, of course, Calgarians from every walk of life went on to do just that, with the no-holds-barred gusto that is typical of the city.

Udderly Art organizers asked Calgary sculptor Brian Cooley to go forth and create the model for this life-sized fibreglass creature, a symbol of interactive artistic expression to stand for the ages. A master craftsman with a glittering résumé, Cooley tackled the job with his customary skill and loving attention to detail. But when he unveiled his model, the sputters, gulps and gasps could be heard clear to Black Diamond.

It was a Jersey.

A WHAT?

A delicate, doe-eyed dairy cow? To represent a city built on the brawny shoulders of King Beef?

The venerable cattle barons of the Ranchmen's Club sat bolt upright in their overstuffed chairs, spilling brandies and cigar ashes. Bristling at the news, they thundered through their moustaches in indignant unison, "Great sufferin' briskets, this is unthinkable."

But once the skeptics took a closer look at Cooley's elegant model, indignation melted away, replaced by sighs of admiration. Men and women, wranglers and ranchers, tinhorns and greenhorns all seemed to fall hard for Cooley's princess of the prairie.

Most of the Udderly Art crew, including prime mover and board chairperson Bonnie Laycock, later pleaded ignorance. They hadn't set out to transform Calgary's streets into a beef-free zone. Scout's honour. It just sort of happened that way.

Laycock later admitted she wasn't 100 percent clear on the precise differences between beef and dairy breeds. (Don't worry. She's clear now.) But she remains unrepentant and still considers the languid, pastoral features of the Jersey the most appealing face in the animal kingdom.

Cooley's artistic eye also warned him away from a beef cow model—a Hereford, say, or an Angus—to bring Udderly Art's message to the masses.

"Beef cows are kind of boring," he explained, meaning no offence and hastily reassuring beef producers everywhere that he spoke strictly in visual terms.

"A beef cow is all meat-kind of blocky and bulky," he explained. But God assembled the Jersey with the artist in mind.

The inspiration for Cooley's model of bovine beauty was Pleasantview Jersey Farm's Pleasantview Galaxy Serena, a four-year-old cow-quette with classic lines and stunning confirmation. She's the Naomi Campbell of Jersey lilies. A show cow in hot demand at fairs and exhibitions throughout Western Canada, Serena is a certified heartbreaker, able to bat one long, sexy eyelash and set the pulse of any self-respecting bull to racing. In short, she's everything a bovine artwork ought to be.

And let's face it, Serena had a great deal to live up to. Though sometimes udder . . . er . . . underrated and occasionally taken for granted, the Universal Cow commands respect for a variety of qualities considered attractive by the human race.

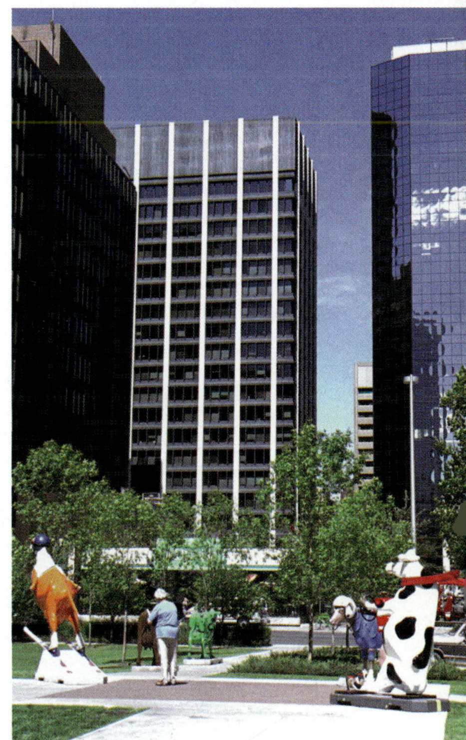

The cow represents both fertility and responsibility. She gives birth to new life and uncomplainingly nurtures the young. She symbolizes growth. Familial support and strength. Peaceful domesticity. While bulls garner the glory, cavorting around the Western ranges, the steadying spirit of the cow holds down the fort, keeping the home fires burning.

Herself a mother, artist and longtime supporter of the Alberta arts scene, Udderly Art godmother Bonnie Laycock always shared this unspoken respect for the Universal Cow though she never dreamed she'd wind up spending so much time in Her company.

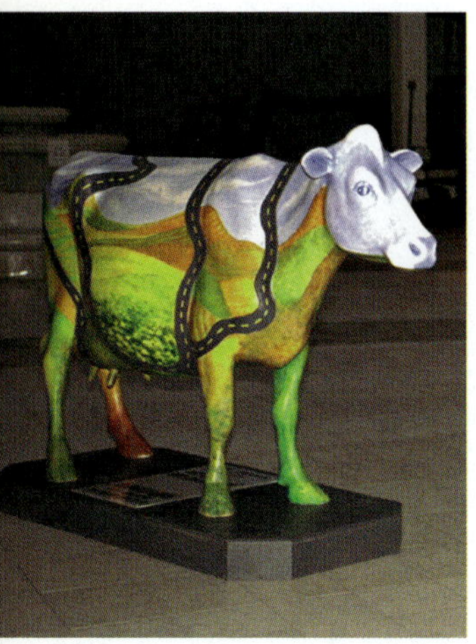

But one summer night in Chicago, Laycock ran smack-dab into destiny. She found herself squinting through the gathering dusk on the Magnificent Mile strip of Michigan Avenue.

"Are there cows on this street?" she asked, half-afraid to hear the answer. Of course, the answer was yes. On closer inspection, Laycock confirmed that this cow was a shocking lime green.

Something clicked. Such fabulous, fabulous cows, she thought. Without doubt, they belonged in Cowtown.

Within a day or two, she had caught up with shoe magnate Peter Hanig, a key organizer of the Chicago herd, in his Michigan Avenue store. Hanig was eager to help. Not only did he brief her on the concept, but he offered her a great deal of practical advice, which later proved useful.

Fired up for action, Laycock landed home in Calgary. By the following day, she had recruited her right-hand man, the second Udderly Art board member, Calgary businessman and family friend, Jim McCartney. With McCartney, a nuts-and-bolts detail man, on board, the cattle call went out in earnest. One by one, Laycock's handpicked herd bosses answered the call.

Straight off the top, Laycock's breathless pitch sounded a little wacko, a bit loopy, even slightly bizarre. One of those Udderly converted was Ann MacDiarmid, who recalled, "When we tried telling our friends about the public-spirited project, a lot of people thought we were talking about real cows. None of us thought we'd ever find ourselves sitting around a table in a law office debating whether we should put steel-reinforced tails and ears on a fibreglass cow." But those initial recruits shared an innate faith in Laycock's judgement. Besides, they were swept up in her exuberance, like tumbleweeds in a dust devil.

Subsequent volunteers took on many jobs, but few members of Laycock's art posse took on so much responsibility. McCartney was in charge of dotting legal *I*s and crossing technical *T*s, clearing Udderly Art's path of potential cow pies.

One of these was liability insurance. To McCartney fell the challenge of explaining to insurance companies that he needed coverage for nothing less than a herd of fibreglass cows.

That issue settled, there were the matters of a logo, copyrights, licensing deals for everything from T-shirts to trading cards to books.

And there was a herd of lovable, eminently paintable cows to be sold in the causes of art and charity—a specialized job for a panel of volunteers with drive, relentless energy and an irresistible sales patter.

People such as sleepless powerhouse Willa Duclos, who figuratively pounced on Calgary financier Rob Peters and dozens of other targets. Always a soft touch for a worthy cause, Peters came through like a champ, buying four cows. He then donated them to STARS Air Ambulance, the Alberta Adolescent Recovery Centre, Glenbow Alberta Institute and the Alberta Film Commission.

Laycock's sales committee grew ever more relentless and ubiquitous. Sales volunteers called in markers from every quadrant of the city and beyond. They jammed a toe in every door, revolving or otherwise.

Suddenly, wealthy hoteliers felt their arms being twisted by insistent spouses burning with cow fever. In self-defence, the twisted arms reached for their wallets. City service clubs saw a terrific chance to add to their already impressive track record of lending helping hands wherever and whenever needed. Energy companies and brokerage houses, law firms and convenience stores, even other charitable organizations heeded the persistent siren song of Laycock's sales team.

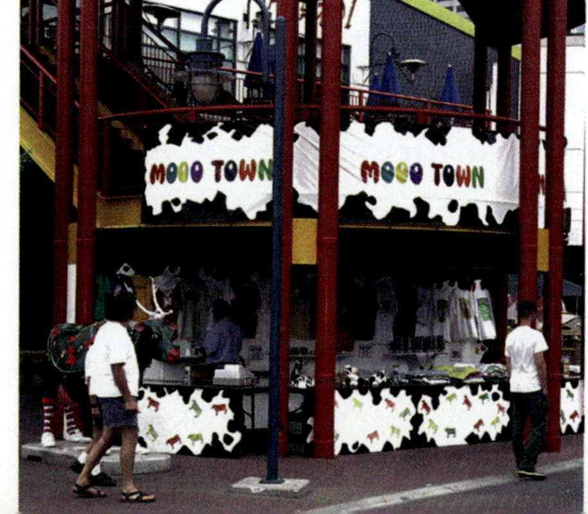

Another Laycock lieutenant, Judy Hunt, served as liaison for Terry Napper when the general manager of newly renovated Chinook Centre went Udderly cow crazy in a large way. Napper wanted to round up a small herd for Chinook's exclusive use, and Hunt was only too happy to oblige.

Several Chinook businesses, plus contracting firms involved in the spectacular redevelopment, carried the ball, laying out cash for a dozen cows.

Badly bitten by the bovine bug, Napper then donated the use of his mezzanine Food Fair to play host to an Udderly Art Herd Owners Roundup on May 29, 2000, during which the organizers paid special homage to the 20 Mavericks. Some 200 people attended.

And once in a while, bedazzled purchasers would stop wondering which hurricane had just blown through his or her chequing account, and start to wonder exactly what had just set them back more than five grand.

A pig in a poke? Not even close. More like a lily-white cow in a delivery truck with a bell on her neck and a bucket of hay nestled between her hooves.

Almost 100 pounds of queenly fibreglass moulded from Brian Cooley's sculpted prototype, the so-called "plugs" were manufactured at Calgary's Marine Clinic, a boat repair service owned and operated by two partners, Dieter Schlaffke and Greg Arich.

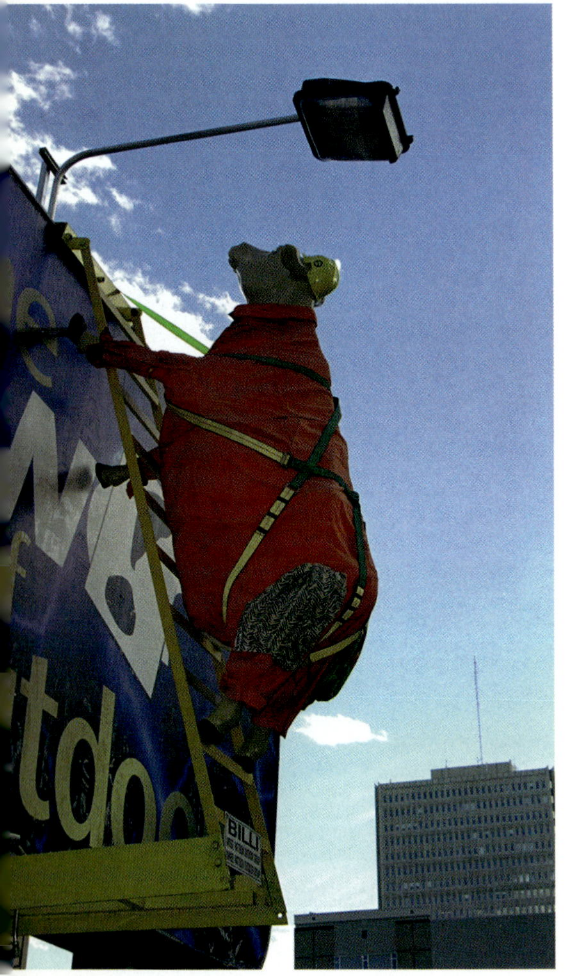

According to one report, Laycock created a stir in the 12,000 square-foot shop when she telephoned to casually ask Schlaffke for an estimate on fibreglass cows.

The upshot was that for a period of about three months, Marine Clinic staff were up to their elbows in Udderly Art.

Arich and Schlaffke's clinicians toiled 12-hour shifts, seven days a week (spending 30 hours on each piece) to produce 125 replicas of Serena, the cutest darn Jersey who ever sashayed past a shedrow.

The remarkably lifelike result—true in every detail to Cooley's design—was then shipped to 125-odd studios around town. One or two even got itchy feet, travelling as far away as Florida.

Most artists stepped forward from the old hometown. But one or two imports managed to crack the roster-including the celebrated commercial artist Romero Britto, a U.S.-based, Brazilian wunderkind who currently rules the world of pop art.

Britto expressed interest, so gallery owner Dennis Smith of Art Mode on 17th Avenue S.W. crated his cow—later reborn as the butterfly and blossom-splashed *Garden of Cow*—and shipped it to Britto's studio in Miami.

"Britto had been in Zurich two years ago and fell in love with the cow exhibit over there. He got so excited about Calgary that he donated his work," explained Smith, who's enjoyed a long business association with the artist.

Art Mode's cow is easily the herd's most widely travelled prodigal. A mixup on Britto's

Miami loading dock sent the crated, completed *Garden of Cow* on a tour of New York State before she was finally rerouted to western pastures.

As a first recruitment step, McCartney approached a former law partner, Cam Mack, to draft the all-important "Cow Service Agreement." This was signed by representatives from both Udderly Art and each corporate supporter. All were asked to pay for their stock up front. Cost per critter: $5,000.00, including GST.

Udderly Art pledged:

1. to mount each fibreglass cow on a concrete base;
2. to produce a definitive herd guide;
3. to place the herd of 120-plus cows in a variety of suitable spots around Calgary and to ride fence, inspecting the herd weekly.

In turn, supporters were required to jazz up their cows' appearance in suitably creative—and weatherproofed—style.

Naturally, Laycock and company tapped into the expertise of Calgary's artistic community, which embraced the concept virtually *en masse.*

"The art snobs—people in New York, say—would probably pooh-pooh this kind of project. But this isn't New York," said Calgary gallery owner Paul Kuhn, who sits on the city's advisory committee for public sculpture.

"But it's a great way to have fun with an art focus. A lot of people got involved, had a good time with it, and even advanced their artistic education a little," added Kuhn, who also served as a volunteer liaison between cow buyers and the Calgary art colony.

Meanwhile, an agreement clause entitled "Option to Purchase" enabled supporters to purchase clear title to their stock prior to an auction on October 28, the date set for the wildest, woolliest urban cattle sale since the doors closed on the Calgary stockyards many years ago.

Some 50 cows were to be put under the hammer by professional auctioneers at the Calgary Stampede Roundup Centre, with all proceeds earmarked for the respective charity of each supporter's choice. The remaining cows would to be m-o-o-o-ved via both a silent and a cyber-auction.

Cyber-auction? Absolutely.

Thanks to an indefatigable volunteer named Mo Keshavjee, Udderly Art staked its claim on the Internet in a large way. Keshavjee

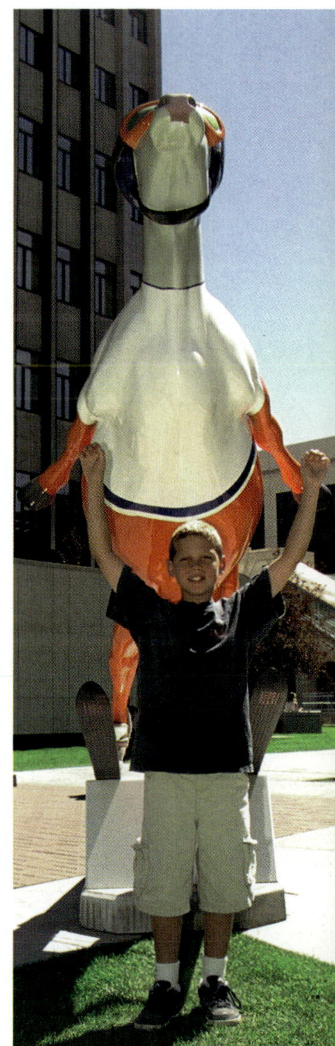

spent an estimated 150 hours building and maintaining the project's award-winning website. Crammed with information and light-hearted graphics, the site quickly galloped to the top of the charts, logging 300,000 visits for a three-month period in spring of 2000 and nailing two awards for creativity and design.

In the days leading up to the auction, the enormity and significance of this whimsical and fabulously feel-good civic project began to sink in. More than 100 richly deserving Southern Alberta causes were about to receive a cash windfall large enough to flatten the billfold of even the most diligent, give-until-it-hurts philanthropist.

Thousands of men, women and especially kids had received a playful visual gift that had enriched their summer days and nights beyond measure. Lifelong friendships had been forged. A dormant sense of artistic appreciation had been kindled within untold numbers of strollers, ordinary folks who set out for a brisk walk at lunch and returned to the office with a herd of colour-drenched cows m-o-o-o-ving their imaginations.

And why? Because a farseeing Canadian visitor had squinted for a better look at a lime-green apparition on a dark Chicago street. One hundred twenty-five artists then girded their loins, grabbed brushes, smocks and paintpots, and got painting.

And as soon as the cows hit city streets on a sun-splashed day in May, lips in Calgary started flapping and flashbulbs began popping.

"It's incredible. People seem to get so much fun out of this," cooed a visiting tourist, running an admiring hand over *Midnight Cowgirl*'s illuminated flank.

Herd guides in hand, kids dragged their parents hither and yon on the most elaborate hunt for multi-coloured treasures since Easter Sunday. Among the hundreds of affirmative messages sent via e-mail to UdderlyArt.com, the following was written by a footsore Calgary mom after completing a six-hour Cow Caravan with two goggle-eyed youngsters. It brought real tears to the eyes of Bonnie Laycock: "My kids are six and three," wrote the correspondent, "and they had the most absolutely wonderful day 'hunting' for cows. . . . The pure joy and wonderment in their eyes is worth every blister we will soon be sporting. Thank you for giving the entire city such a beautiful and precious gift." For an apt summation of the Udderly Art experience, the message said it all.

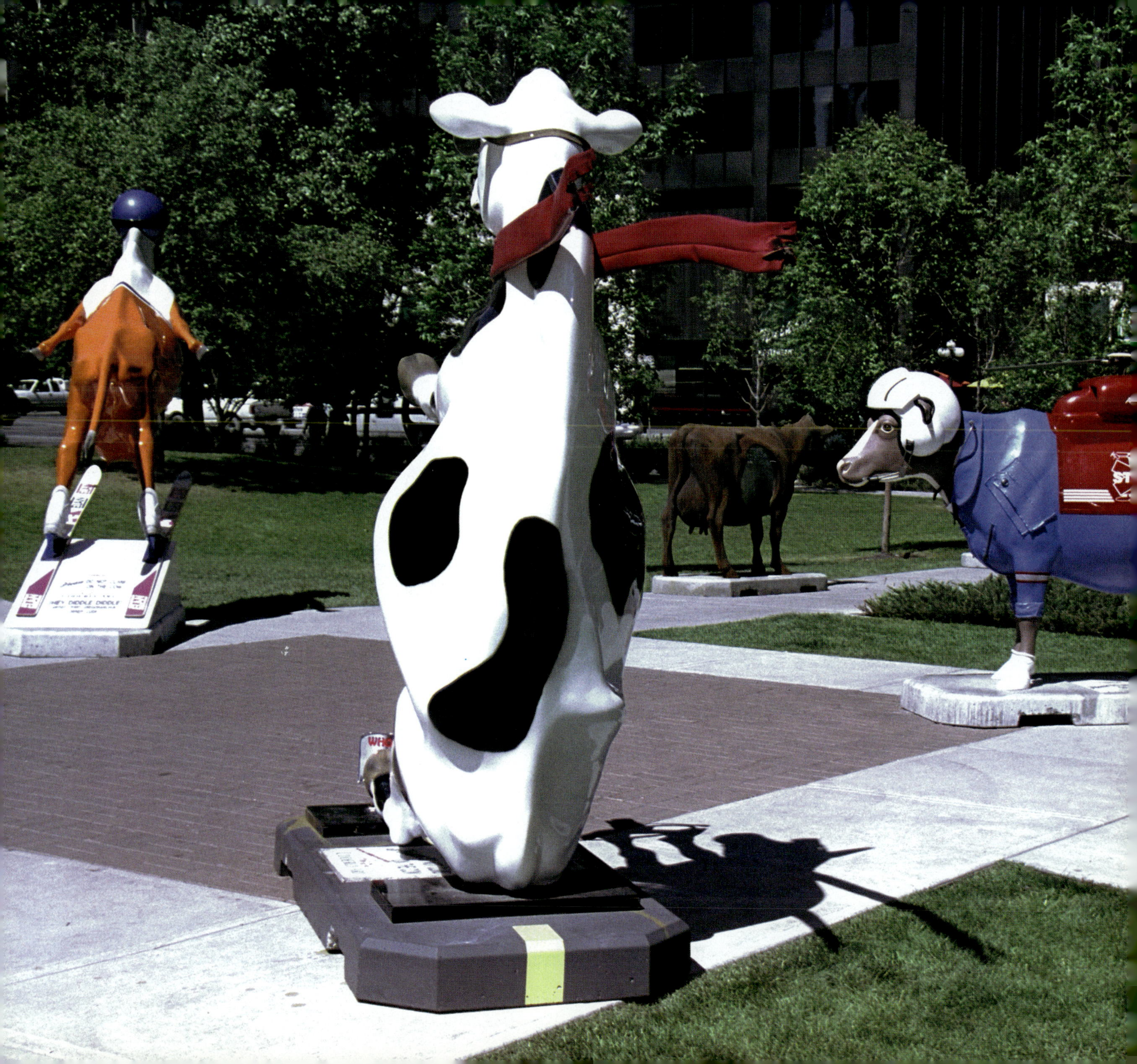

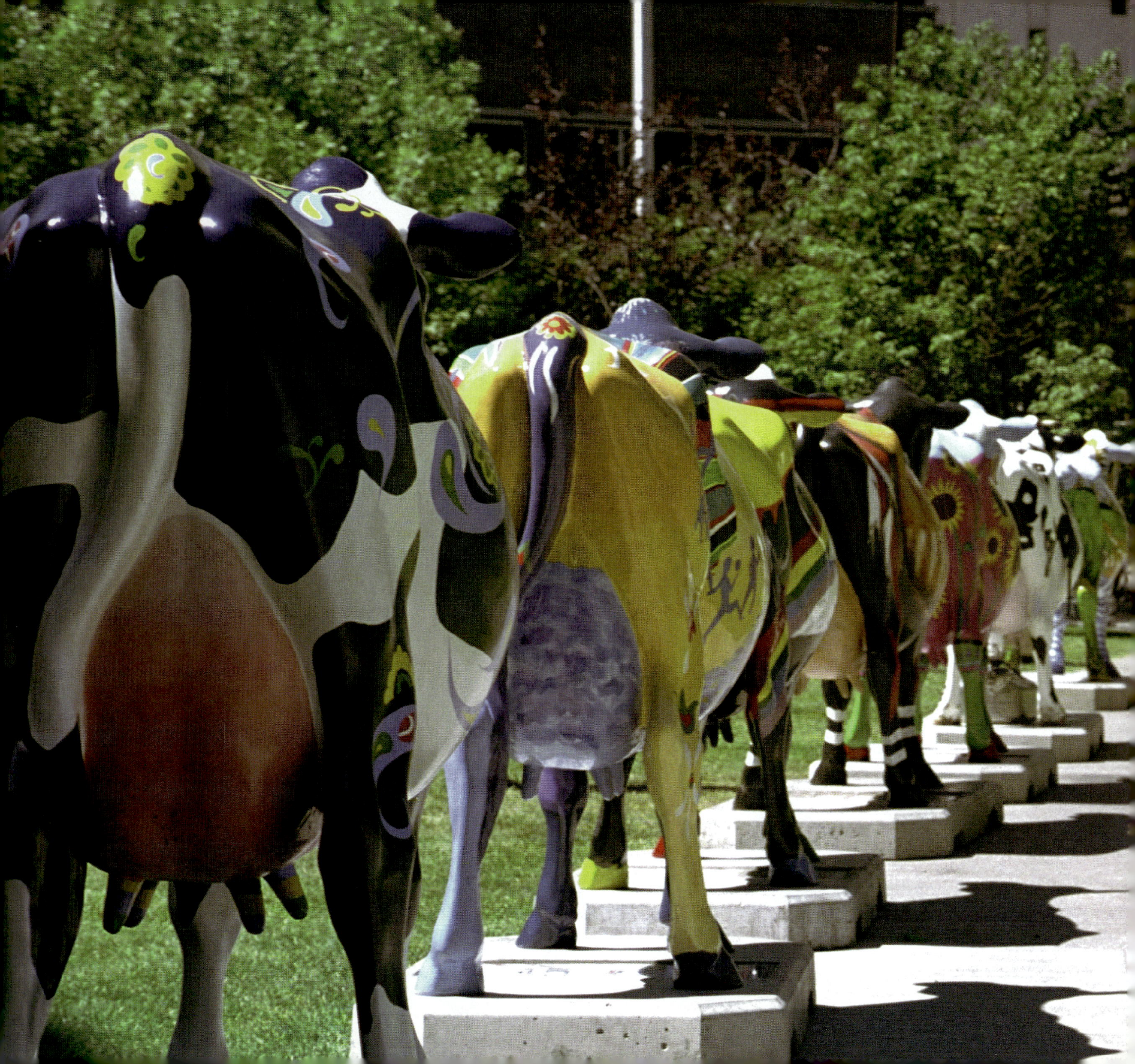

The Herd Guide

I never saw a purple cow,
I never hope to see one;
But I can tell you, anyhow,
I'd rather see than be one.

GELETT BURGESS [1895]

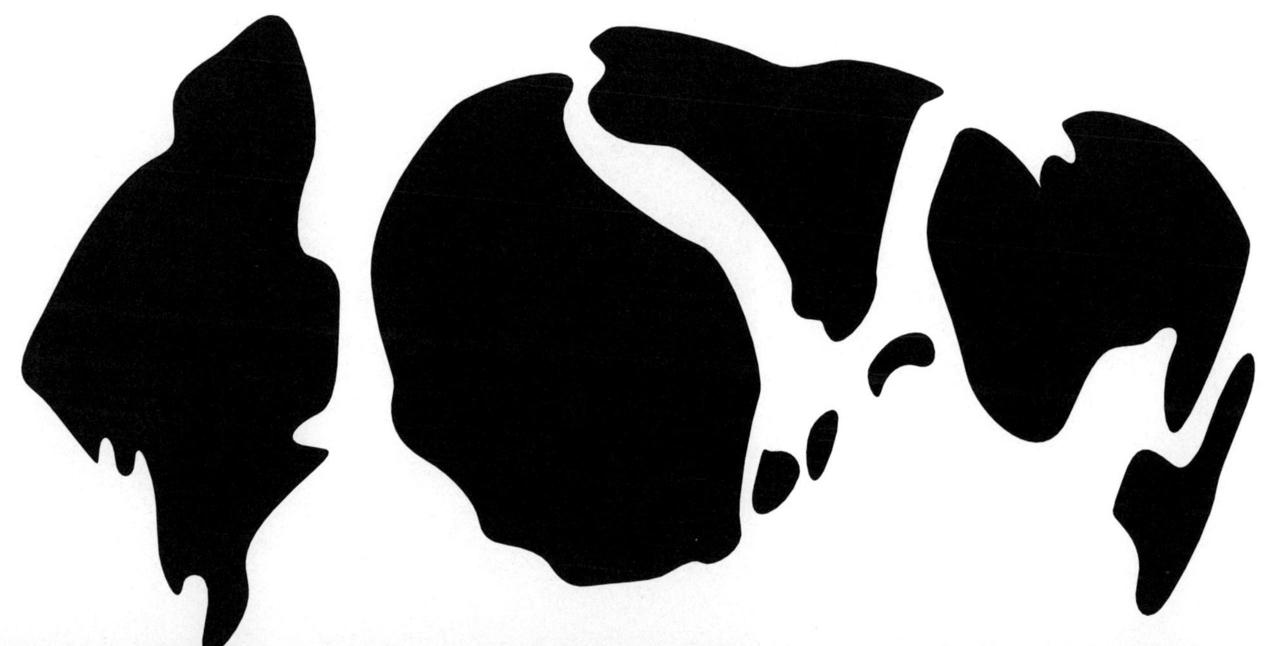

3Moos

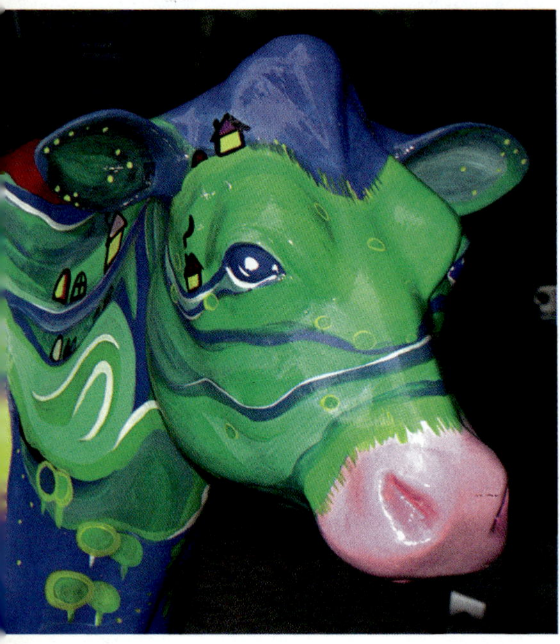

Artist: Sandra Stahl

Owner: 3M Canada Company

Charity: Alberta College of Art

This cow raises your spirits as high as one of those charming, nostalgic prints by Grandma Moses or Norman Rockwell. Innocence, laughter, love and exuberant good times are evoked by Sandra Stahl's colourful splashes of blue, red and green. Happy faces, peaceful sailboats and a good time are being had by all.

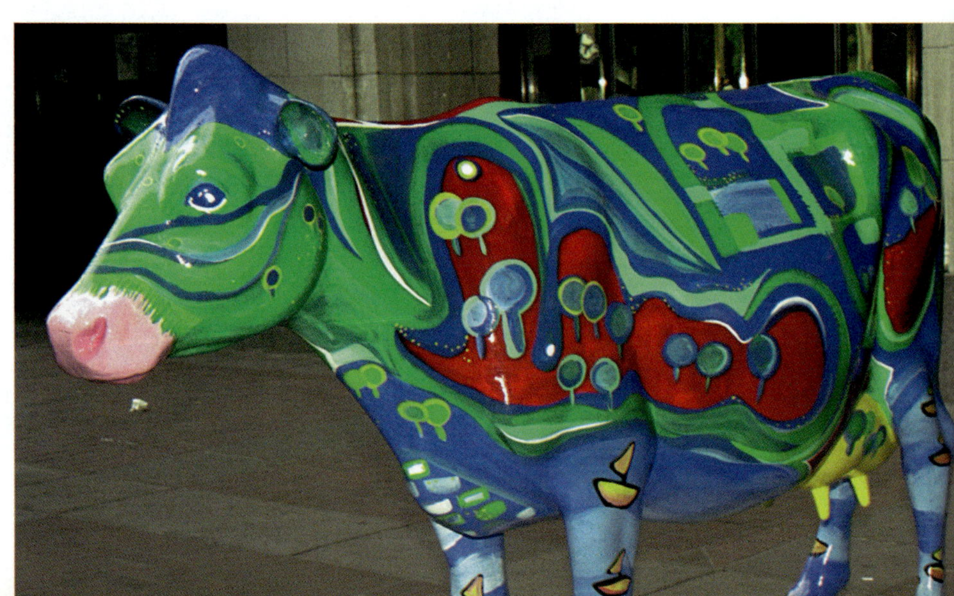

Au Ag Cu

Artist: Errol Lee Fullen

Owner: Carscallen Lockwood Barristers & Solicitors

Charity: Canadian Breast Cancer Foundation

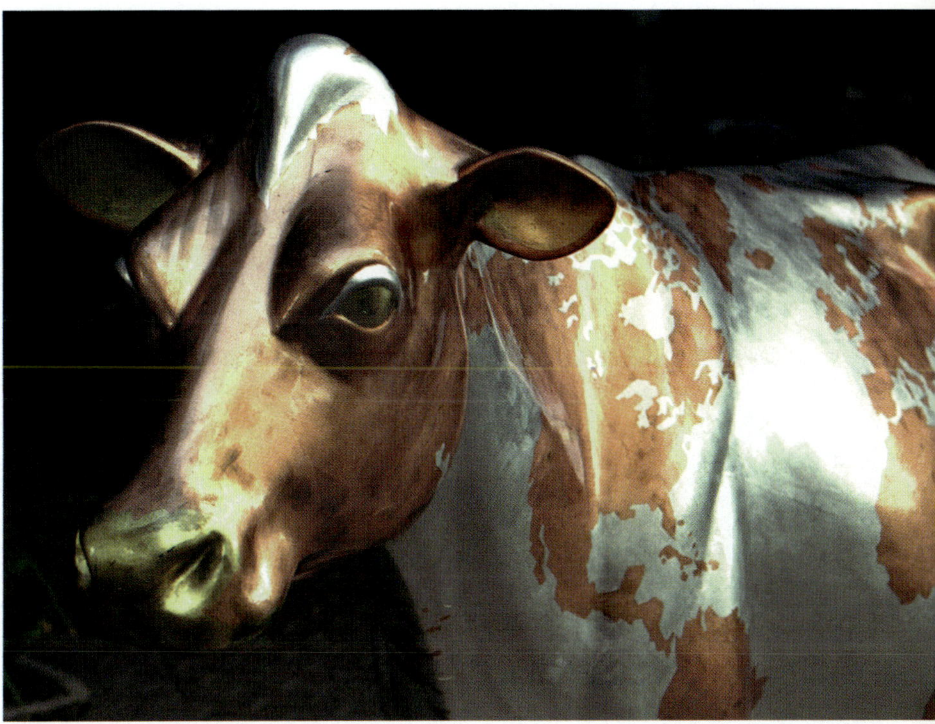

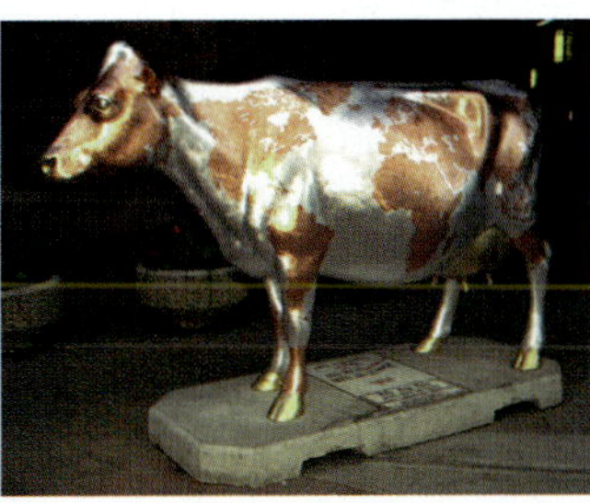

Some onlookers were baffled by the name of this bovine unit—particularly those who ducked out of chem class. The not so mysterious letters are the chemical symbols for gold, silver and copper. Of course, these are the colours Errol Lee Fullen used to produce this piece.

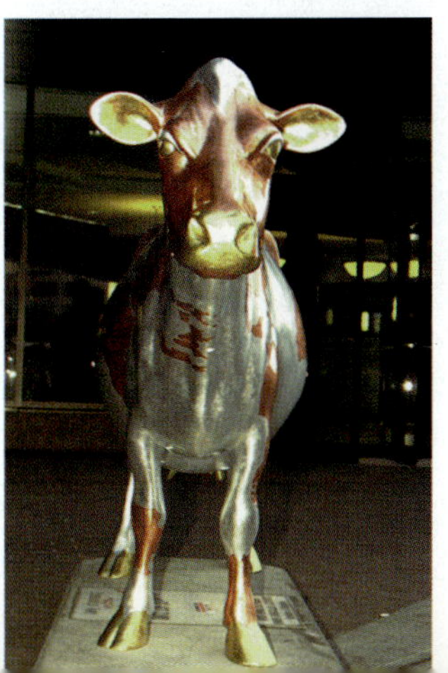

Aurora Cow-Ealis

Artist: Rick Janzen

Owner: Ledcor Industries Limited

Charity: Calgary Homeless Foundation

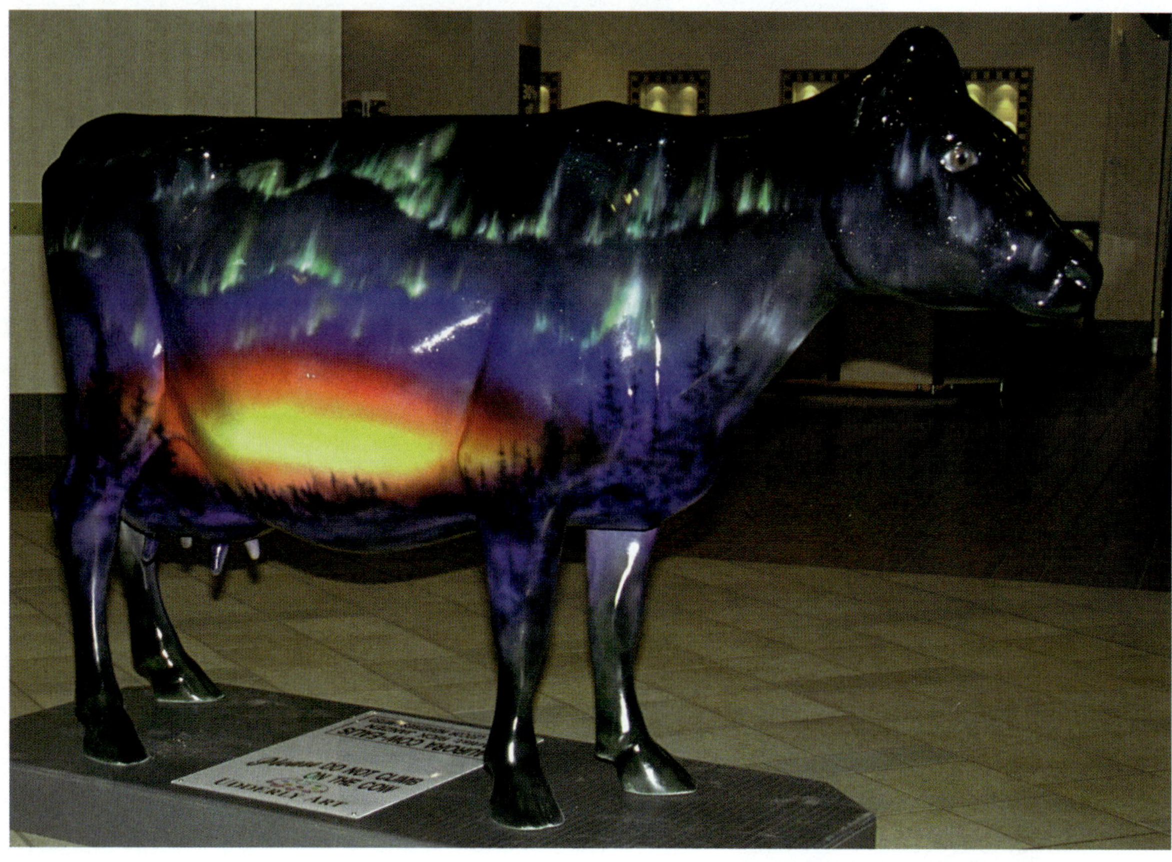

Another of Rick Janzen's cows, *Aurora Cow-Ealis* wouldn't look out of place hanging on the walls of an elite gallery—okay, maybe just a tad awkward. This one gives Janzen's impression of nature's unique light show, a stunning, blue and turquoise display of northern lights backgrounded by a galaxy far away.

Automoobile

Artist: Terry Gregoraschuk

Owner: United Way of Calgary and Area (donated by Macleod Dixon Barristers & Solicitors)

Charity: United Way of Calgary and Area

Like his ski-jumping *Hey Diddle Diddle*, Terry Gregoraschuk's cow-cum-crazycar is a visual smorgasbord. Man, that's some Boss-y Machine-hot wheels, sleek cockpit and flaming hot-rod paint job. For the axles, Gregoraschuk modified his cow's legs, offering us a rare glimpse of a spread-eagled, speed-demon cow.

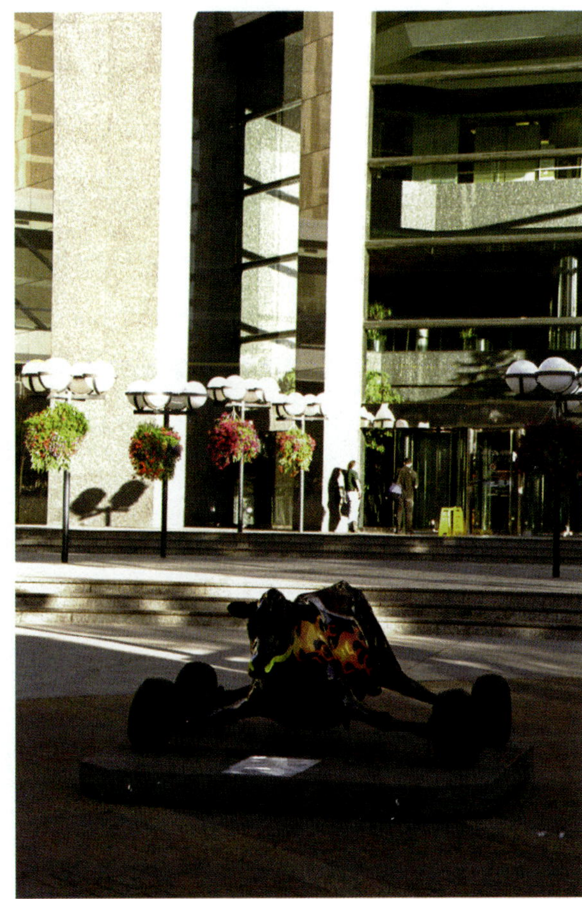

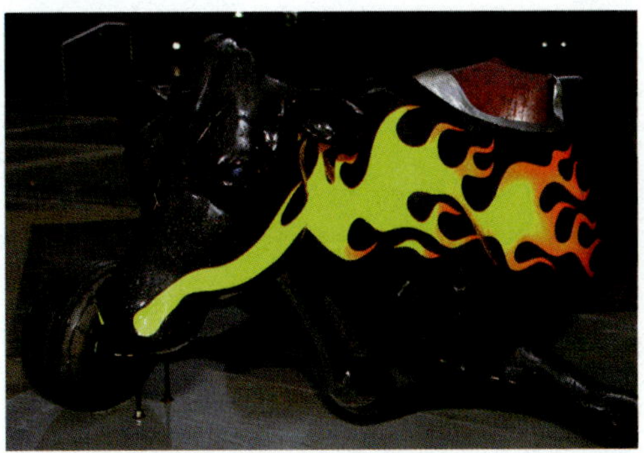

Baywinkle

Artists: Hope Johnson and Brian Smith
Owner: The Bay Downtown
Charity: Calgary Native Women's Crisis Centre

Even a casual eye can spot the stripes a mile away. They mean *Baywinkle* has to be the most comfortable cow in the Udderly Art herd or at least the warmest. Those distinctive red, green, yellow and blue bands on a beige background also immediately suggest a Canadian icon: the Hudson's Bay blanket.

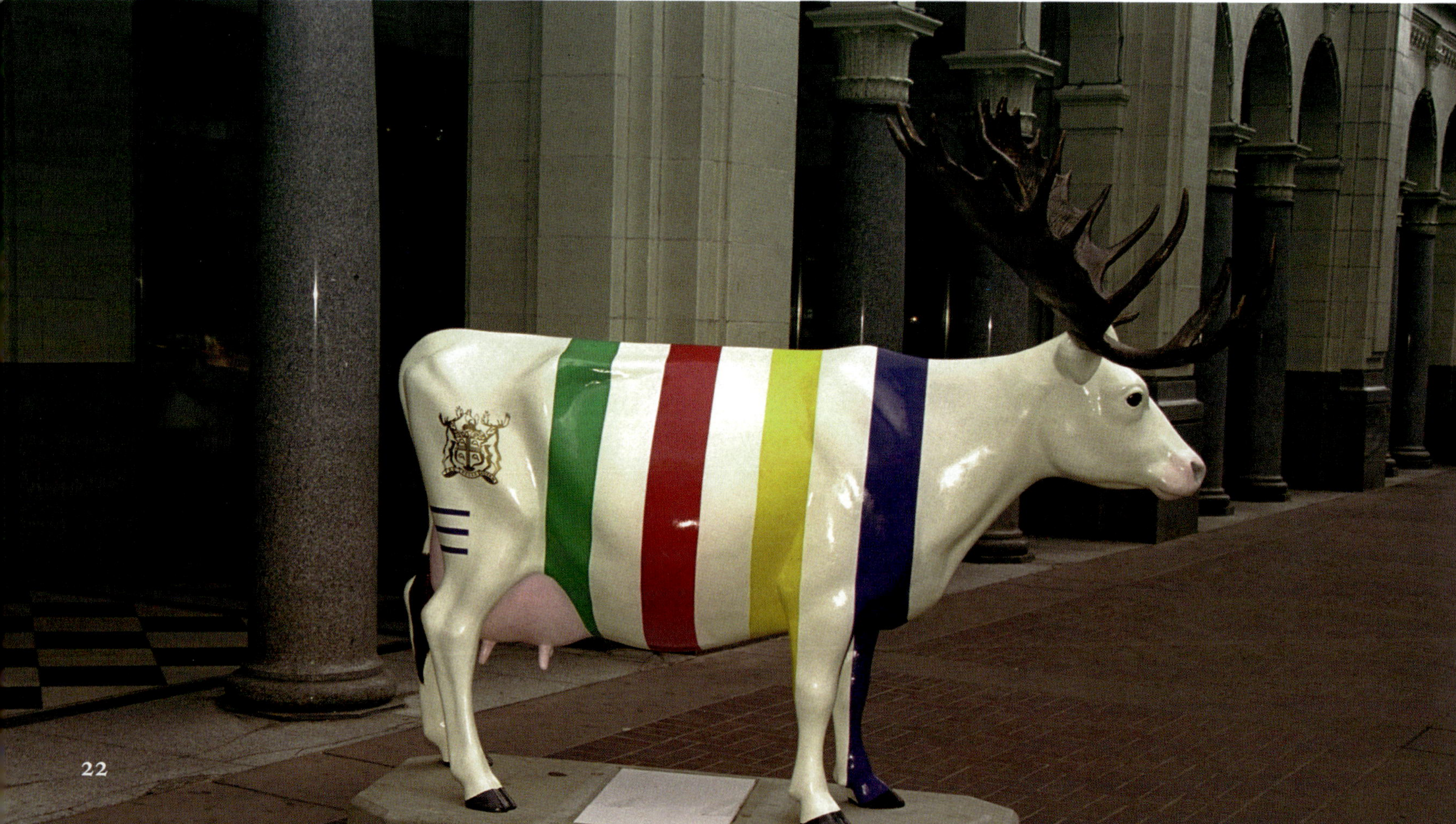

Belle

Artist: Gary Olsen

Owner: Agrium Inc.

Charity: 4-H Millennium Fund

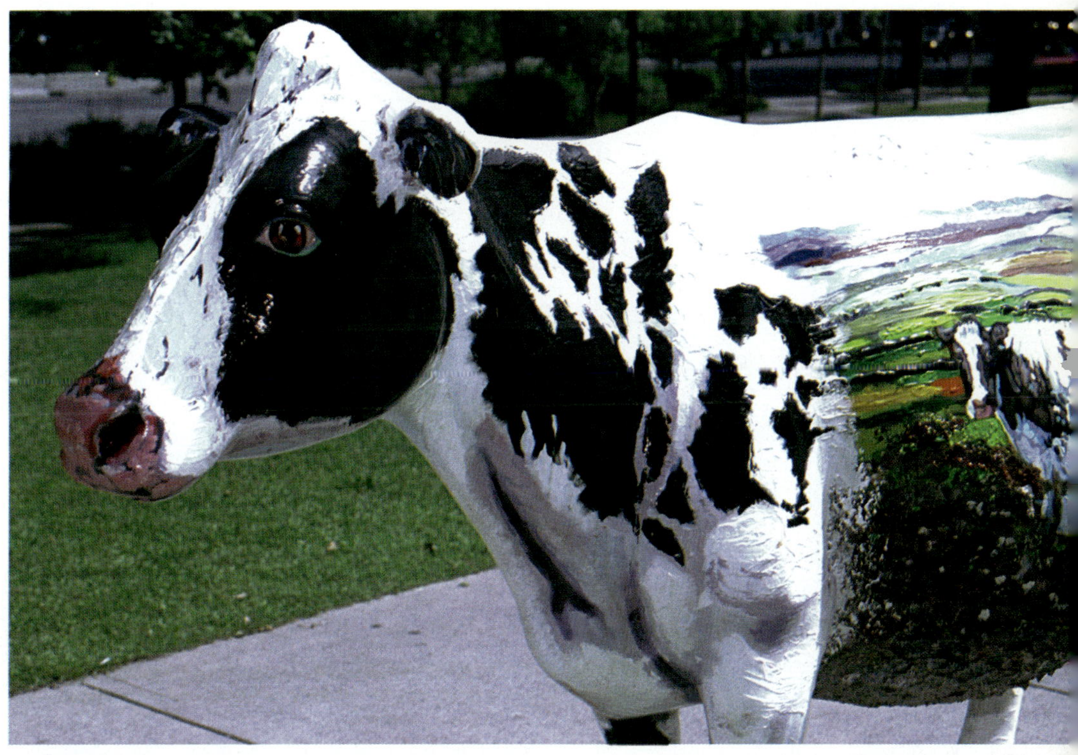

In French, it means "beautiful," and no other word adequately describes the masterly detail work of artist Gary Olsen on *Belle*. She's a self-contained self-portrait—a cow within a cow, if you will. And she stands in an ultrarealistic, well-trodden field portrayed by means of carefully sculpted, mounded layers of paint.

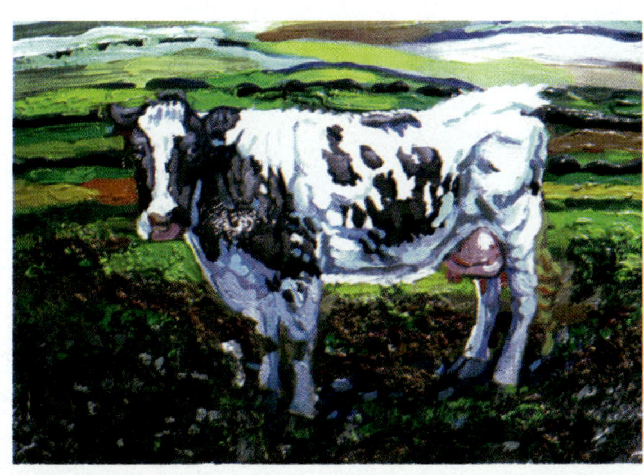

Billi

Artist: Pattison Outdoor Group
Owner: Pattison Outdoor Group

A joint effort from the creative, sales and bill-posting staff of Pattison Outdoor Group resulted in this ultra-clever cow. After the Pattison team hoisted *Billi* skyward via cherry-picker express, she spent her entire summer on a ladder, posting a billboard at 6th Avenue and Centre Street South.

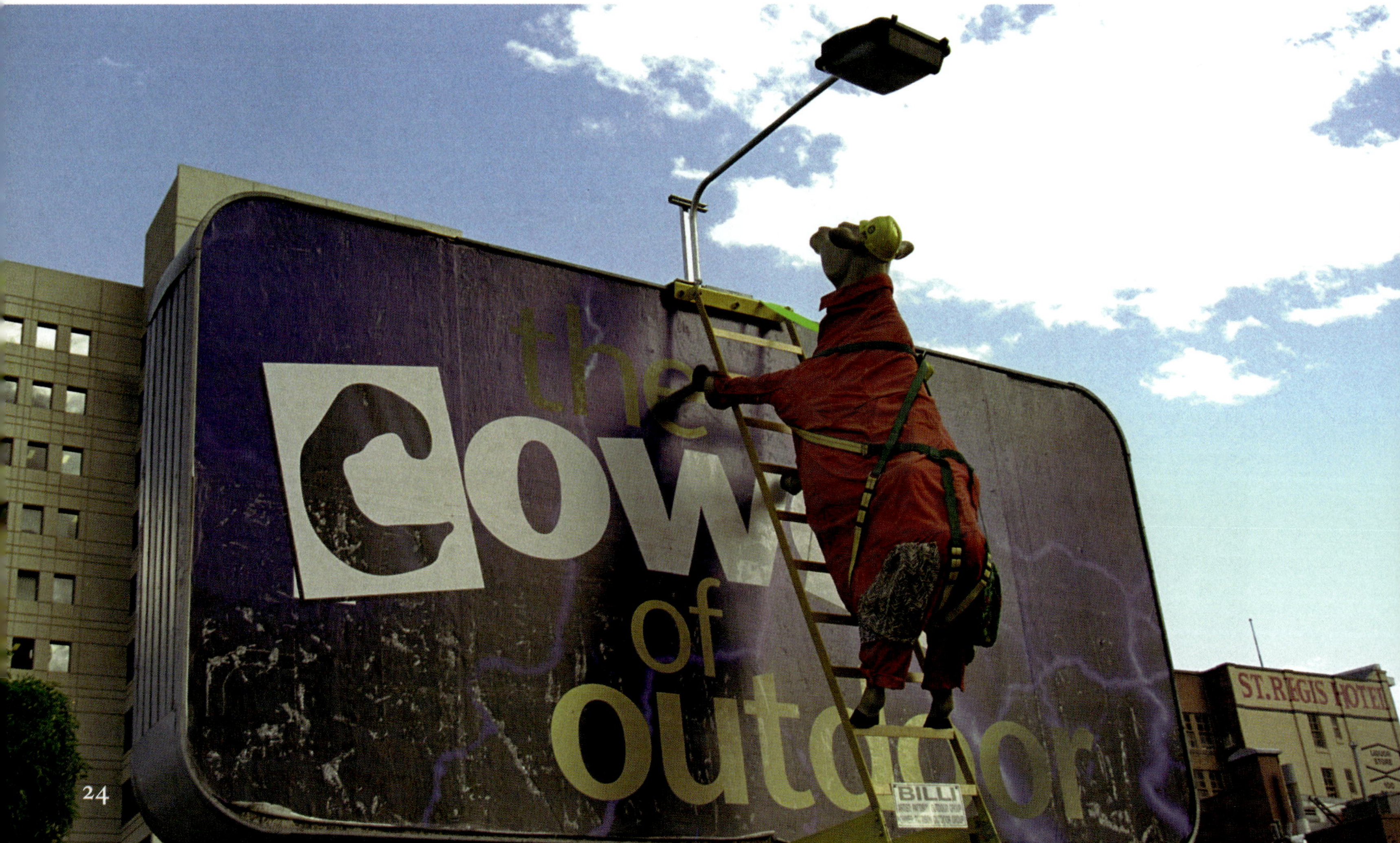

Blue Skies

Artist: Ron Moppett

Owner: Burnet, Duckworth & Palmer

Charity: Institute for Modern and Contemporary Art

Calgary artist Ron Moppett wanted to catch a summer country breeze and carry it all the way downtown. With *Blue Skies,* he turned the trick. Using a base of pale blue and a hint of lavender, Moppett added a few of his trademark artistic touches—including the top hat and the artist's palette on the checkered tablecloth "saddle."

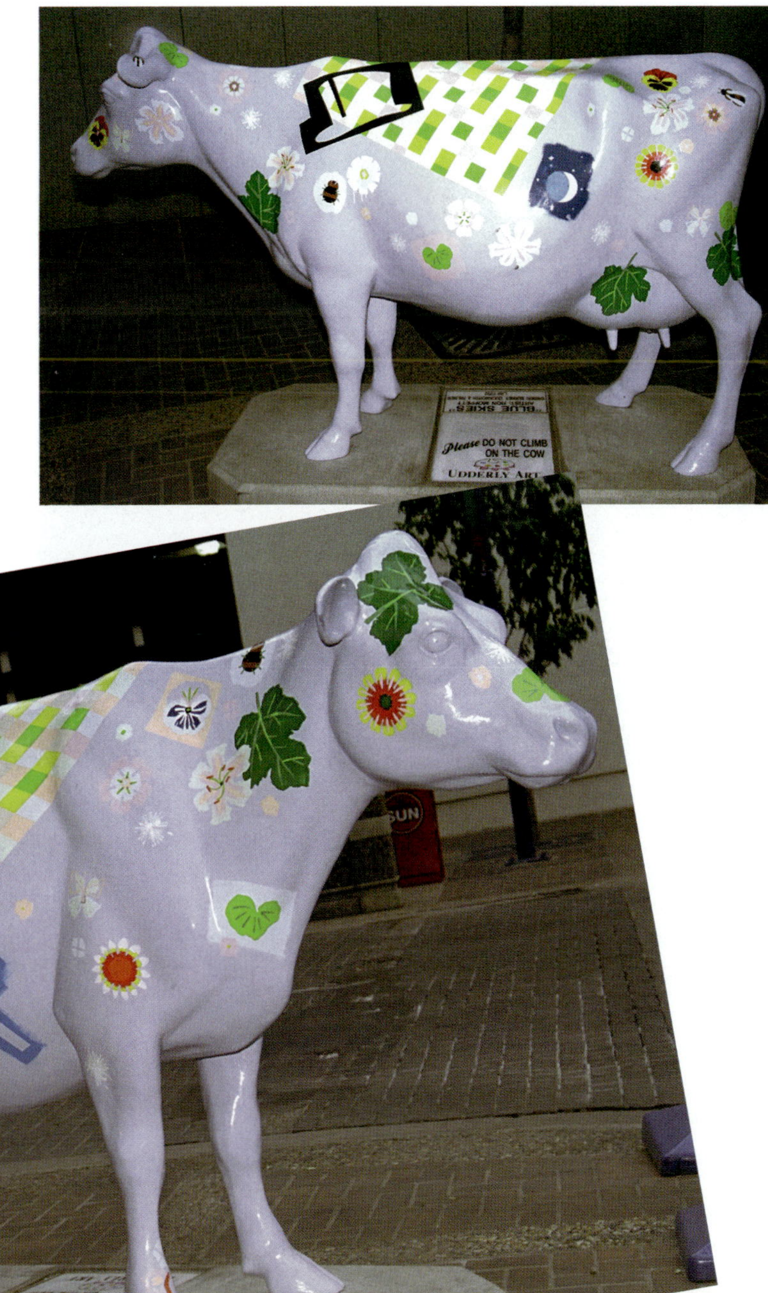

Blueline Bovine

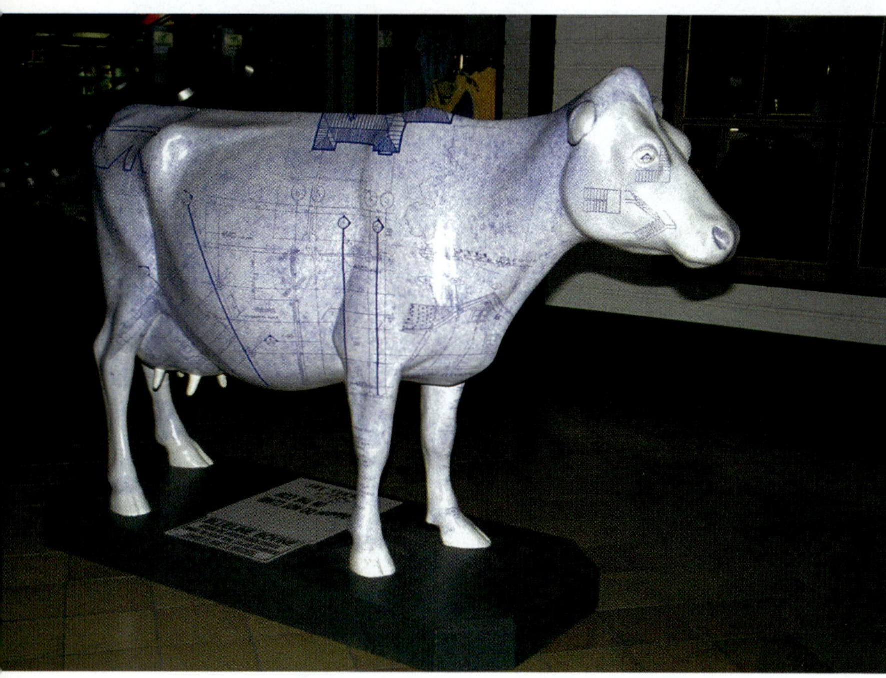

Artist: Mount Royal College Interior Design Students

Owner: Mount Royal College Foundation (donated by Bissett & Associates)

Charity: Mount Royal College Foundation

Judging by their work for Udderly Art, the Mount Royal College interior design students have found their blueprint for success. During the cow's long sojourn at Calgary International Airport, weary travellers had the pleasure of tracing the floor plans of a variety of classic structures on the back of this co-operative blue bovine.

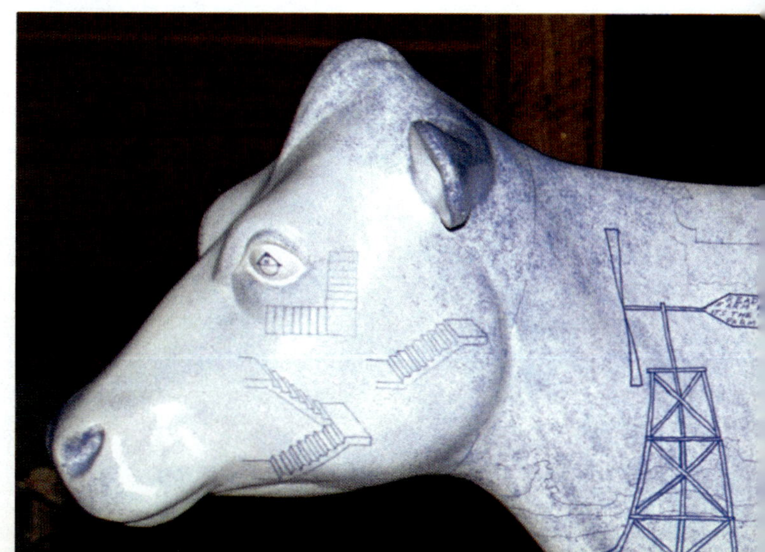

Bovine Skyline

Artist: Scott McLean

Owner: HSBC Bank of Canada

Charity: Calgary Interfaith Food Bank

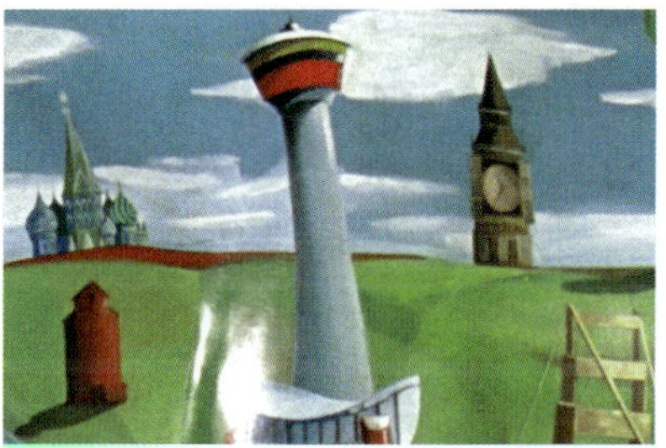

A skyline from where? Just about everywhere that matters. Scott McLean has tossed in the Eiffel Tower, Big Ben, the Golden Gate and, in a nod to the 2000 Olympic Games, the Sydney Opera House, all watched over by an orbiting telecommunications satellite. And he didn't leave out the landmark dear to the hearts of Calgarians—the Calgary Tower.

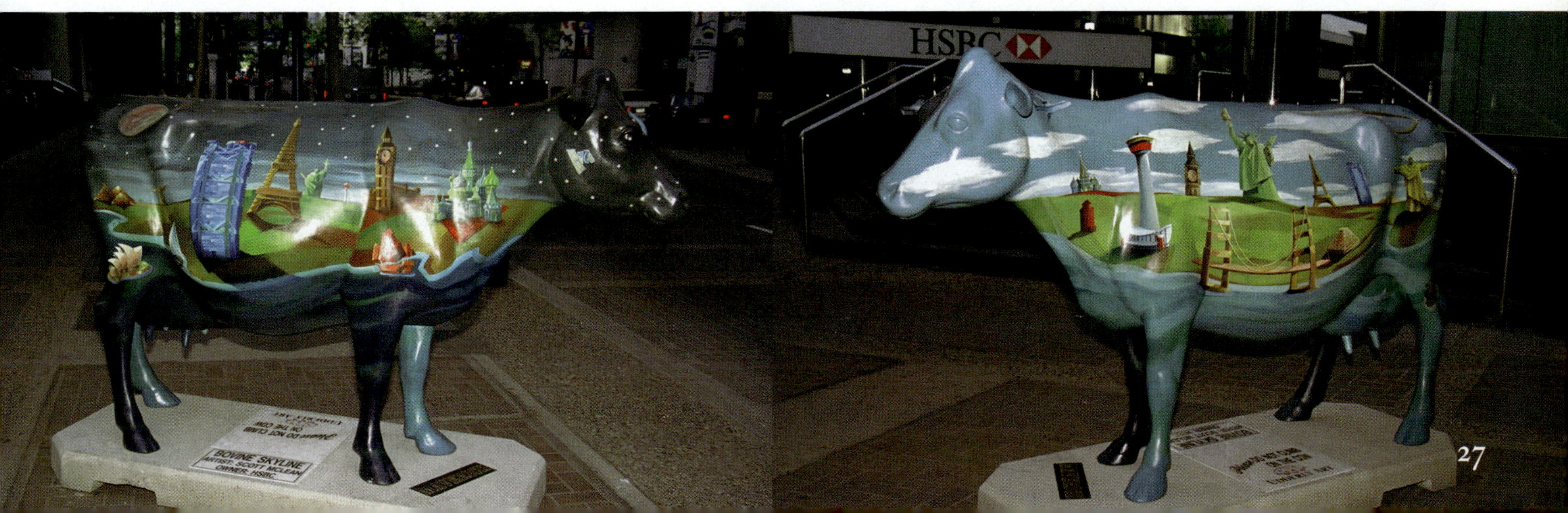

Bovine with a Cause

Artist: Jerald Blackstock

Owner: Canada Safeway Ltd.

Charity: Crime Stoppers

In this case, the cause seems to be eat right and keep fit. This vegetarian spent the summer of 2000 tethered in the courtyard of Kensington Safeway, where she made a statement about the benefits of a healthy diet: broccoli, fresh fruit and corn on the cob.

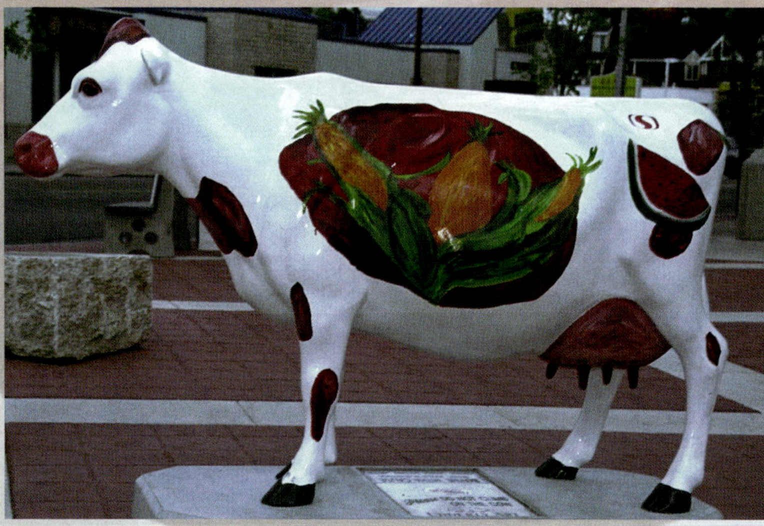

Bovinus Illuminatus

Artist: Petronella Overes

Owner: Enslin Associates Ltd.

Ever read a book by starlight? You could manage it sitting beside this silver-splashed, illuminated beastie. The artist spent hours wiring *Bovinus Illuminatus* before fitting her exterior with trails of white lights. Fortunately, Petronella Overes's cow spent her formative months in Chinook Centre, where a handy pillar provided the requisite plug-in.

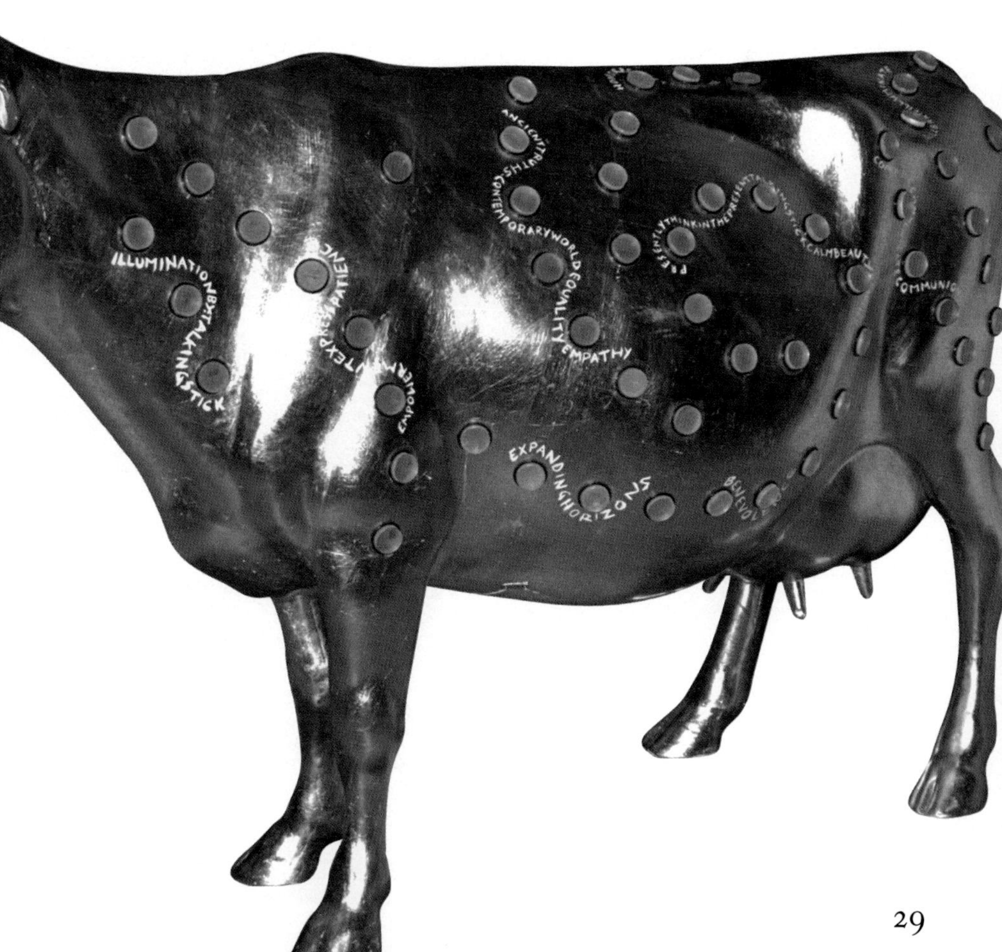

Bow-Vine

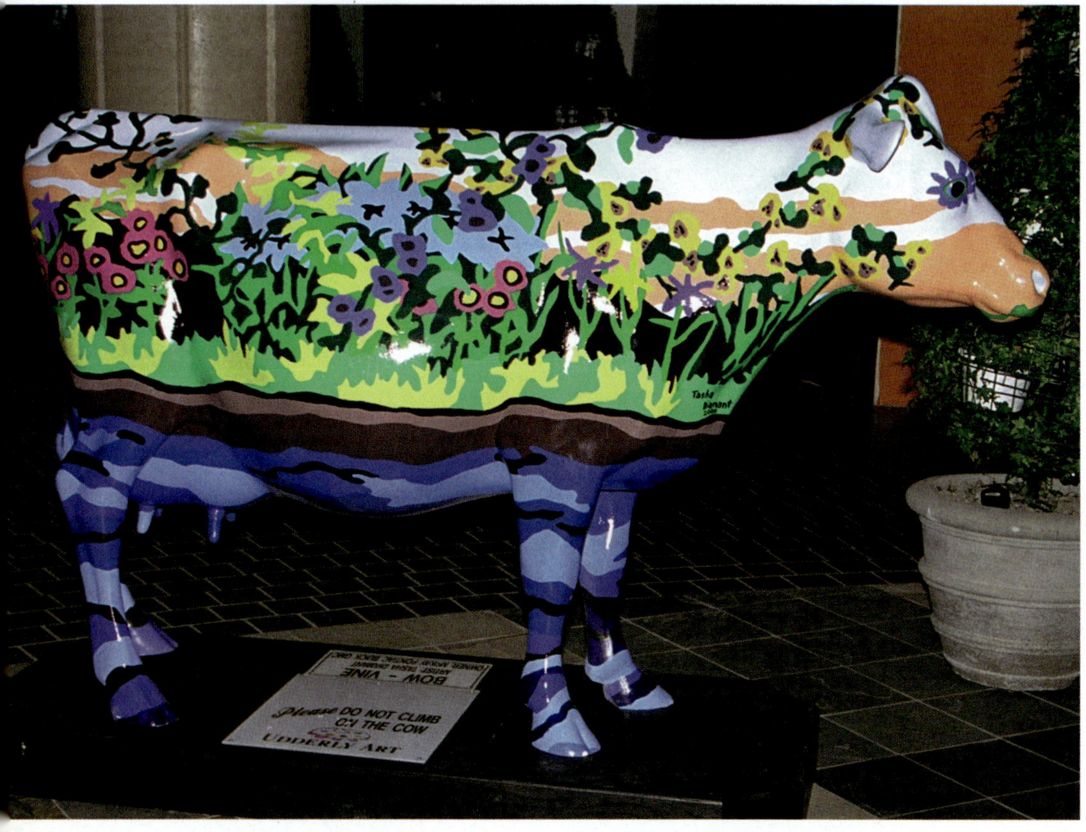

Artist: Tasha Diamant

Owner: McKay Pontiac Buick GMC

Charity: Tom Baker Cancer Centre

Bow-Vine's blue legs indicate she's grazing along the Bow River's edge, and her outdoor motif includes the river's brown banks, a spray of vivid flowers and blue sky. But this cow's no idle lounger. When sold at auction, proceeds will be set aside for breast cancer treatment at the Foothills Hospital cancer clinic.

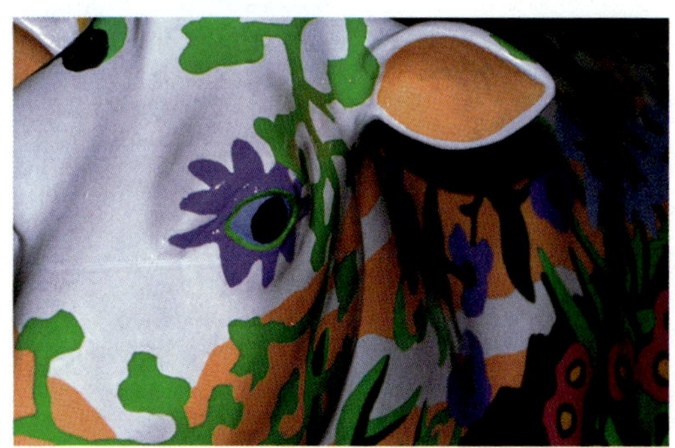

Brace Yourself

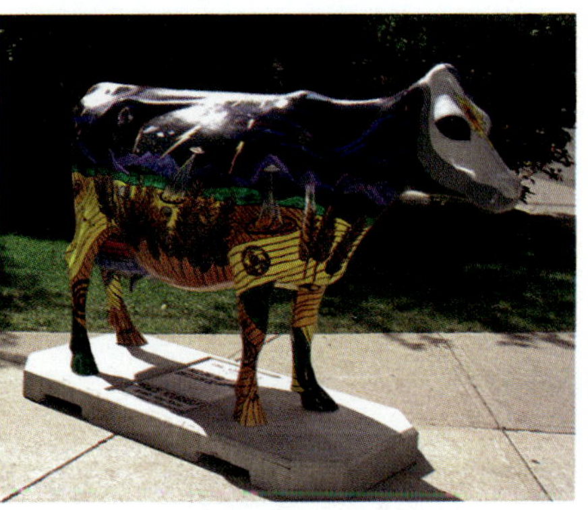

Artist: Kay Enns

Owner: Antosz Orthodontics

Brace Yourself? That's gotta be a reference to the profession of Dr. Mark Antosz, one of Calgary's top orthodontists. But the artist seems to think there's more to worry about than a pronounced overbite. Kay Enns is bracing for a space invasion, led by grinning aliens with the straightest white teeth this side of the Milky Way.

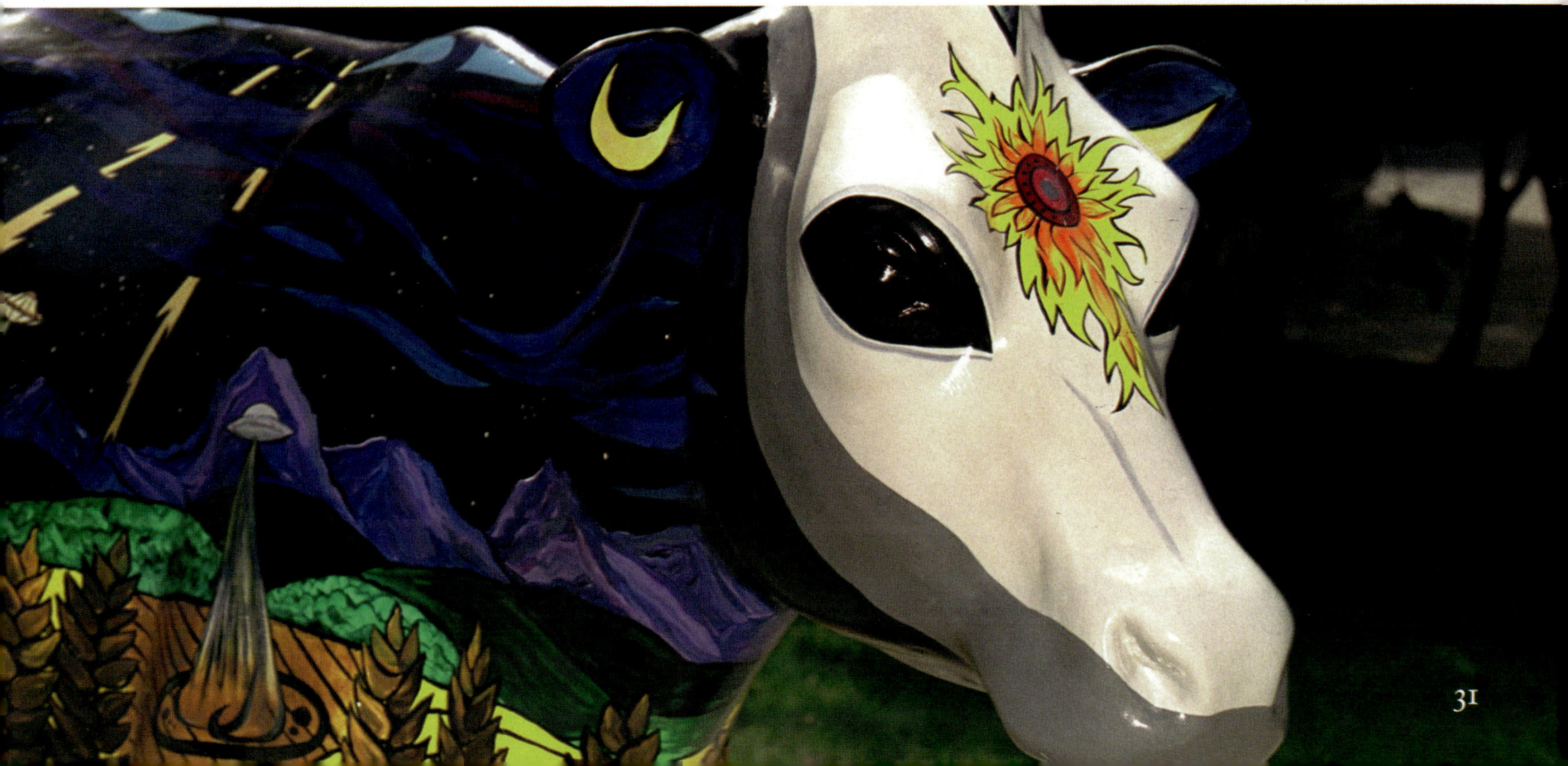

Brandy

Artist: Mac MacKenzie
Owner: Cowgirl Cattle Company
Charity: Western Heritage Centre

It took exactly five days for the Cowgirl Cattle Company to establish a blue-chip credit rating at the Cochrane branch of Scotiabank.

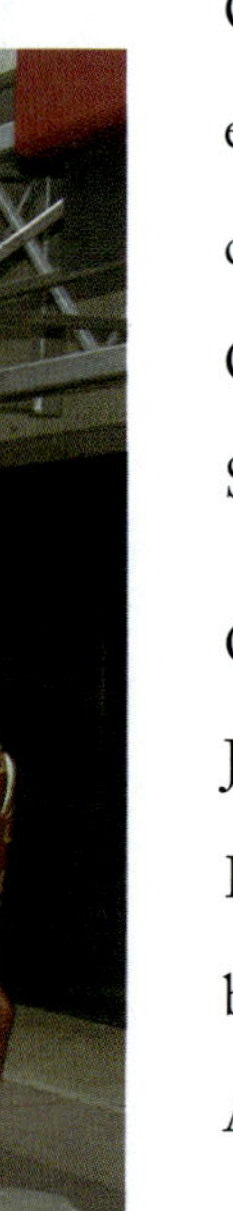

On March 30, twin sisters Judy MacKenzie and Jill Richards marched up to branch manager Jan Austin and launched an unusual pitch: they needed a fast $5,350 loan on behalf of the CCC.

Why? To buy a fibreglass cow, of course.

At the time, the twins were unknown to Austin. But something about their story tickled her fancy. She approved the loan and was only mildly shocked when it was repaid in full (including $10.16 in interest) by April 4.

Longtime Cochrane-area ranchers, Judy and Jill had been captivated by the Udderly Art concept from the start. But they lacked the ready cash to get in the game.

That's when they dreamed up the Cowgirl Cattle Company, a consortium of far-flung females with country roots and home addresses ranging from Dawson Creek, British Columbia, to Milk River, Alberta, to Fir Mountain, Saskatchewan.

Membership requirements:

1. no cowboys need apply;
2. mandatory dues of $110 to finance Brandy;

3. access to a currently registered brand in the family by birth or by marriage.

Once they got a thumbs up on their loan, the twins began working the phones. Within a day they doubled their original goal of 50 stockholders. Soon after, they cranked the numbers in support of Brandy beyond 180. She was painted by Judy MacKenzie's husband, Mac, and dressed up with 100 genuine Southern Alberta cattle brands.

Today, the roster of the Cowgirl Cattle Company reads like a Southern Alberta Who's Who, including names such as Copithorne (11 members), Cross, Daines, Edge (9 members), Lammle and Harvie.

The newly formed CCC was born to run. Its original objective was to raise funds for Cochrane's Western Heritage Centre, and with that goal in the bag, the cowgirls plan to address future causes as they come along.

They've already booked the Centre's boardroom for annual meetings 10 years down the road.

This blue-chip outfit is in for the long haul.

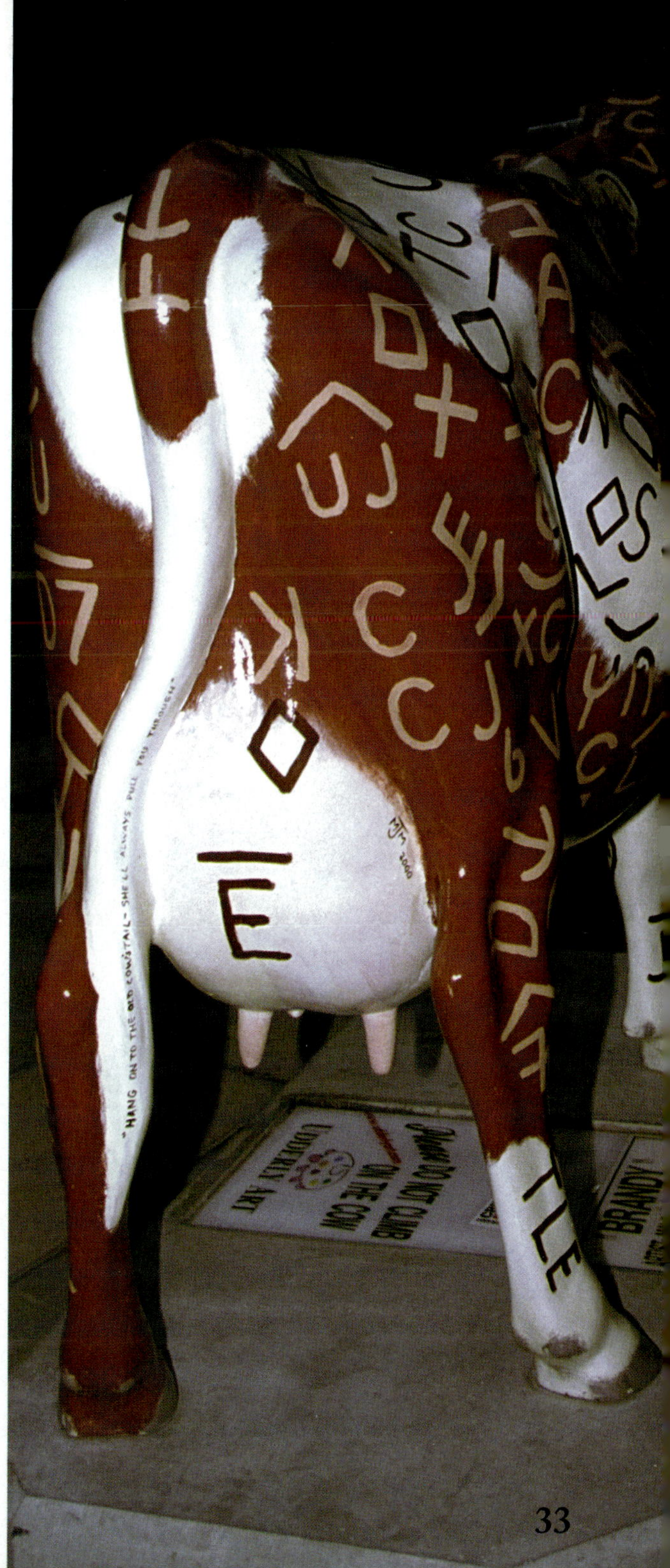

Broadband Besi

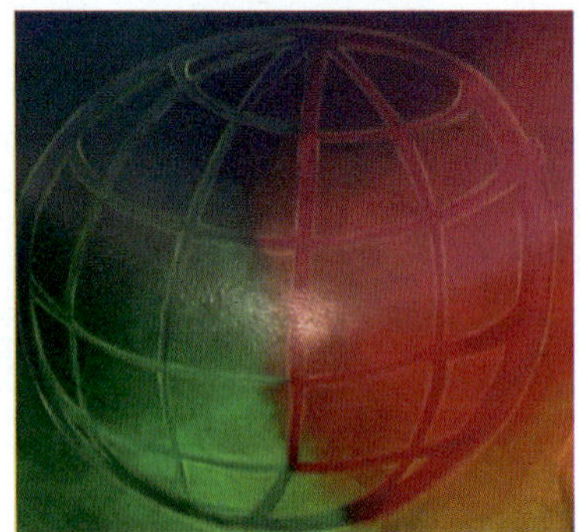

Artist: Rob Mabee

Owner: Bell Nexxia

Charity: Southern Alberta Institute of Technology Alumni Scholarship Fund

Broadband Besi is a symbol of Bell Nexxia's telecommunications commitment to next-generation technology. And you thought she was just a cow.

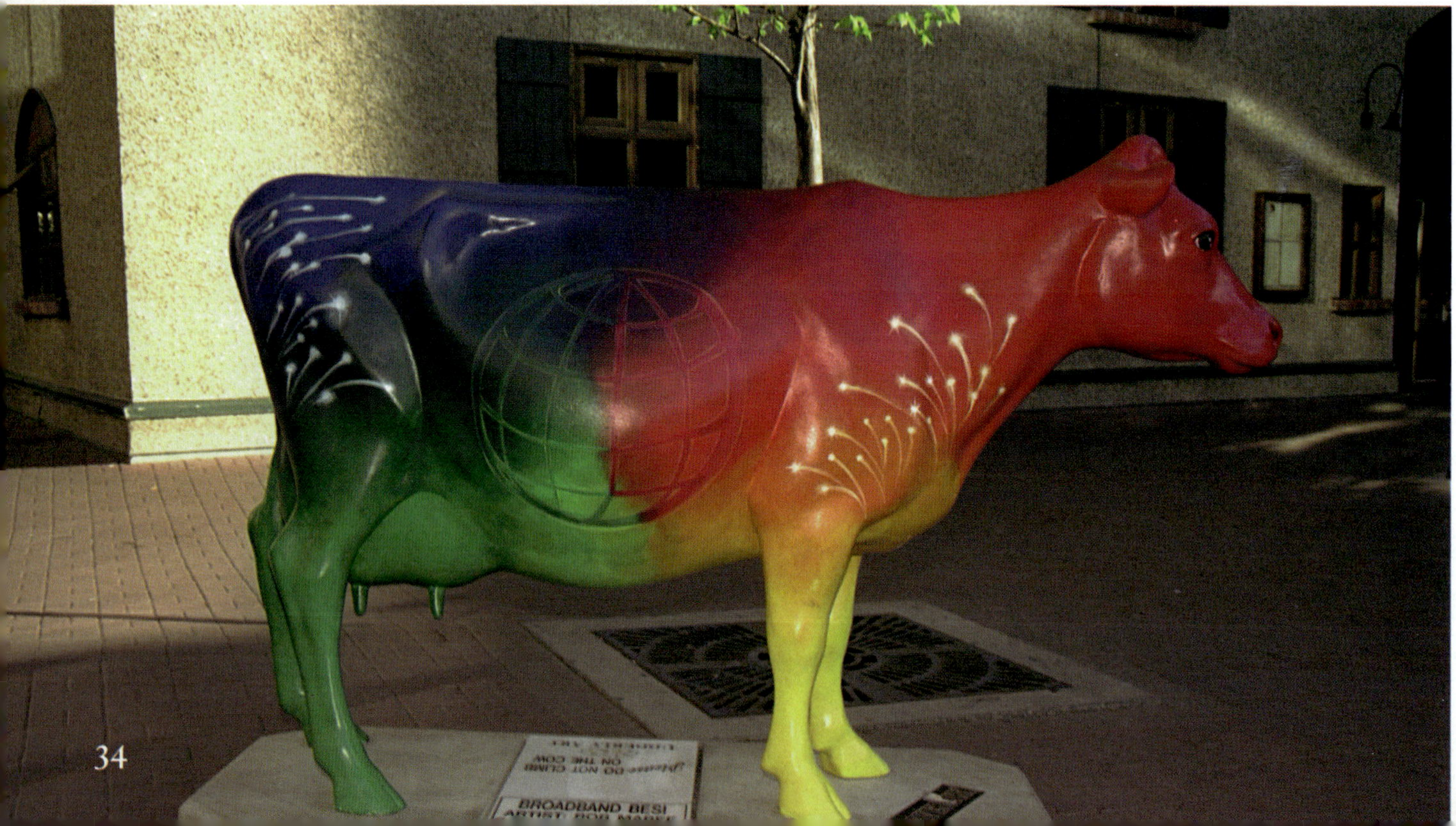

Canabelle

Artist: Cynthia MacKenzie
Owner: CANA Construction Co. Ltd.

For artistic reasons, Calgary sculptor Brian Cooley created the Udderly Art cow prototype in the shape of a milk-yielding Jersey. But Cynthia MacKenzie's *Canabelle* has a bit more meat to her. With her broad brown back and white face, this Jersey is either on steroids or is a beefier breed—maybe a Hereford.

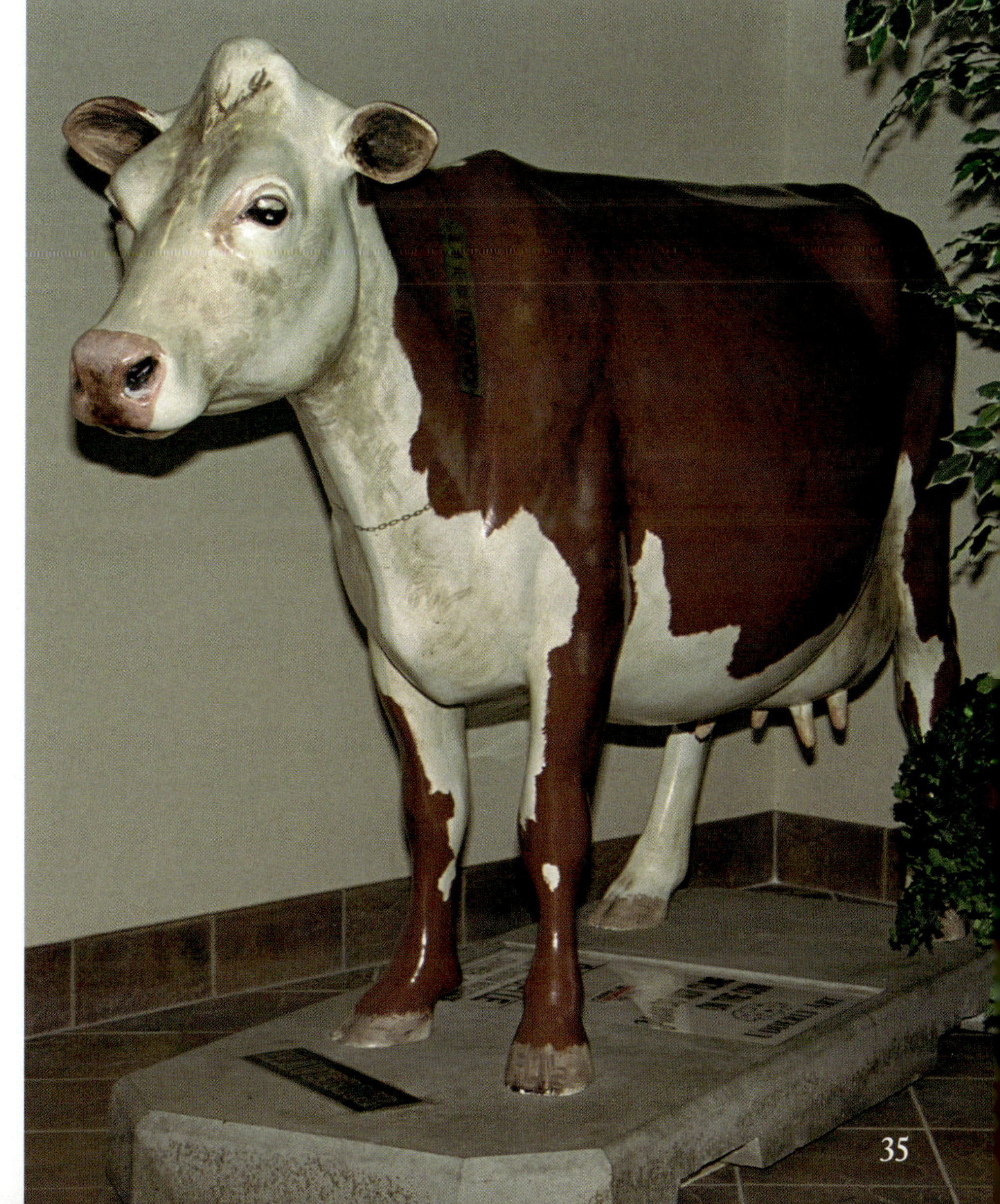

Cattle Drive

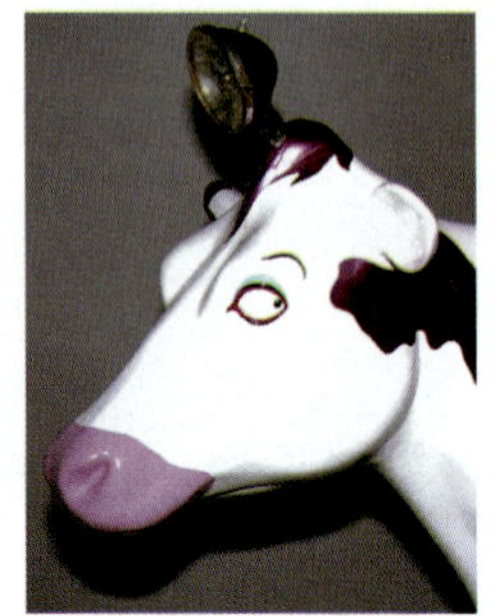

Artist: Ben Crane

Owner: Calgary Stampede

Charity: Calgary Stampede Foundation

Cattle, the open range and the Calgary Stampede are a natural fit, like favourite old boots of soft leather. Understandably, then, the Calgary Stampede went deep into cattle country to find their artist, drafting Eckville's Ben Crane to create this bovine ode to the glory days under the Big Sky.

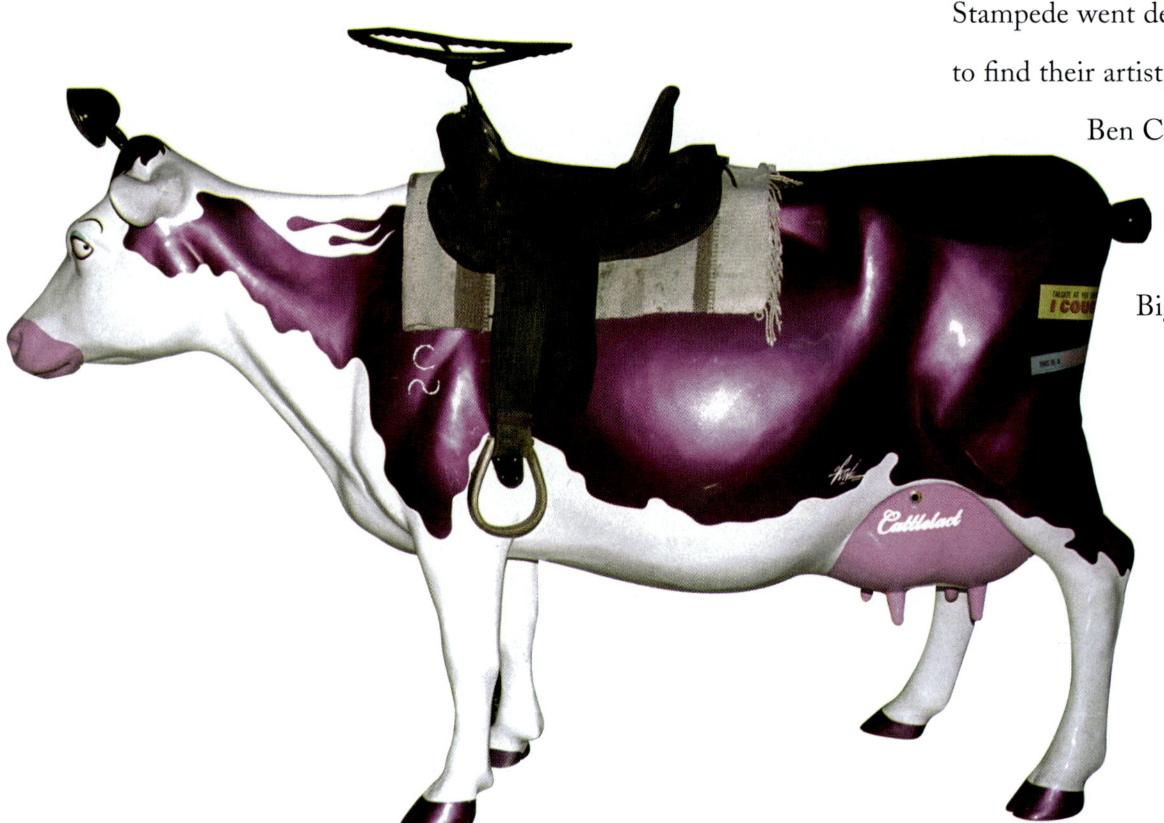

Chew-Choo

Artist: Damien Manchuk

Owner: Canadian Pacific Railway

Charity: Calgary Inter-Faith Food Bank Society

Damien Manchuk, a recent Alberta College of Art grad, combined urban skyline and locomotive motifs in making this cow bow to the CPR's role in building the Canadian West. The artist even supplied an inside look at the "engine works," through a window. Everything's where it should be, right down to the pipeline filter.

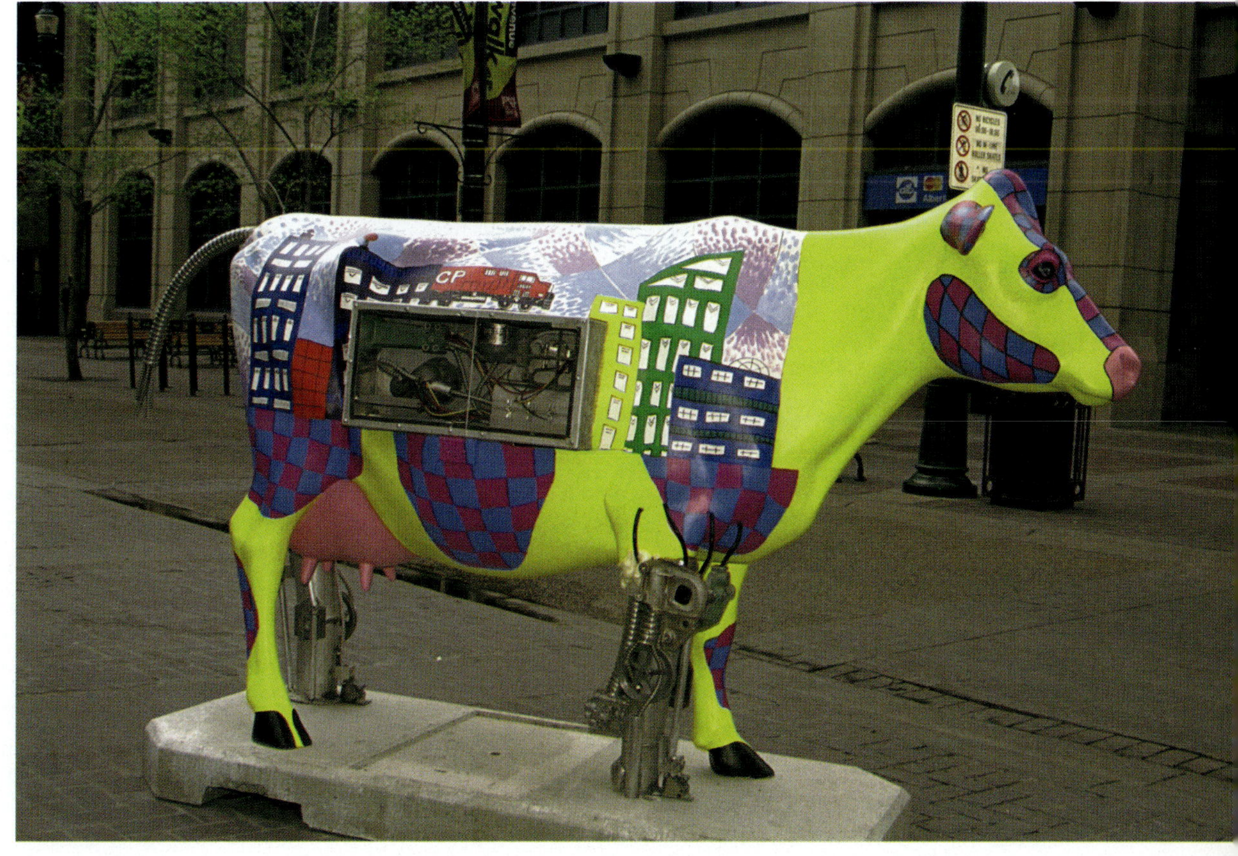

Chewing the Cud

Artist: Evelyn Grant

Owner: Calgary Downtown Association

It was probably inevitable that one of the Udderly Art creations would try to horn in on *The Conversation,* the popular sculpture on Stephen Avenue Mall.

Briefcase dangling from her jaws, Evelyn Grant's bronzed bovine sch-moo-zer fits right in with the two portly gents who've been bending each other's ears in downtown Calgary for the better part of two decades.

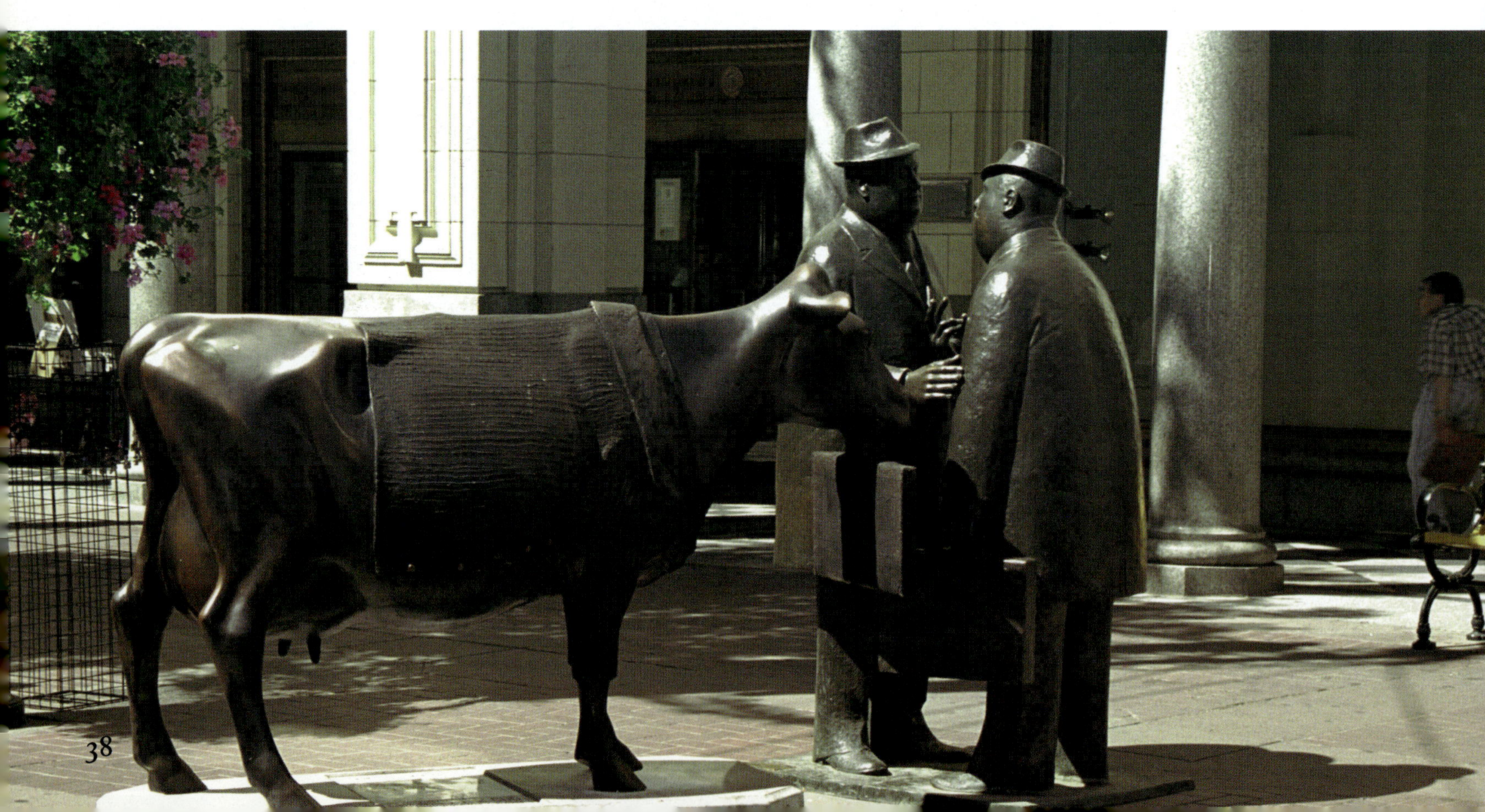

For much of the summer of 2000, Grant's creation turned two's company into an entertaining and popular crowd, judging from the pleased reaction of passersby on the mall.

All the more remarkable, then, to learn that Grant was exploring uncharted territory when she received her commission from the Calgary Downtown Association. A specialist in fine ceramics, her preferred medium is clay. But she found the challenge irresistable.

And like so many other artists on the project, her creativity enabled her to find help from unexpected sources. The two chatty crows on the cow's rump, for example, were discovered lounging on a shelf at Ribtor. And the briefcase is actually a sturdy, collapsible storage container, its handle wrapped in drywall paper and held in place with vandal-repellent metal brackets.

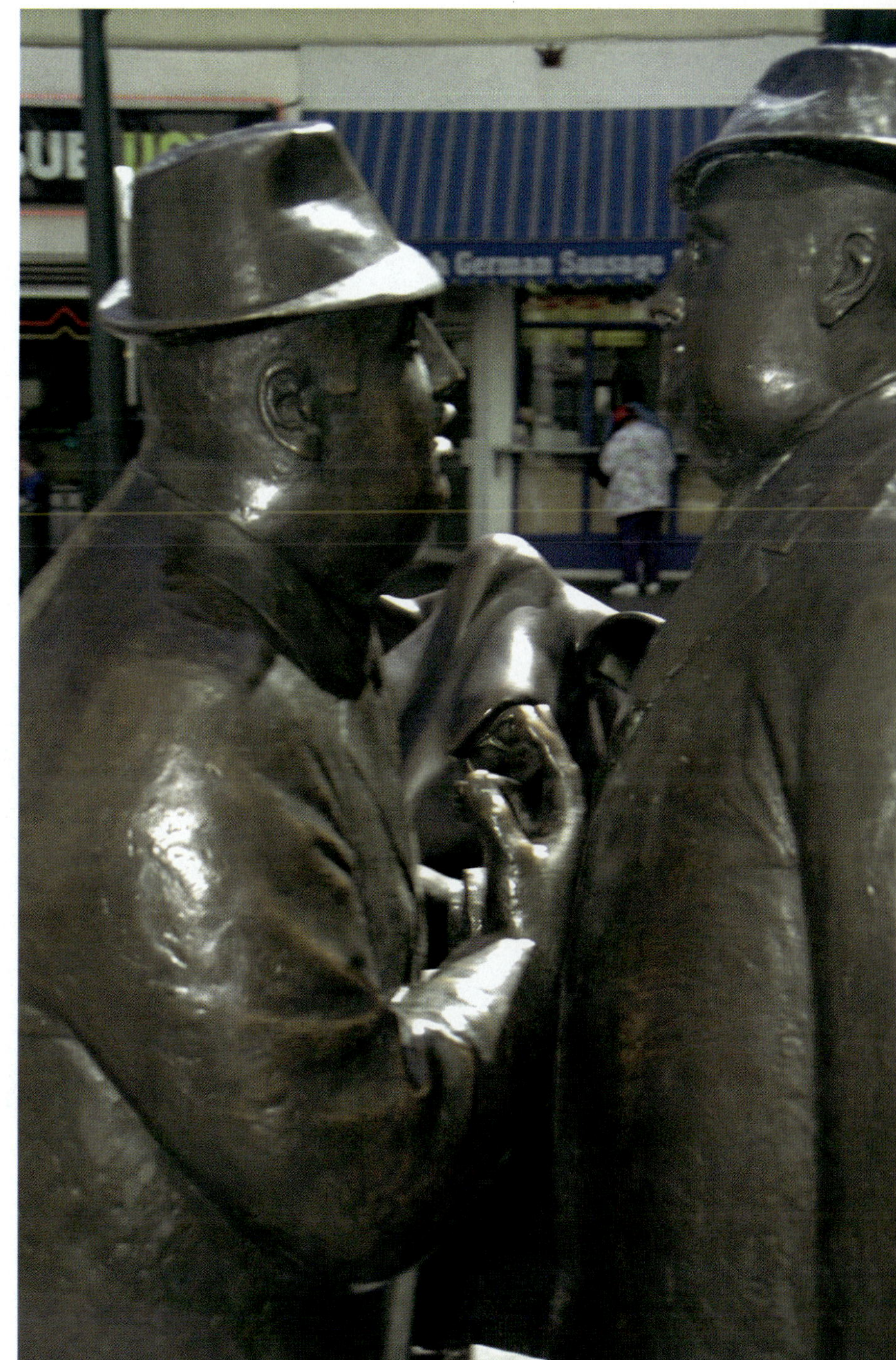

Chloë the COW-Muter

Artists: Stan Phelps, Carole Bondaroff and Amber Phelps Bondaroff

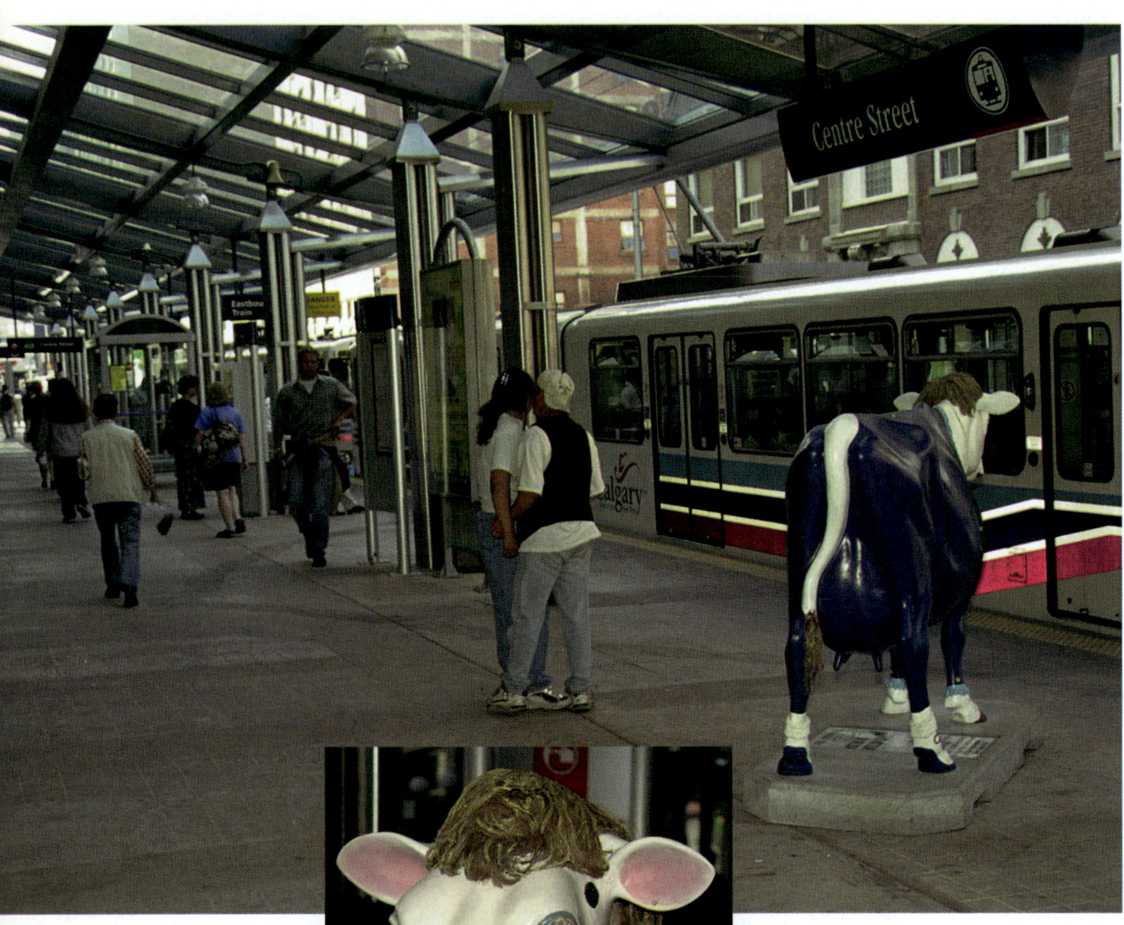

Owner: Calgary Transit

Charity: Calgary Handi-Bus Association

Calgary Transit employees have already adopted *Chloë* as an unofficial mascot. Small wonder. She's the quintessential C-train rider. Her artists adorned her with a businesslike pantsuit, wig, painted sneakers and honest-to-gosh socks. She's done up in Calgary Transit's colours—navy and magenta—and, yep, that's a transit schedule peeking out of her pocket.

City on the Bowvine "Under Construction"

Artist: Pam Weber

Owner: Remington Development Corporation

According to the gag, Calgary will be a heck of a city if they ever finish it. Pam Weber's nod to the building industry is a cow primed and ready to punch in for a full shift. She's been outfitted with a hardhat and a fully equipped toolbelt, probably a size 60, judging from the girth of that midsection.

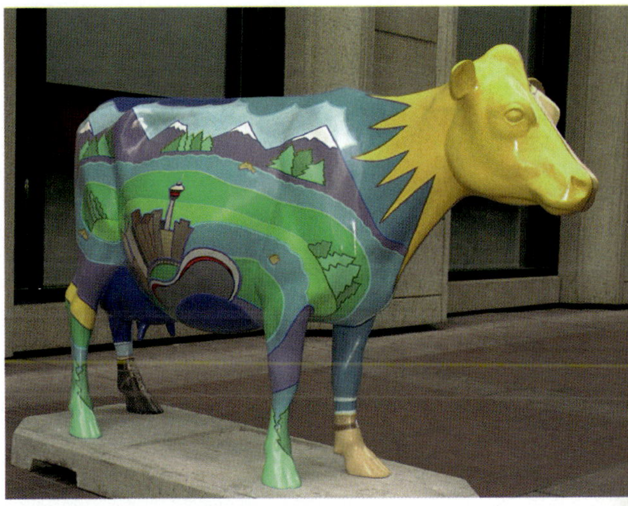

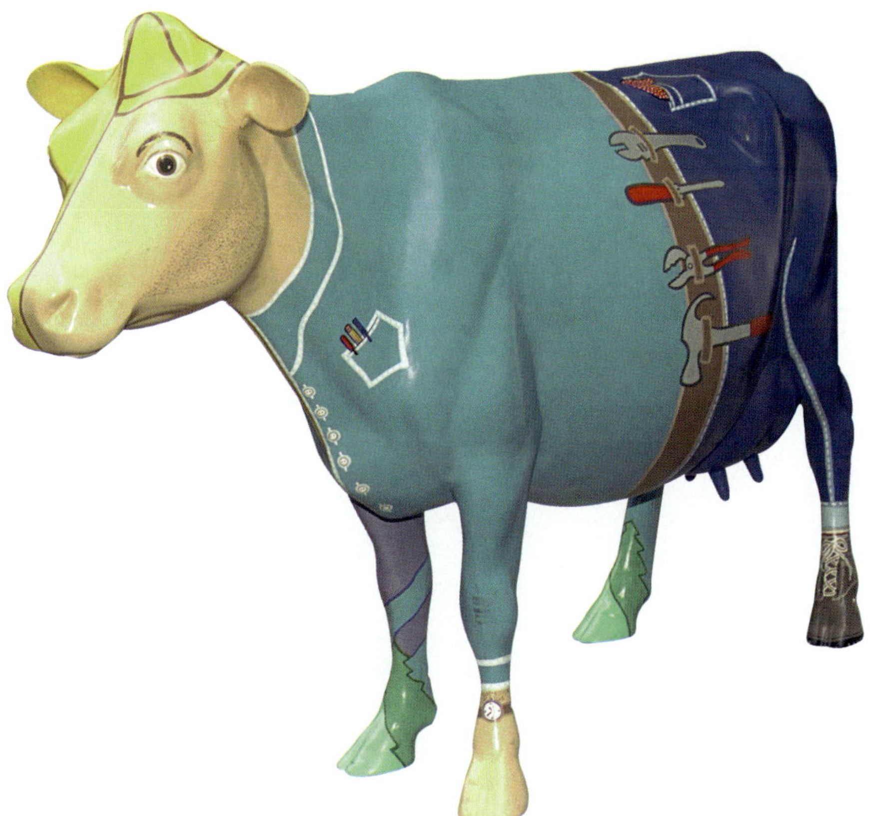

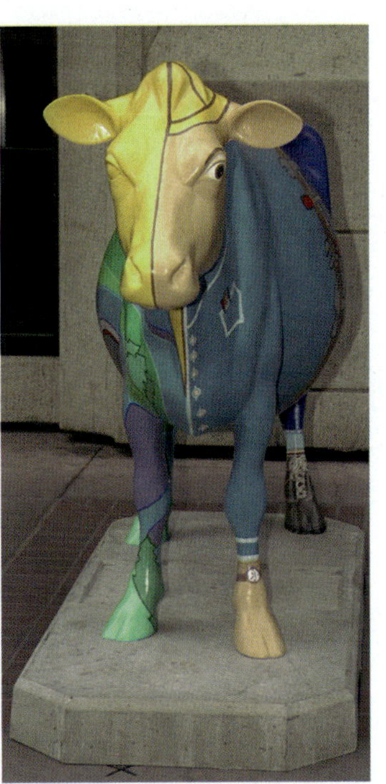

Clara B-Ellis

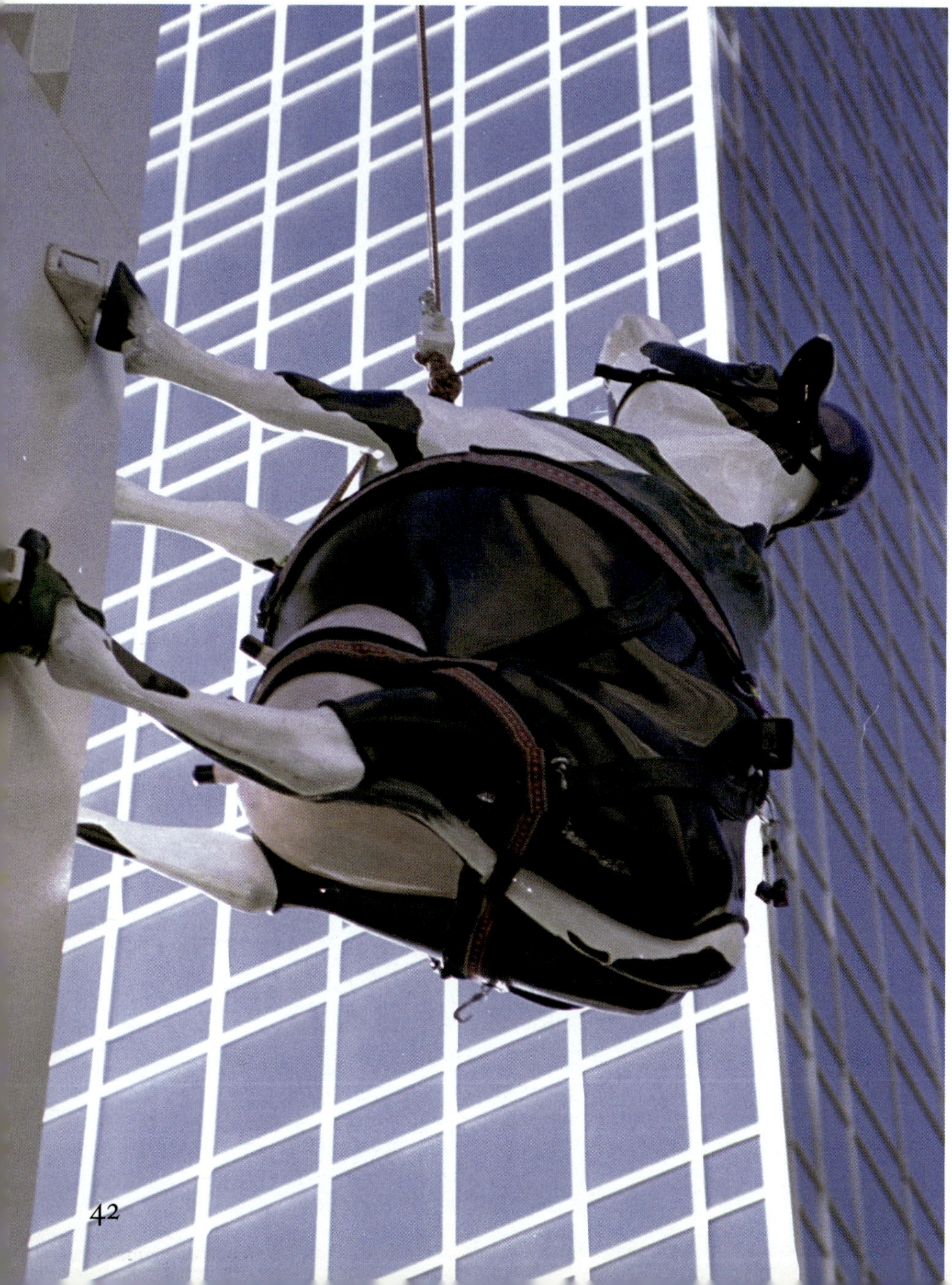

Artists: Debra Beres and Karen Aasen

Owner: CB Richard Ellis

Charity: Canadian Breast Cancer Foundation

She's a real social climber. Well, a mountain climber, anyway. Outfitted with crampons and ropes, *Clara B-Ellis* scaled the exterior of the old Alberta Wheat Pool building in downtown Calgary, where she liked the view so much, she stayed most of the summer.

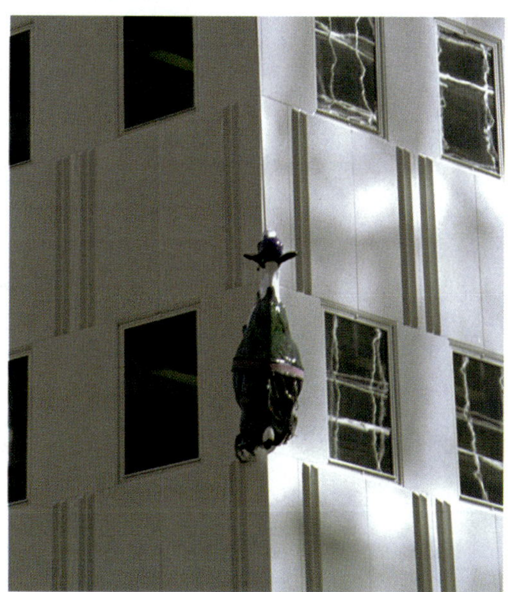

Climbing the Cowporate Ladder

Artist: Carrie Bozohora

Owner: Bankers Hall

Charity: Calgary Humane Society

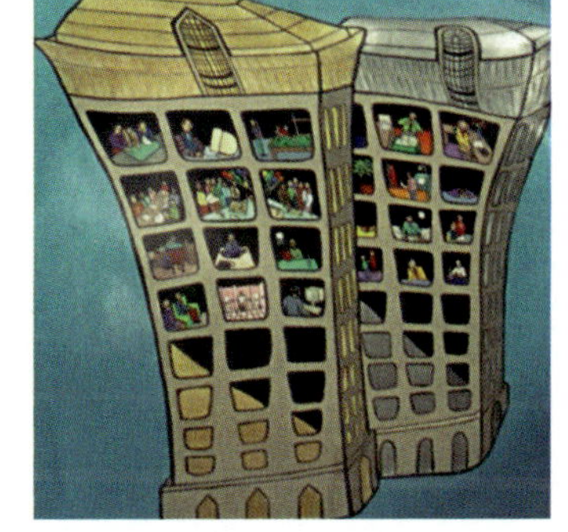

One of several artists to poke gentle fun at Calgary's downtown business community, Bozohora made sure this piece was dressed for success: corporate climber's jacket, power tie, the works. As a bonus, the artist included a candid, cutaway glimpse of some of the action within the offices of the Bankers Hall twin towers.

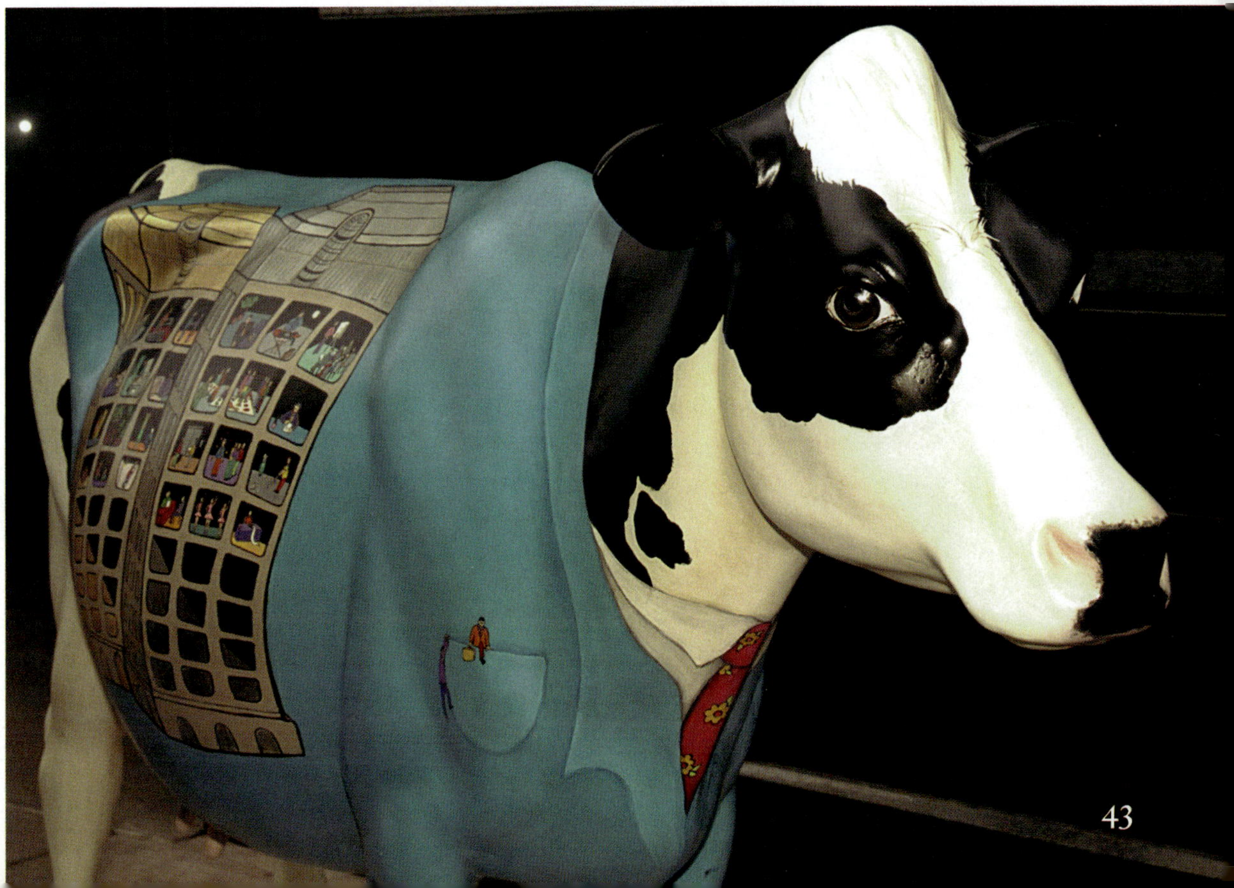

Cow Belle

Artist: Brad Polak

Owner: Westin Calgary

Charity: Calgary Children's Foundation

She's a one-woman band. A bovine or-cow-stra. A moo-rimba, if you will. Bells everywhere, each one eminently ringable. Visitors to the Westin Hotel spent the summer of 2000 having a bell . . . er . . . ball playing tunes on this marvellously interactive critter.

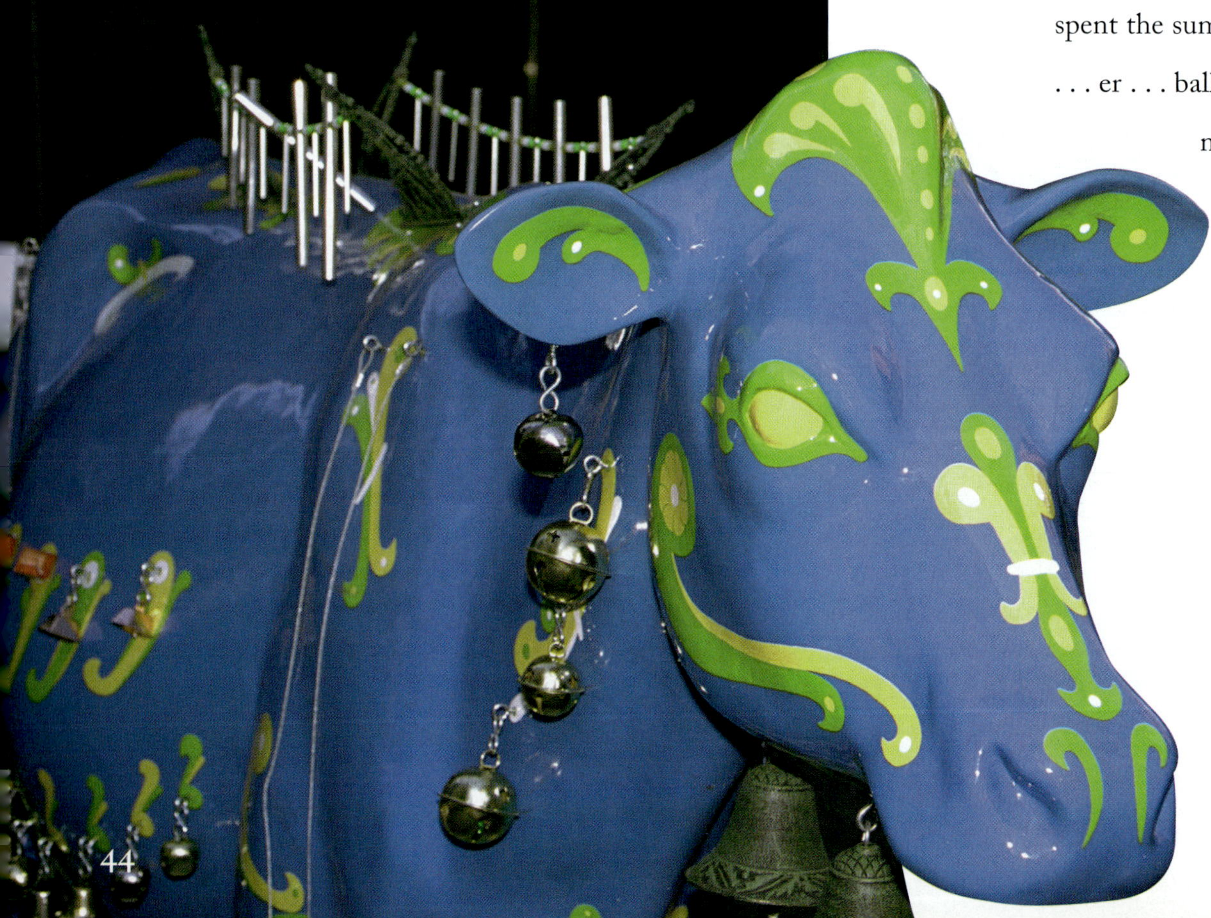

CowGary

Artist: blake@cross-eyed Illustration

Owner: Coast Energy Canada Inc.

Charity: Calgary Flames Foundation and Institute for Modern and Contemporary Art

Now the Calgary Flames' flaming *C* stands for *CowGary*. Another of Blake McCully's bovine babies, this example of pinpoint brushwork in the colours of the NHL Flames echoes the occupation of some of McCully's favourite clients. Blake's handiwork adorns the face masks of some of pro hockey's best-known goaltenders.

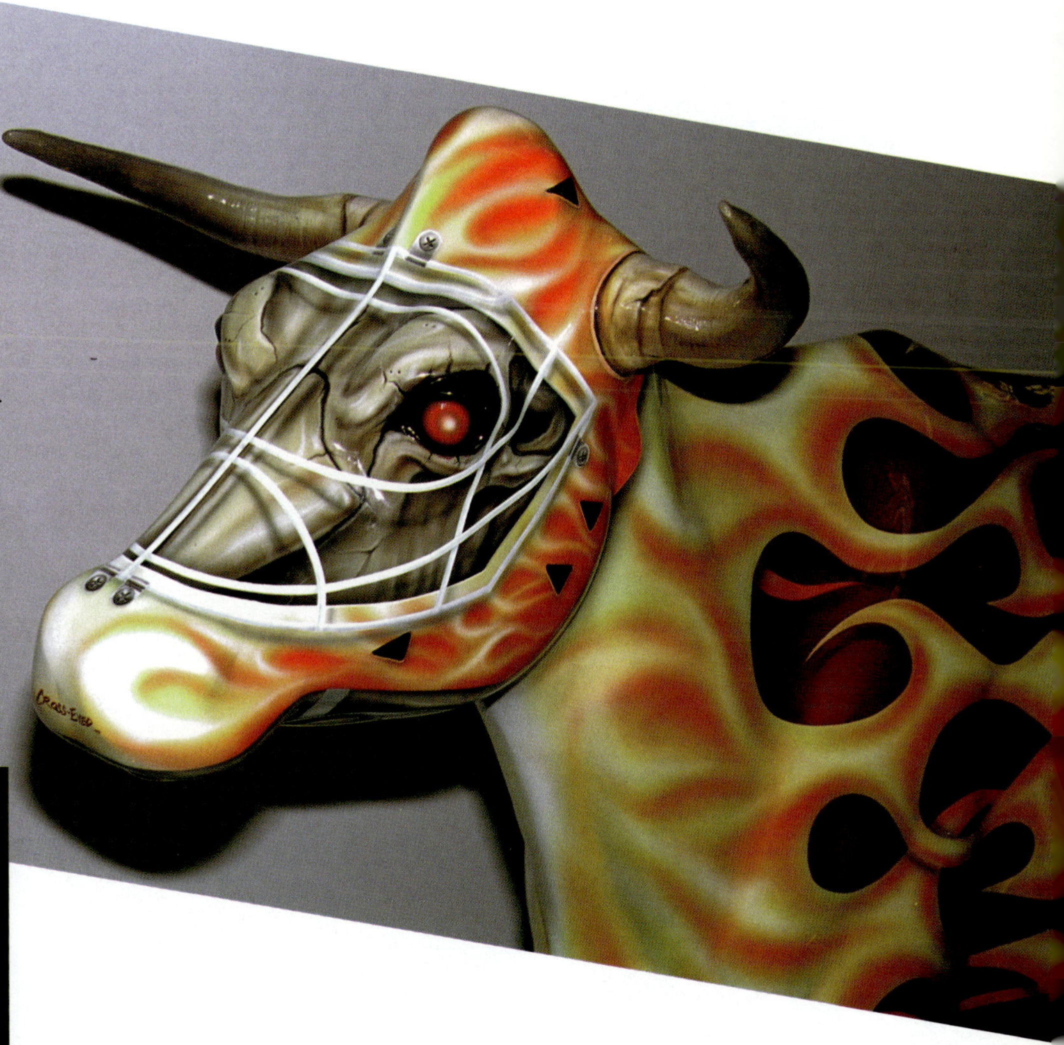

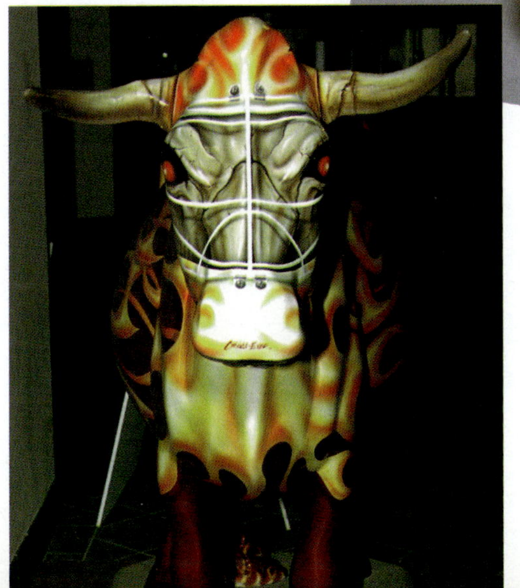

The Cow on Top of the Moon

Artist: Diane M. Anderson

Owner: Attaché Stables

Charity: Cerebral Palsy Association of Alberta

Where's the riding crop? This red-coated equestrian high-stepper got enough altitude out of her mount to make it all the way up to the moon. Wait a minute, forget the riding crop. What happened to the horse?

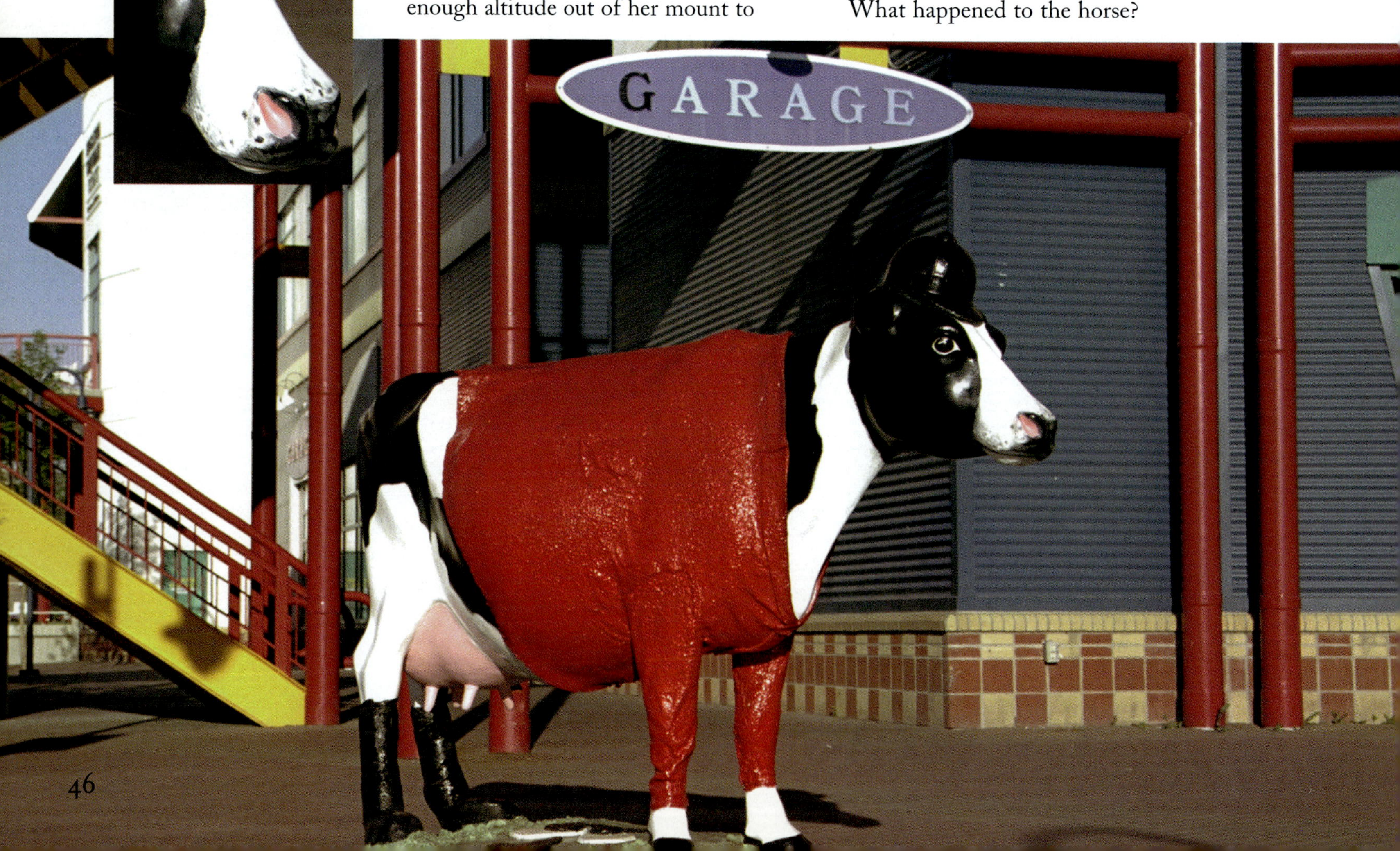

Cowabunga

Artists: Helen Archer and Nancy Diamond

Owner: Mayfair MRI

Charity: Peter Lougheed and Rockyview Hospital Foundations

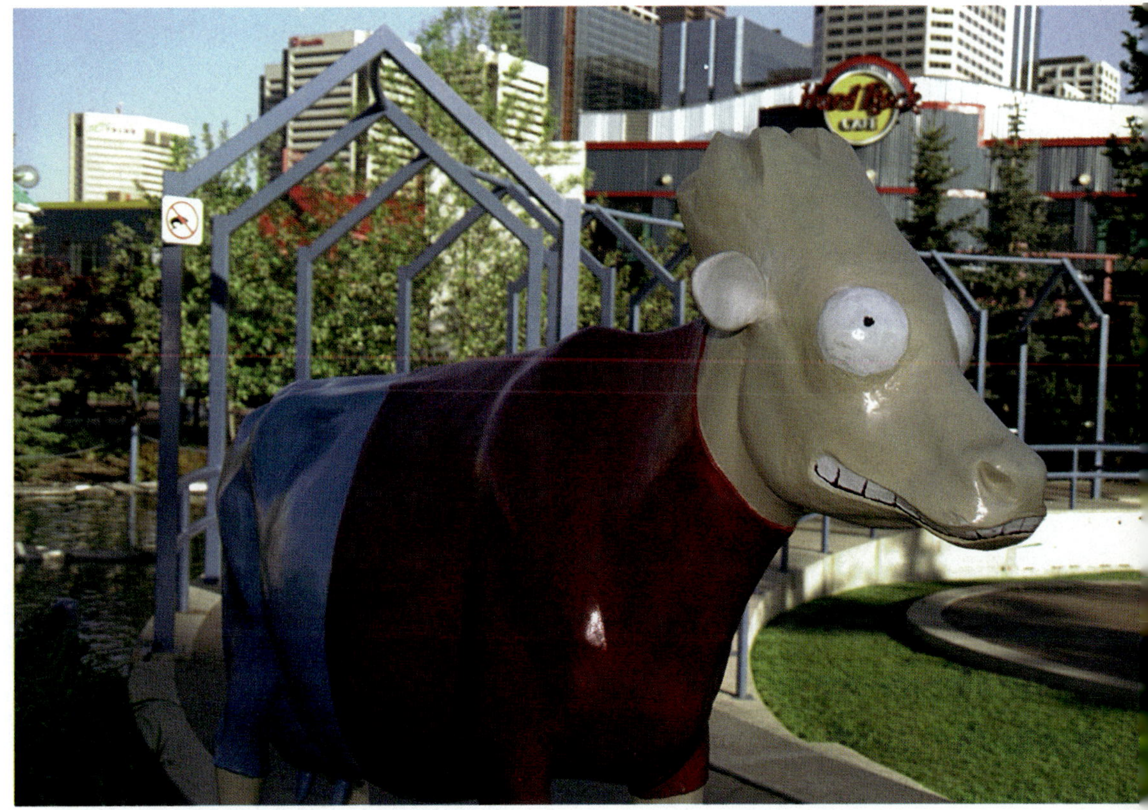

Cowabunga, dude, it's rascally Bart Simpson. But don't have a cow, man. As usual, he's just out for a good time and dressed for speed: shorts, T-shirt, and a cow-sized, racing-striped skateboard beneath his hooves.

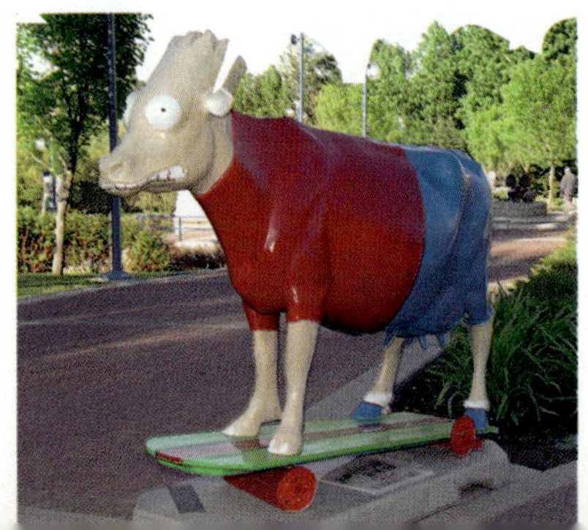

Cowardly Lion

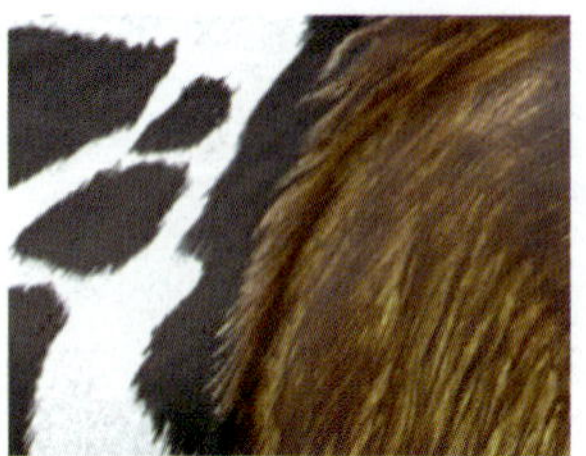

Artist: James Lutzko

Owner: Calgary Eastport Lions Club

Charity: Lions Eye Bank

Lions International service clubs refer to themselves as Knights of the Blind, so it's fitting that proceeds from the auction sale of *Cowardly Lion* will benefit their eye bank. By means of a golden mane, feline whiskers but a distinctly bovine backside, artist James Lutzko has skillfully combined two highly appropriate animal symbols.

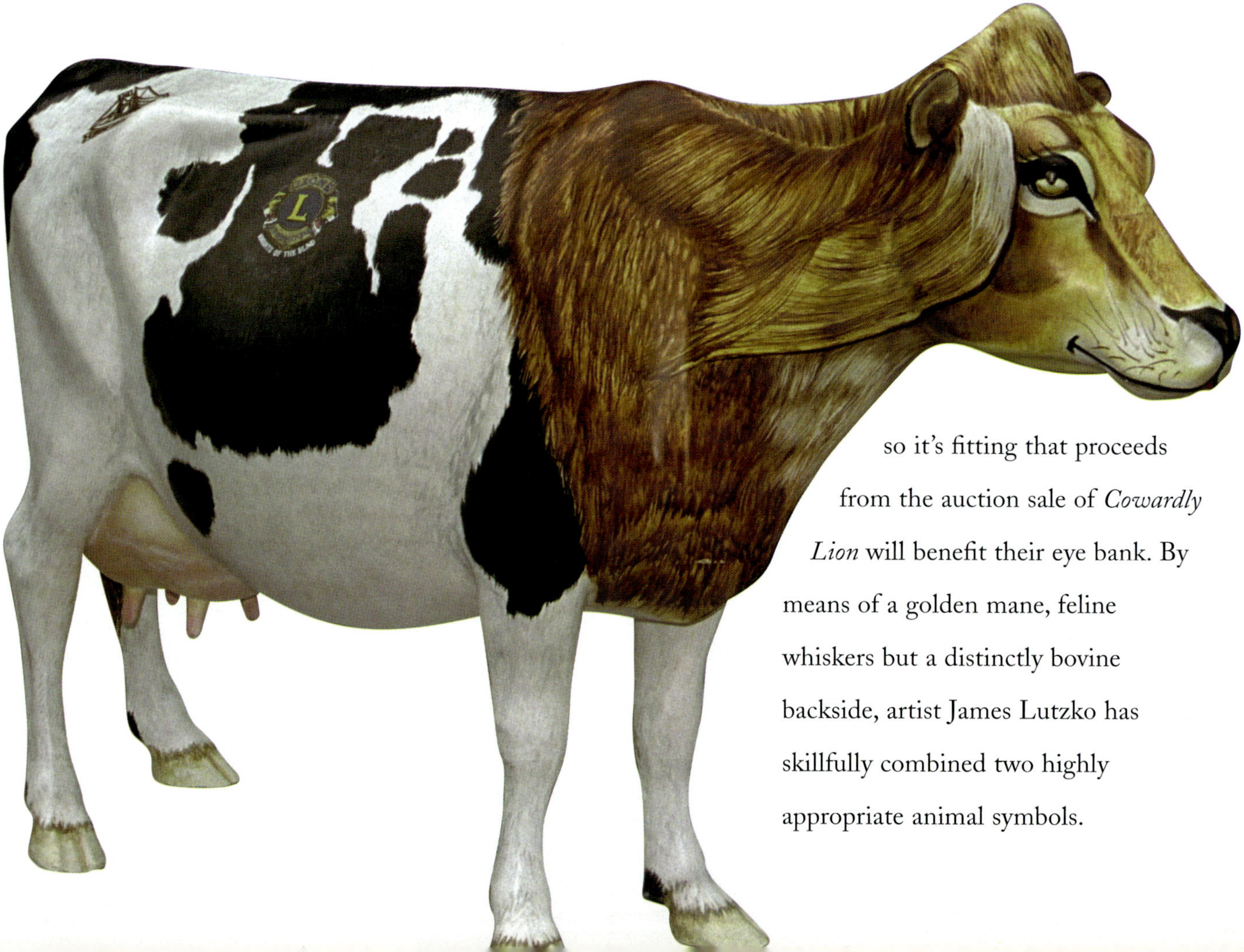

CowGary Tower

Artists: Dustin Hagerud and Ron Barreth

Owner: Calgary Tower

Charity: Habitat for Humanity

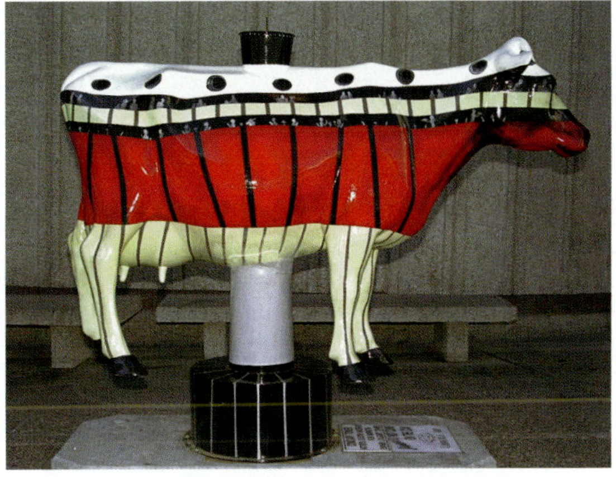

Of course, the artists did a spectacular job. But so did Calgary Tower staffers, who took big-time pride in their personal replicow of the landmark tower. Tower staffers formed a Cow Committee, and broad-shouldered volunteers helped lug their 100-pound baby to various sites for touch-ups and repairs.

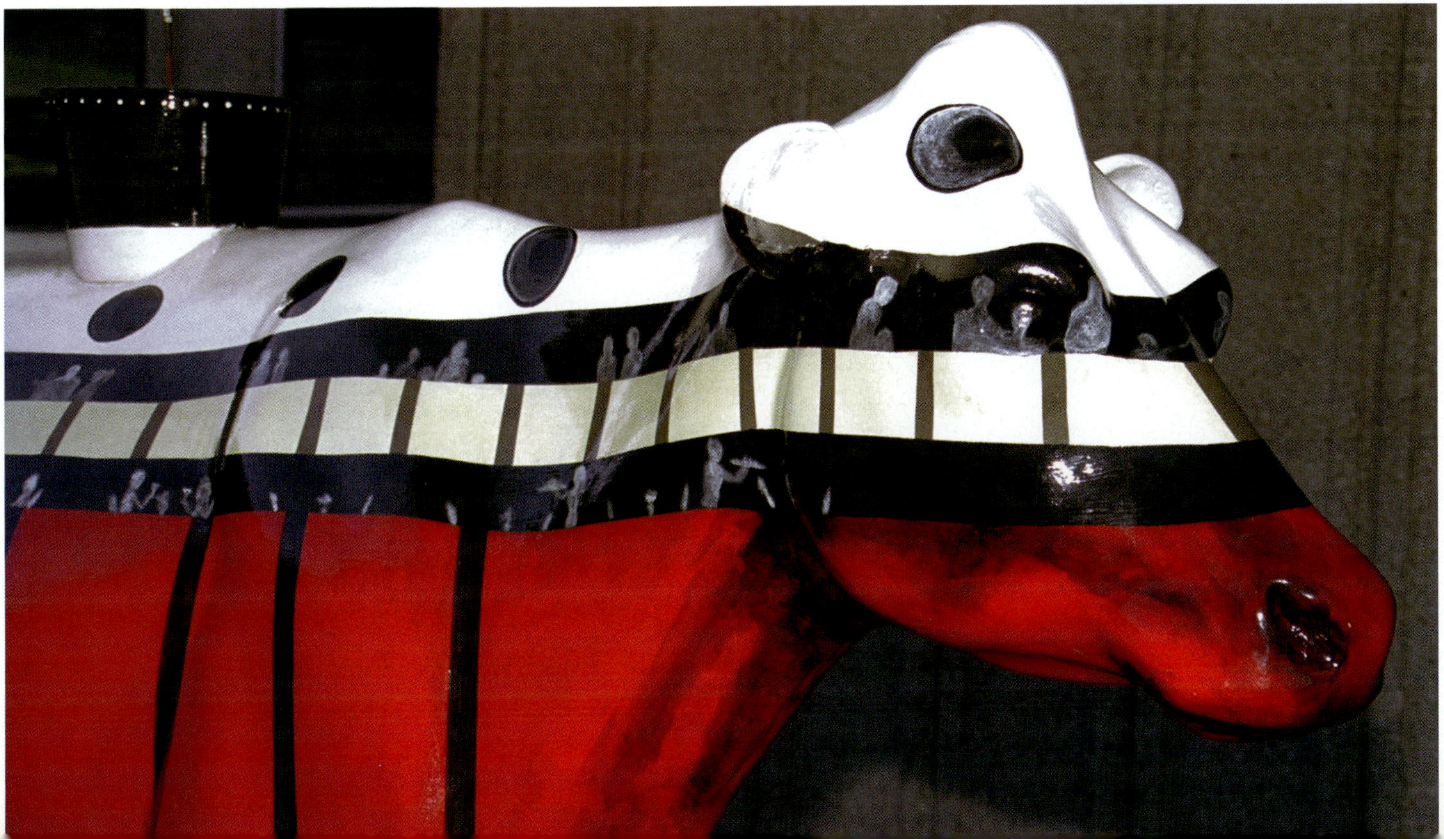

Cowatrina Witt

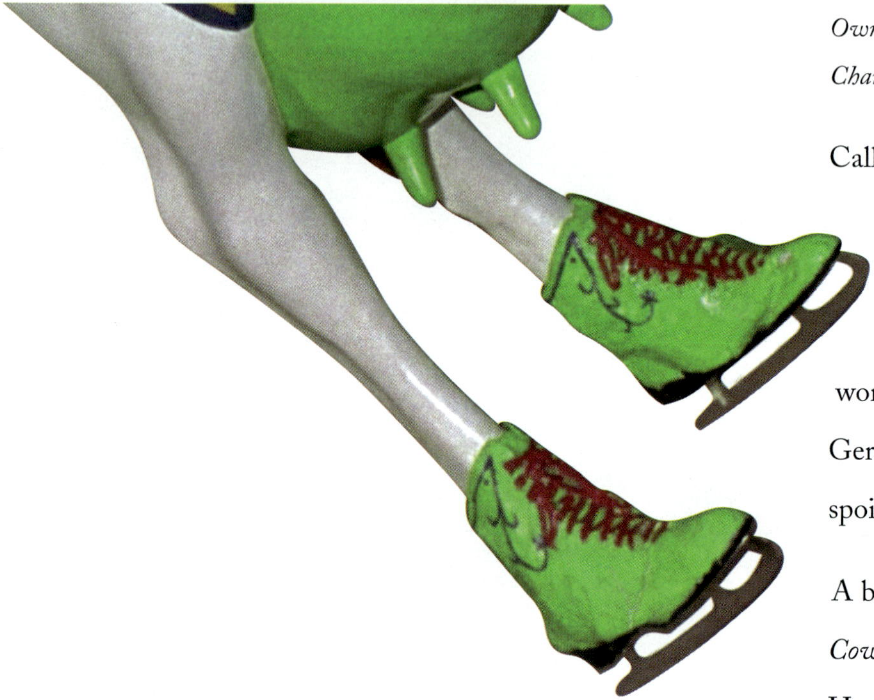

Artist: Keesa Hutchinson

Owner: Ken Hutchinson Architect Ltd.

Charity: Westside Regional Recreation Society

Call it a manifestation of Old Man Winter's warped sense of humour. But at the time, Keesa Hutchinson, a Calgary artist and architect, wasn't laughing. Her Udderly Art tribute to a world-famous star of the Olympic Winter Games, German figure skater Katarina Witt, had her debut spoiled by a freak Southern Alberta snowstorm.

A beskirted, beskated ballerina of the blades, *Cowatrina* was to be hauled by pickup truck from Hutchinson's Cochrane studio to a photo shoot in Calgary. But the impromptu spring blizzard stopped both the truck (it was stuck in a snowdrift most of the day) and the shoot.

"We'd bundled her up in blankets to protect her," explained the artist, but the cold, cold cow had to wait for the tow truck to make it back to the barn.

At least she was equipped for the weather. Hutchinson had *Cowatrina* with a Witt-style bolero jacket, loosely based on the outfit her namesake wore while skating in Calgary during the 1988 Winter Olympic Games.

And the skates? One pair came from Keesa's mom. The second came from Sport Swap. And don't look too close at those. One's a size 9, the other checks in at size 10.

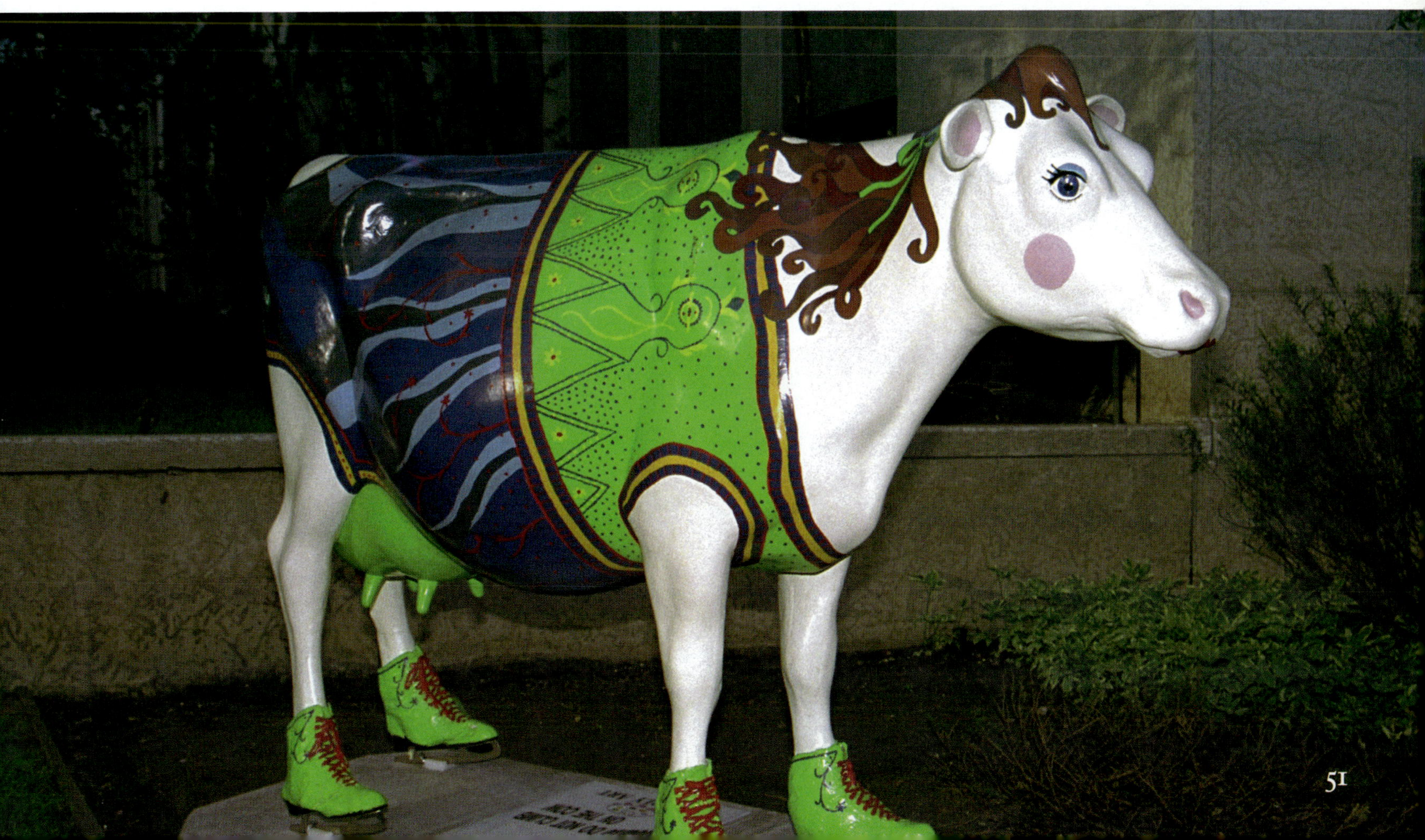

Cowley Ridge

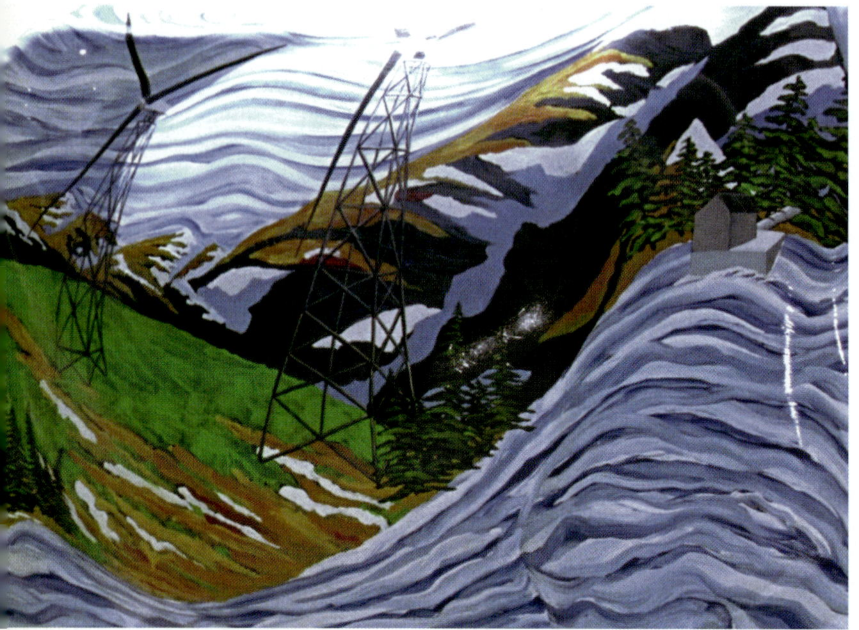

Artist: Scott Mushens

Owner: Canadian Hydro Developers Inc.

Charity: Pincher Creek Historical Village

If real, live cattle graze near the Cowley Ridge wind plant, they'd better be tethered to an anvil. Gusts in the area—east of the Crowsnest Pass, on Highway 3—have been recorded up to 120 kilometres an hour. Some of the plant's 52 wind turbines are strikingly depicted on the rib cage of Cowley Ridge's fibreglass namesake.

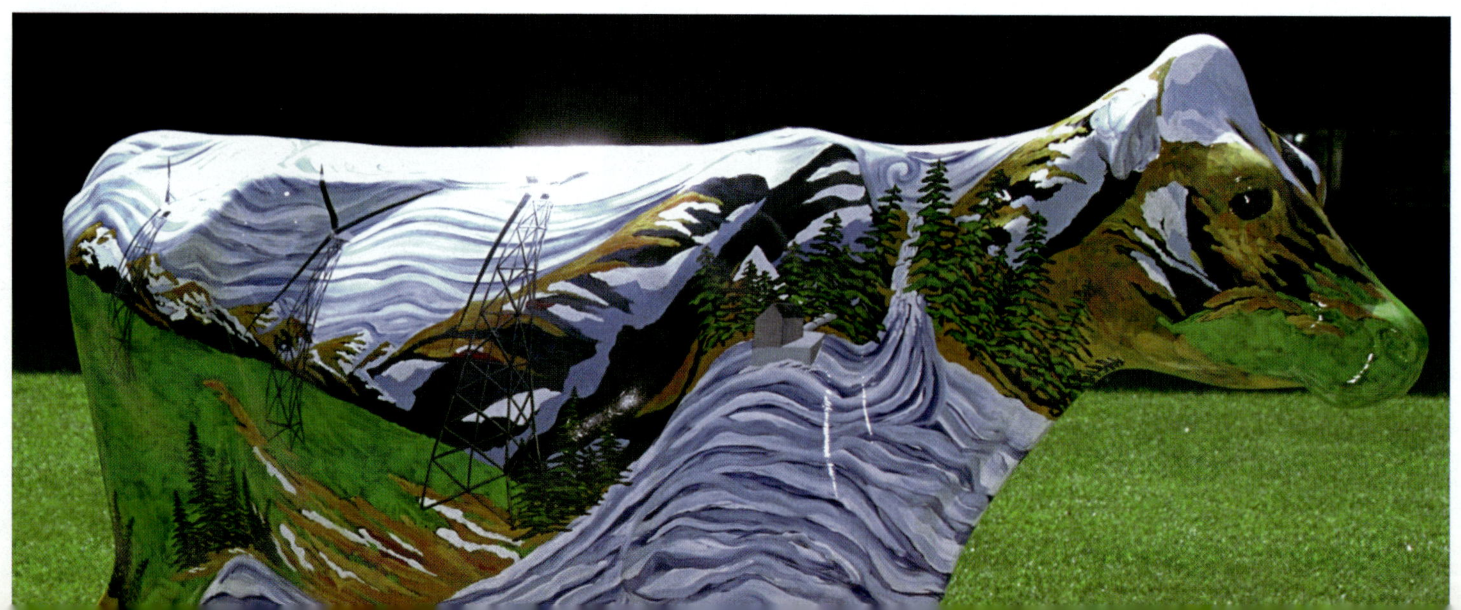

Cowlune

Artist: Effie Lecky

Owner: The Bow Valley Club

Charity: Alberta Children's Hospital Foundation

One fabled cow jumped over the moon. *Cowlune* landed on it and melded with the moonscape. Now she's a hooved, uddered moon rock herself. Cratered and corrugated, she's also playing benign host to two mice perched above her eyes. Maybe the moon really is made of green cheese.

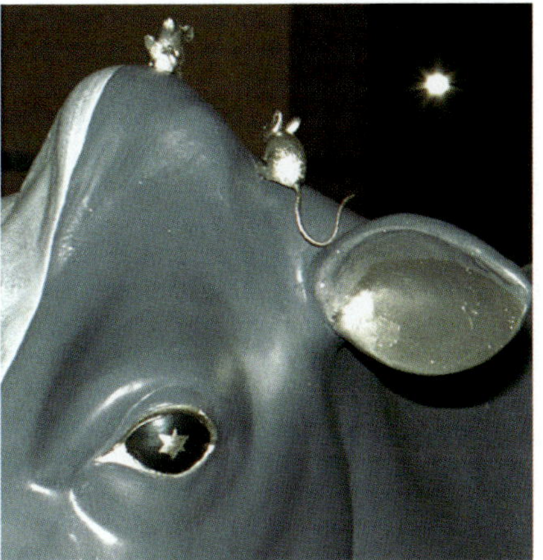

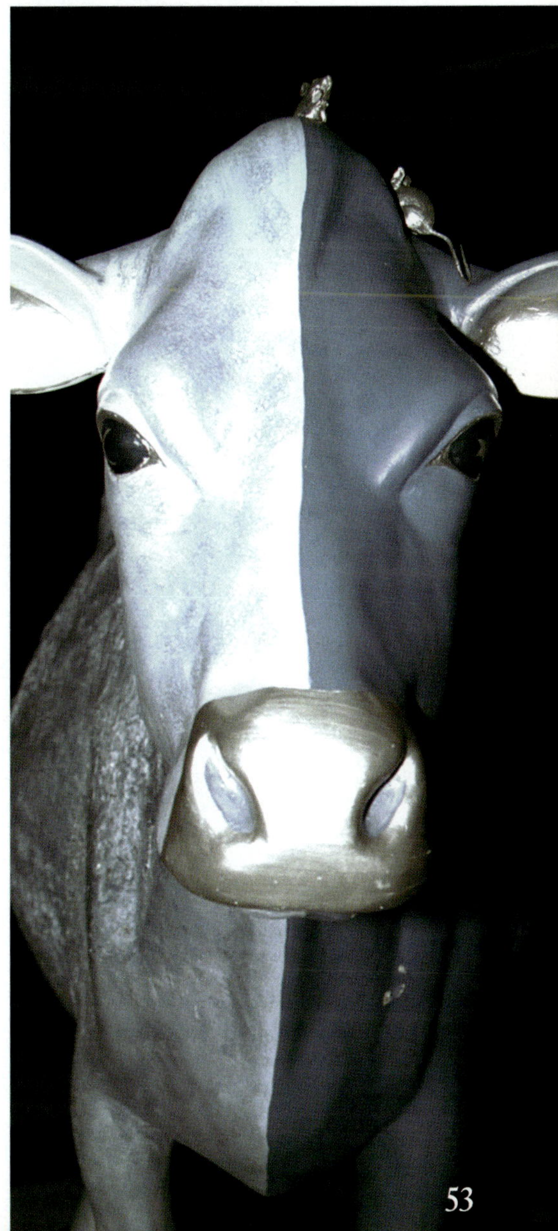

Cow.meleon

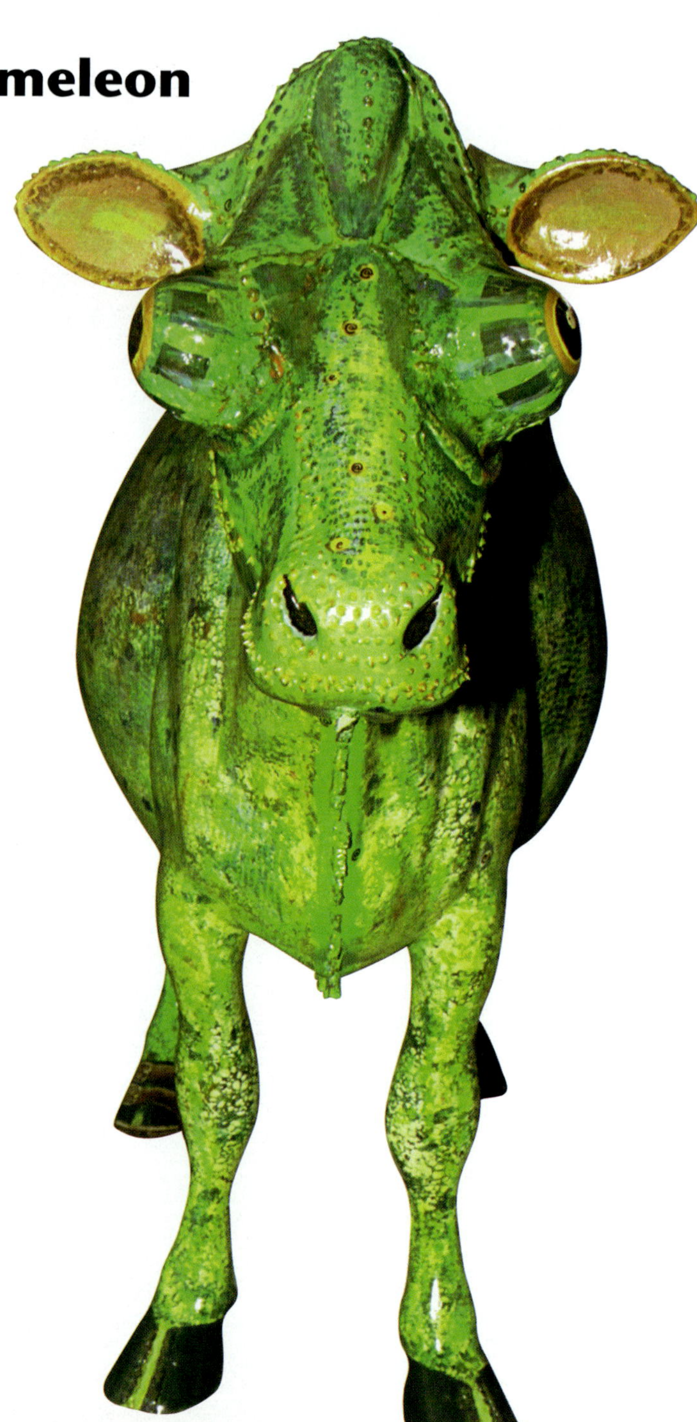

Artist: Janet B. Armstrong Design

Owner: iPlanet e-commerce solutions and Burntsand Inc.

To survive in the high-flying world of 21st century computer cow-merce, you've got to adjust to new environments in nanoseconds. You've got to be on the ball round the clock, virtually sleepless in fact. Rare qualites in your basic, garden-variety milk cow, but part of the standard equipment of any self-respecting chameleon.

So Calgary artist Janet Armstrong dreamed up this lizardlike hybrid to cow any obstacle the day-to-day business grind might toss in her path.

Since Janet's cow was purchased from Udderly Art by two high-tech software companies, she wanted to make her creation as computer friendly as possible.

Her research told her chameleons constantly change colours to match their changing surroundings and look two ways at once. They never close their eyes, not even to blink—ideal qualities for the modern-day e-marketer, who can never afford to be caught snoozing.

Equipped with painted Beefenstocks on each hoof, *Cow.meleon* also sports tiny software signs and computer keyboard symbols on her lizardlike "scales."

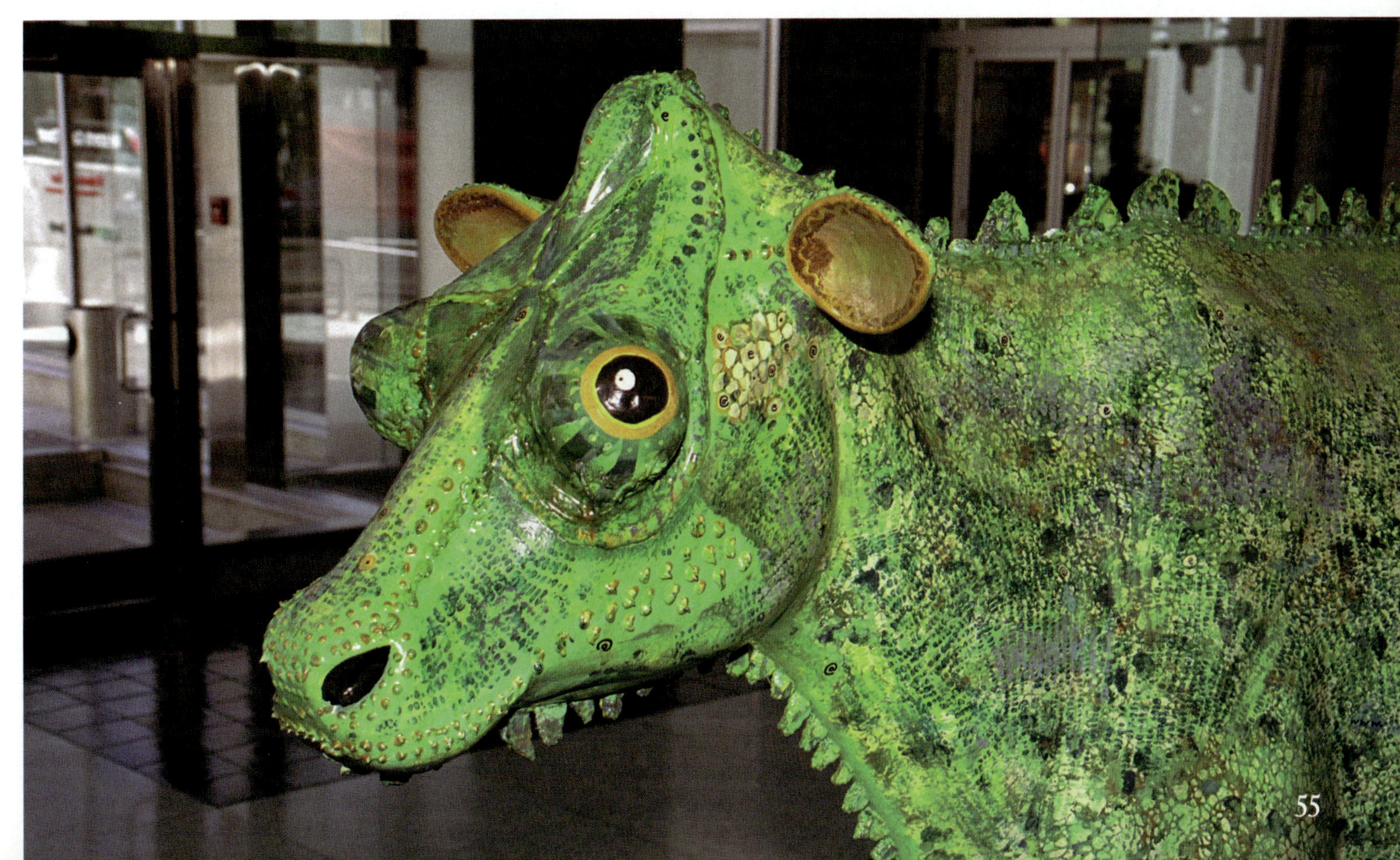

Cows on Cows

Artist: Rick Sealock

Owner: Highwood Communications Ltd.

Charity: Calgary United Way

Rick Sealock splashed a carload of appealing—and kinda crazy—cartoon cows on his humorous creation, intermingling a musical motif from the *Great American Songbook.* Ever imagine a cow warbling "Fly Me to the Moon," or "I've Got You Udder My Skin?" Give *Cows on Cows* the once-over, and you'll get the general idea.

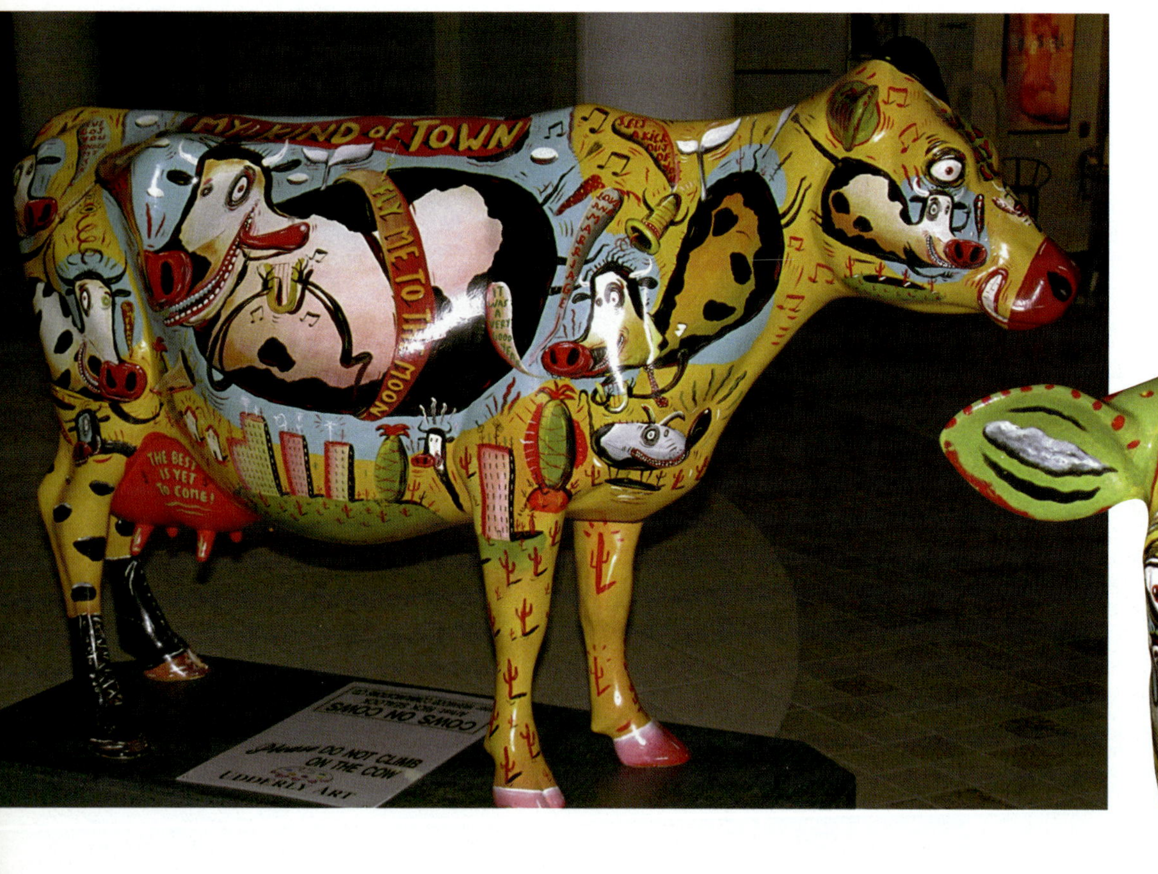

Cows R Us

Artist: Brenda Campbell Burrows

Owner: Alberta Cattle Commission

Charity: Boys & Girls Clubs of Calgary and Rainbow Society of Alberta

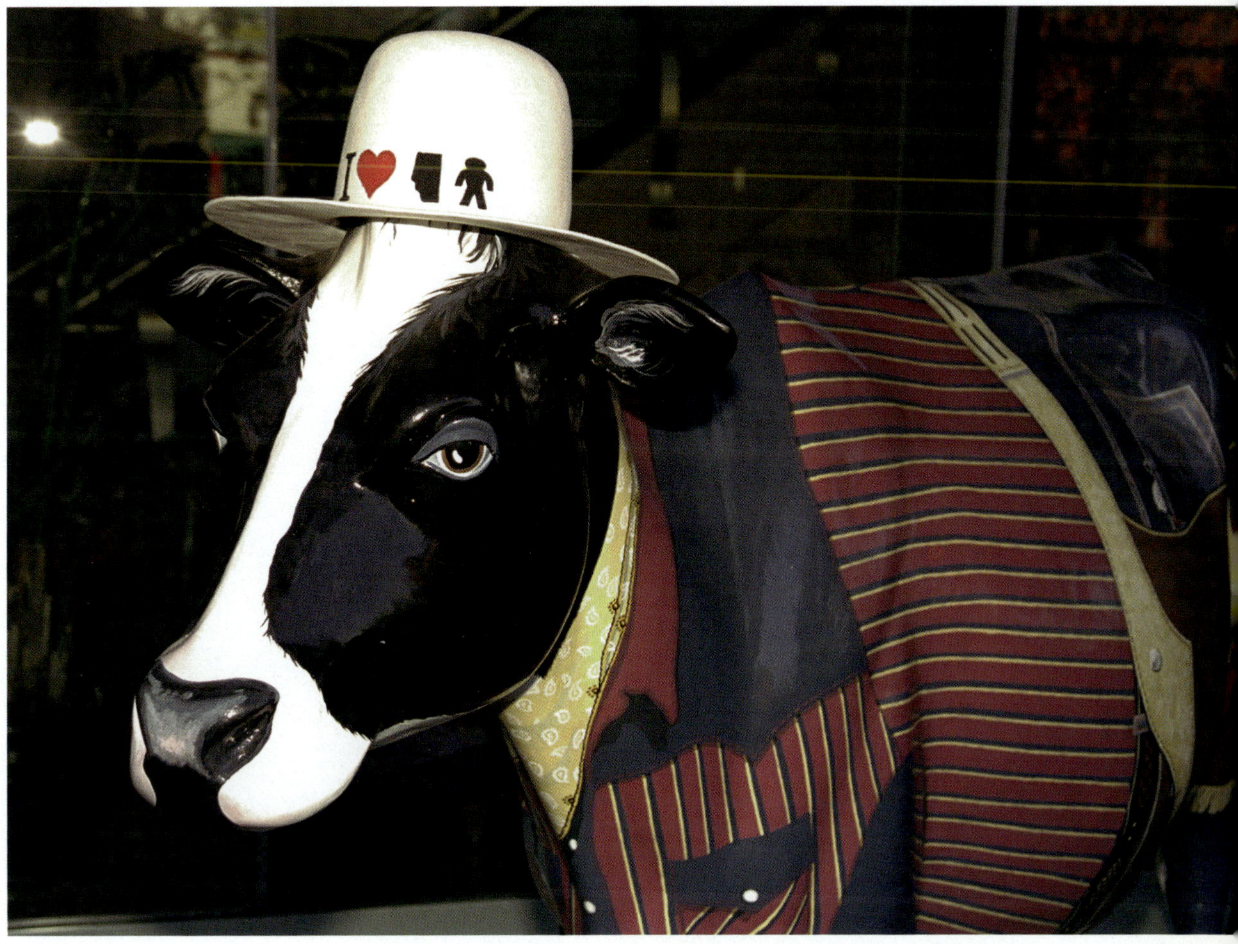

Considering the cow's original purchaser, Irricana's Brenda Campbell Burrows chose the ideal theme. This range roamer is duded up in the latest western wear, right down to her designer jeans and chaps. To boot, the artist serves up her hilarious variation of the I Love Alberta Beef insignia on the cow's 10-gallon lid.

Cowtown

Artist: Gordon Reid

Owner: Calgary Stampede Foundation (donated by Bennett Jones)

Charity: Calgary Stampede Foundation

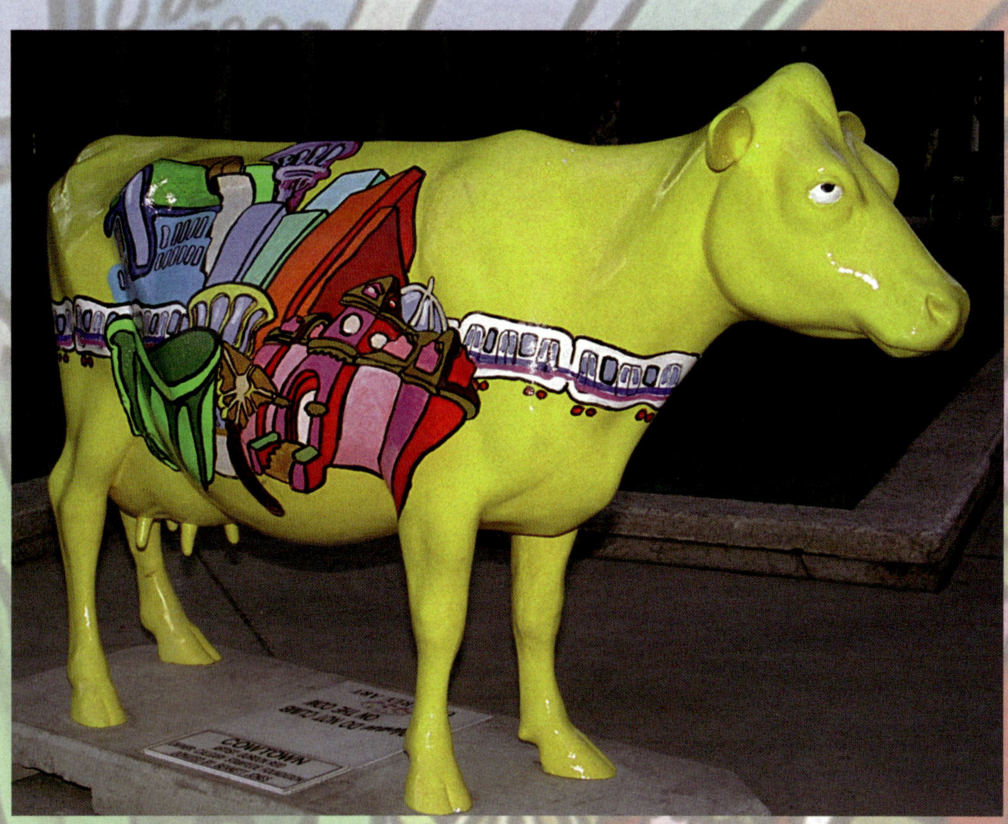

Gordon Reid's highly stylized city skyline leaps out from a brilliant yellow base. This cow was donated to the Calgary Stampede Foundation by the venerable law firm of Bennett Jones. So Reid wrapped the gift by means of a round-the-cow ribbon, which looks suspiciously like a C-train.

Cowtown Sundown

Artists: Jeanette Moran and Nancy-Lynne Hughes

Owner: Colliers International

Charity: Safe Haven Foundation

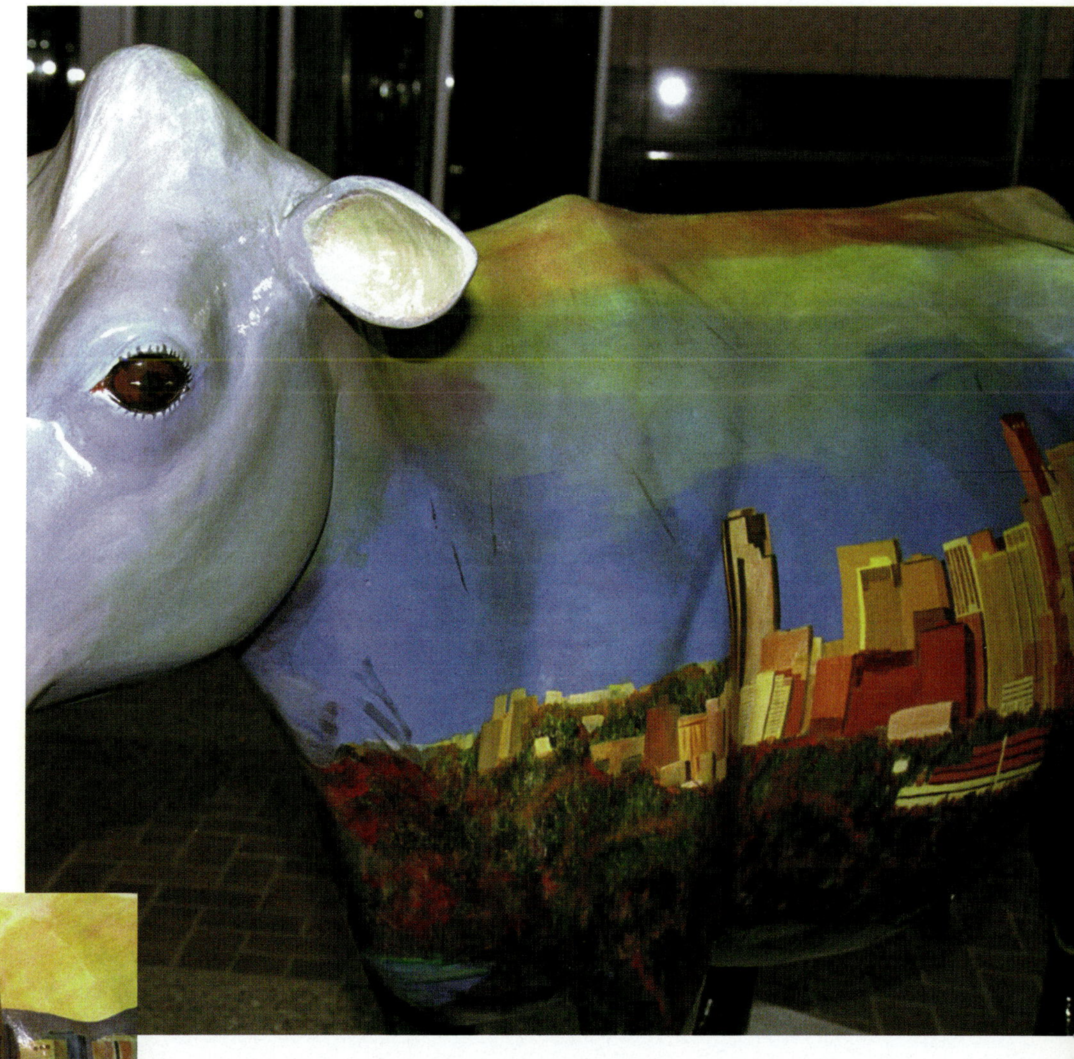

The name of the Safe Haven agency helped inspire this twin perspective of the Calgary skyline at sunset. Artist Nancy-Lynne Hughes has always considered her home city a safe haven in itself. So the artists provide viewers with east-to-west and west-to-east perspectives of the downtown core, with the Saddledome down under on the udder.

Coyuse

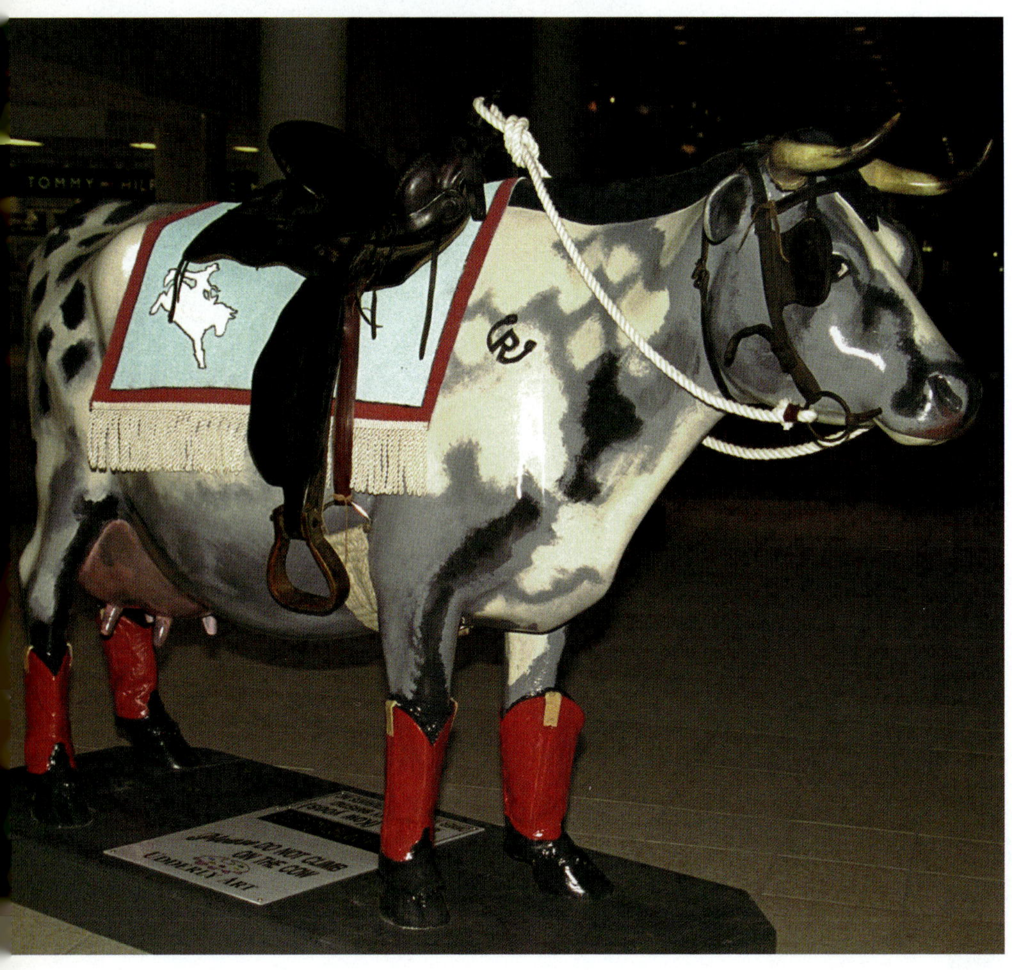

Owner: Ranchman's Restaurants Inc.

Artist: Rocky Barstad

Multitalented artist Rocky Barstad of High River has a fetish for getting things right. A Westerner to the bone, he has no use for anything false or artificial, particularly when it comes to his work.

So when he set out to craft a distinctive fibreglass cow for his pal, Harris Dvorkin of Ranchman's Restaurants, Barstad went to the source.

"Harris was kind of hoping to turn that cow into a horse," Barstad explained of his booted, saddled, cow-cum-cayuse.

"No problem," Barstad nodded in assent, "just so long as we do this thing right."

He insisted on borrowing an antique saddle from Dvorkin, who had to retrieve the leather accessory from high in the rafters of his Macleod Trail restaurant, where the saddle had been on display for years.

Then Rocky set to prowling rural antique shops until he came up with a splendid set of high-end cattle horns in Nanton. He searched high and low for two pairs of matching scarlet boots until his search ended successfully right in his own backyard, a High River boot shop. As for that gorgeous saddle blanket, it's Rocky's own creation.

And for the final delicate touches?

"Good old western house paint," laughed the dyed-in-the-wool purist.

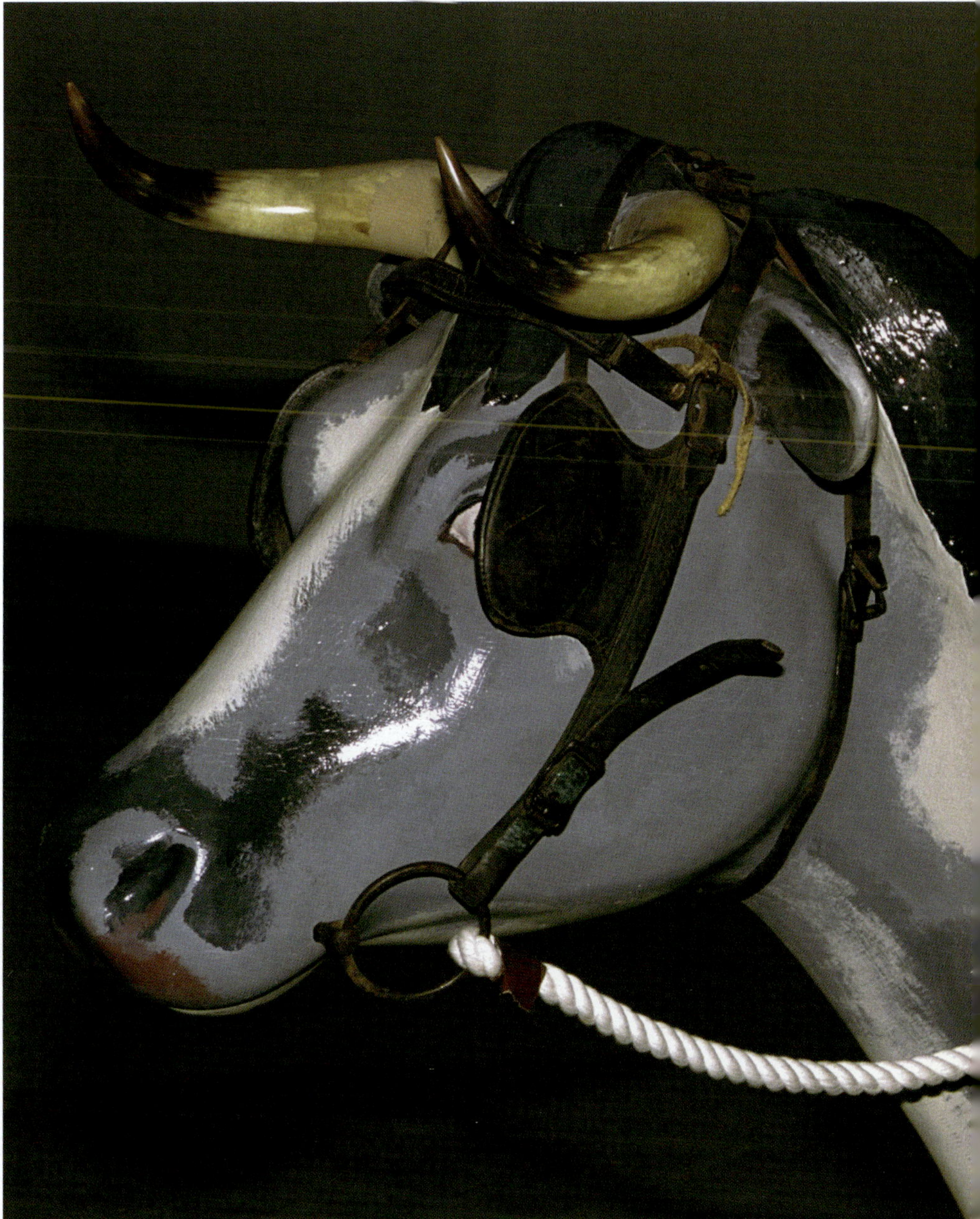

Crocus Dancer

Artist: Joane Cardinal-Schubert

Owner: Don McGregor

Charity: Calgary Aboriginal Arts Awareness Society

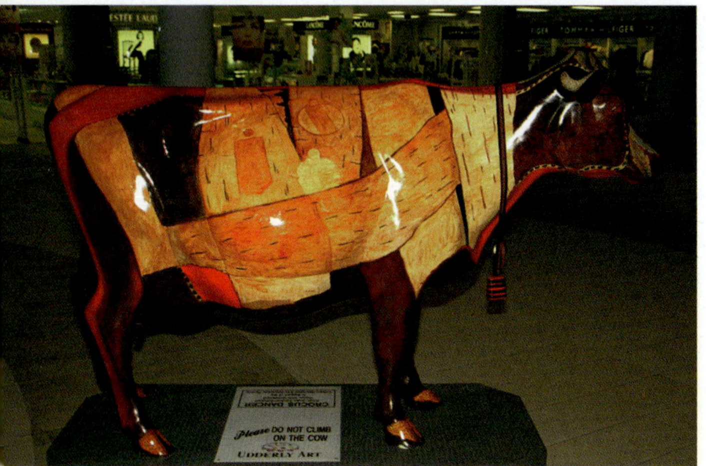

One of several Calgary cows decorated in tribute to North American aboriginal culture, *Crocus Dancer* wears her heart on her sleeve and a long, beautiful Plains Indian feather down the length of her snout. She is a picture of placid dignity caught during a meditative moment between dances.

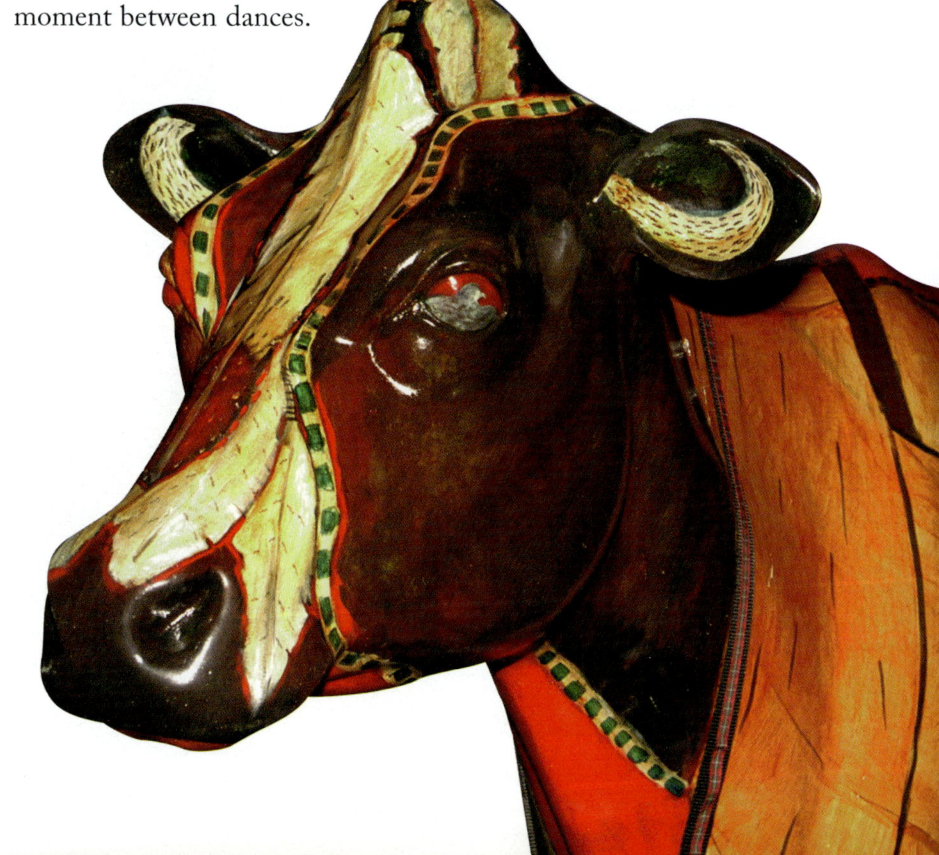

Daisy the Calgary Cowgirl

Artists: Dana Schnirer and Kieran Gelfand

Owner: Denim Pipeline Construction

Charity: ALS Society of Alberta (Lou Gehrig's Disease)

Western to the soles of her triple-E-width cowboy boots, *Daisy*'s as feminine as the next gal—after she's finished her shift at the ranch. Despite the pink, daisy-drenched shirtfront, those funky coveralls make it clear that she's a working cowgirl.

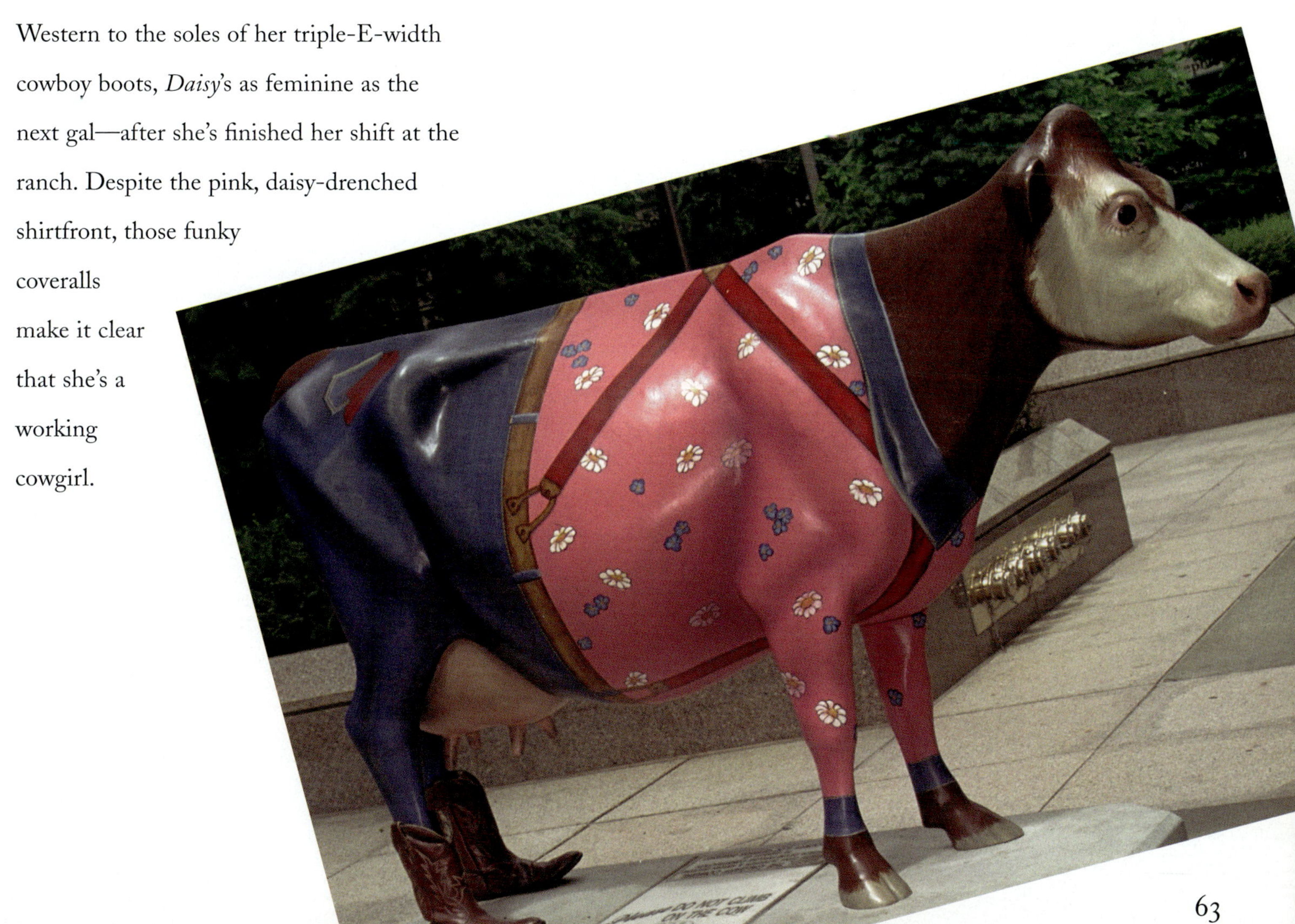

Daisy Deco

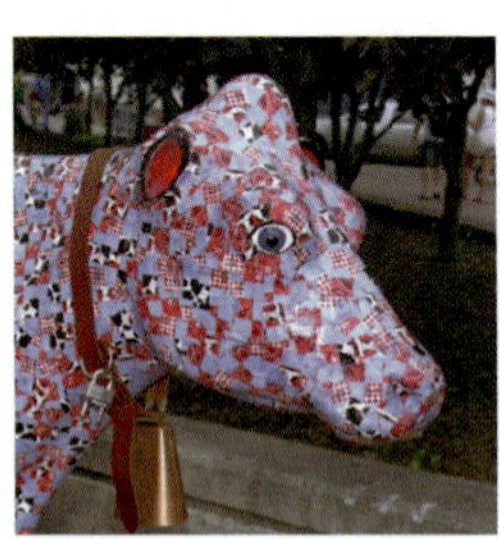

Artist: Children from the Calgary Children's Festival

Owner: Alberta Milk Producers

Charity: Calgary Children's Milk Fund

She's a match made in milk-cow heaven: milk producers and kids joined forces to create this sweet-tempered provider of strong bones and straight teeth. The kids created a labyrinthine patchwork of cute cow faces and red calico.

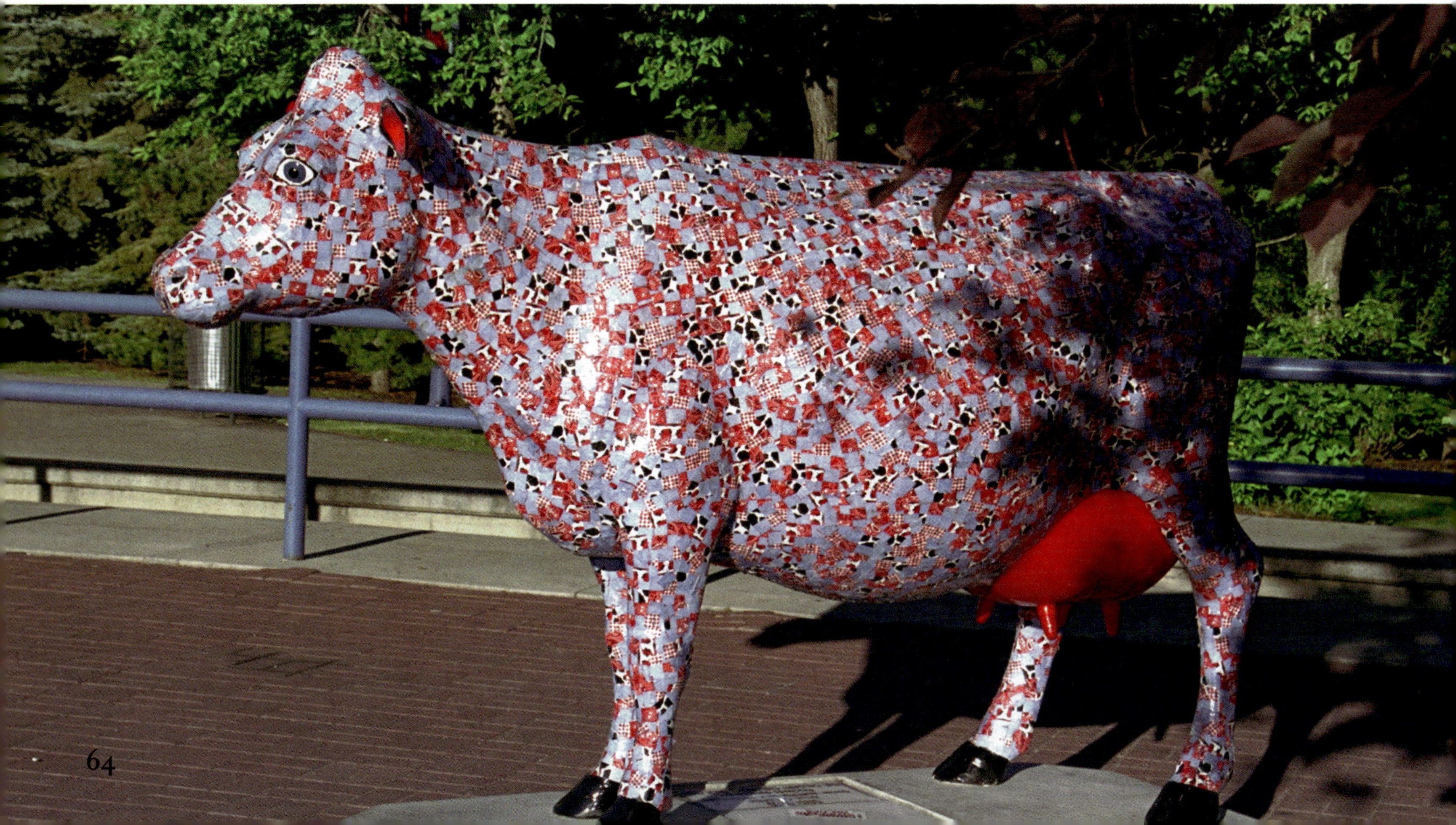

Daisy Mae

Artist: In-Definite Arts Society

Owner: Marine Clinic

Charity: In-Definite Arts Society

This rodeo clown (and the rest of the herd) comes to you courtesy of Greg Arich and Dieter Schlaffke, owners of the Marine Clinic. Marine Clinic staff spent three months producing all the hollow fibreglass cows for Udderly Art. The partners' personal cow wears a straw hat drenched with daisies. It looks good enough to eat—if you're into that, and some cows are.

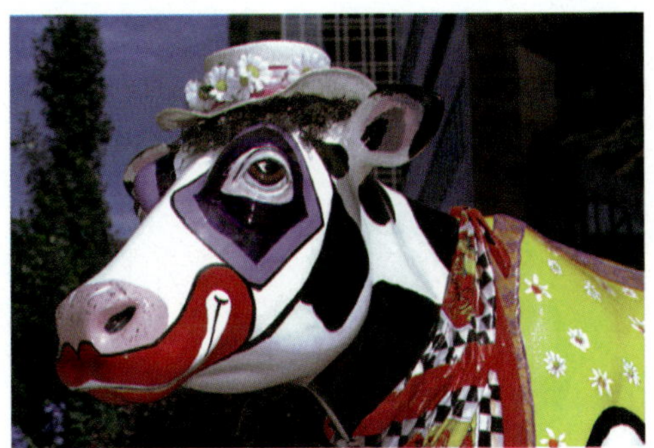

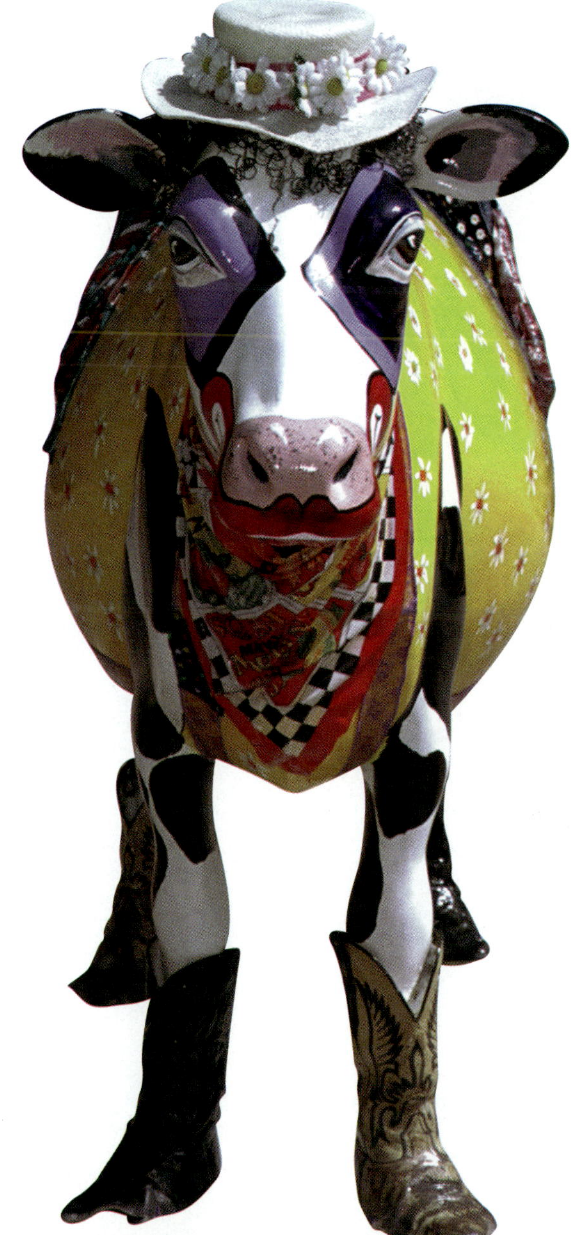

Daisy Springtime

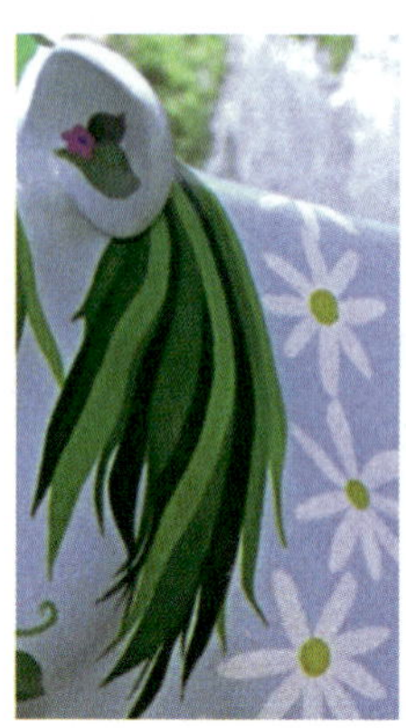

Artist: Maggie Pringle
Owner: Maggie Pringle

An optimistic harbinger of eternal spring, Maggie Pringle's uplifting piece reminds us that the wheel of time never stops turning. *Daisy Springtime*'s delicate daisy-chain necklace reminds us to pause and reflect: when a prairie winter descends, can spring be far behind?

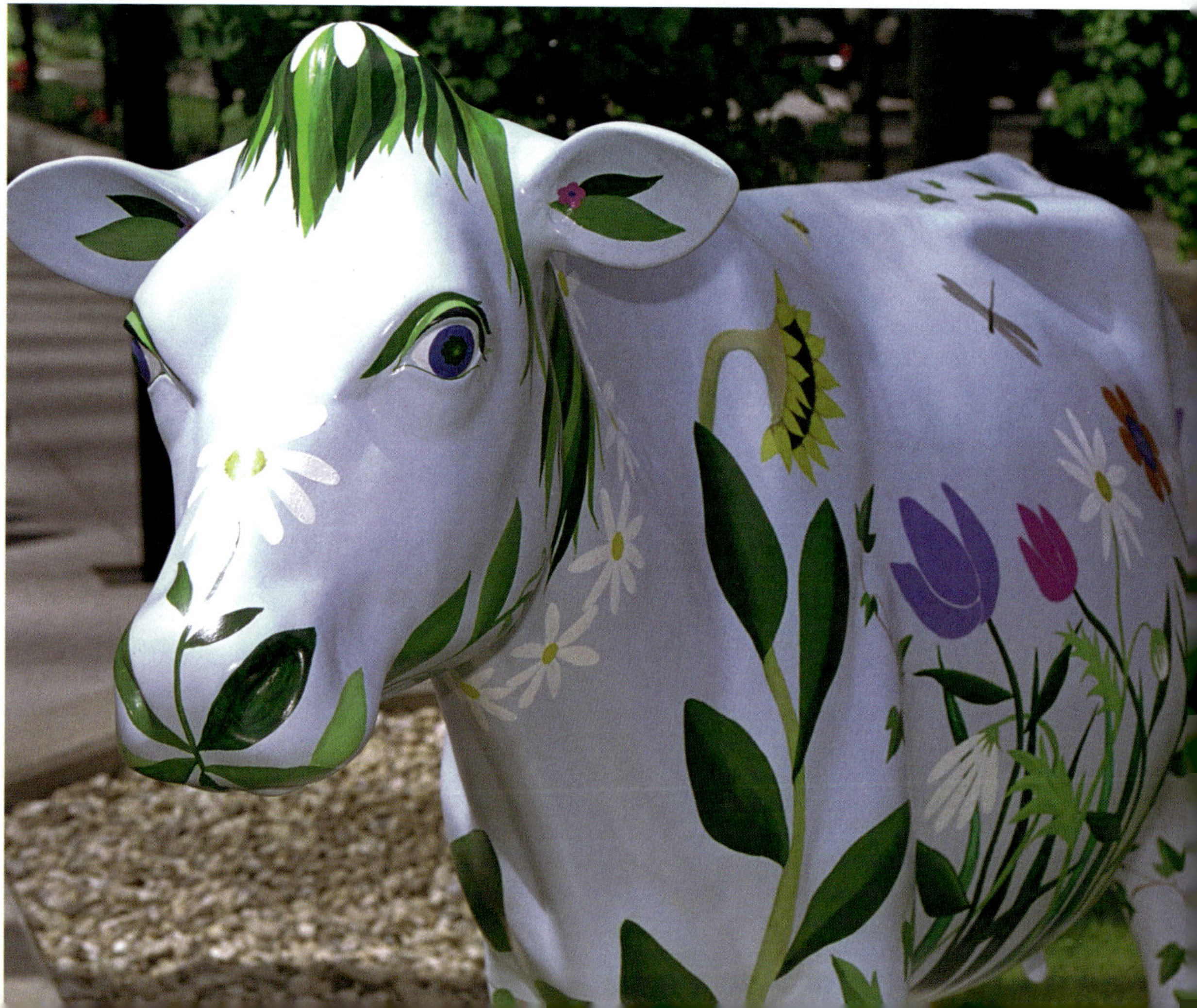

Deep Moo

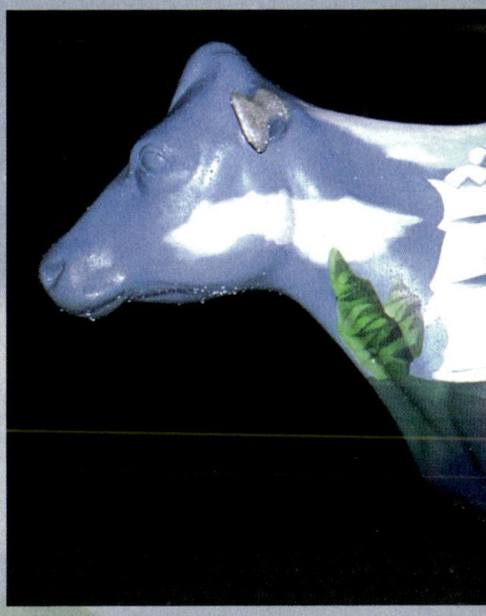

Artist: Scott McLean

Owner: IBM Canada Ltd.

Charity: Calgary Women's Emergency Shelter

The slightly surrealistic chessboard on the broad back of *Deep Moo* holds all the traditional pieces—from pawn to rook—but a newer player stands out from the crowd. Three guesses. Not to give away secrets, it wears the crown of an undisputed digital business king with a mouse (no, not the furry kind) attached.

The Duchess of Paisley

Artist: Jim Clark

Owner: Duke Energy Marketing

Charity: Alberta Ballet Company, Nat Christie Centre

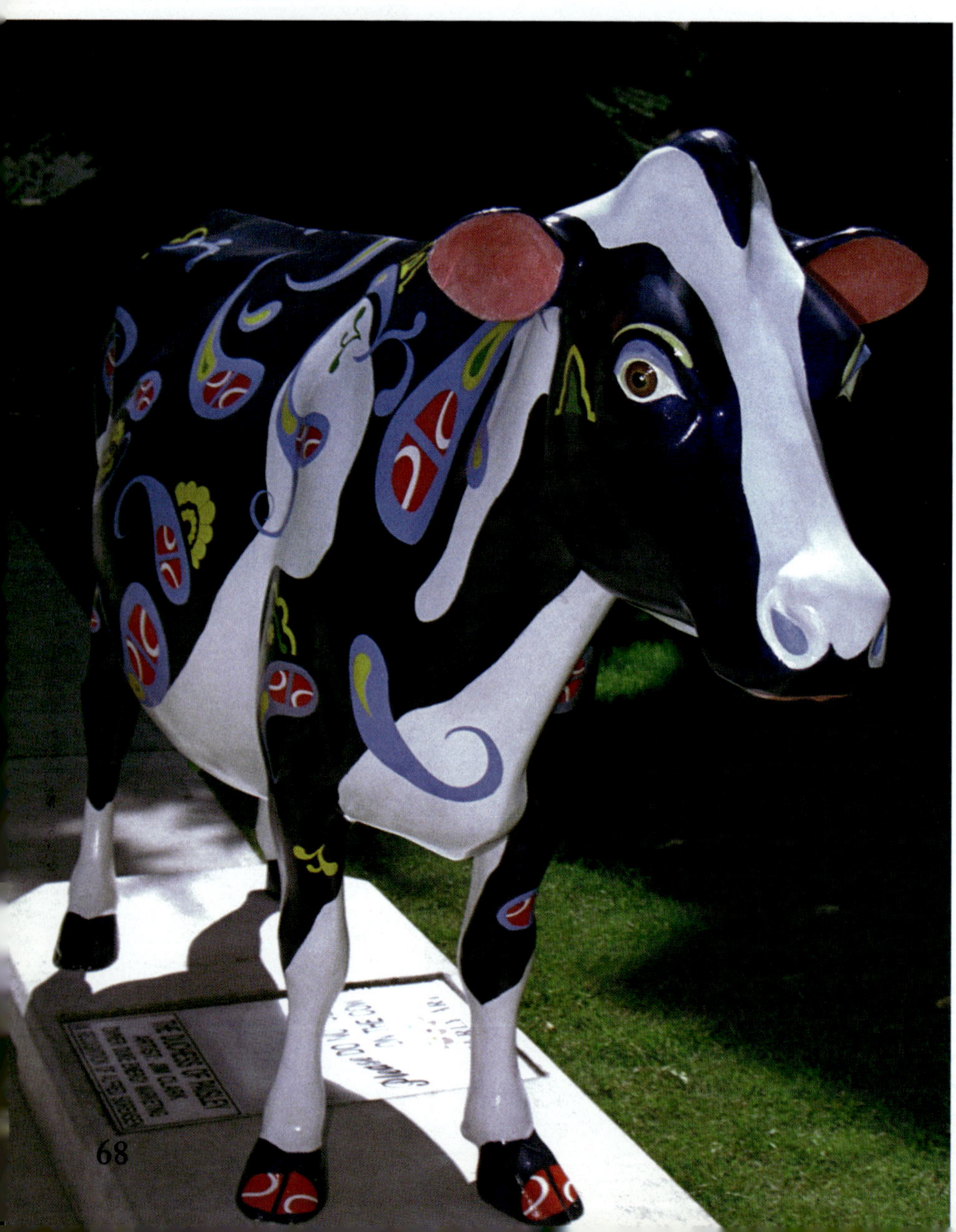

A visual treat, Jim Clark's *Duchess* is flashing more deep blue, white and red paisleys than one of those kaleidoscopic men's shirts from the 1960s. Proceeds of the auction sale will go to the Alberta Ballet Company, in recognition of Duke Energy's former Canadian president, Alfred Sorensen, now based in London, England.

Ellie, The Environmental Cow

Artist: Jolie Bird

Owner: IKEA Calgary

Charity: DAREarts

Think g-r-e-e-n. Passing by Jolie Bird's study in rich, deep green, it's hard not to. A timely reminder that she who clutters up her own pasture may be forced to lie in it. Along with her ecologically correct green blanket, Ellie wears a diadem of flowers and carries a green sack, presumably to collect litter wherever she finds it.

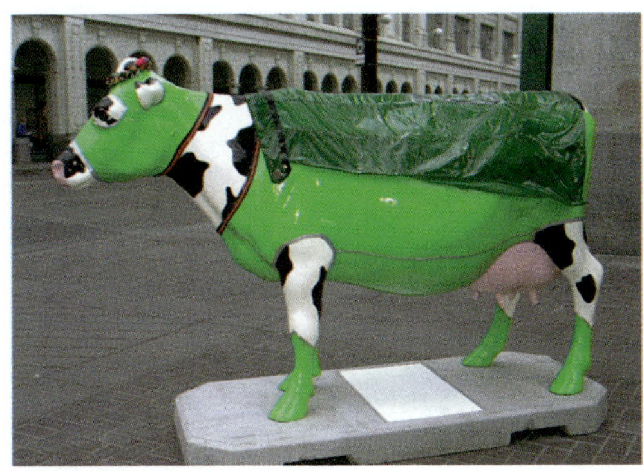

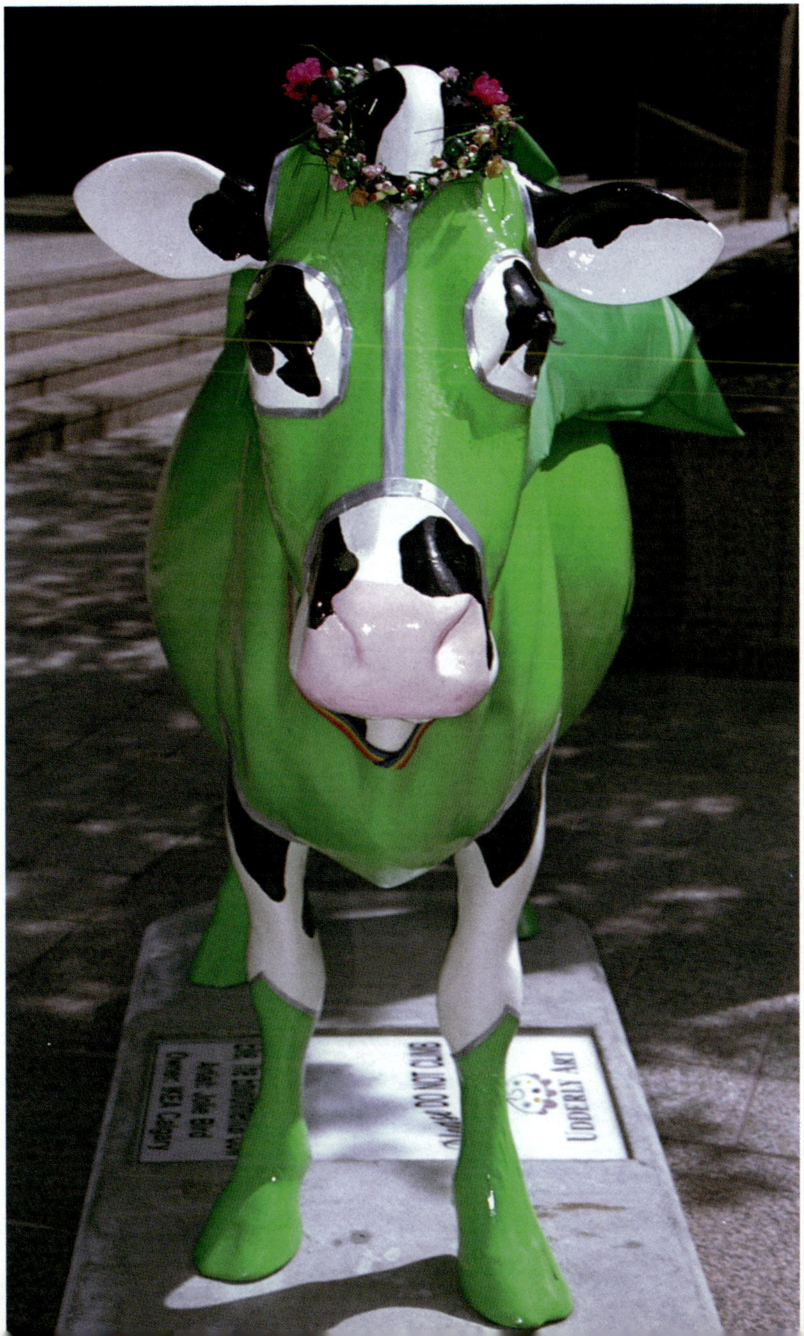

Entrepre"MOO"rial Cow

Artist: Jack Rigaux

Owner: Pinnacle Breakfast Club

Charity: Gord Laing Memorial Foundation

The shades are firmly in place. The cell phone in the jacket pocket is switched off as this slick, moustachioed, corporate cowboy takes a breather. With shirt and trouser sleeves rolled up, Jack Rigaux's bovine slickster spent the summer of 2000 chilling in a shallow pool behind Calgary's Fifth Avenue Place.

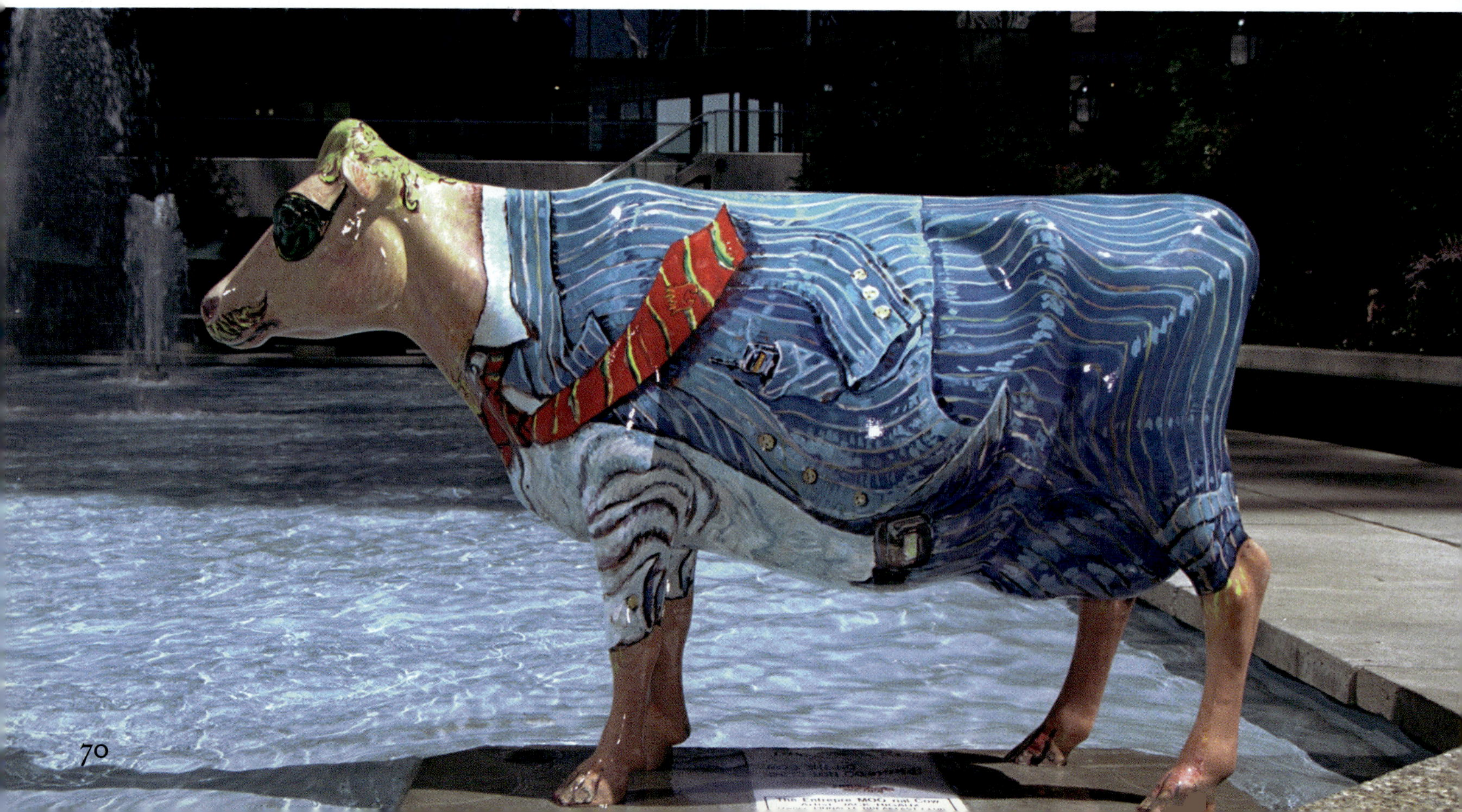

The Garden of Cow

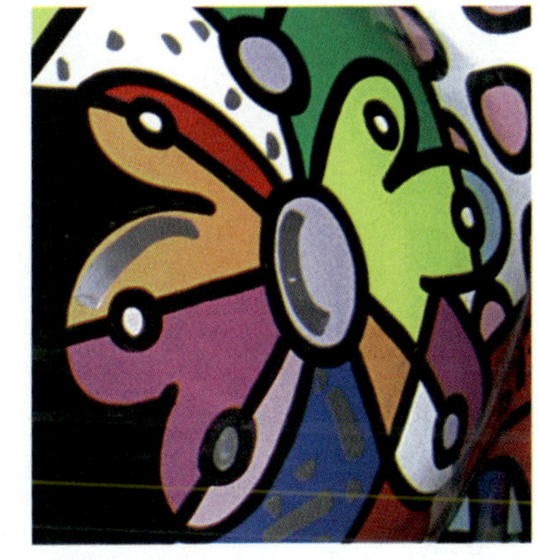

Artist: Romero Britto

Owner: Theatre Calgary (donated by Art Mode Gallery and West Canadian Graphics)

Charity: Theatre Calgary

The most widely travelled cow in the herd, *The Garden of Cow* took a junket to Miami, Florida, to be decorated by Romero Britto and his staff. One of the hottest commercial artists south of the border, Britto got a kick out of the Udderly Art concept. He asked Dennis Smith of Art Mode Gallery how he could get involved. What you see is the answer.

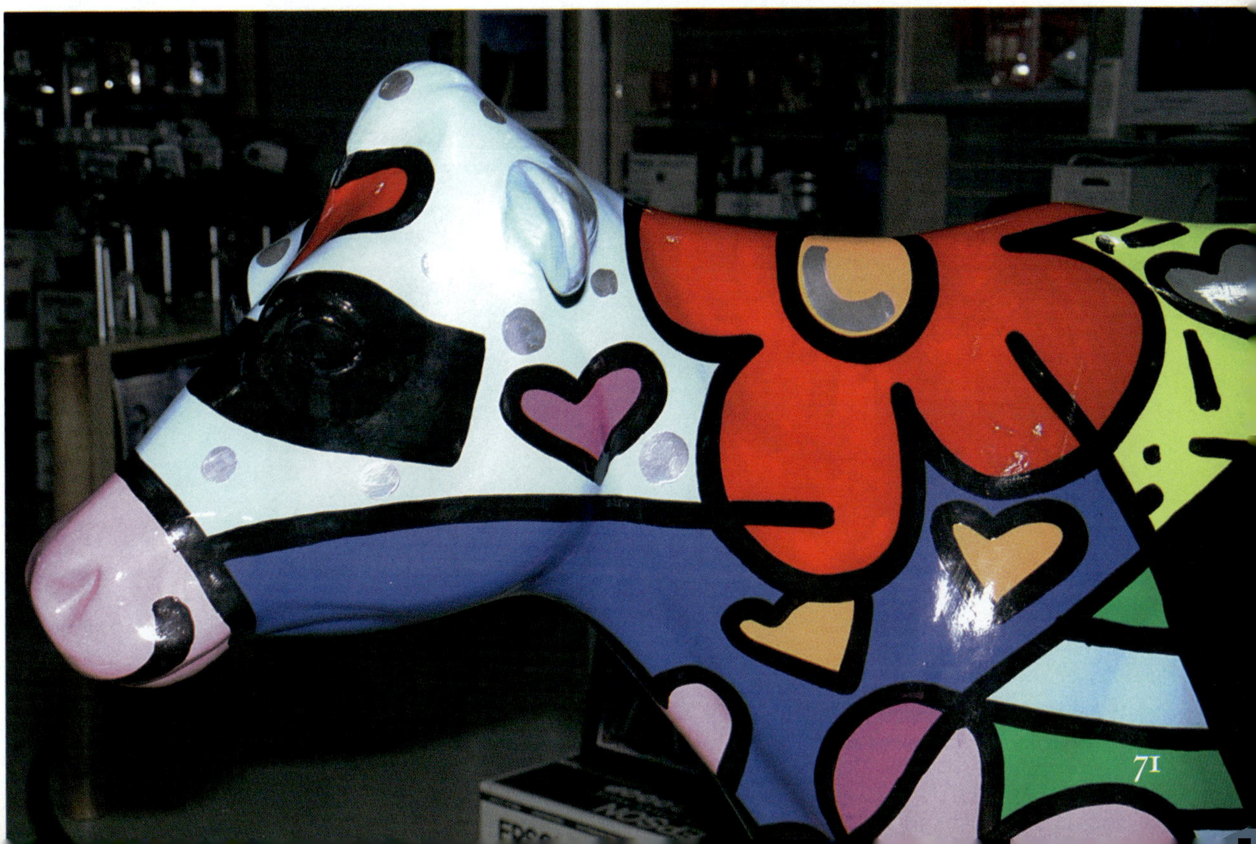

Foothills

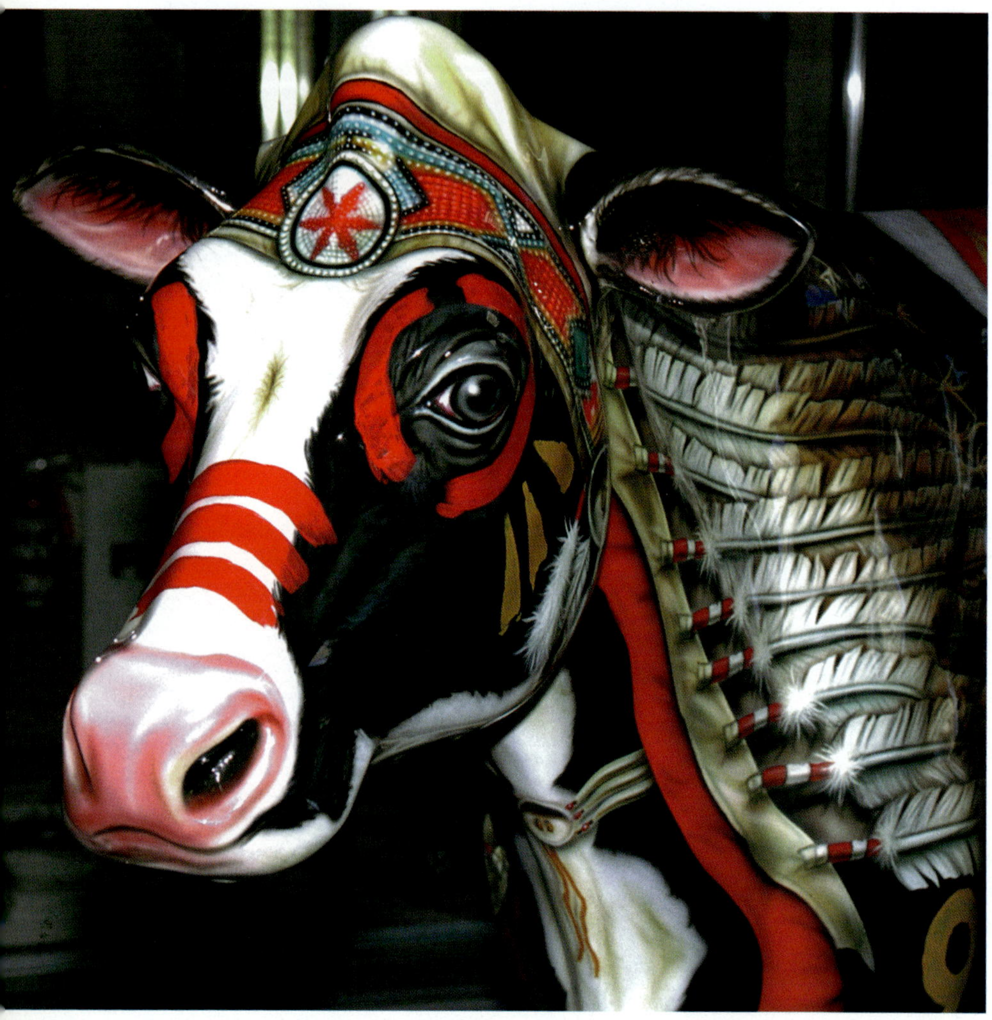

Artist: blake@cross-eyed Illustration

Owner: International Hotel

Charity: Foothills Hospital Foundation

One of the busiest and most meticulous artists in Calgary, Blake McCully serves the needs of an eclectic client base. Professional hockey players such as Rick Tabaracci and Trevor Kidd wear his signature work on their goaltender masks. And untold numbers of motorcycle enthusiasts prowl the highways aboard Blake's custom-painted show bikes, Harley Davidsons a specialty.

A painstaking detail man, McCully applied himself to two Udderly Art cows, including one known as *CowGary*, a dazzler decked out in a Calgary Flames motif.

But *Foothills* represented something of a departure though Blake's breathtaking brushwork immediately identifies this tribute to the Plains Indians as another McCully masterpiece.

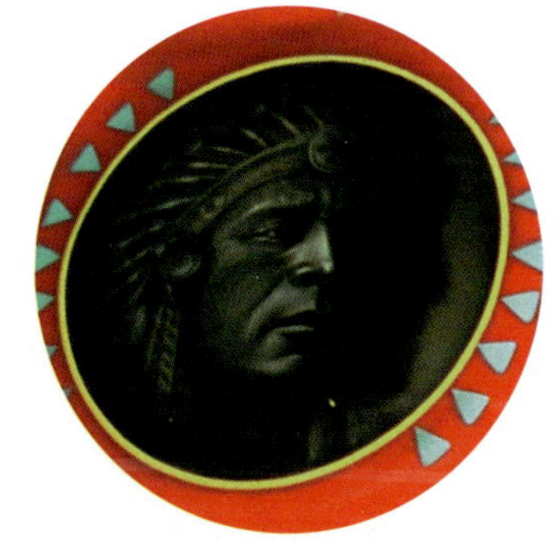

"This is not a social comment, just a nod of respect to the Blood, Blackfoot and Cree," he says. "It's a generic concept rather than a representation of a specific people. I was trying to show how Native culture is reflected within our city."

Foothills was endorsed by the undisputed experts. A group of elders from the Blood reserve blessed McCully's creation.

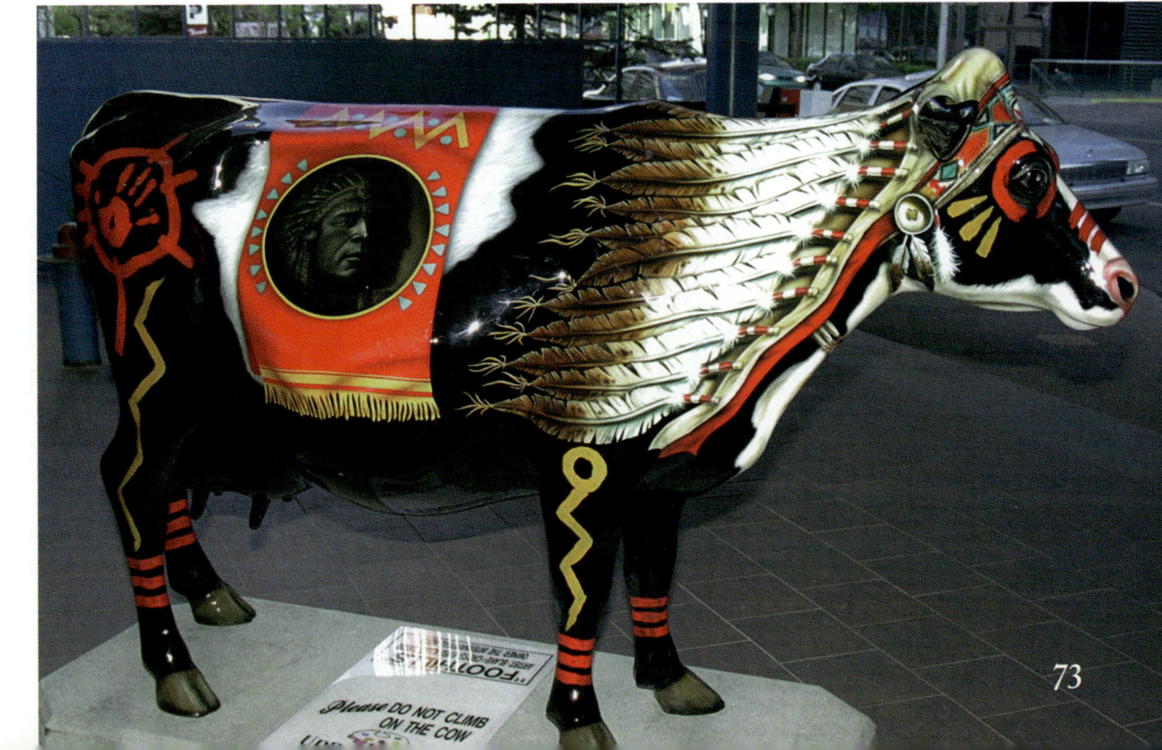

Genesis (Gennie)

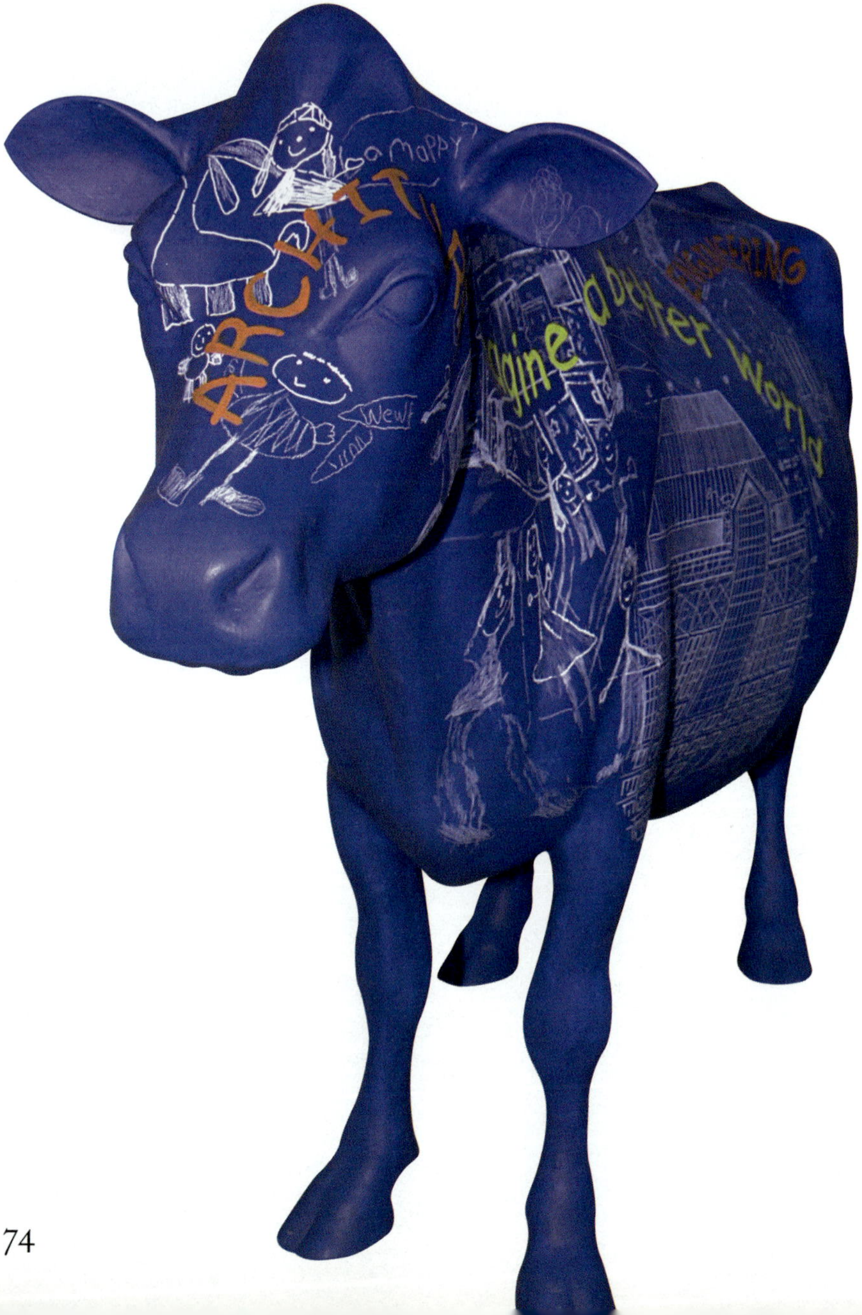

Artist: The Firm

Purchased: Cohos Evamy Partners

Charity: Alberta Children's Hospital Foundation

Let's face it, the most rabid fans of Udderly Art cows are children. So Cohos Evamy Partners' idea was to imagine a better world as seen through the children's eyes. Structural drawings depicting various architectural disciplines were applied first then overlaid by samples of the kids' own vision.

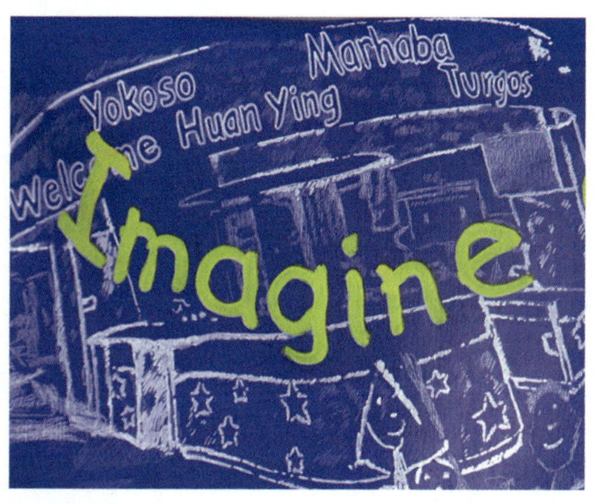

Goepel McDermid Raising Alberta Stock

Artist: Jack Rigaux

Owner: Goepel McDermid Inc.

Charity: Alberta Children's Hospital Foundation

If Cézanne or Monet had been raised in the shadow of the Rocky Mountains, they may have created a landscape in the style of Jack Rigaux's impressionistic prairie scene. But those wild roses around the hooves make it clear this is Rigaux's Alberta, not Monet's Giverny.

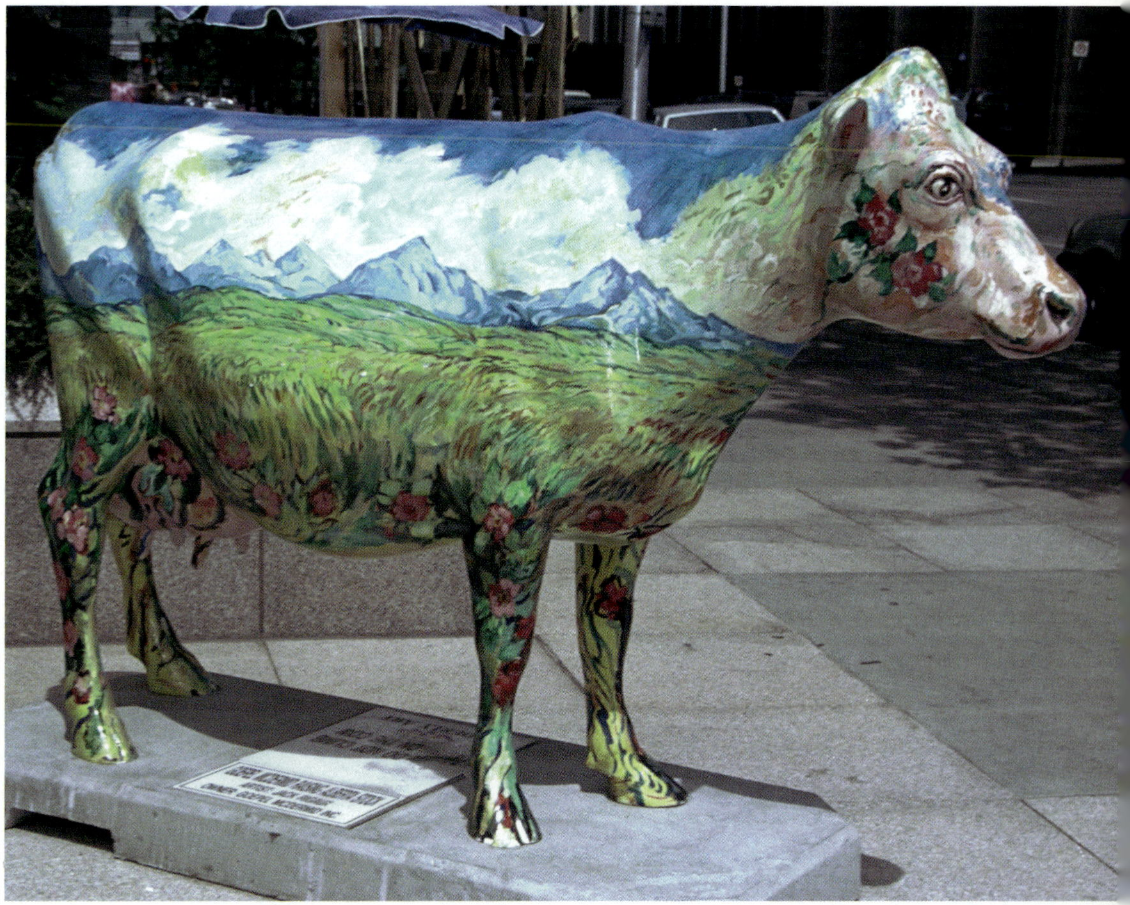

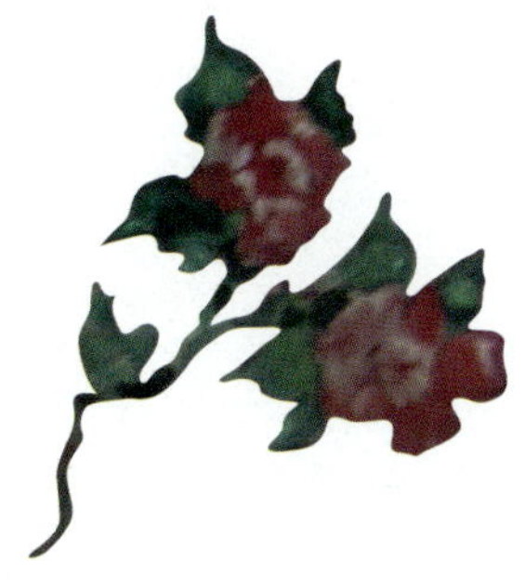

Gracie

Artist: Lesley Gallagher

Owner: Grace Foundation (donated by the Winfield and Desbarats Families)

Charity: Grace Foundation

The white picket fence is the key to interpreting this cow-borne ode to domestic bliss. Among other objectives, the Grace Foundation aims to promote harmony within the family. Lesley Gallagher's piece symbolizes the ideal while acknowledging that even the happiest backyard has to endure an occasional mosquito.

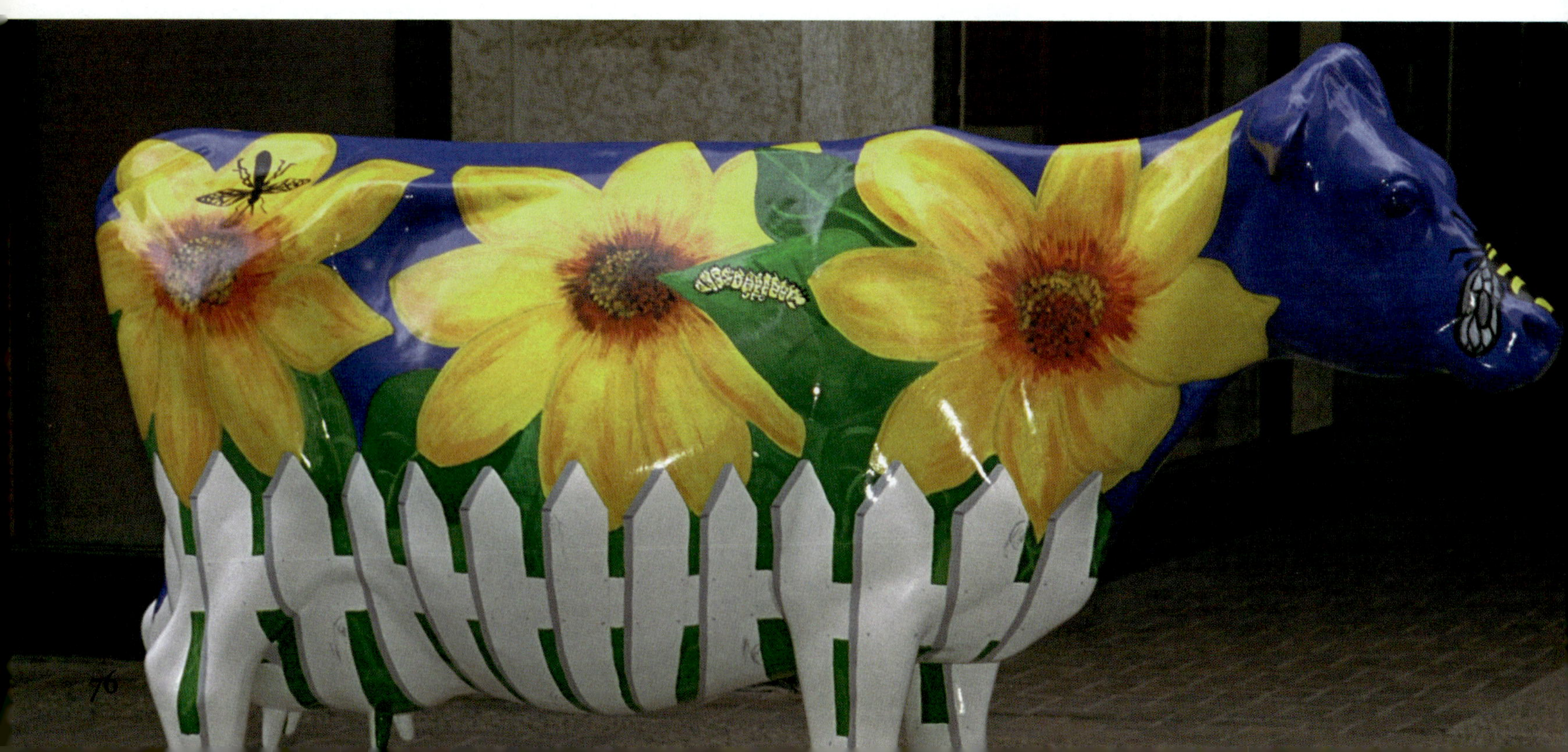

Grant

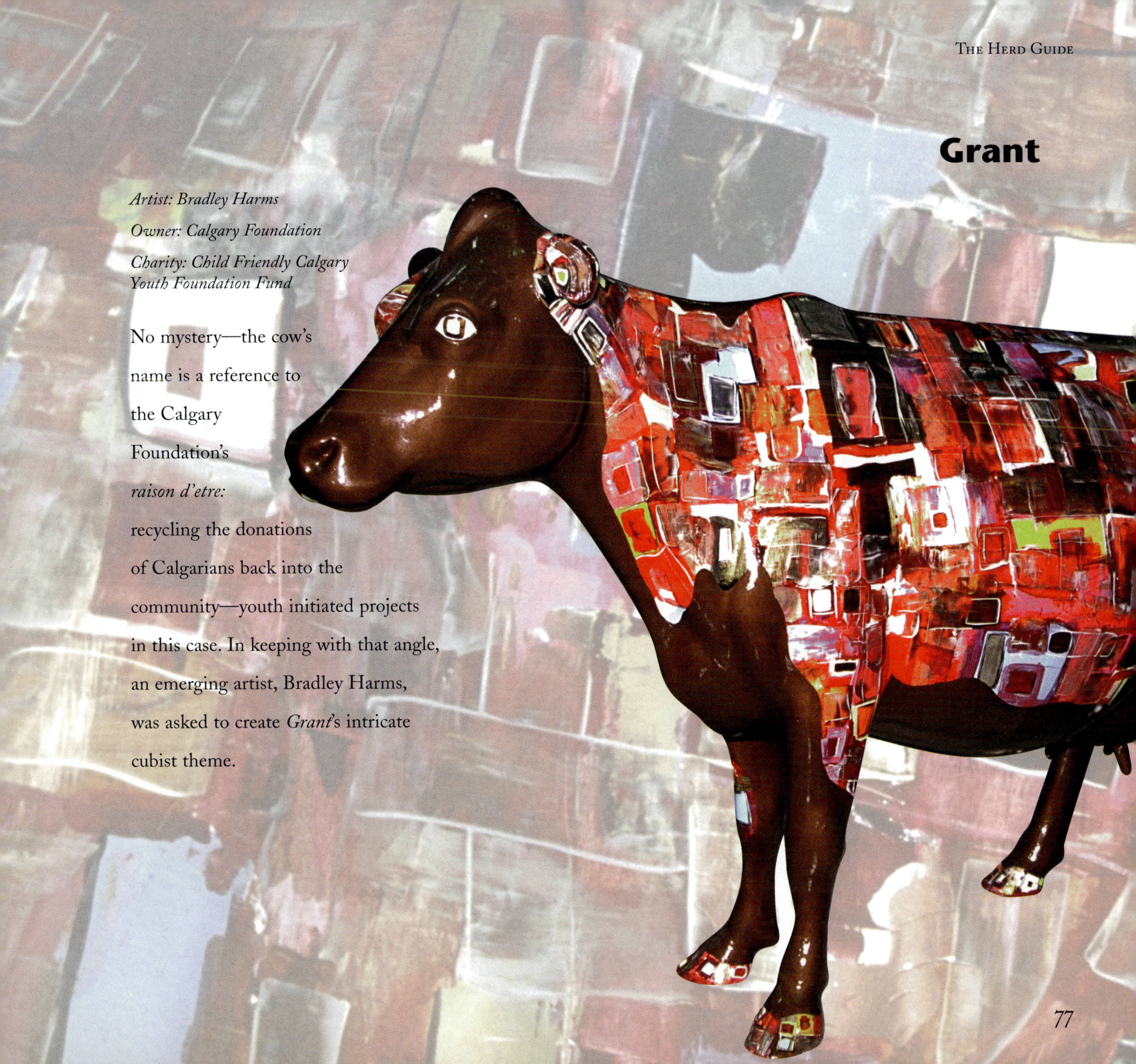

Artist: Bradley Harms

Owner: Calgary Foundation

Charity: Child Friendly Calgary Youth Foundation Fund

No mystery—the cow's name is a reference to the Calgary Foundation's *raison d'etre:* recycling the donations of Calgarians back into the community—youth initiated projects in this case. In keeping with that angle, an emerging artist, Bradley Harms, was asked to create *Grant*'s intricate cubist theme.

Handrietta

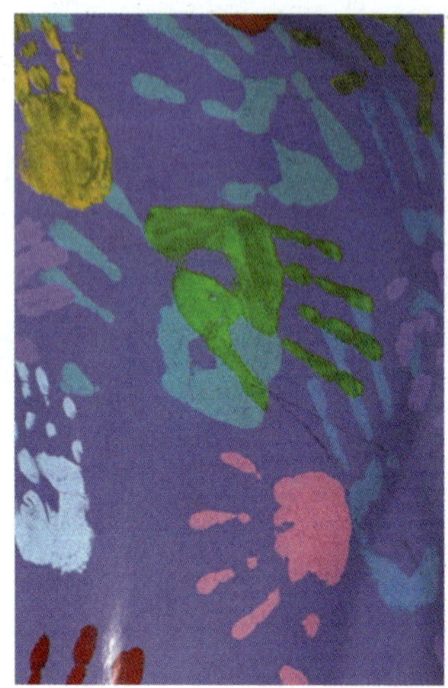

Artists: Julie Hamilton and Children Affected by Childhood Cancer

Owner: Kids Cancer Care Foundation (donated by RBC Dominion Securities)

Charity: Kids Cancer Care Foundation

Two nights running, Julie Hamilton's garage was crammed with laughing, smiling, paint-spattered kids—young cancer patients, and their brothers and sisters. Hamilton invited many kids with cancer and their siblings to leave a palm print on *Handrietta,* and 60 youngsters raised their hands to volunteer. The children got to pick their own colour. In return for the artistic help, Hamilton provided cookies and Kool-Aid.

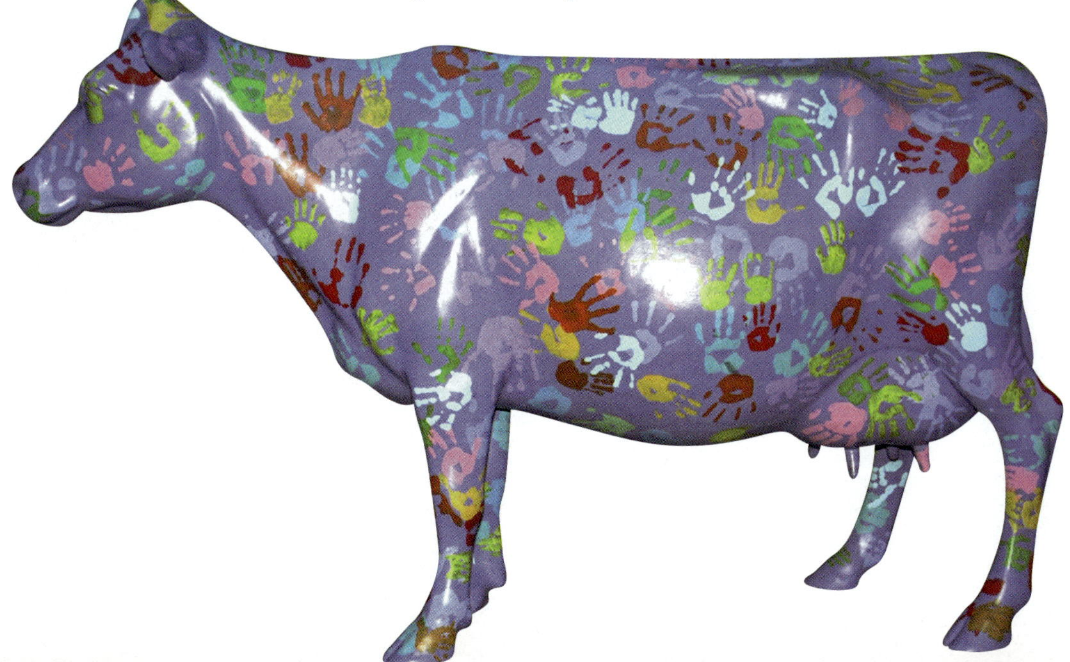

Haute Cowture

Artist: Laura Pope

Owner: Mac's Convenience Stores Inc.

Charity: Servants Anonymous Association

The pun in this cow's name is a spin on the French phrase routinely applied to the Parisian world of fashion runways and pencil-thin super models. But Laura Pope's purpose was to honour western heritage with a high-fashion cow. Although *Haute Cowture* is swathed in a Pope design of warm red, ochre and blue, it'd look perfectly at home in fancy western shirts, boots or trousers, too.

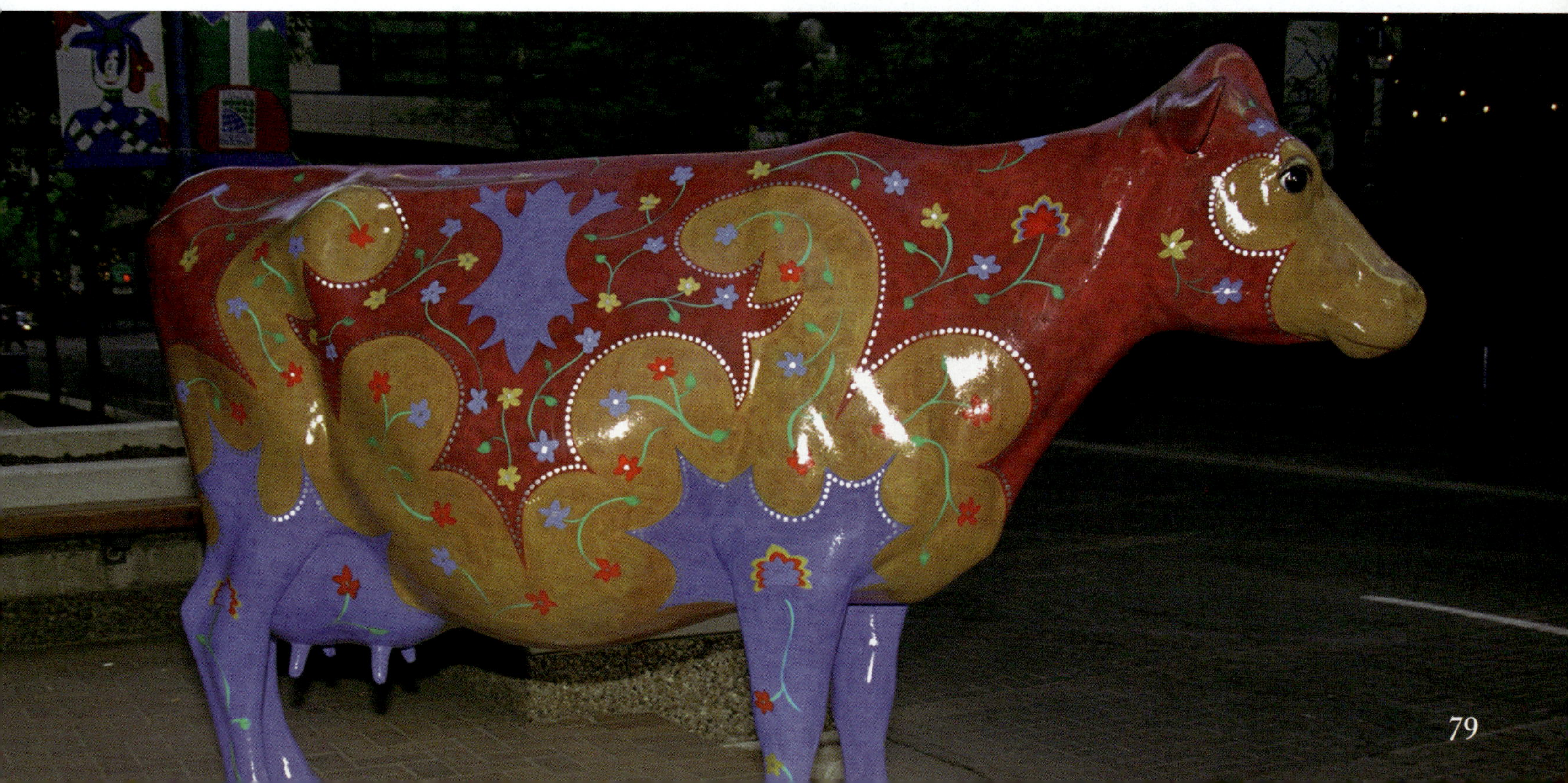

Hey Diddle Diddle

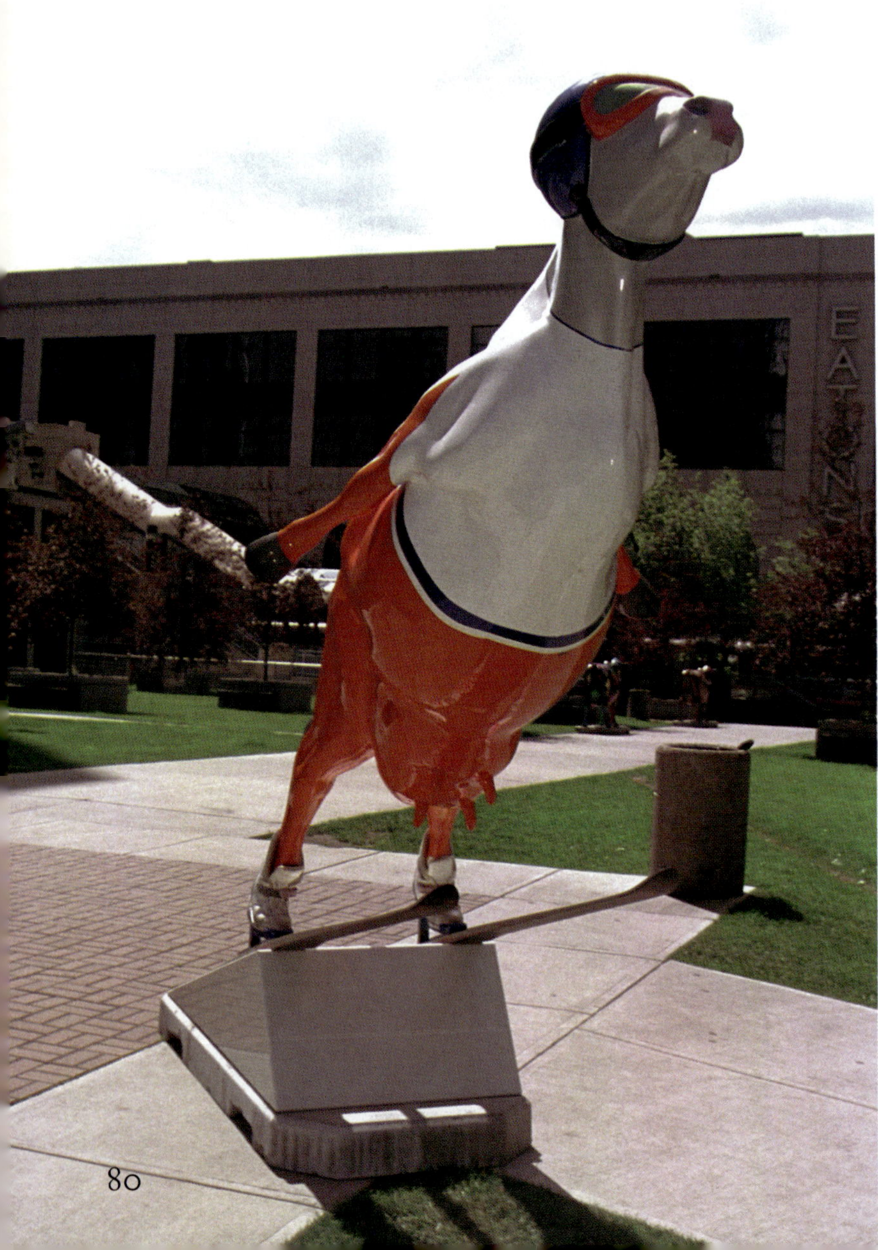

Artist: Terry Gregoraschuk

Owner: Calgary Olympic Development Association

Charity: Calgary Special Olympics

She's a high-flyin' striver with the kind of athletic gear, skill and determination that almost makes you believe the nursery rhyme might come true. This jet-fueled cow looks as though it really could ski jump over the moon. The Calgary Olympic Development Association endorsed this design for precisely that reason. *Hey Diddle Diddle* exemplifies the Olympic ideals of fitness, drive and spirit, which enable athletes to achieve goals they never dreamed possible.

A certified eye-widener, this piece is one of the undisputed stars of Udderly Art's herd.

But visual artist Terry Gregoraschuk, a former art director for *Western Living* magazine, originally had an even wilder design in mind.

"My idea was a cow ski jumping down a half-moon," Gregoraschuk explained. But to bring that startling vision to life would have broken the budget, requiring, among other things, a 20-foot steel infrastructure.

Olympic Development officials gently urged Gregoraschuk to reconsider and were more than pleased with the result. As it is, the upright skier was reinforced with heavy steel piping up the rear legs and steel plating on the boots.

For an authentic touch, Canada Olympic Park nordic-combined coach Greg Poirier chipped in his boots and skis.

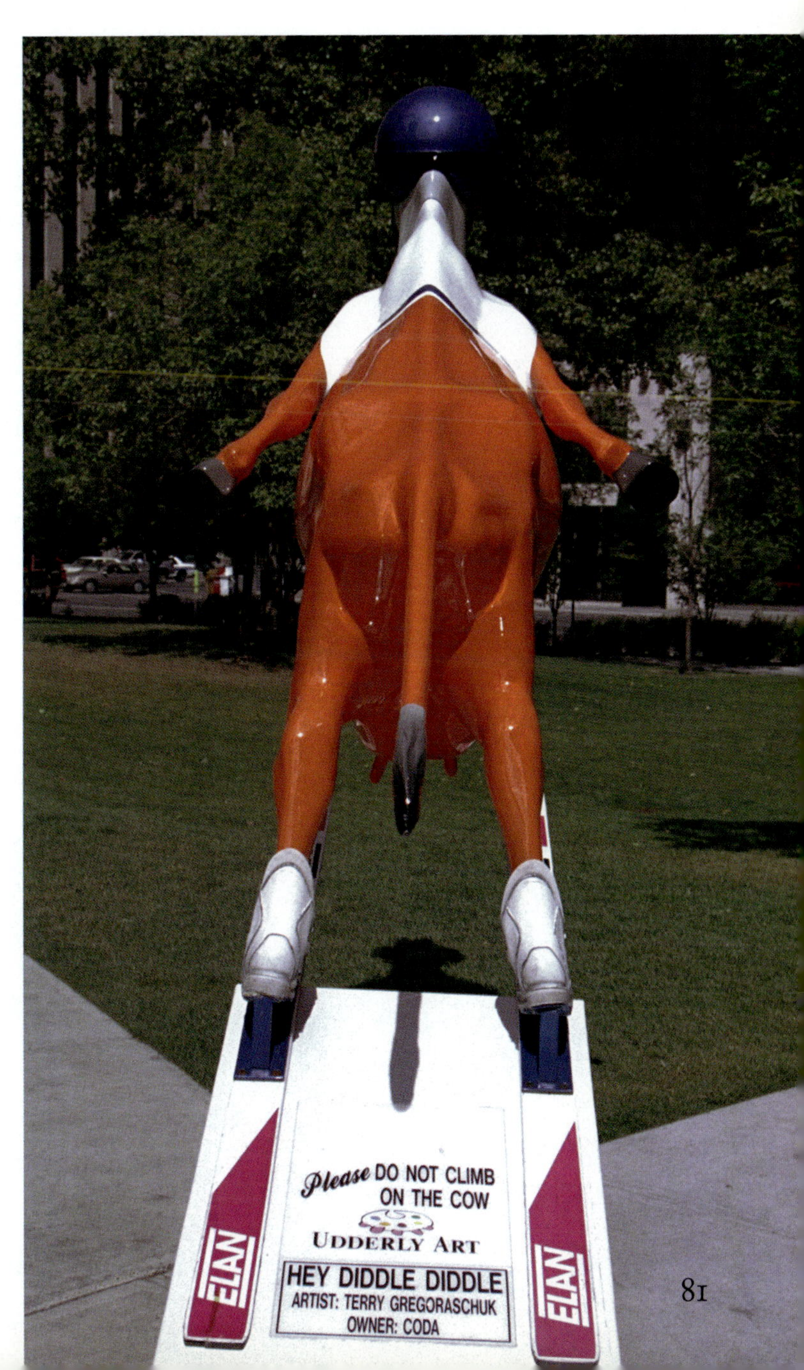

Hockeycow

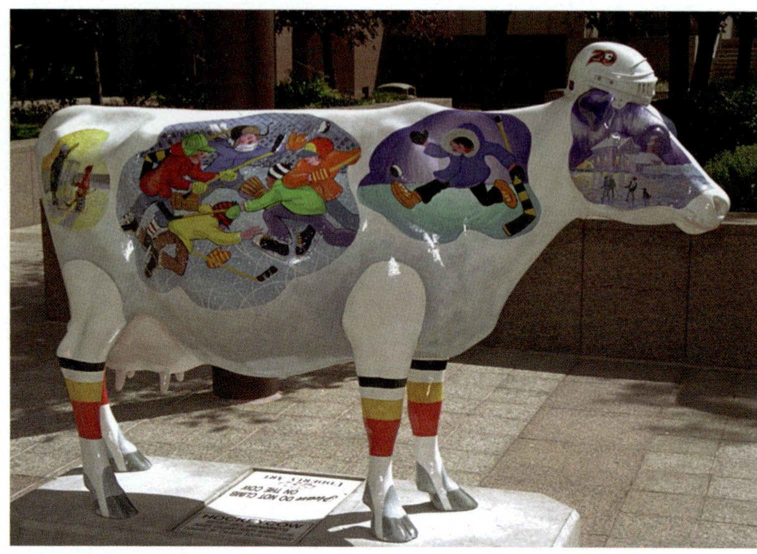

Artist: Bill Brownridge

Owner: Calgary South Rotary Club

Charity: Rotary Challenger Park

Bill Brownridge's nostalgic prints are steady sellers in galleries across Canada. *Hockeycow* gives us a half-dozen of the Calgary artist's instantly recognizable scenes: kids shooting, scoring and choosing up sides on prairie outdoor rinks. But take a closer look at that goalie. He wears moccasins, because he can't skate. A portrait of the artist as a young man? Why not ask him?

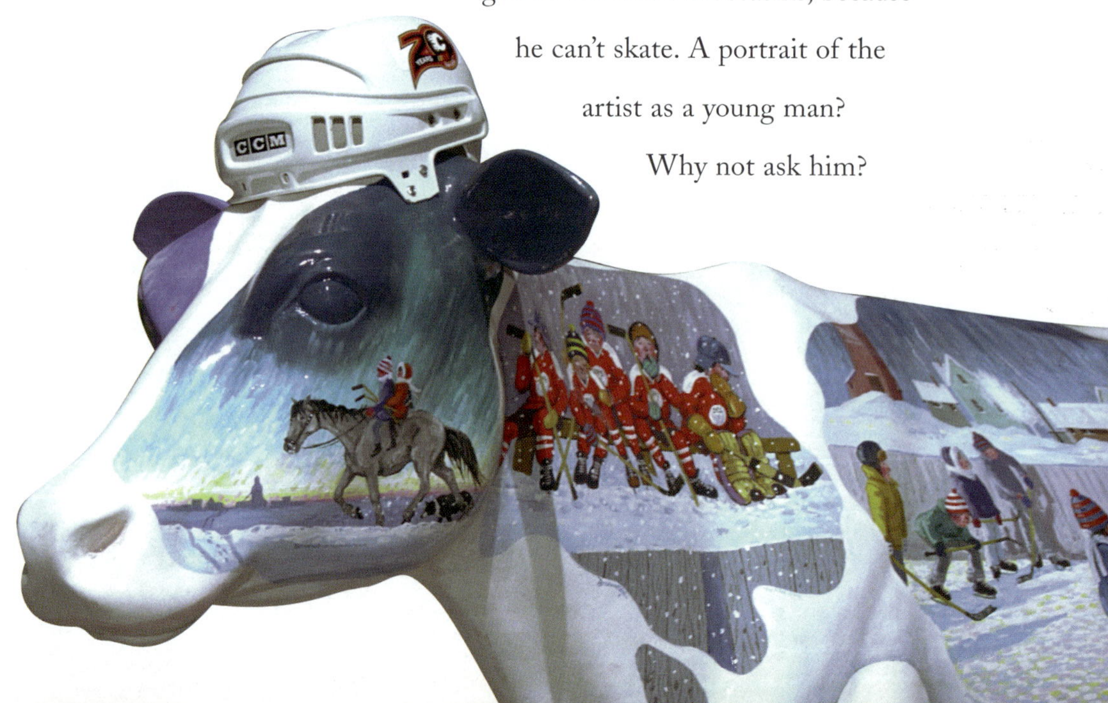

Hollywood and Bovine

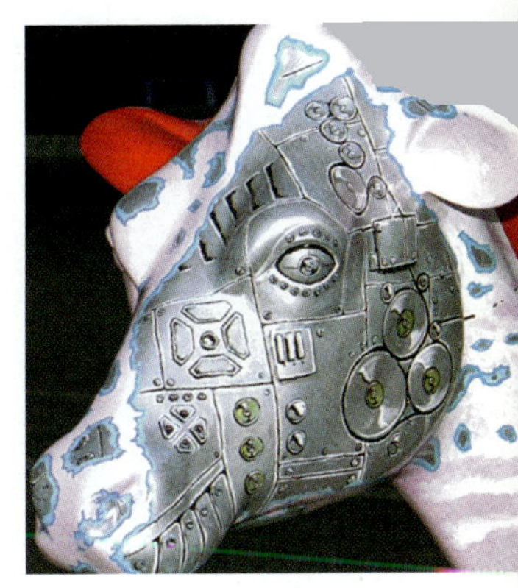

Artist: The Gizmo Shop Ltd.

Owner: Alberta Film Commission (donated by Rob and Ruth Peters and Family)

Charity: Alberta Film Commission

This is one star-struck milk machine. And she's tangled in a kilometre or two of unspooled reels of film. Among other things, the piece lets the onlooker in on some of the boffo box-office smash hits currently playing to packed pastures everywhere. They include *Honey, I Shrunk the Calf* and *Unforhooven.*

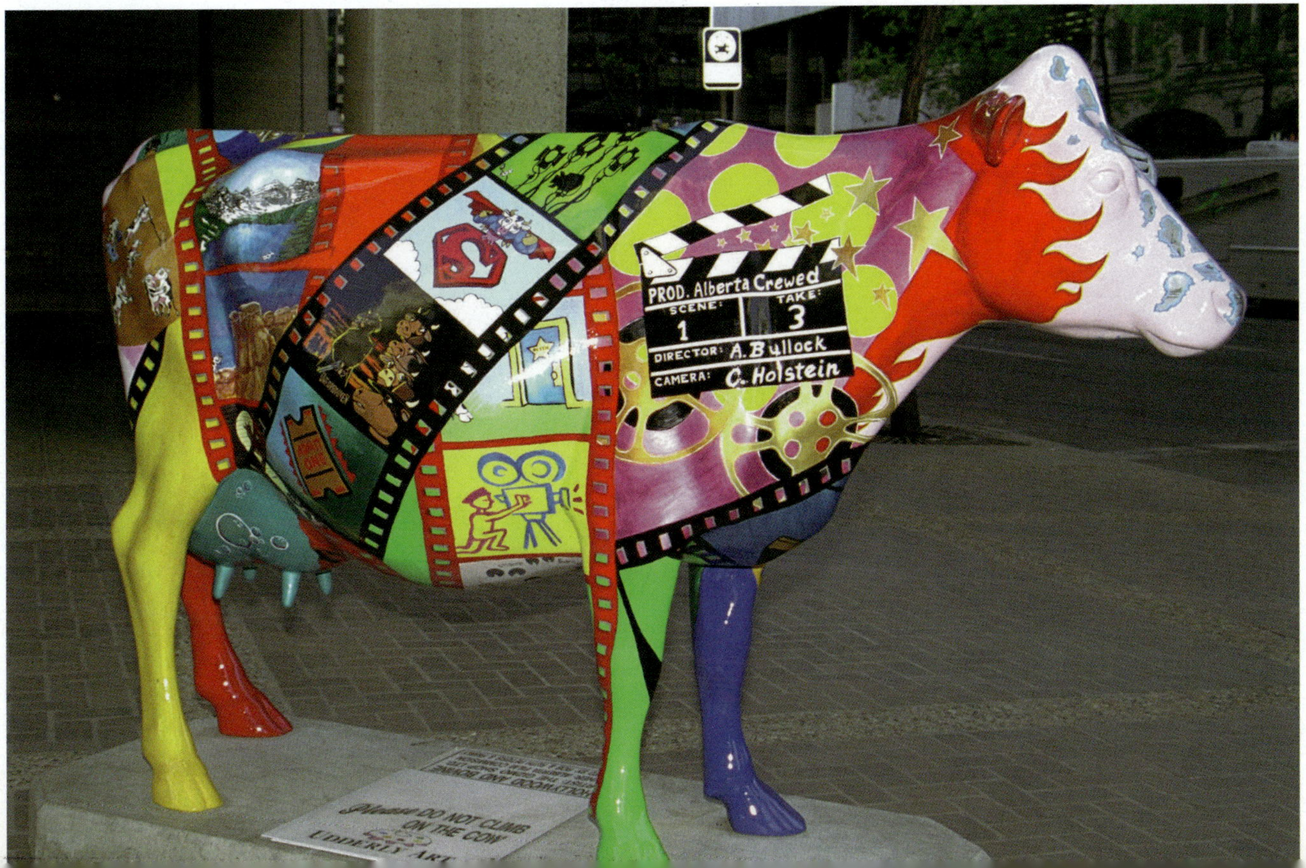

Homer

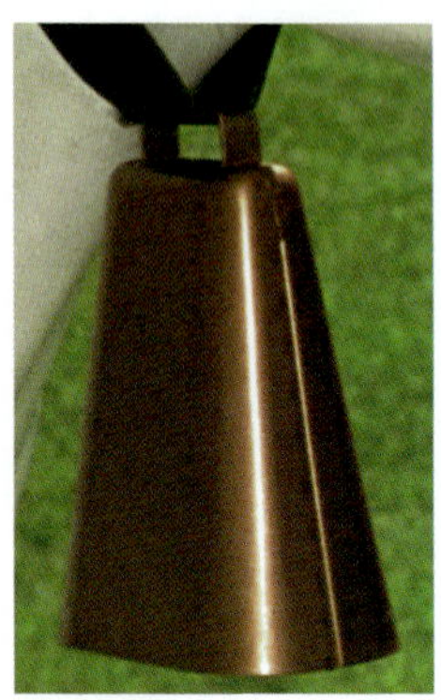

Artist: Sandy Farr

Owner: 411 HomeNet Inc.

Charity: Calgary Homeless Foundation

A companion piece to Sandy Farr's *Hopebelle,* pink-uddered Homer is decked out in similar style: designer black on a creamy white base. Homer was the bell cow of this inseparable twosome, which spent several months as a pair of attractive bookends bidding welcome to visitors to the new city hall on Municipal Plaza.

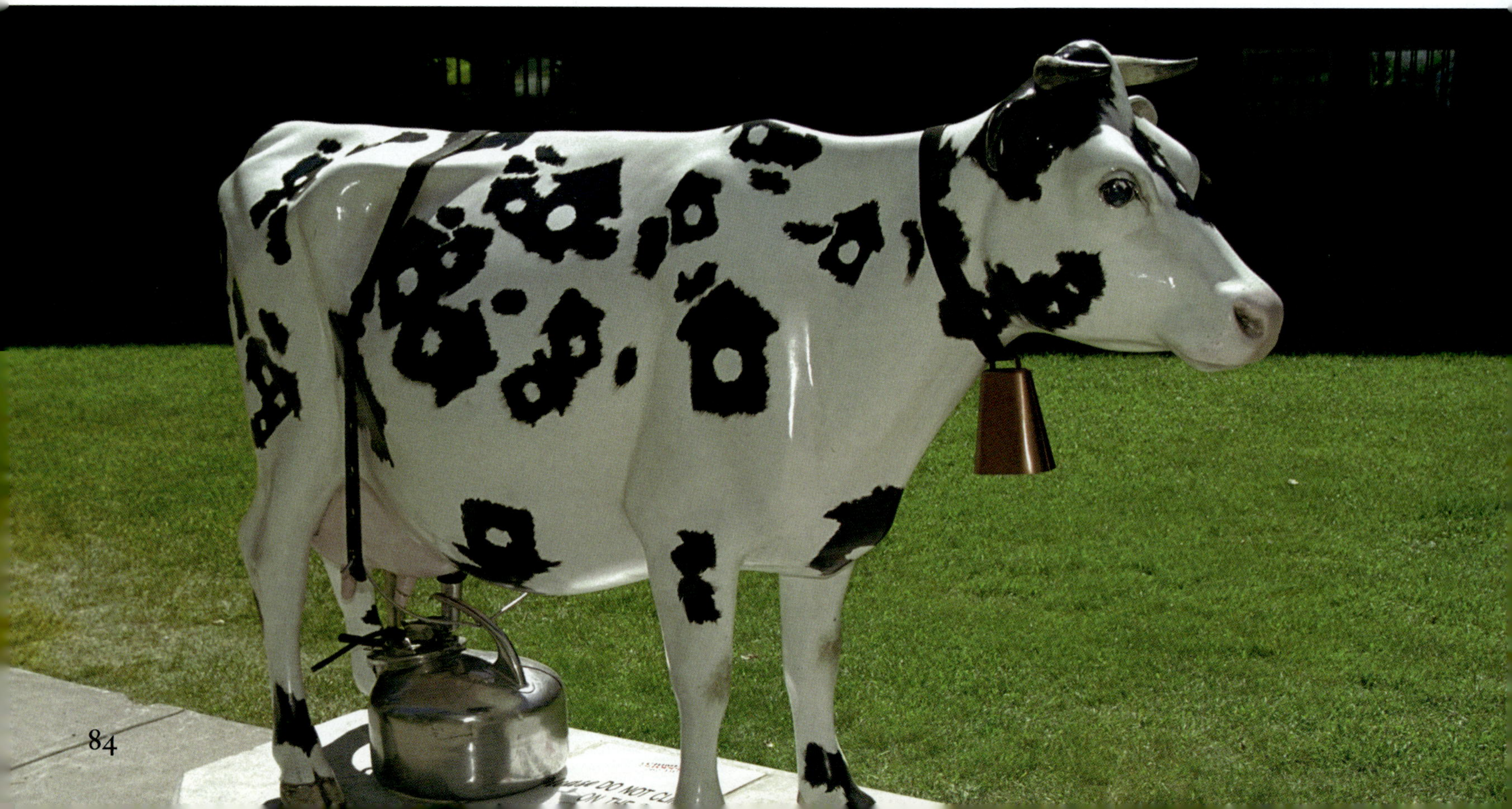

Hopebelle

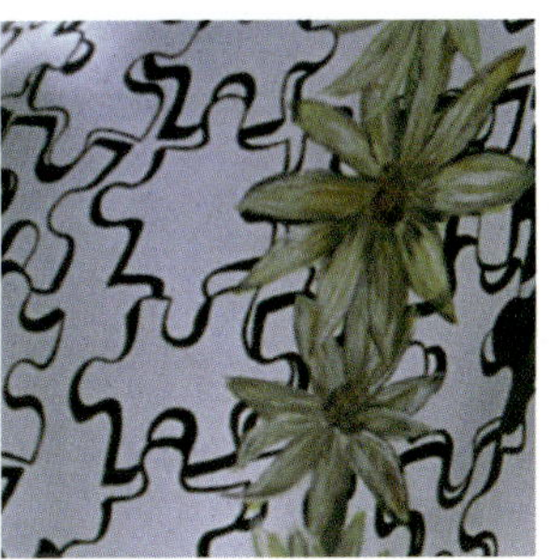

Artist: Sandy Farr

Owner: Hopewell Group of Companies

Charity: Canadian Cancer Society

Hopewell Group bought this cow in the name of employee Ryan Colhoun, diagnosed with third-stage Hodgkin's disease last year. But after several months of treatment and rest, the accounting manager for the company's logistics division was able to return to work. Who says Udderly Art cows don't bring good fortune?

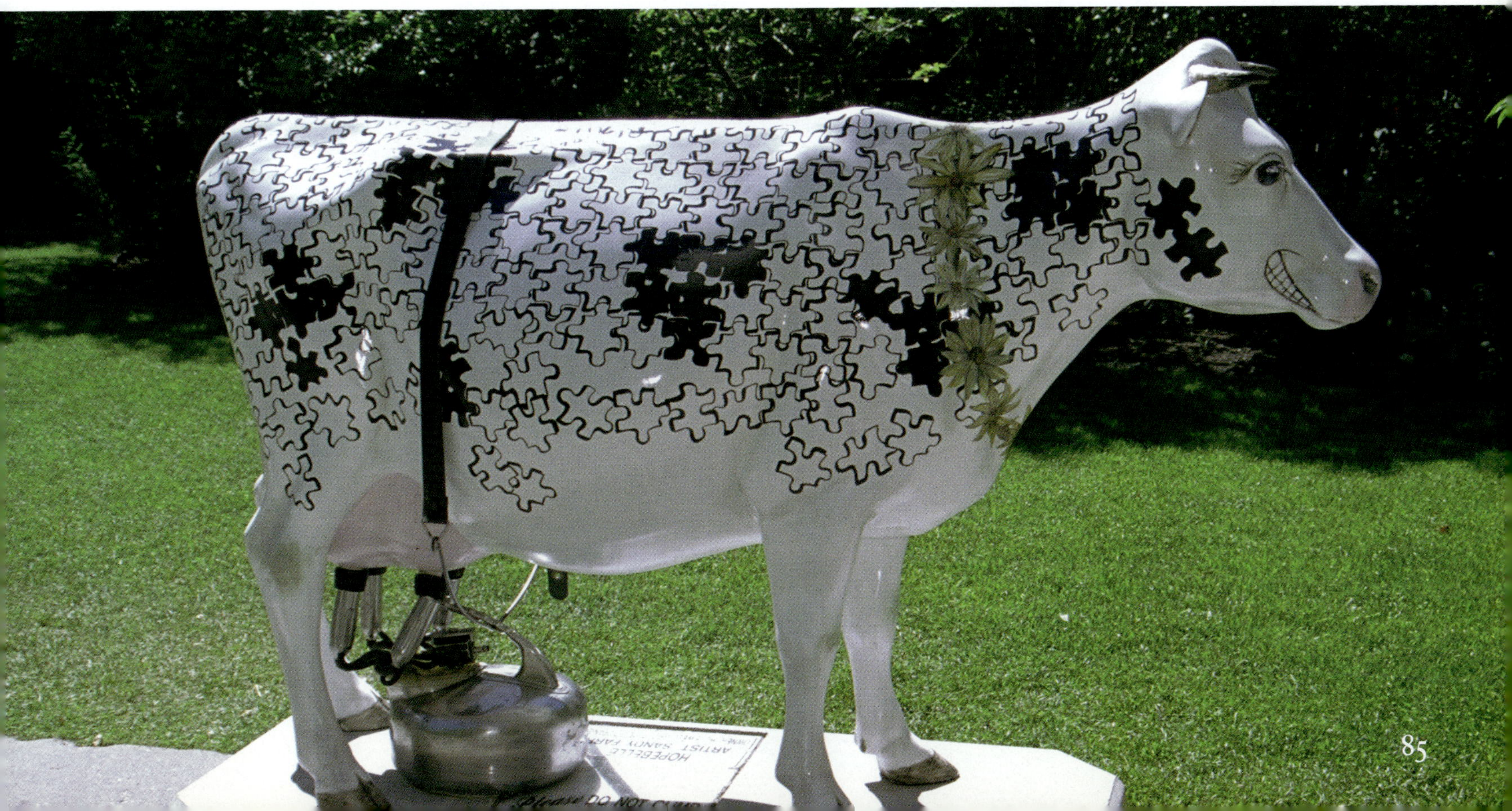

If Cows Could Fly, STARS Ammoolance Helicowpter

Artists: Joan Bailey, Bryan Pfahl and John Furneaux of Brown Bag Design

Owner: Alberta Shock Trauma Air Rescue Foundation (donated by Rob and Nancy Peters and Family)

Charity: STARS Air Ambulance

It was around midnight when a paint-stained artist named Joan Bailey raced into the Alberta Children's Hospital and buttonholed the first doctor she saw.

This was an emergency. A medical problem? No, not exactly.

"I had to look at his stethoscope," the perfectionist explained, a little sheepishly. "He was very kind about it."

Bailey's on-the-spot research led to her creation of an artistically correct stethoscope, which hangs around the neck of the rotor-powered paramedi-cow.

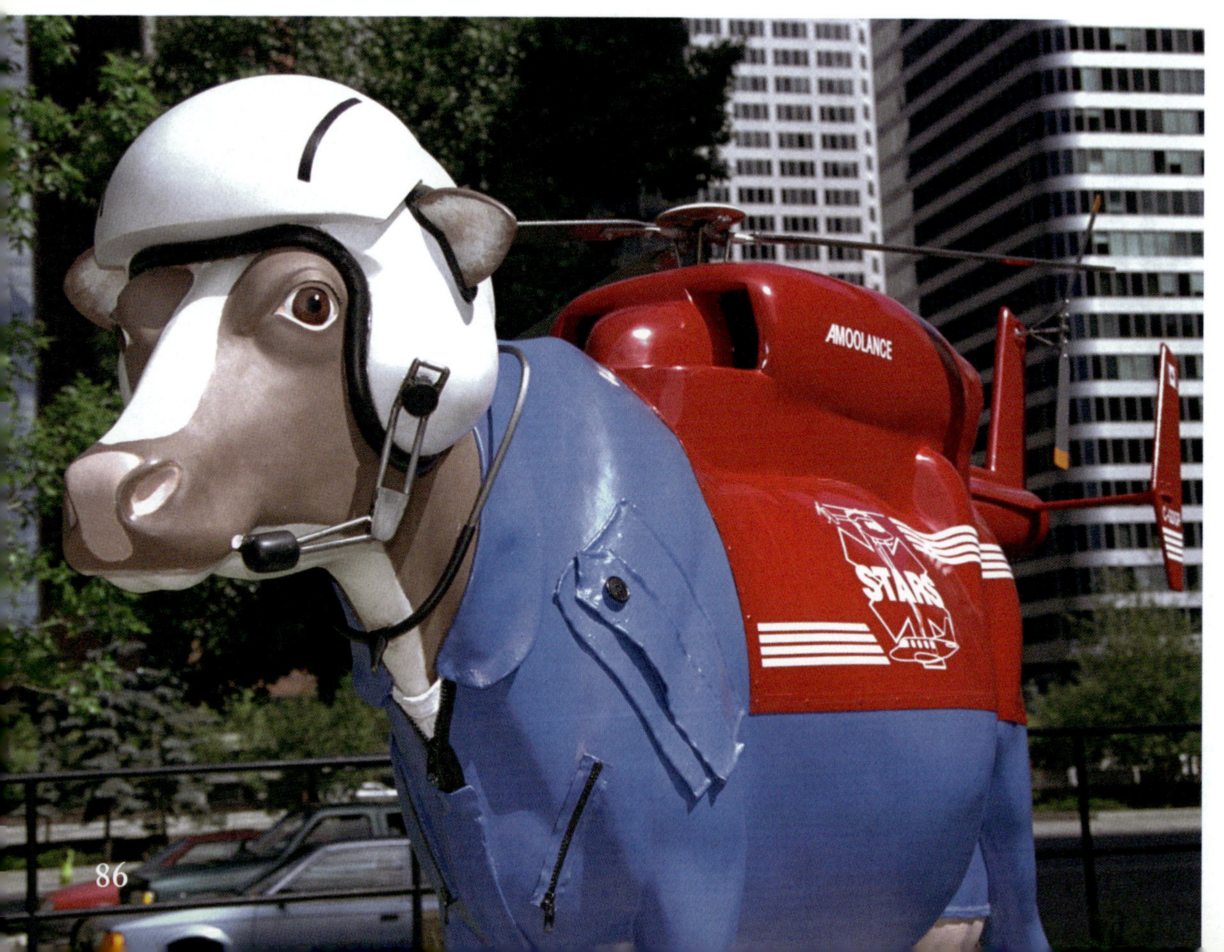

Fashioned from a hank of hair, a piece of bone, wood, fibreglass, foam, wire and countless buckets of Bondo, this high-flying beauty came together after a flurry of dawn-to-midnight shifts packed into about a dozen days.

A potpourri of delectable detail, the airborne bovine wears the snappy blue coveralls so important to flying paramedicattle everywhere and protective latex gloves on her front hooves.

And when it came to suitable hoofwear to bring up the rear, Furneaux gamely offered up the supreme sacrifice: the paramedi-cow is wearing his boots.

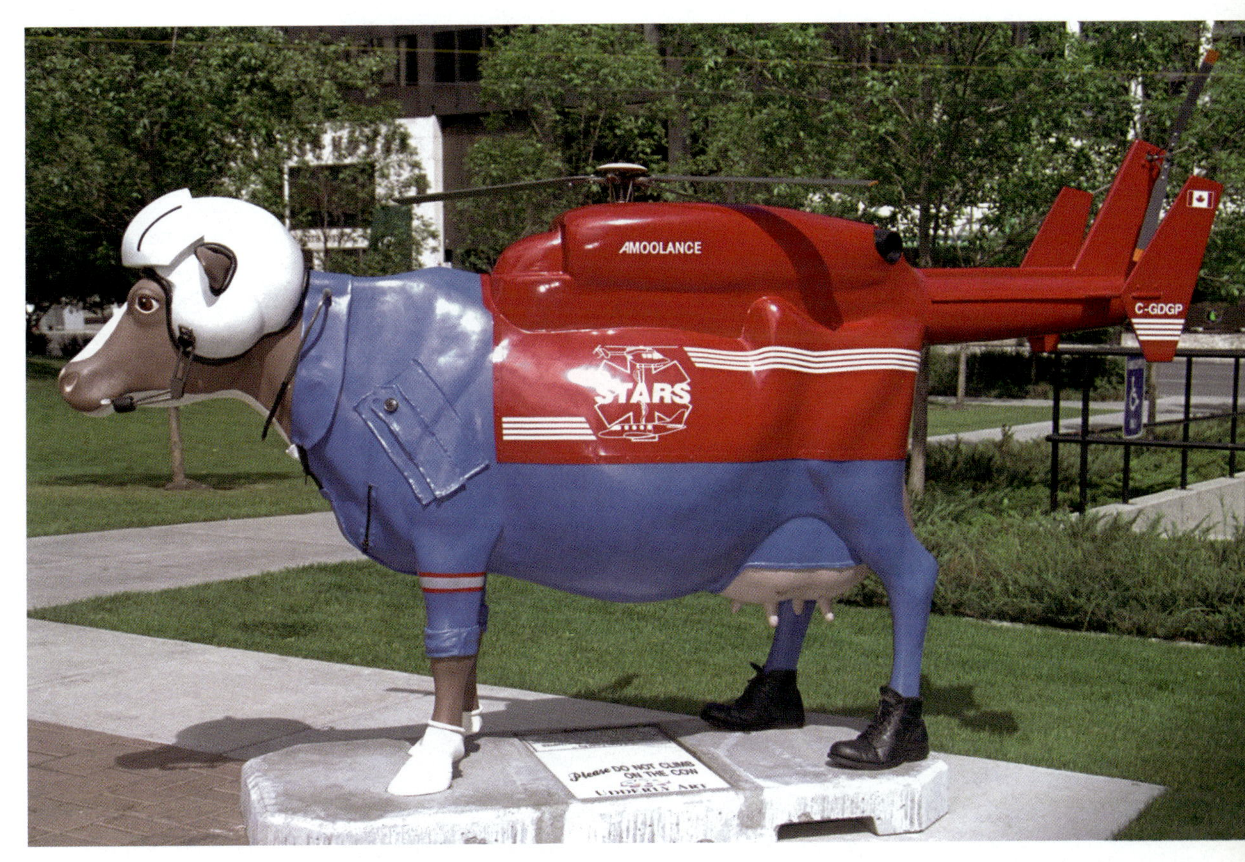

In Cybernetic Metal

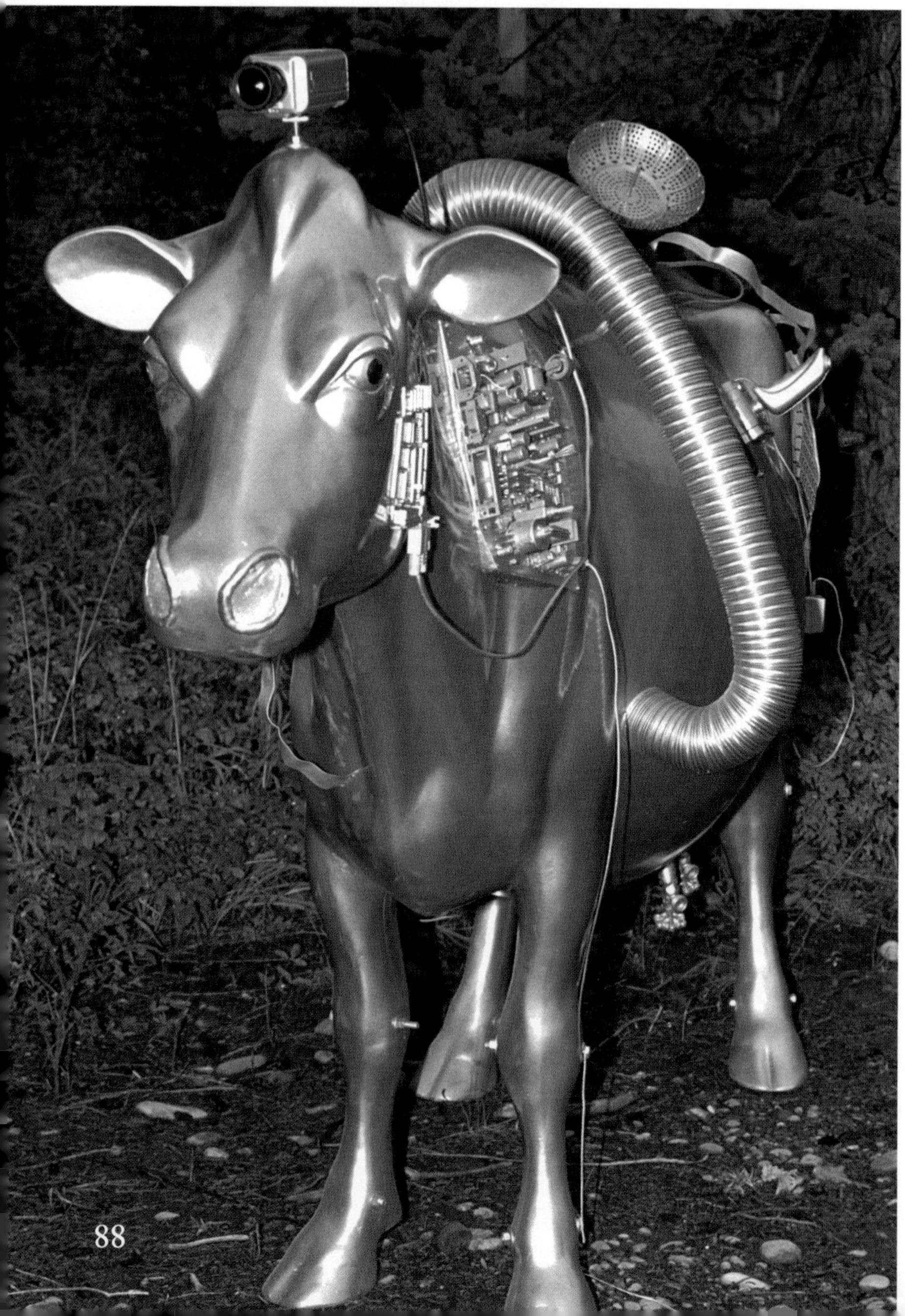

Artist: Rhianna Edwards

Owner: Calgary Stampede Foundation (donated by Jack Steen)

Charity: Calgary Stampede Foundation

A major beneficiary of Udderly Art's charitable mission has been the Calgary Stampede Foundation, recently created to help the youth of Alberta increase awareness of its heritage and cultural roots. Foundation-funded programs enhance personal growth, citizenship and education. Five Uderly Art cows, including this one, have been donated to the cause.

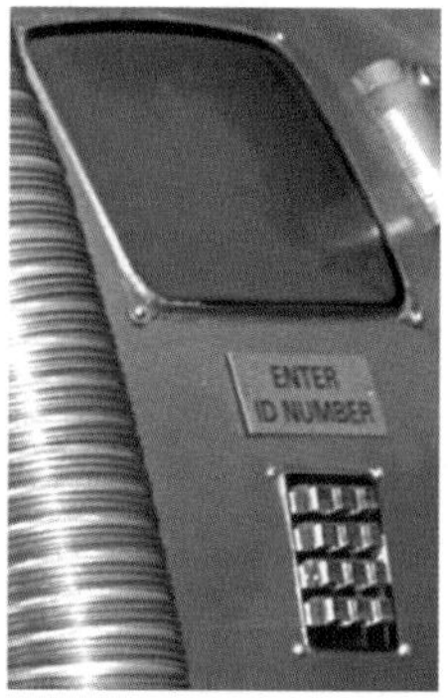

Jackson Cowlick, Incidental Bovine

Artist: Ivan Zadravec

Owner: Glenbow Museum (donated by Rob and Ruth Peters and Family)

Ivan Zadravec works in Glenbow's production department and confesses to an affection for the work of the late American abstract painter, Jackson Pollock. In his tribute to the artist, Zadravec applied more than 300 coats of paint and wound up with a subtle, mottled sheen that would have mo-o-o-ved the action-oriented Pollock.

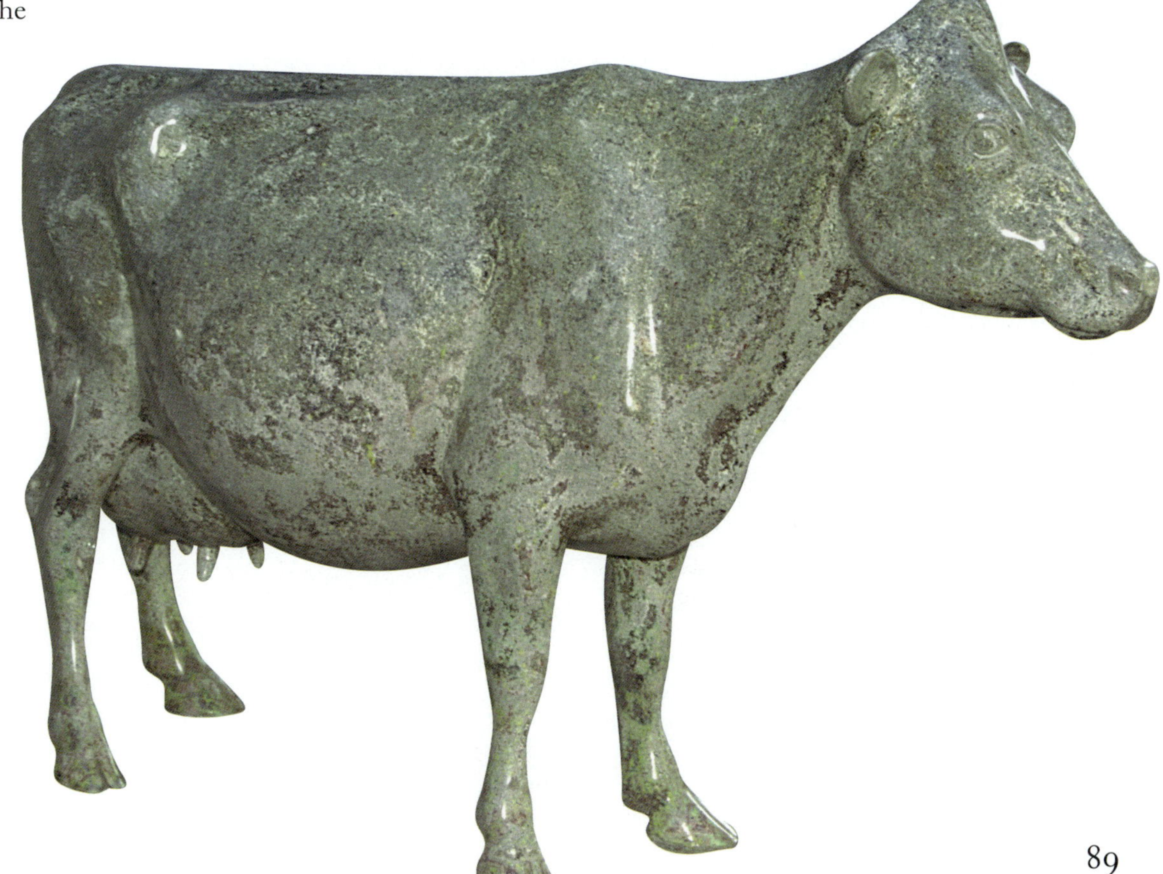

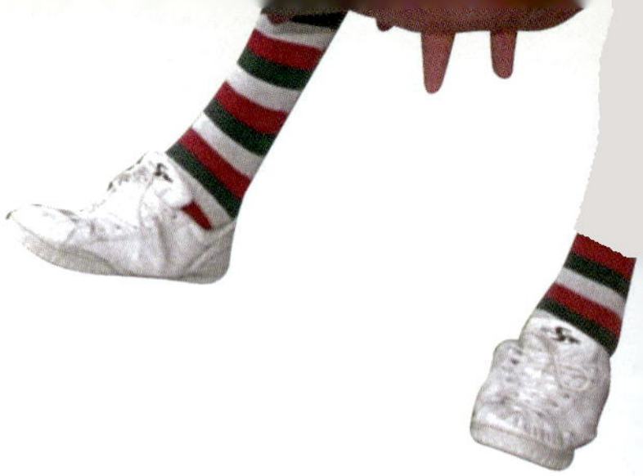

Jingle Belle

Artist: Barry W. Fairbairn

Owner: Super Drug Mart

Charity: Arthritis Society

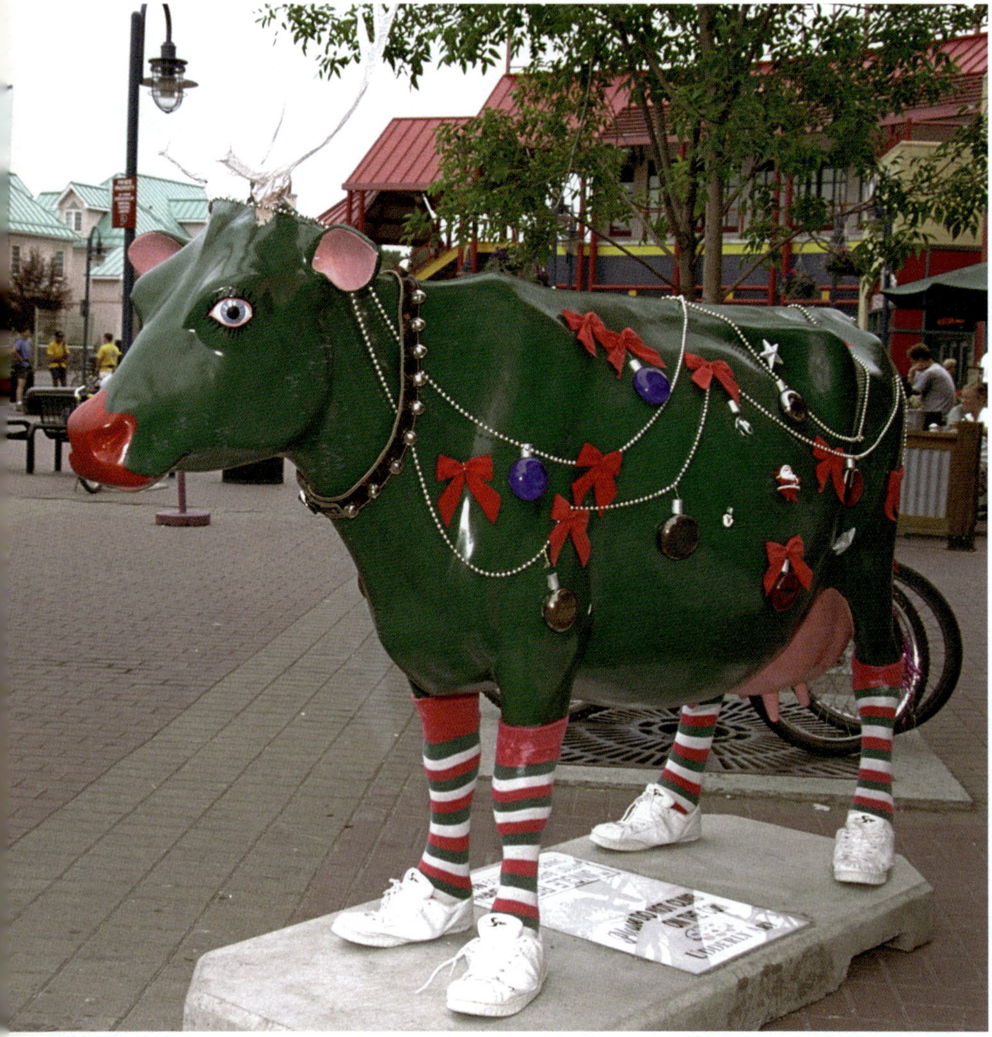

A not-so-distant cousin of Rudolph the Red-Nosed Reindeer, *Jingle Belle* displays all the family characteristics: Christmas colours, antlers, scarlet snout, sleigh-bell collar and white rubber-soled sneakers for those slippery roof landings. Look to the skies this Christmas for her arrival at a rooftop near you.

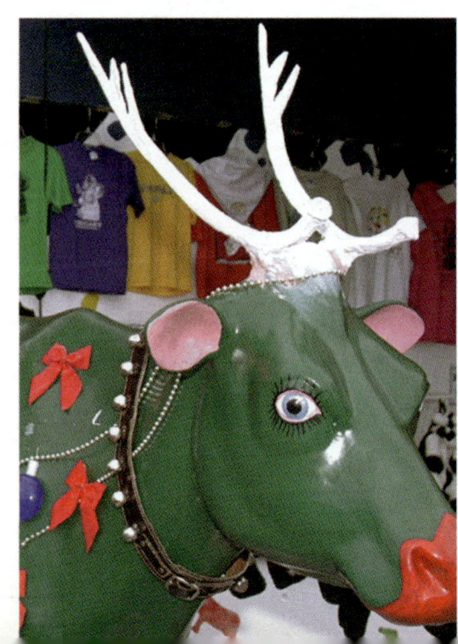

Latest Graze in Cowcarey

Artist: Pam Weber

Owner: Frank Carey Family

Grazin' in the grass, Pam Weber's work is washed from hoof to snout in artful splatters of wild, bright, feel-good colours. As a group, Udderly Art is more than slightly pun-happy, so it shouldn't surprise anyone that the cow's name is a tongue-twisting curtsey toward the initial purchasers.

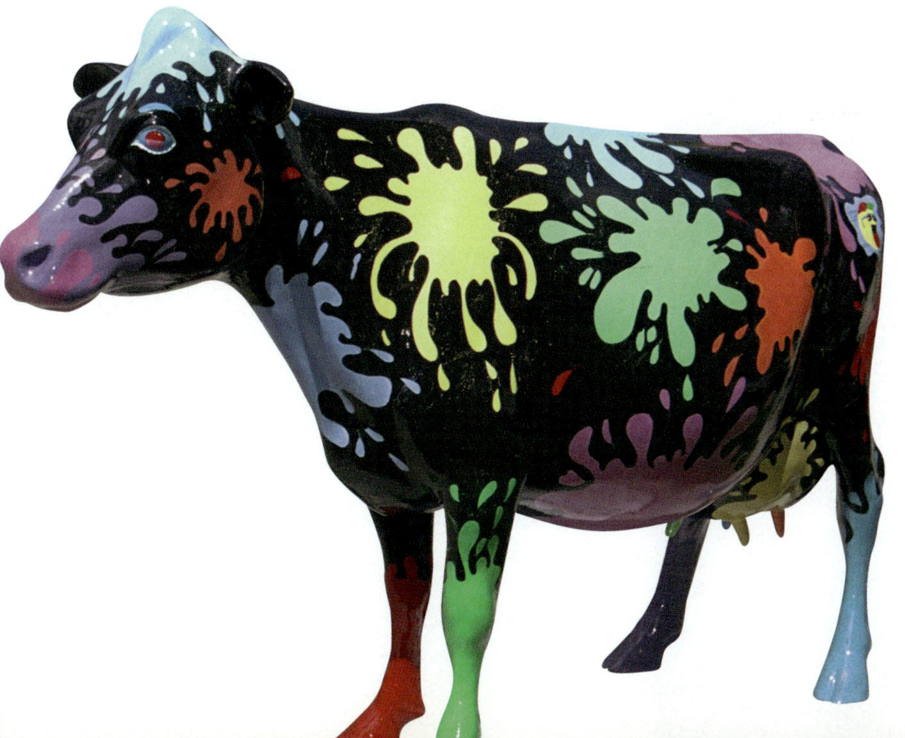

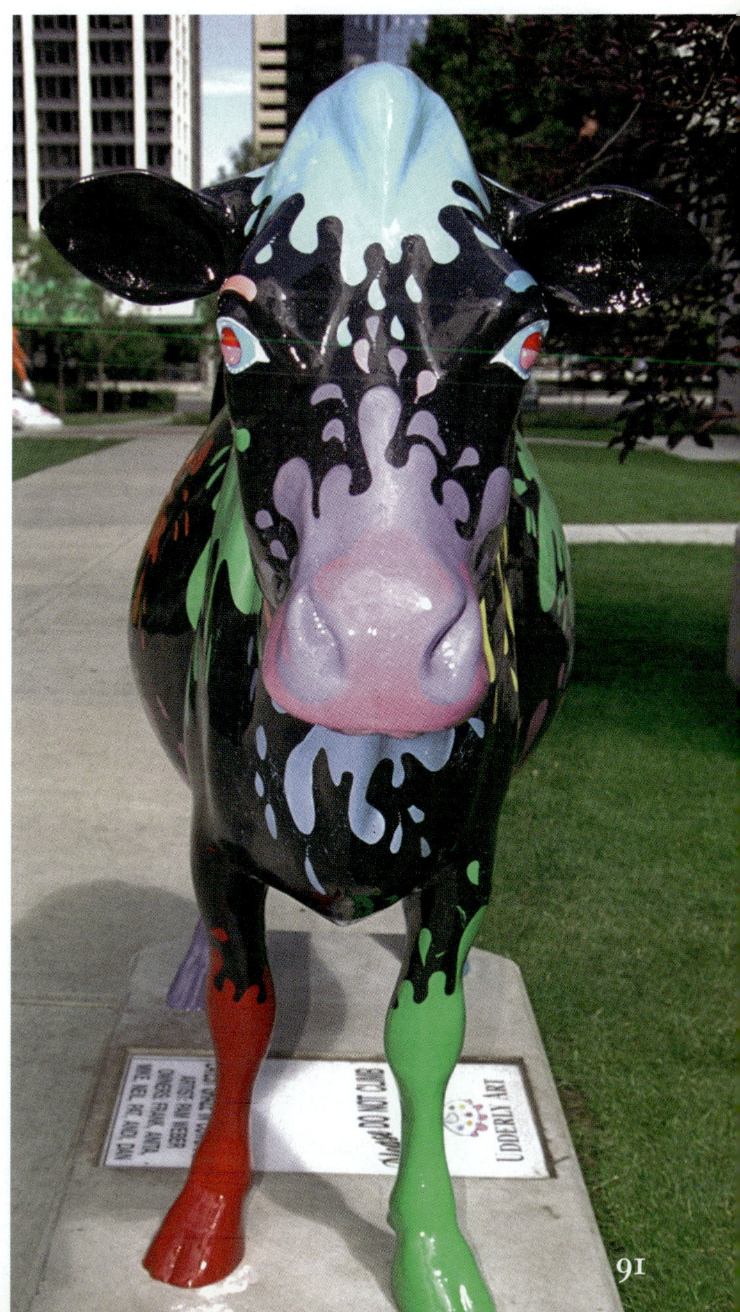

Knee Deep in Wild Flowers

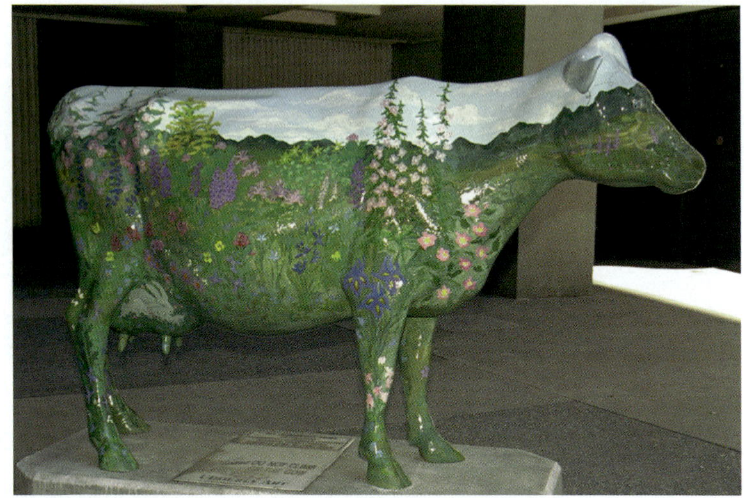

Artist: Lynnie Wonfor

Owner: Calgary Stampede Foundation (donated by Viking Management Ltd.)

Charity: Calgary Stampede Foundation

A longtime friend of the Stampede Foundation, Viking Management CEO Kirk Purdy was happy to donate this wonderful, wild-flowered cow. But Purdy didn't anticipate that his wife, Barbara, would fall udderly in love with *Knee Deep in Wild Flowers,* one of two Udderly Art cows decorated by Calgary's Lynnie Wonfor.

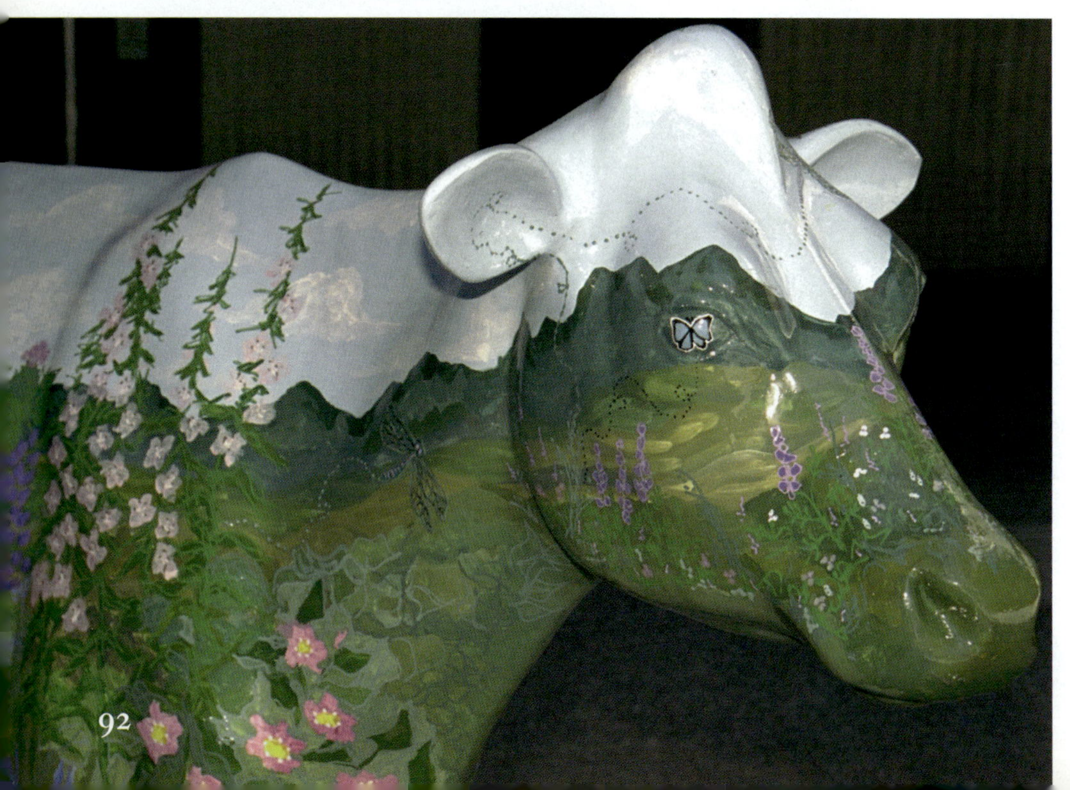

Prior to the October 2000 auction, Barbara had begun to apply subtle pressure to persuade her husband to buy back the cow.

No surprise, really. Both Purdys are longtime admirers of Wonfor's work. A close friend of the family, she has painted murals on the walls of their home, a rambling country place with a splendid mountain view. The distinctive Wonfor touch has also been applied to the interior of the Purdy family recreation vehicle. And those roses painted on the Purdy's fence are Wonfor originals, too.

The mutual-admiration relationship began when Wonfor painted the couple's chicken coop at Barbara's request. Barbara is a creative person herself, with a highly developed sense of humour. And since she had forged a "friendship" with each feathered denizen of her coop, she persuaded Wonfor to include the name of every chicken—Henrietta and Penelope among them—on her exterior paint job.

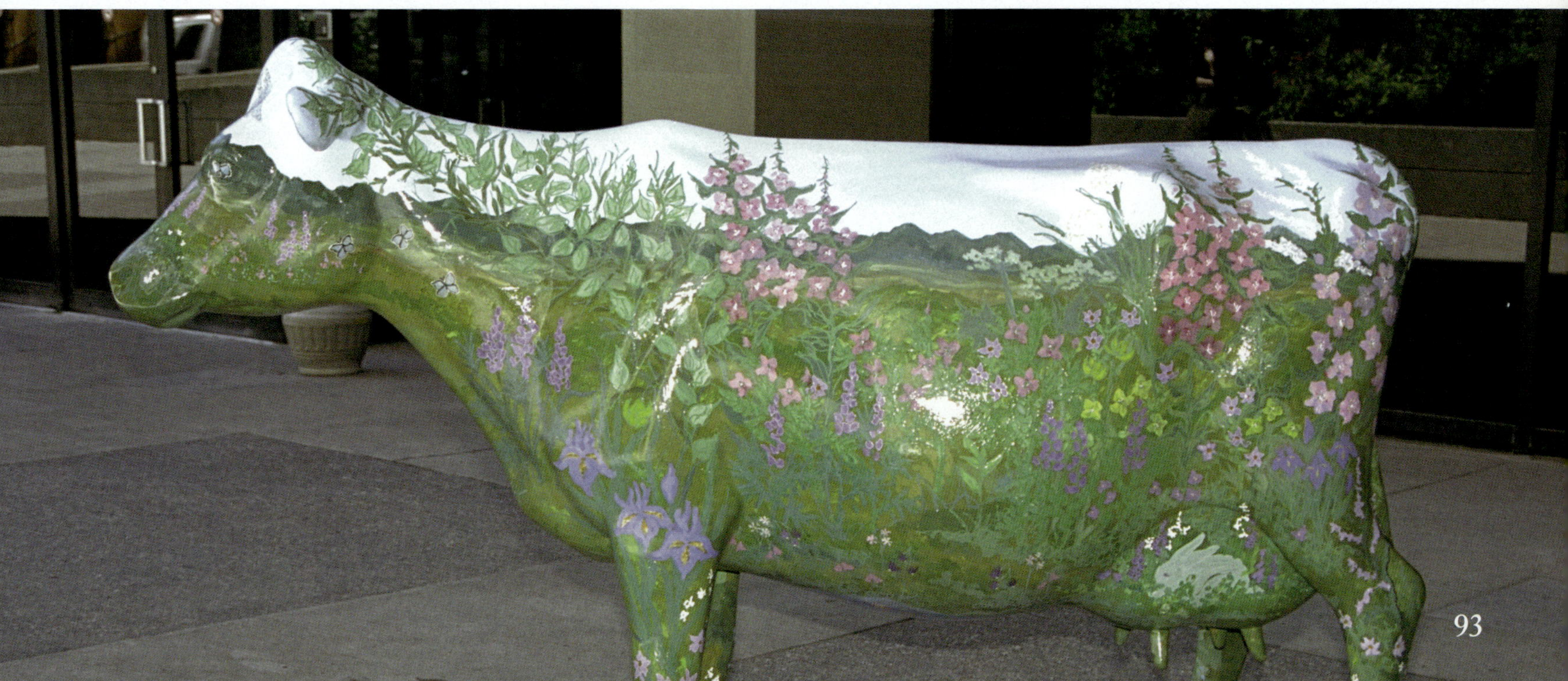

Macow

Artist: Luella Gilchrist

Owner: Eau Claire Market

Charity: Alberta Youth Outreach Foundation

Birds of a feather flock together, but *Macow* is unique—solitary fowl and unusally silent for a parrot prototype. Still, the blue wing feathers and yellow belly are unmistakable. She's one big bird on the hoof.

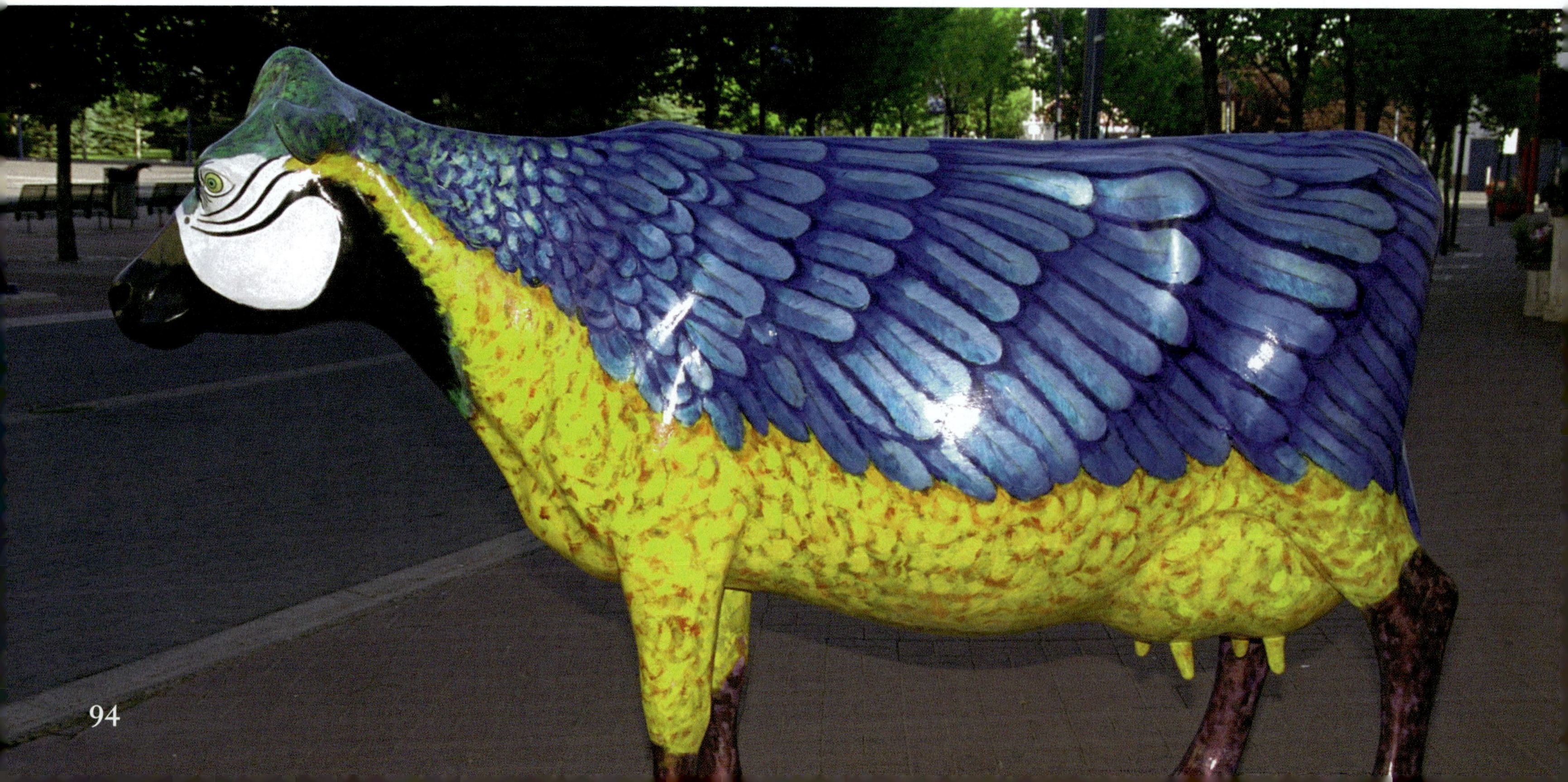

Milk Chocolate

Artist: Karen Teskey

Owner: F&D Scene Changes

Charity: Alberta Children's Hospital Foundation

What kid could resist munching on such a tempting hunk of milk chocolate? It emerges from the golden wrapper like the most humungous sweet-tooth satisfier since the Easter Bunny blew town. Ooops, take a look at that bite out of the cow's neck. Somebody couldn't wait.

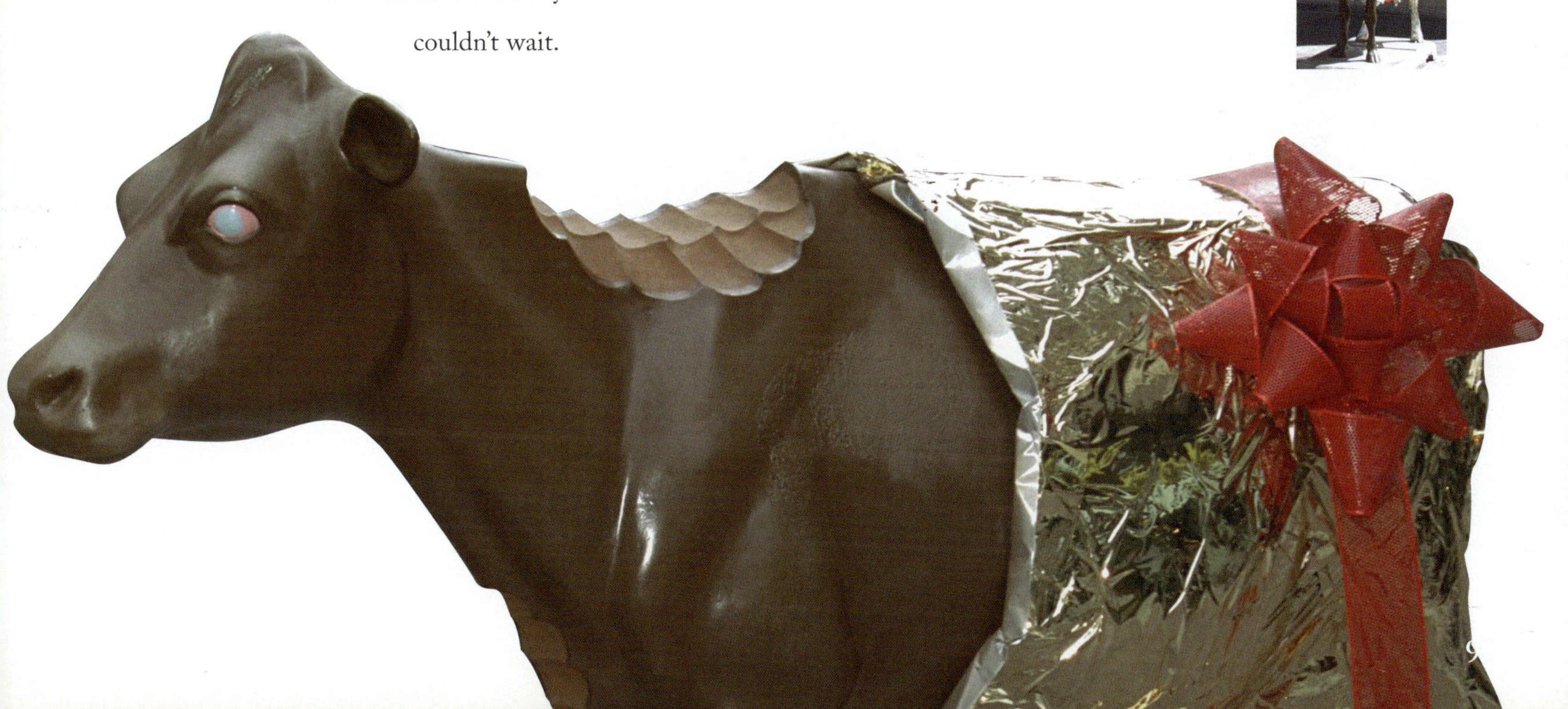

Midnight Cowgirl

Artist: Laura Pope

Owner: Mac's Convenience Stores and Dairyland Milk Company

Charity: Diabetes Association (Foothills)

It's a truly stunning piece of public work, a combined urban and rural landscape worthy of any traditional canvas hanging in any traditional art gallery. But it just so happens that Laura Pope's most talked-about new creation is painted on a cow, one of Udderly Art's placid fibreglass herd, which has spent much of its time grazing on the concrete plaza outside Calgary's Court of Queen's Bench.

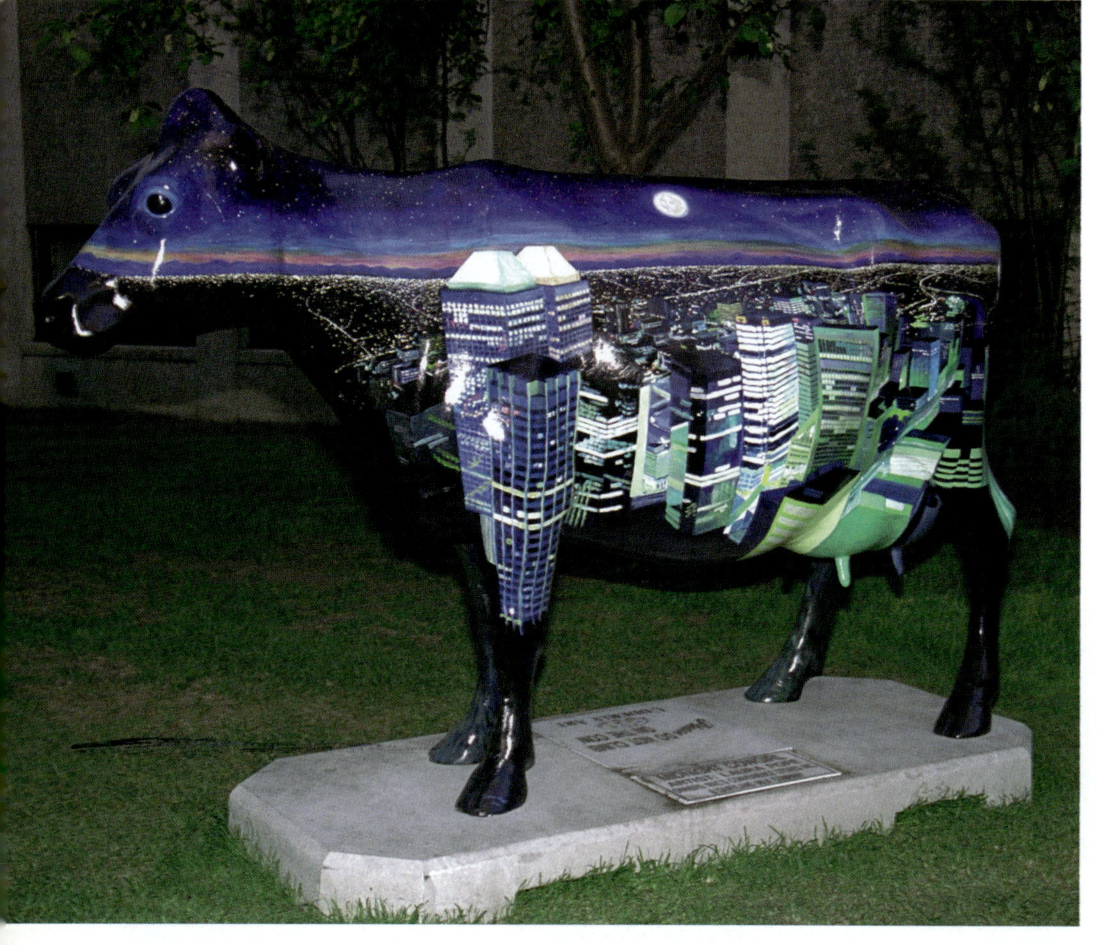

The denizens therein—judges, Crown and defence lawyers, bailiffs and court clerks alike—fell in love with *Midnight Cowgirl.* At last word, this impromptu legal consortium was reportedly pooling its pennies and plotting a coup with the intention of purchasing the cow so it could be tethered nearby as a permanent fixture.

For her part, Pope is proud of such positive feedback. And she's also proud, once again, of her association with Mac's Convenience Stores.

In a previous partnership, Laura worked on a series of murals for Mac's Stores in Victoria. For the current project, she used Mac's Open 24 Hours policy as inspiration for her evening scenes, which include a particularly arresting bird's-eye view of downtown Calgary with the Bankers Hall twin towers as a primary focus.

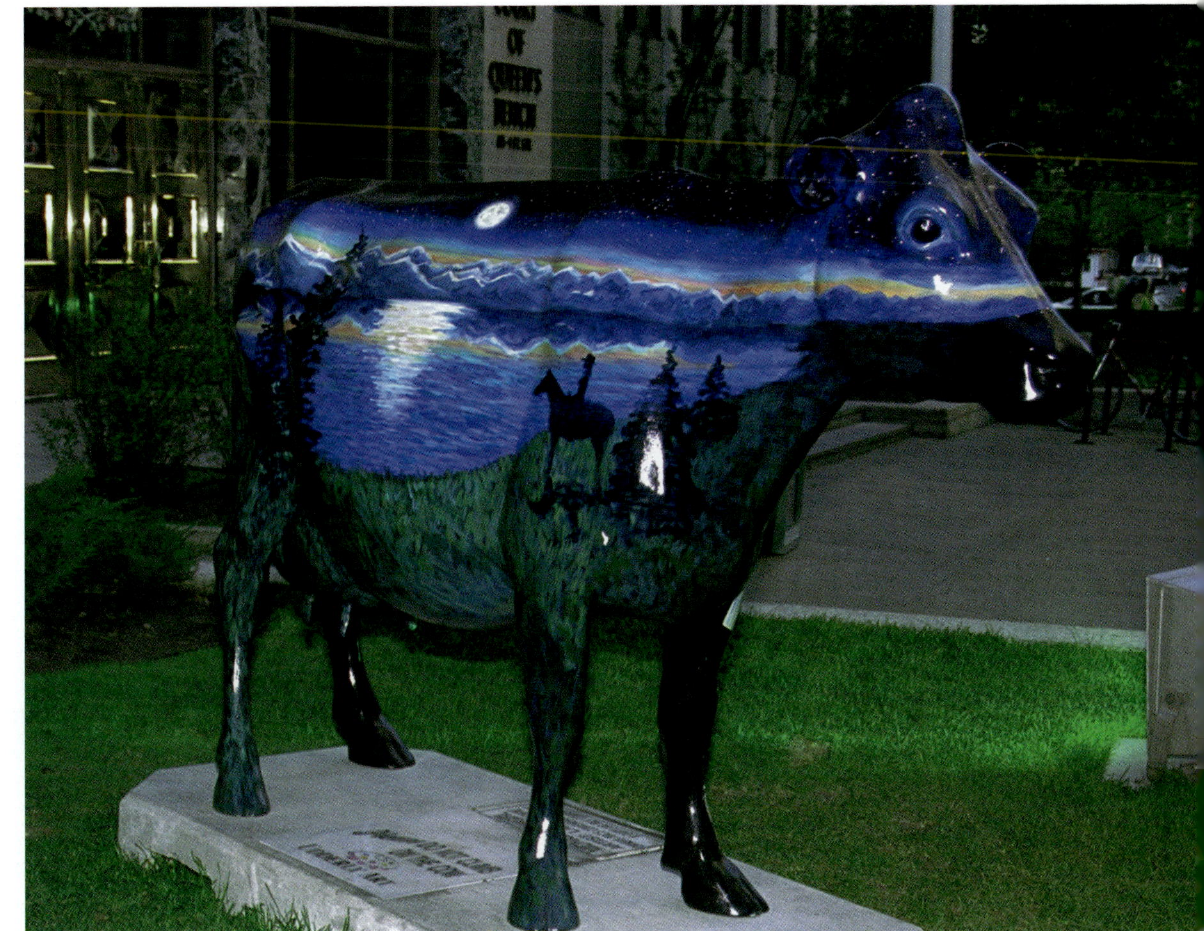

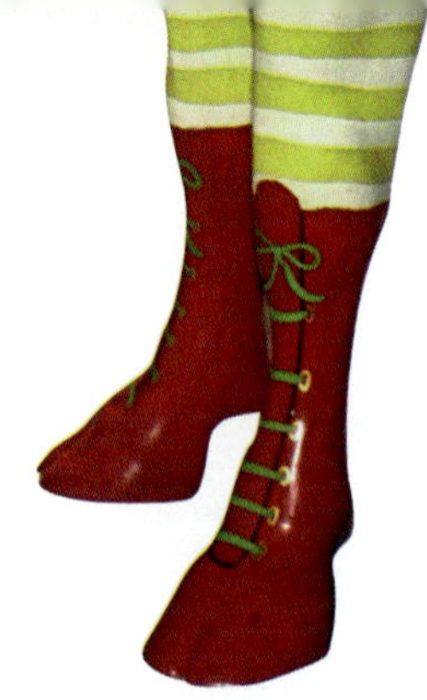

Miss Bella Bovine the Devine

Artist: Audrey Mabee

Owner: Bell Intrigna

Charity: Canadian Mental Health Association and Kids Help Phone Foundation

A longtime fixture in Calgary artistic circles, Audrey Mabee creates works of sublime beauty. Her intense colour palette is guaranteed to improve the blackest of moods. Audrey was kept busy in the spring of 2000 with a triad of Udderly Art cows. Bell Intrigna was so impressed they bought two and commissioned Audrey for both.

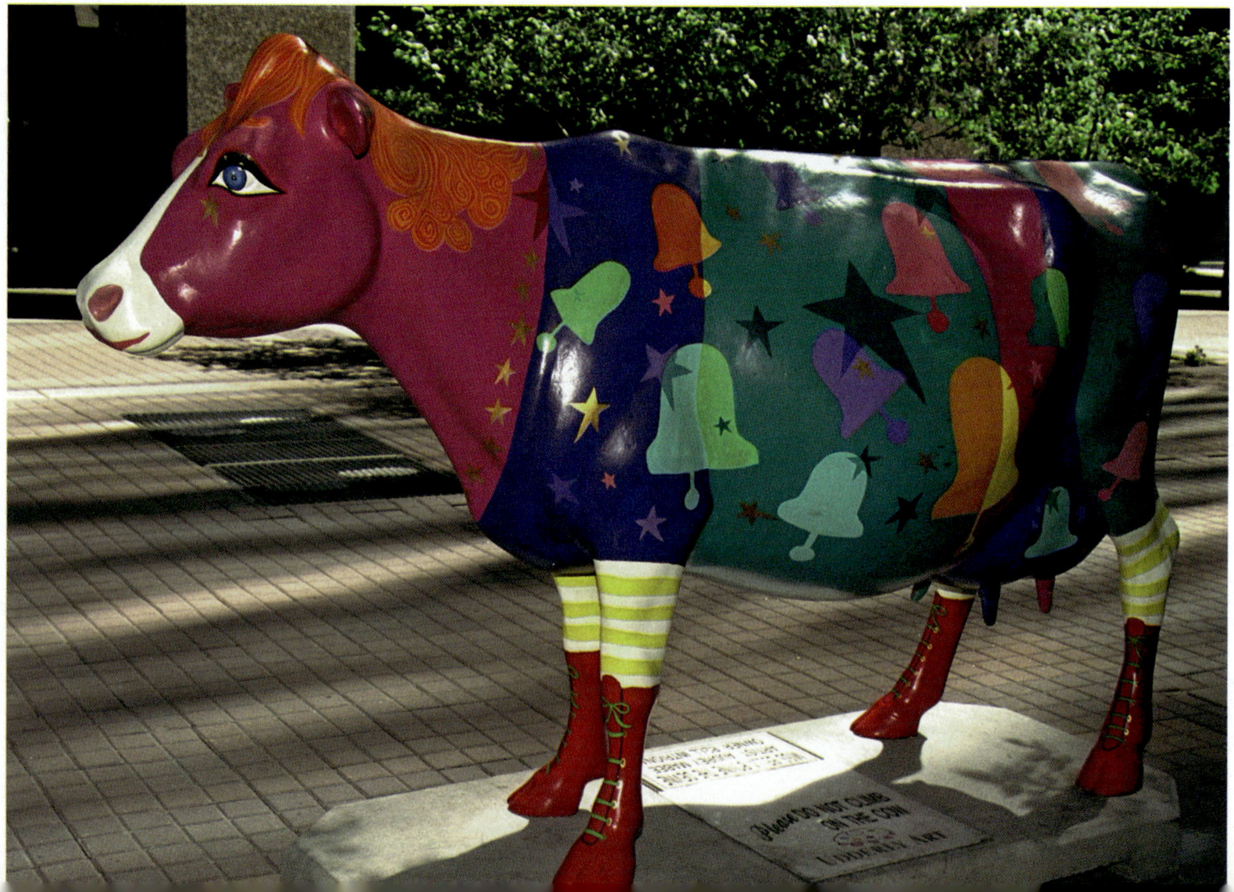

Miss Cowgary International

Artist: Flagworks

Owner: Flagworks Inc.

Flags, flags and more flags. This queen of the walk is festooned with an international smorgasbord of flag insignias with Canada taking pride of place on the face of the royal miss. She's even supported by two cutout "ladies in waiting."

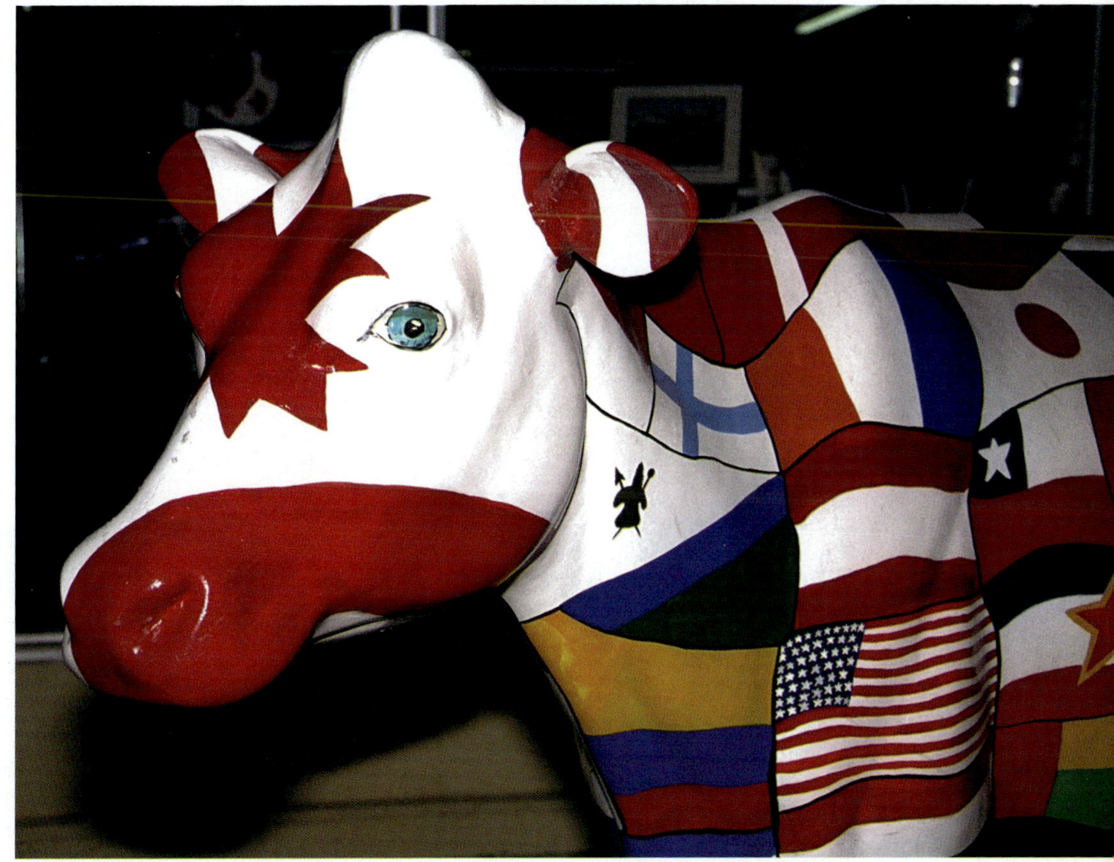

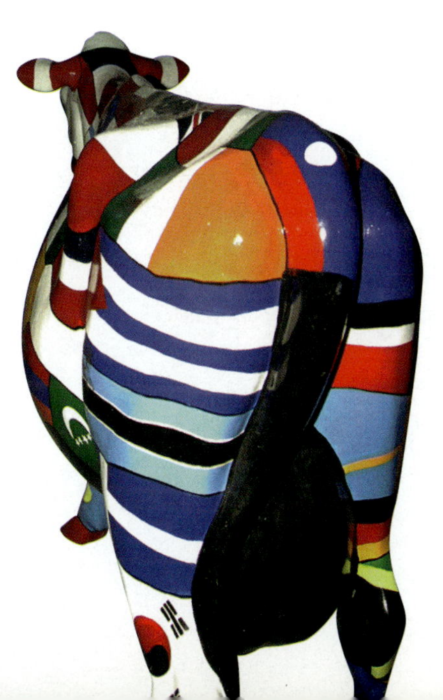

Moo Bella Cluck Cluck

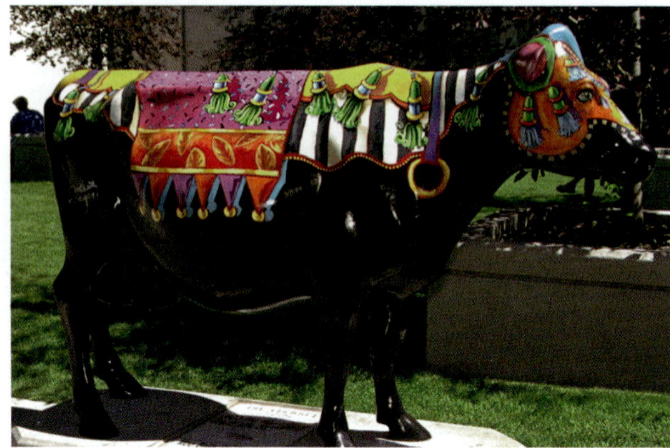

Artist: Grant Leier

Owner: Chickwagon Foundation

Charity: Calgary Women's Emergency Shelter

By now, everyone in Calgary knows the Chickwagon Chicks . . . er . . . ladies . . . er . . . women. They're a posse of fun-loving females who keep one eye on the prize and the other peeled for a cause worth working for. Naturally, the group—which buys an annual canvas in the Calgary Stampede Rangeland Derby chuckwagon auction—found Udderly Art a perfect fit.

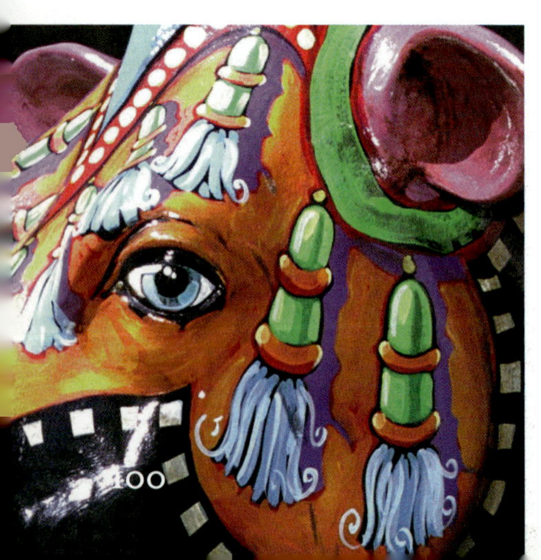

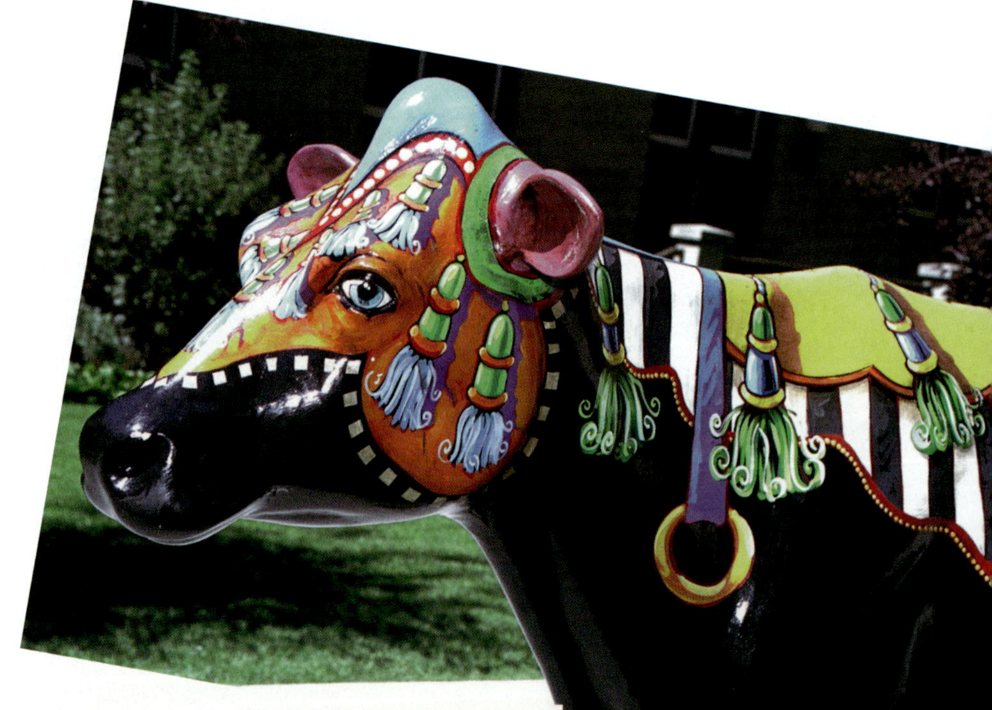

"Moo"lligan

Artist: Dean Stanton

Owner: Country Club of the Hamptons

Charity: Mustard Seed "Moving Mountains Campaign"

In past years, the Country Club of the Hamptons has played host to some of the biggest stars in the golf world, including Nancy Lopez and Chi-Chi Rodriguez. These majestic ex-pros may rarely "take a mulligan," but Dean Stanton's bovine beauty assures the rest of us mere mortals that it's okay to do so.

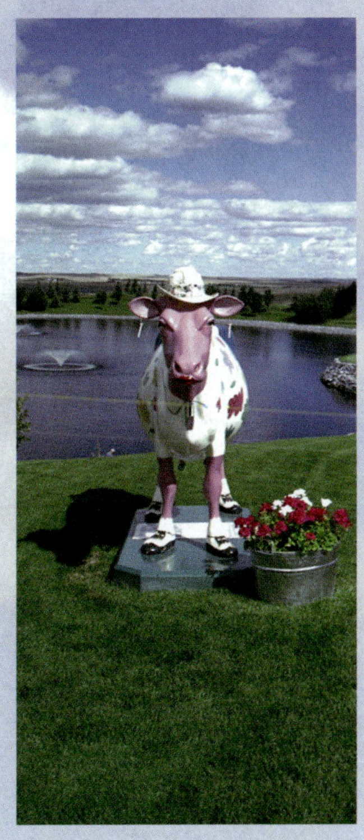

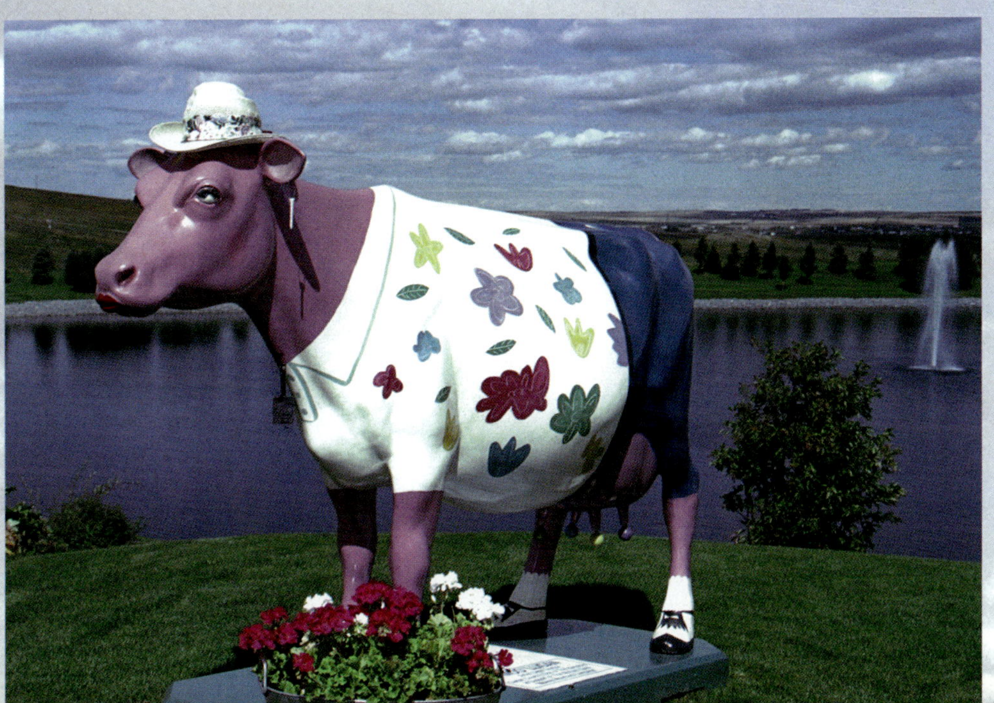

Moo West

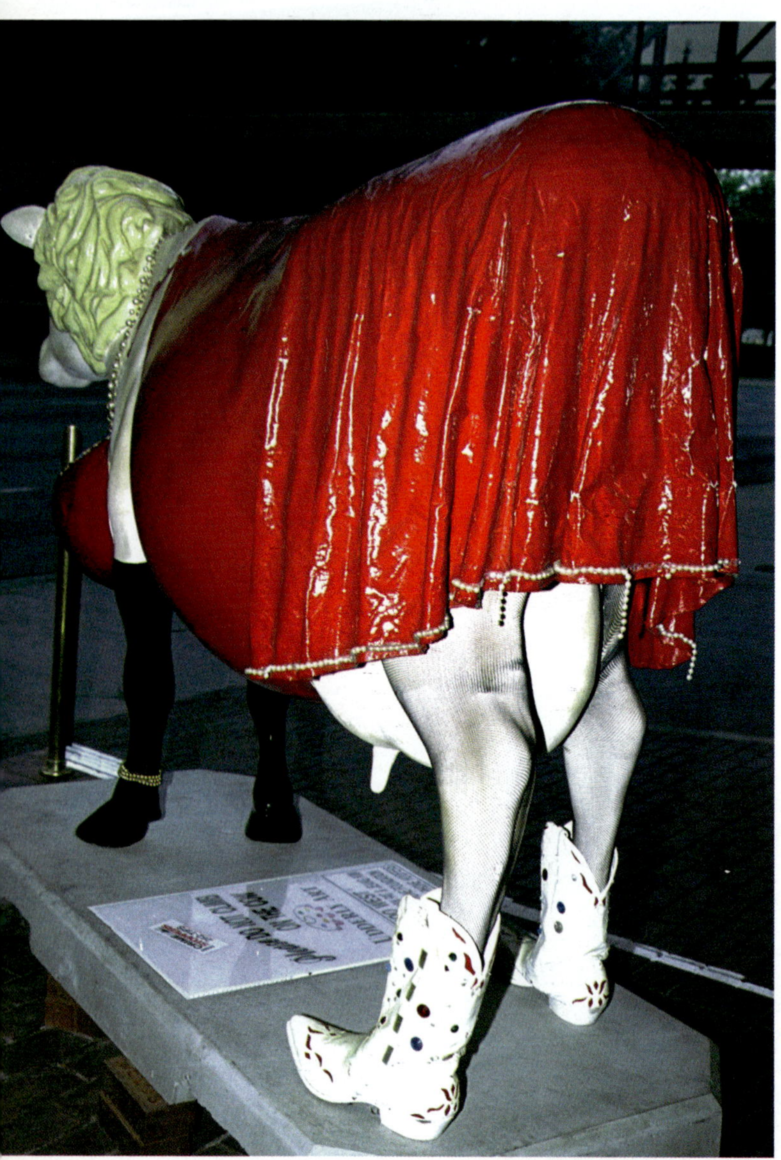

Artists: Margie Kwan Pat and Jeang Kim

Owner: Kids Help Phone Foundation (donated by Kids Help Phone Foundation Hoofers)

Charity: Kids Help Phone Foundation

She's sexy, she's saucy, she's on the sleazy side. Let's face it, the lady is a scamp. But like most shady ladies, *Moo West* has a warm heart. She took up her familiar post at the Delta Bow Valley after Calgary's Barb Ibbotson rounded up 24 other women to buy a cow to benefit the Kids Help Phone Foundation and have a little fun along the way. As for *Moo West*, come up and see her . . . anytime.

Moochas Grassias

Artist: Sonja Billard

Owner: friends in Cowbos

That's *Moochas Grassias.* (Loose translation: "Thanks a bunch for the good grazing grass.") Sonja Billard's cow seems to be saying thanks for a splendid getaway, perhaps on the Gulf of Mexico. This piece evokes an ecstatic celebration of summer from its sailfishing seascapes all the way to its brightly flowered tail.

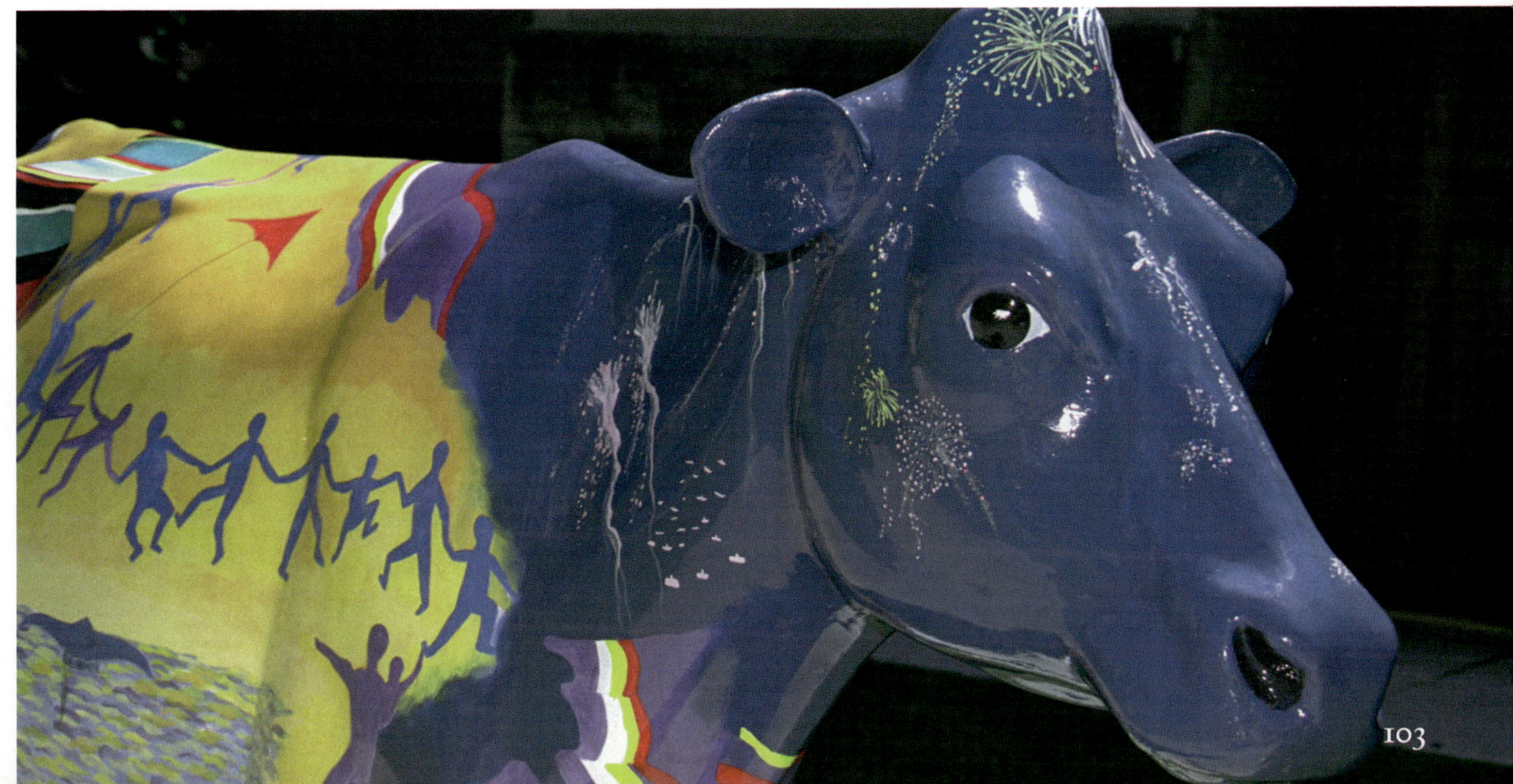

MooCowthy Cow

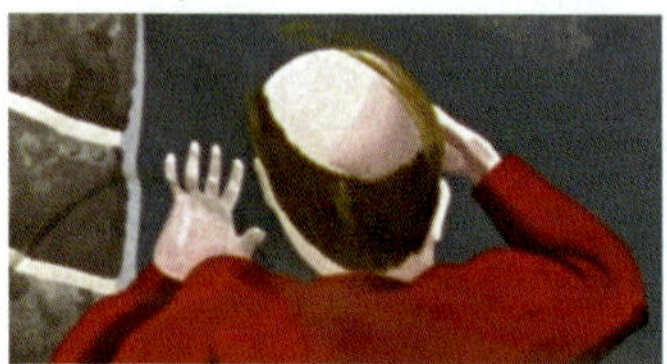

Artist: Mark Farand

Owner: McCarthy Tétrault

Charity: Hull Child and Family Services

Barristers, solicitors . . . and cows? It may strike some as an unlikely alliance, but Calgary artist Mark Farand makes it work beautifully. We're told the lawyers approve, but there's no word yet whether *MooCowthy Cow* will be offered a partnership anytime soon.

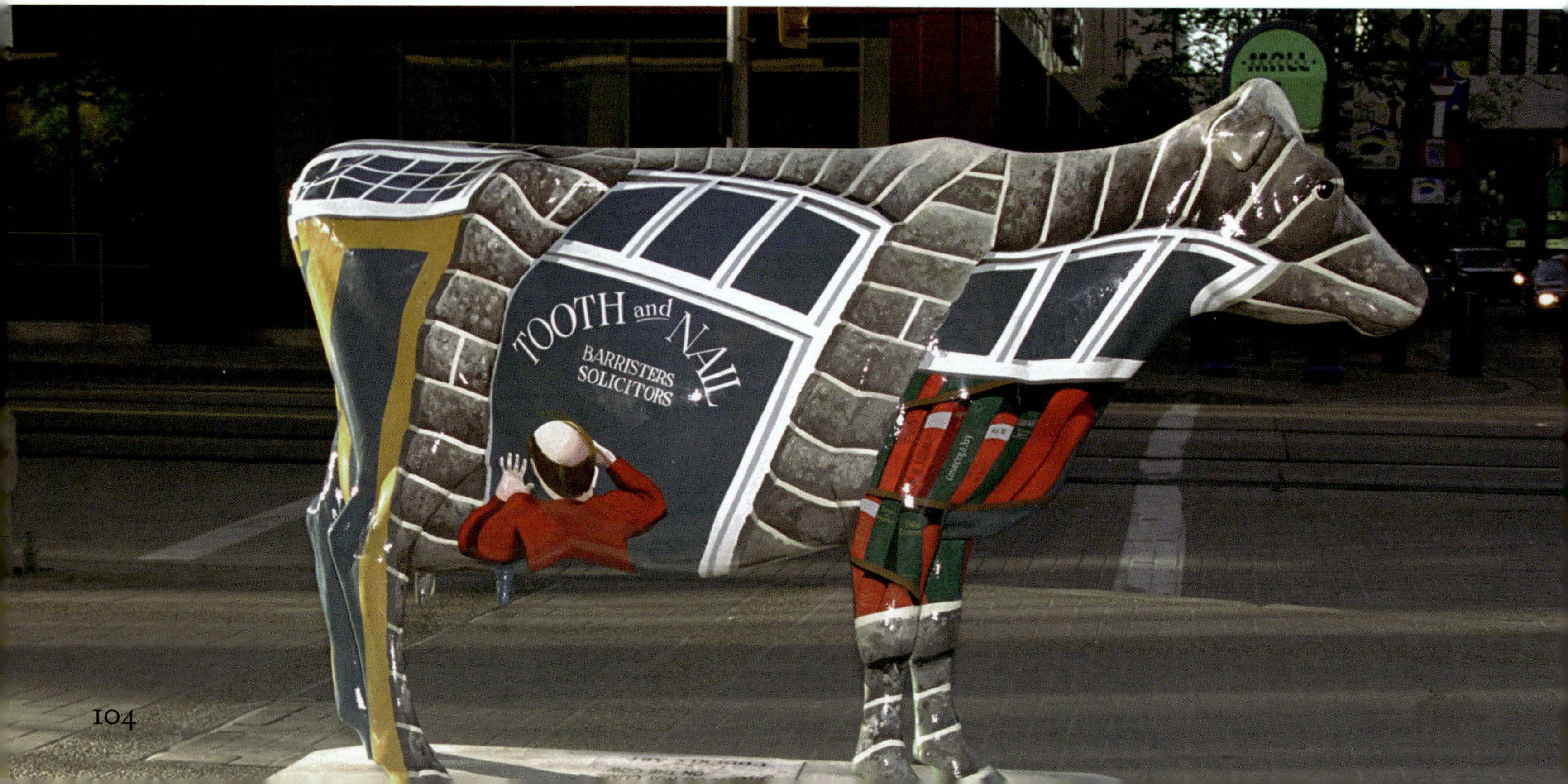

Moolennium

Artists: Jeanette Moran and Nancy-Lynne Hughes

Owner: EFW Radiology

Charity: Wings of Hope and Prostate Cancer Foundation

The radiology clinic was after something fun and magical—a vision of children gazing into the brightest of possible futures. Jeanette Moran and Nancy-Lynne Hughes supplied that and more, including a "cast" of happy children. There's a surprise on the cow's belly, but you have to lie on your back to get the picture.

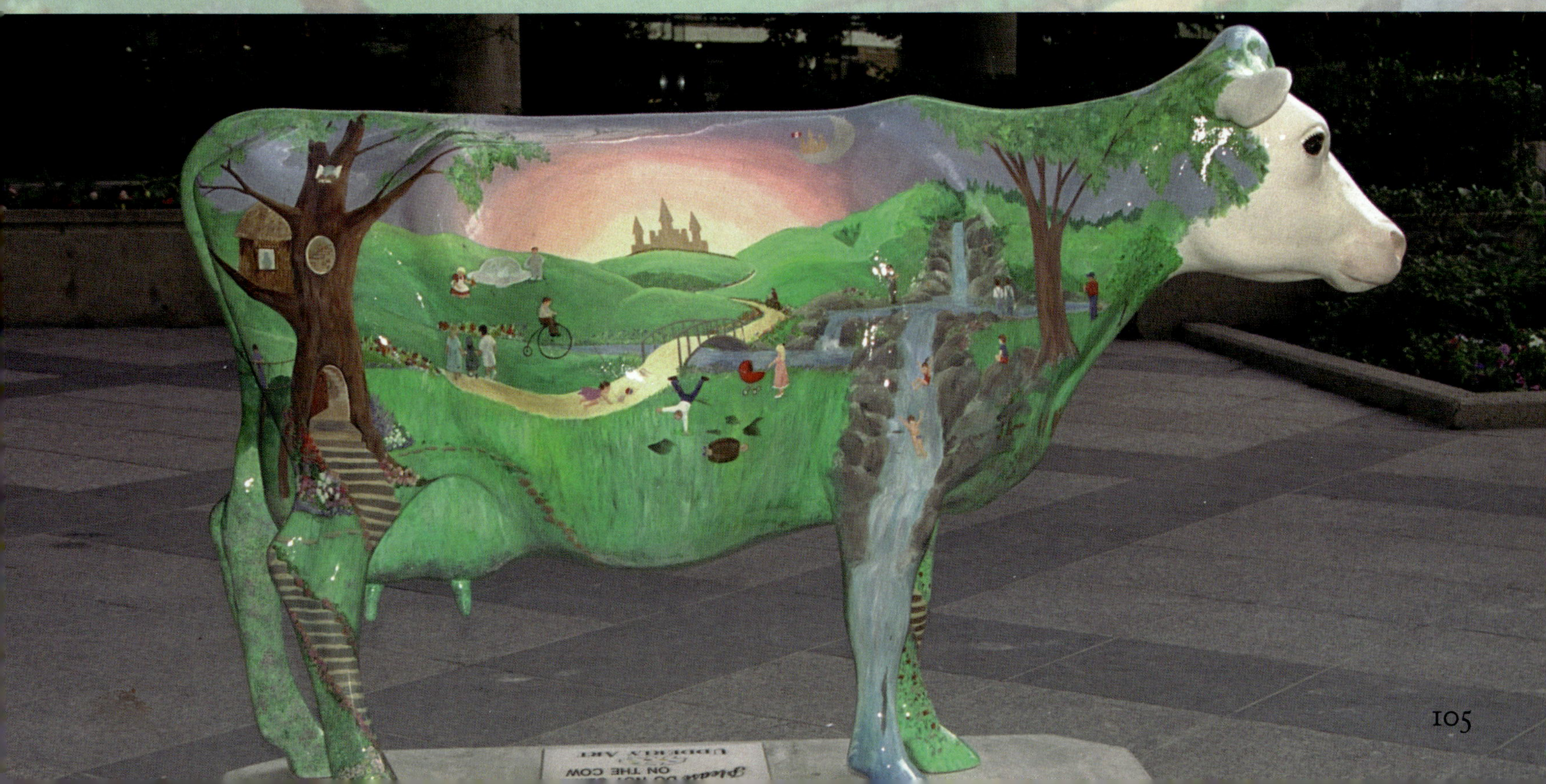

Mooney Trader

Artist: Damien Manchuk

Owner: Calgary Young People's Theatre (donated by CIBC Wood Gundy)

Charity: Calgary Young People's Theatre

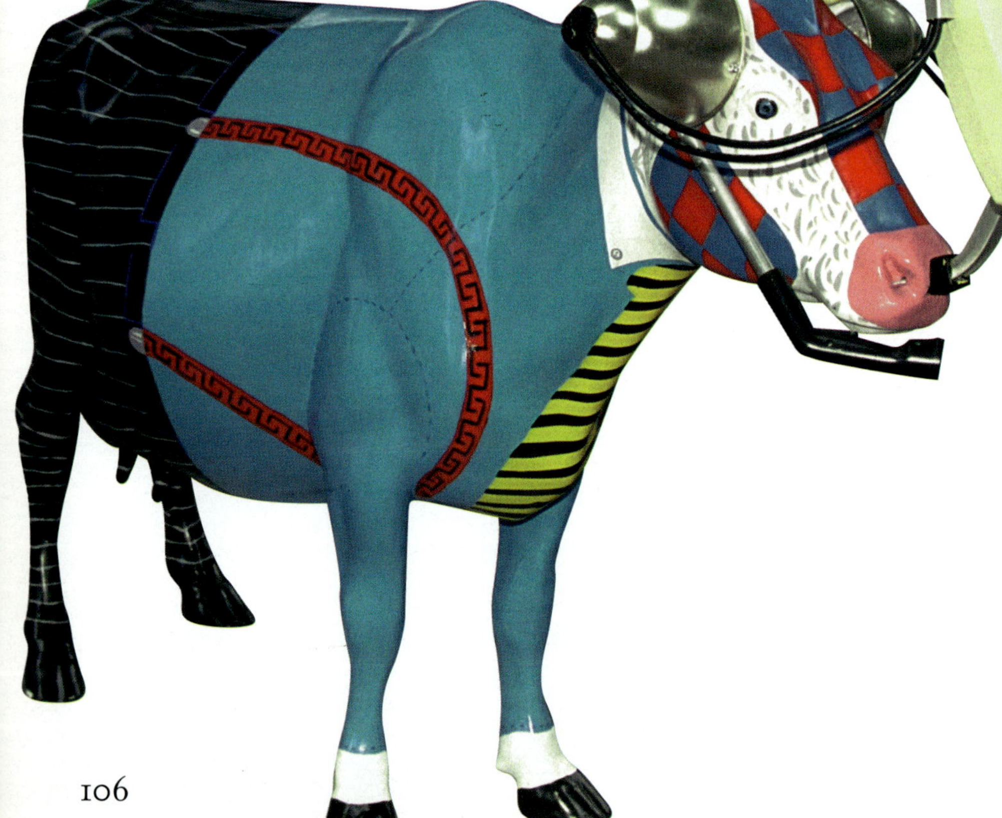

Looking back, it was quite a graduation present. A month or two prior to completing his program at the Alberta College of Art, Damien Manchuk found himself working on not one, but two, of Udderly Art's most appealing bovine sweethearts.

First, thanks to a kind word from ACA professor Gary Olson, Damien was selected to produce the cow known as *Chew-Choo* for Canadian Pacific

Railways, which he did, to the satisfaction of all concerned.

Within weeks, Manchuk had fielded a call from Hugh McGillivray of CIBC Wood Gundy, who had a second proposal in mind—to dress up an Udderly Art cow in the uniform of the stock-trading pit.

That meant a striped yellow power tie, smart blue shirt and the obligatory pinstriped trousers.

"Hugh took me into a men's clothing store to see what well-dressed cows were wearing," Damien explained.

But the young artist dreamed up the most arresting wrinkle—a computer screen ()sturdily held in place by stout aluminum tubing) at the end of the cow's nose, thus allowing the snappily attired *Mooney Trader* to keep up with TSE quotes 24 hours a day.

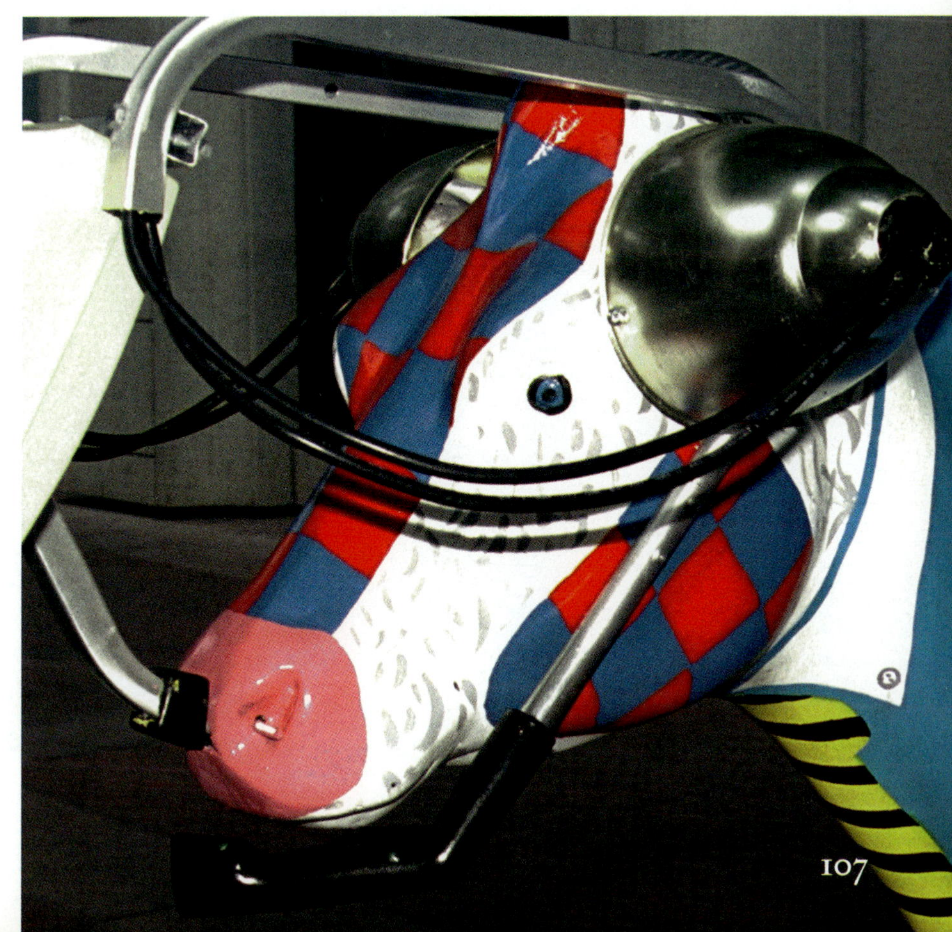

Mooovover

Artists: Randy Ross (designer) and A-1 Autobody Staff

Owner: A-1 Autobody Ltd.

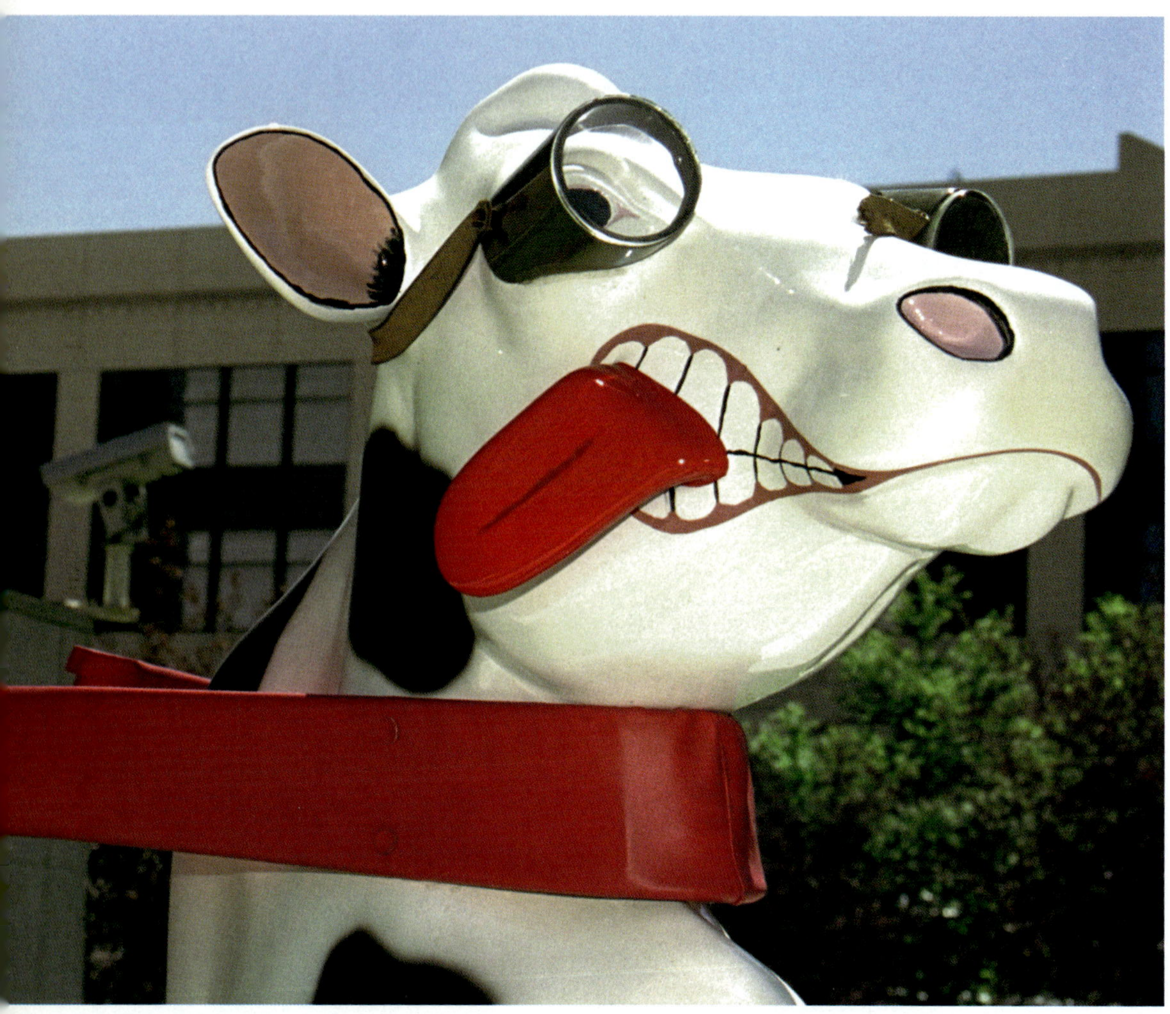

By day, he's a solid citizen and the highly reliable detail inspector in the shop of Calgary's A-1 Autobody. But there's an edgier, more creative side to Randy Ross. For proof, check out his hilarious design for *Mooovover*, the speed-craving, road-raging cow, whose right rear hoof is permanently clamped to the gas pedal.

Ross dreamed up *Mooovover*'s highly visual look after A-1 owner Gary Miller decided his staff might get a kick out of entering two in-house contests. Their challenge was to come up with an original game plan for jazzing up A-1's new cow and to follow up with an appropriate name for the beast.

Turned out to be no contest at all. Ross submitted winning entries in both.

The next step was to bring Ross's design to life. To that end, A-1 employees put in some 120 volunteer hours in the shop, sawing, sanding, bonding, reattaching and painting before *Mooovover* sped out of the shop to delight Calgary residents and visitors alike.

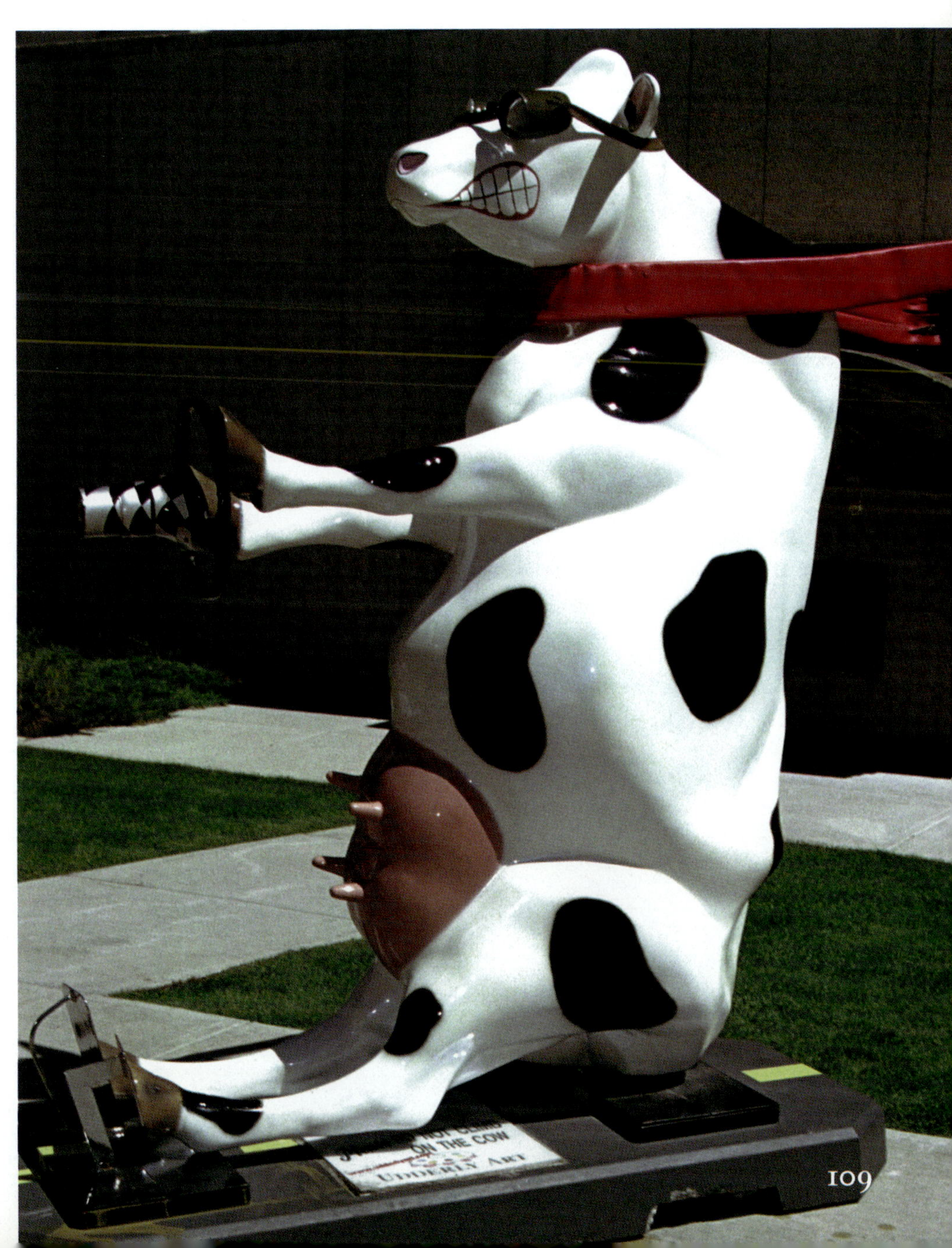

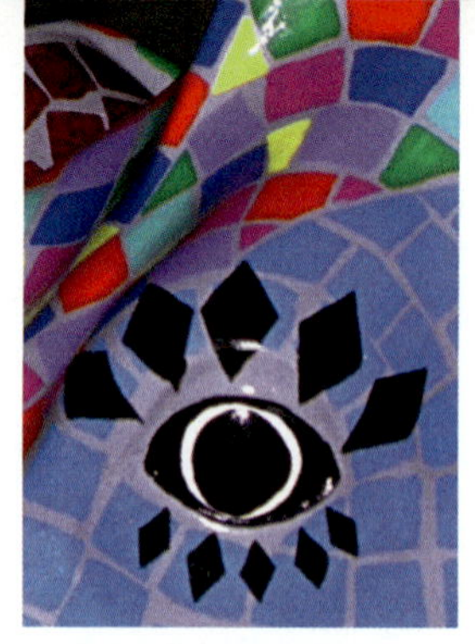

Moosaic Kid's Cow

Artist: Donna Hobbs

Owner: Flesher Marble & Tile and Chinook Centre Maintenance

Charity: Alberta Children's Hospital Foundation

Using materials near to hand, artist Donna Hobbs salvaged some blue tiles used to renovate the floors of Chinook Centre and applied them to the hooves of her cow. It's a bright, multicoloured, whimsical, happy and cheery mo-o-o-saic with several nursery rhymes tossed in as a bonus.

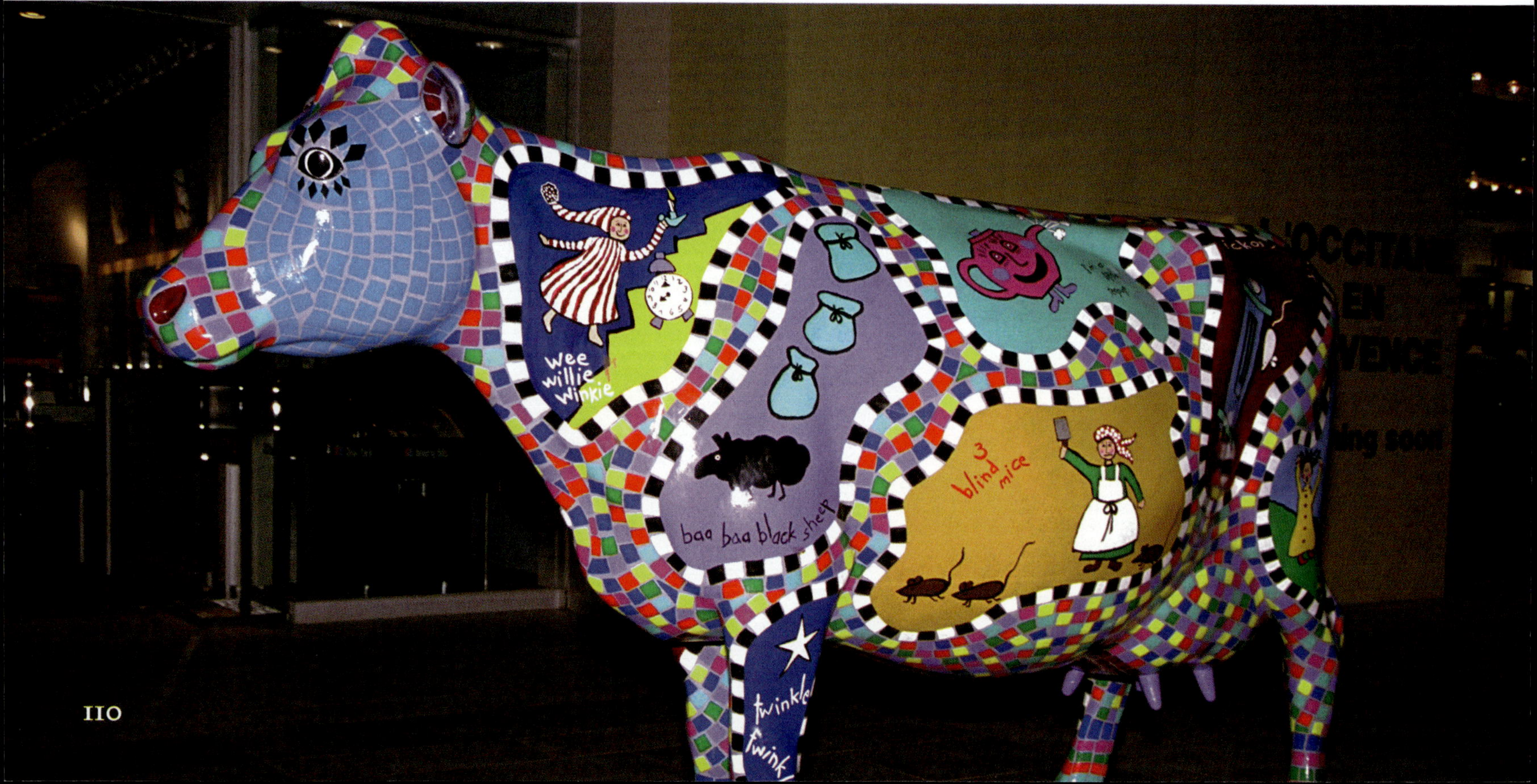

Moosterpiece

Artist: Gordon Oglan

Owner: Calgary Motor Dealers Association

Charity: Discovery House and Calgary Centre for the Prevention of Family Violence

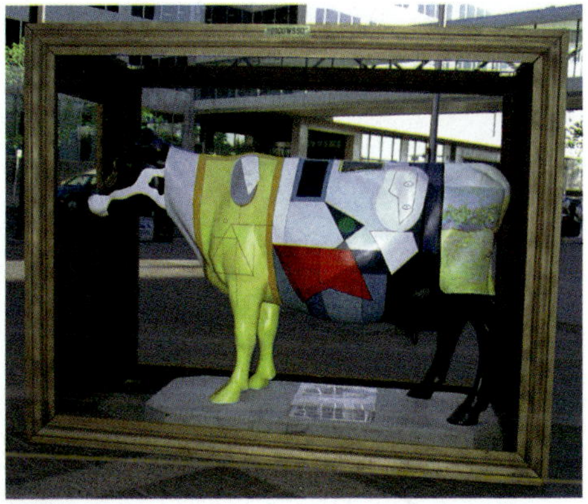

Too clever by half. In a masterpiece of economical, one-stop shopping, Gordon Oglan gives us a survey of art history within a cutaway frame. Oglan has included a taste of every key "ism"—cubism, impressionism and expressionism, including a full frontal "Moona" Lisa and a rearview Claude "Moonet."

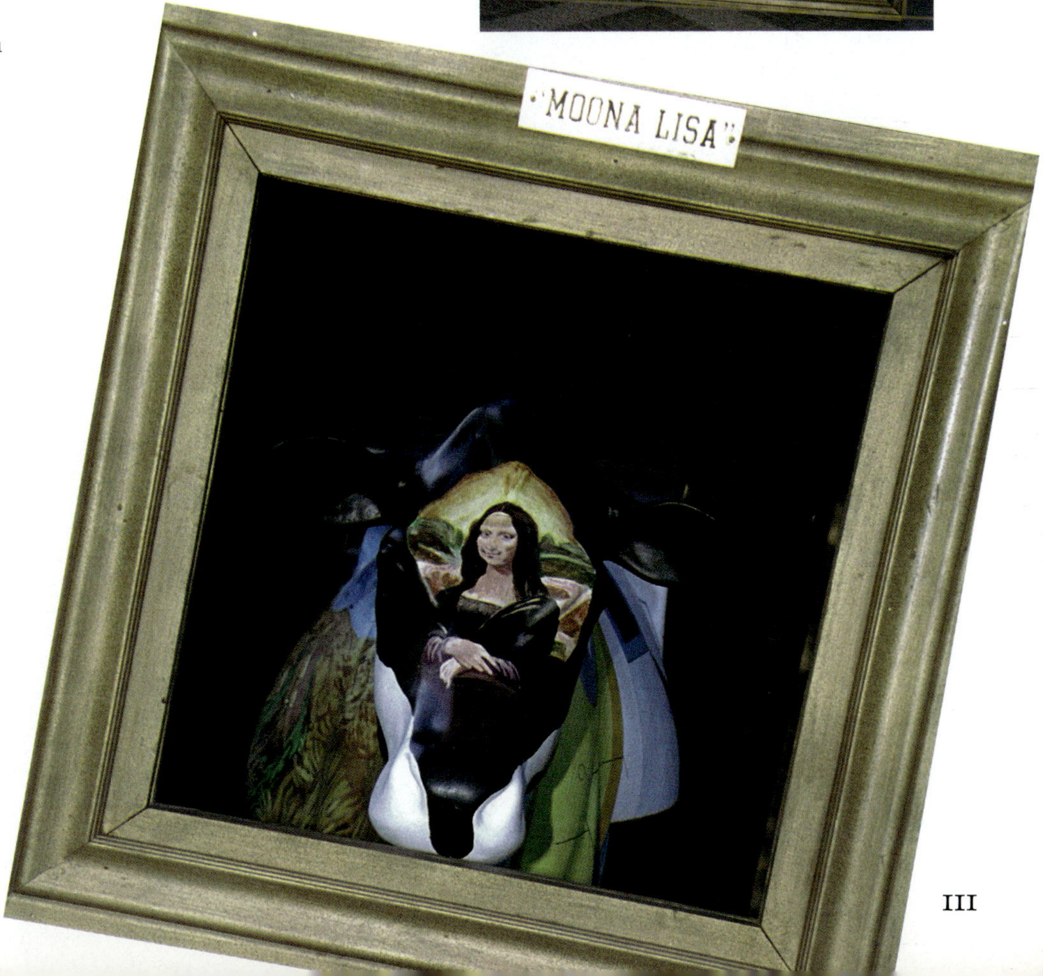

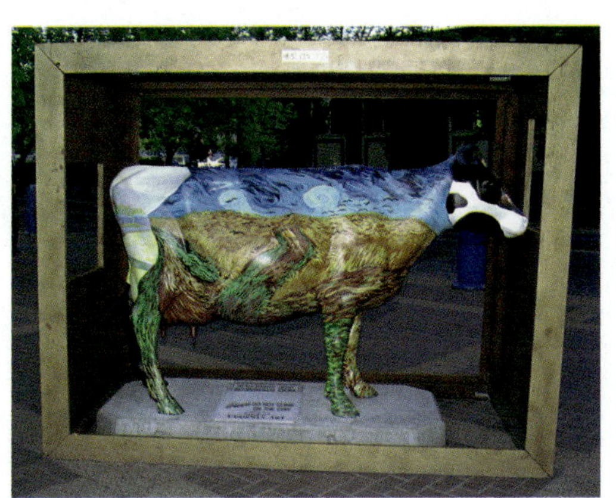

Moovin' On

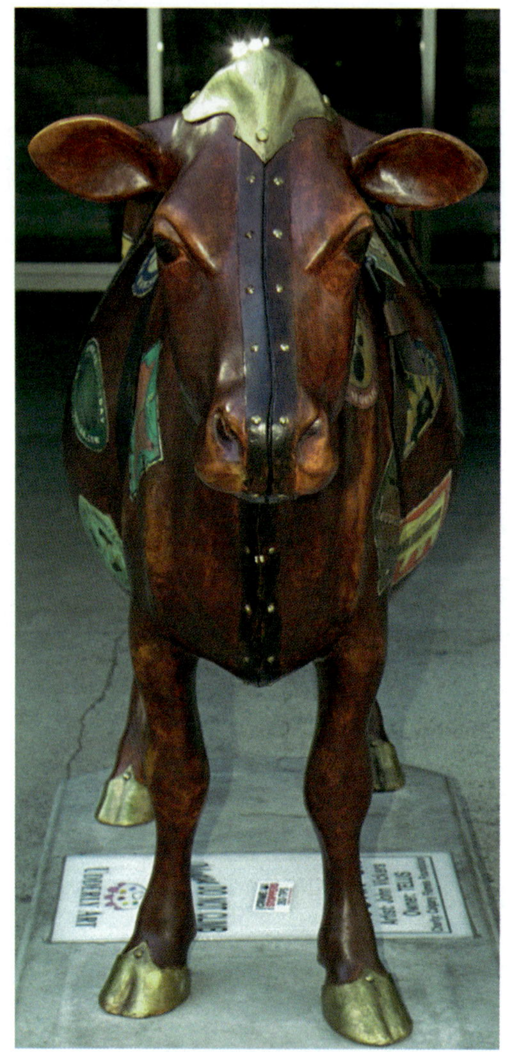

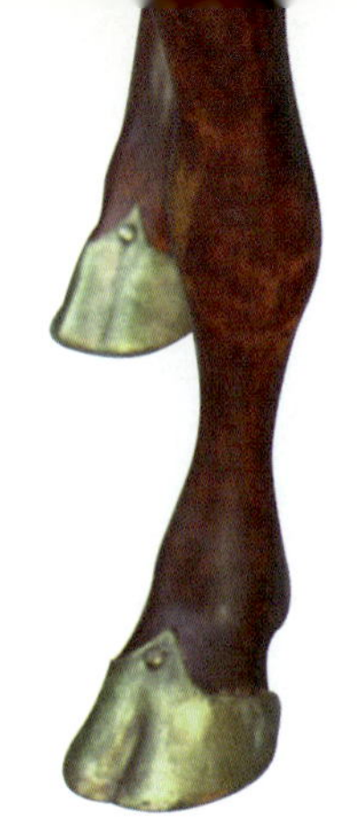

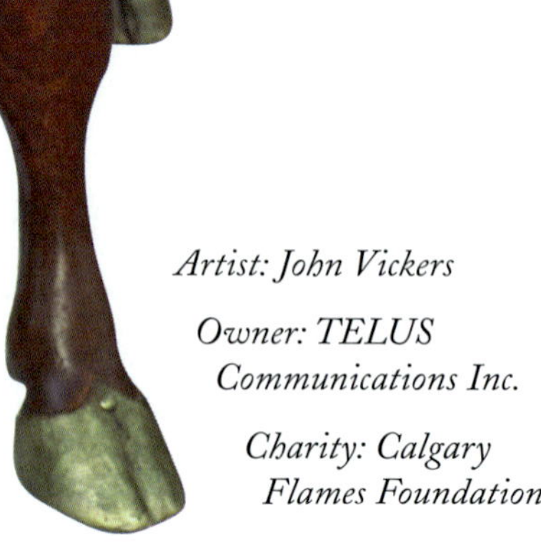

Artist: John Vickers

Owner: TELUS Communications Inc.

Charity: Calgary Flames Foundation

Decked out as a top-quality steamer trunk, *Moovin' On* is packed and ready to hit the highway, although someone forgot to remove the hooves from this snazzy leather valise. She's a symbol of freedom and the open road. For her personal credo, check the internet @ beyourownbossy.com.

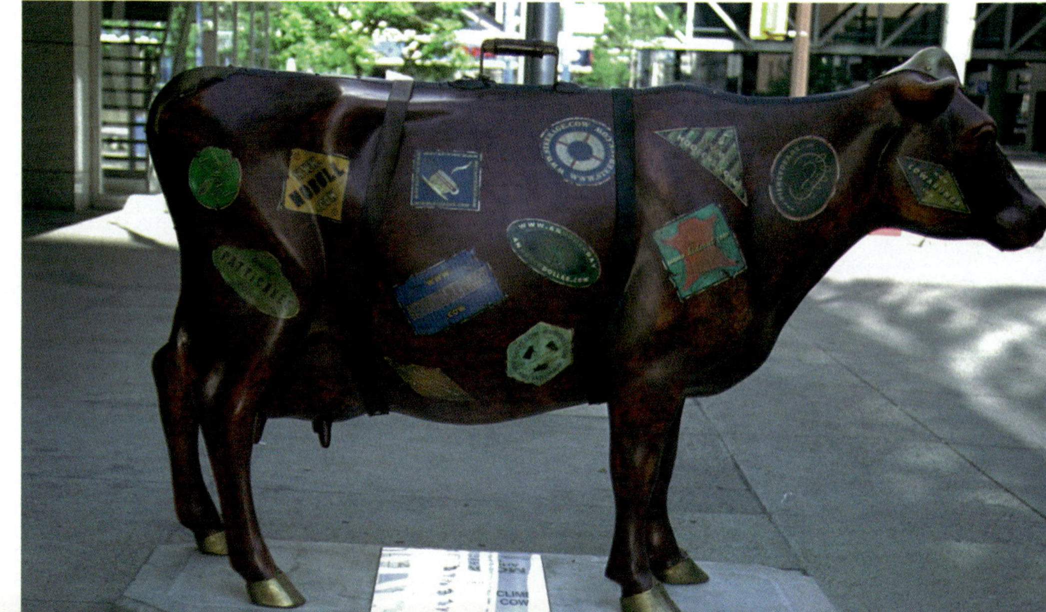

Moowithaview

Artist: Stan Phelps

Owner: Bantrel Inc.

Charity: United Way of Calgary

The staff of Bantrel Inc. wanted a one-stop-shopping cow that reproduced the view from an ideally situated corporate office. Artist Stan Phelps gave them exactly that: one side of *Moowithaview* offers a breathtakingly clear look at the Rockies while the other provides a peek at Calgary office towers. From the bird's-eye vantage, you'll find a wrap-around sunrise.

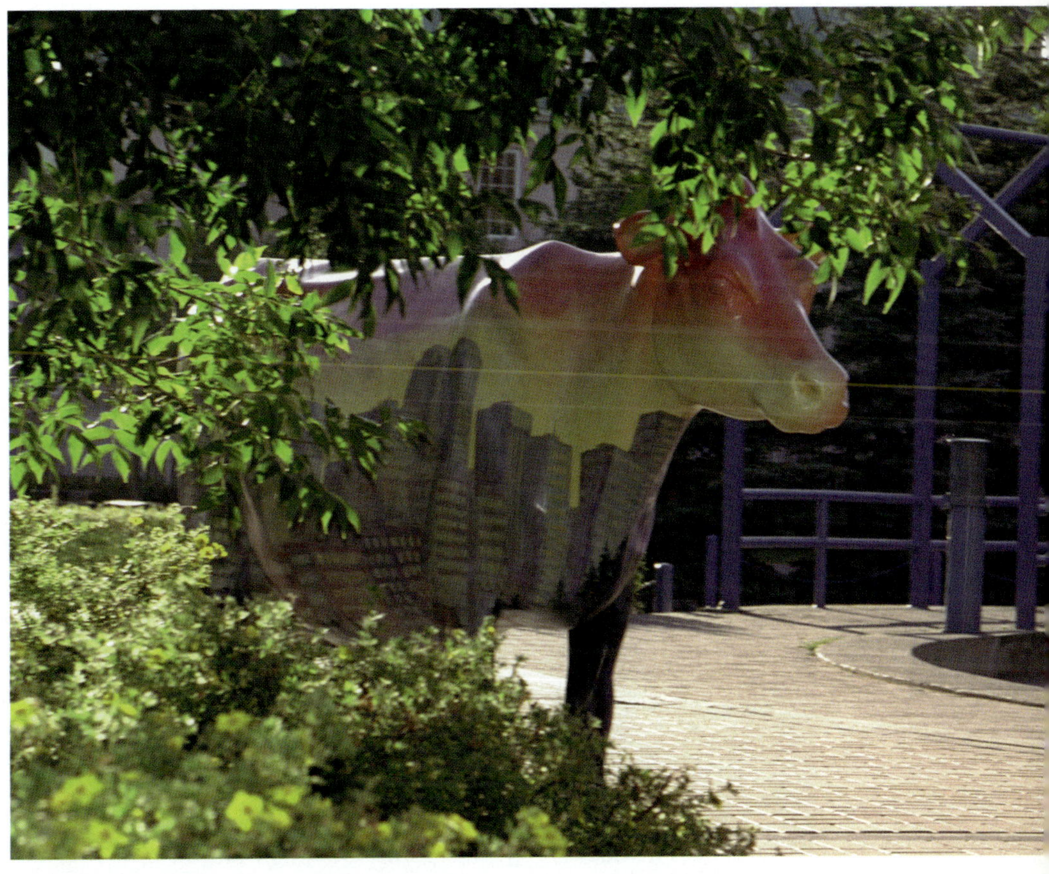

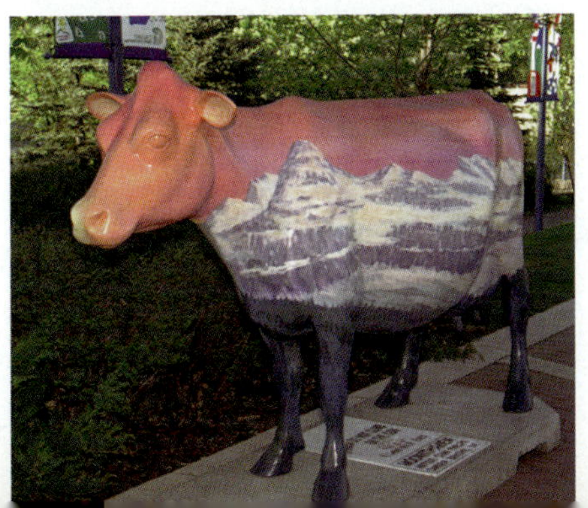

Ms. Mustard Seed

Artists: Barbara Amos and Jean Pederson

Owner: Mustard Seed Street Ministry (donated by Coe & Company International Inc.)

Charity: Mustard Seed Street Ministry

Ms. Mustard Seed feels proud of her association with one of the most humbly unpretentious, yet most effective social agencies in Calgary. The Mustard Seed opens its doors to temporarily house and feed the homeless.

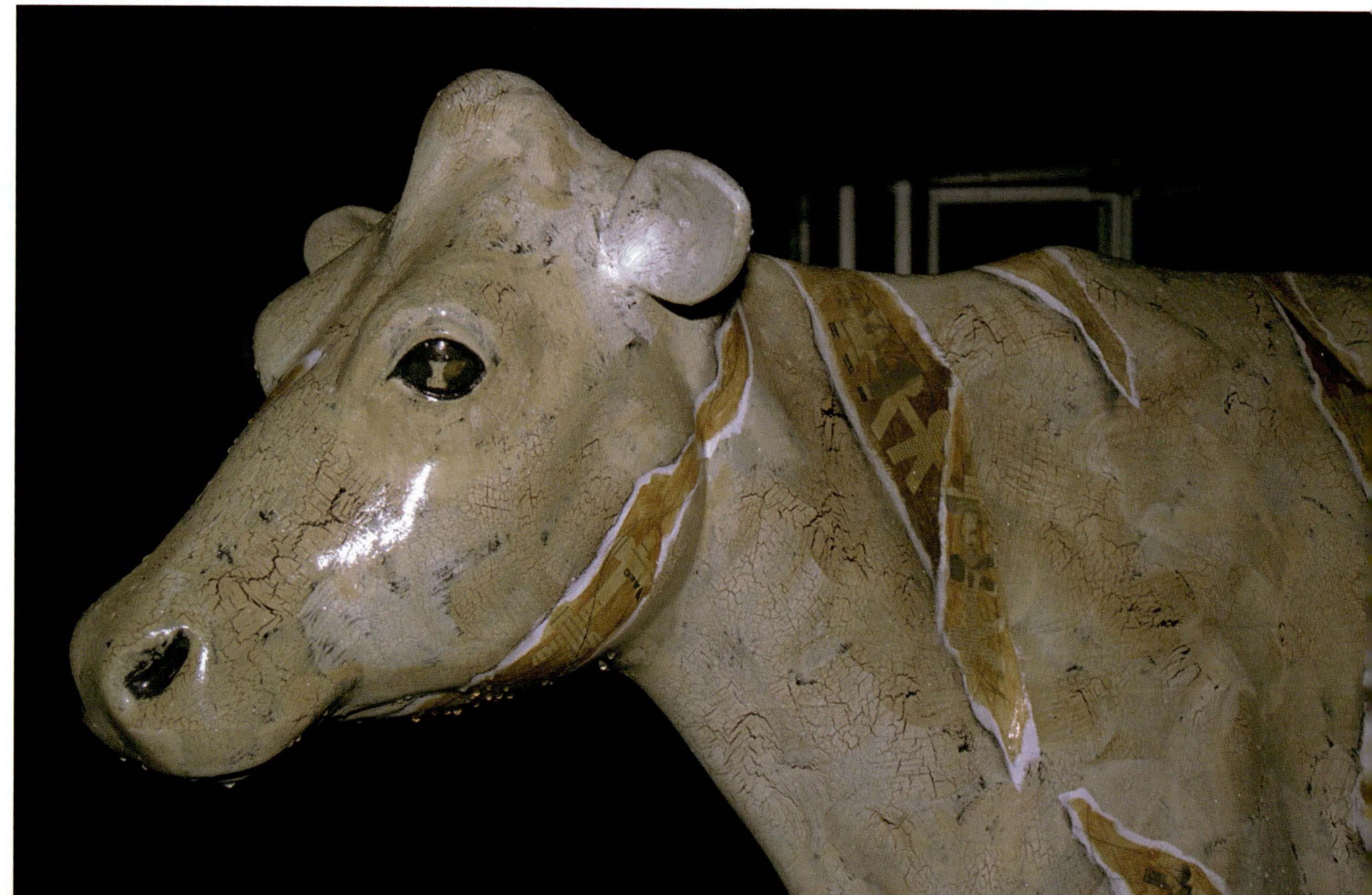

New Sun

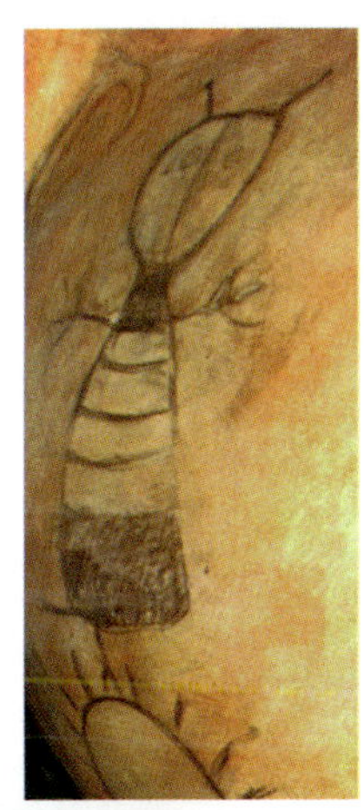

Artist: Joane Cardinal-Schubert

Owner: Calgary Foundation

Charity: Plains Indians Cultural Survival School

She's a longtime friend of the First Nations, who refer to her as New Sun. This Calgary woman, who prefers to remain anoymous, also supplied funds for both cows initially purchased by the Calgary Foundation. So the foundation asked First Nations artist Joane Cardinal-Schubert to create this fine work of art and to name it New Sun in honour of their anonymous friend.

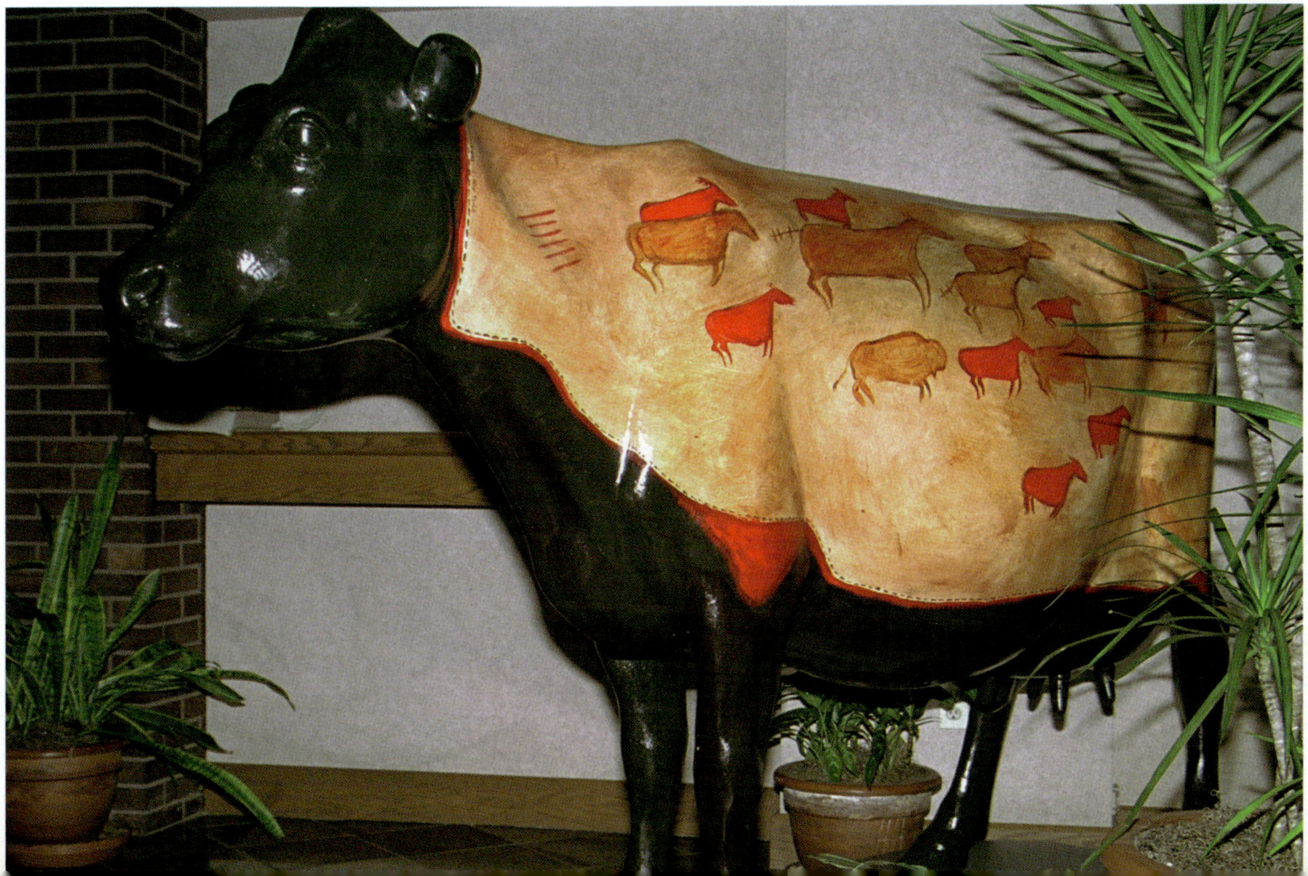

Oil MOOver

Artist: Bert Kniss

Owner: Gibson Petroleum Co. Ltd.

She's already become an international poster cow. Previously written up in Gibson Pete's internal publications, *Oil MOOver* also has been the subject of a photo feature in a magazine published by the Hunting Group of London, England, Gibson's parent company. Created by Bert Kniss of Trail, British Columbia, *Oil MOOver* has been elongated by three feet. Kniss also built up her sides, to simulate a tractor-trailer oil transport.

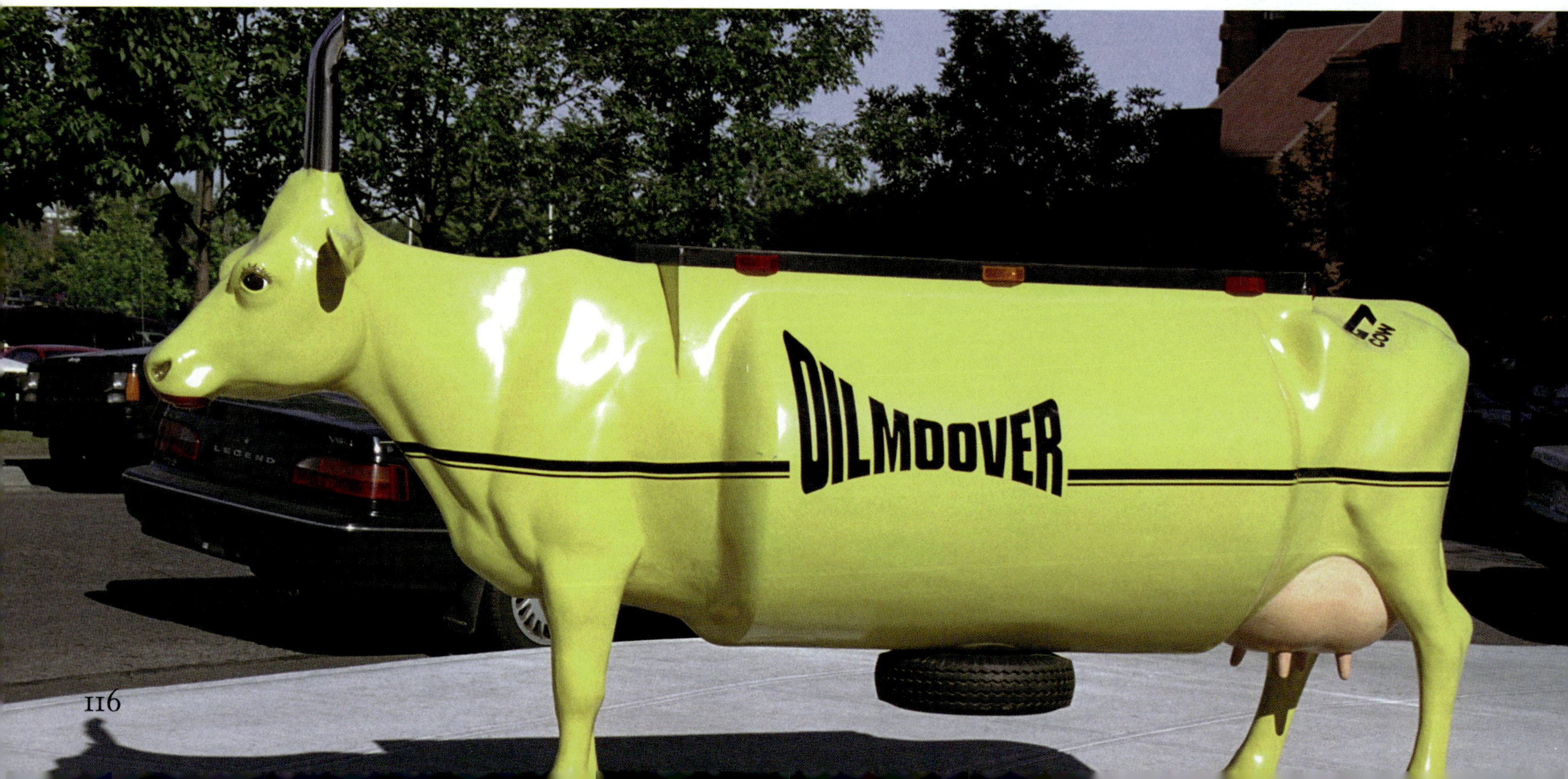

Parallel "Cow Chip"

Artists: Scott Pasishnek and Margo McKee

Owner: Parallel Strategies Group

Charity: Sheriff King Family Support Centre

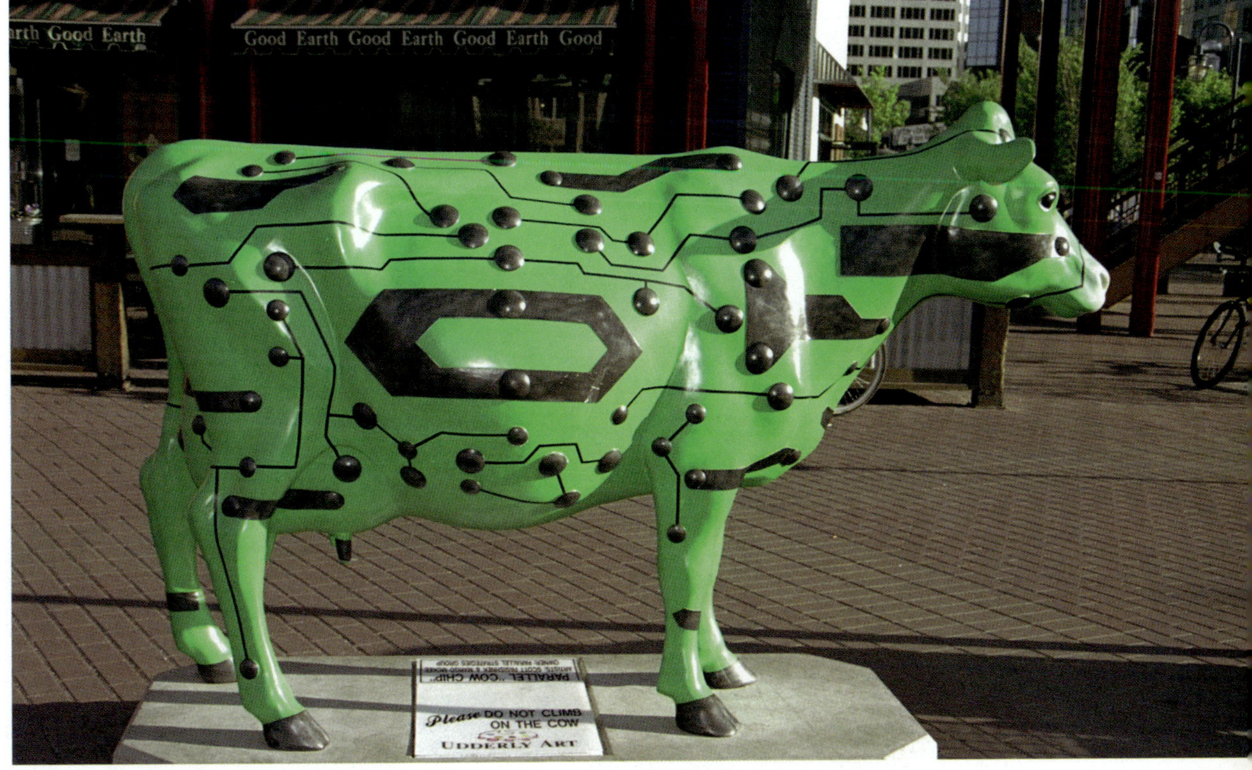

No, we're not talking obnoxious, organic cow chips here. Based on a design by Margo McKee, a senior strategist with Parallel Strategies Group, these chips are of the digital variety. Brought to life by artist Scott Pasishnek, McKee's idea was to represent the computer motherboard so essential to smooth sailing for Calgary's well-wired business community.

Patches

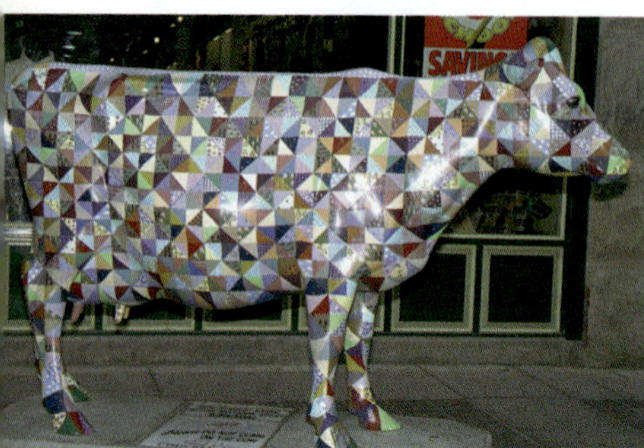

Artist: Madelene Dollar

Owner: Heritage Park

Charity: Heritage Park Foundation

In the new millennium, everybody's quilting. So Madelene Dollar's finely detailed cow is in step with the trend. An ornate tribute to an ancient and honourable craft, *Patches* is deftly stitched from ear tips to hooves. She ties in particularly well with the quilt festival held each spring at Heritage Park.

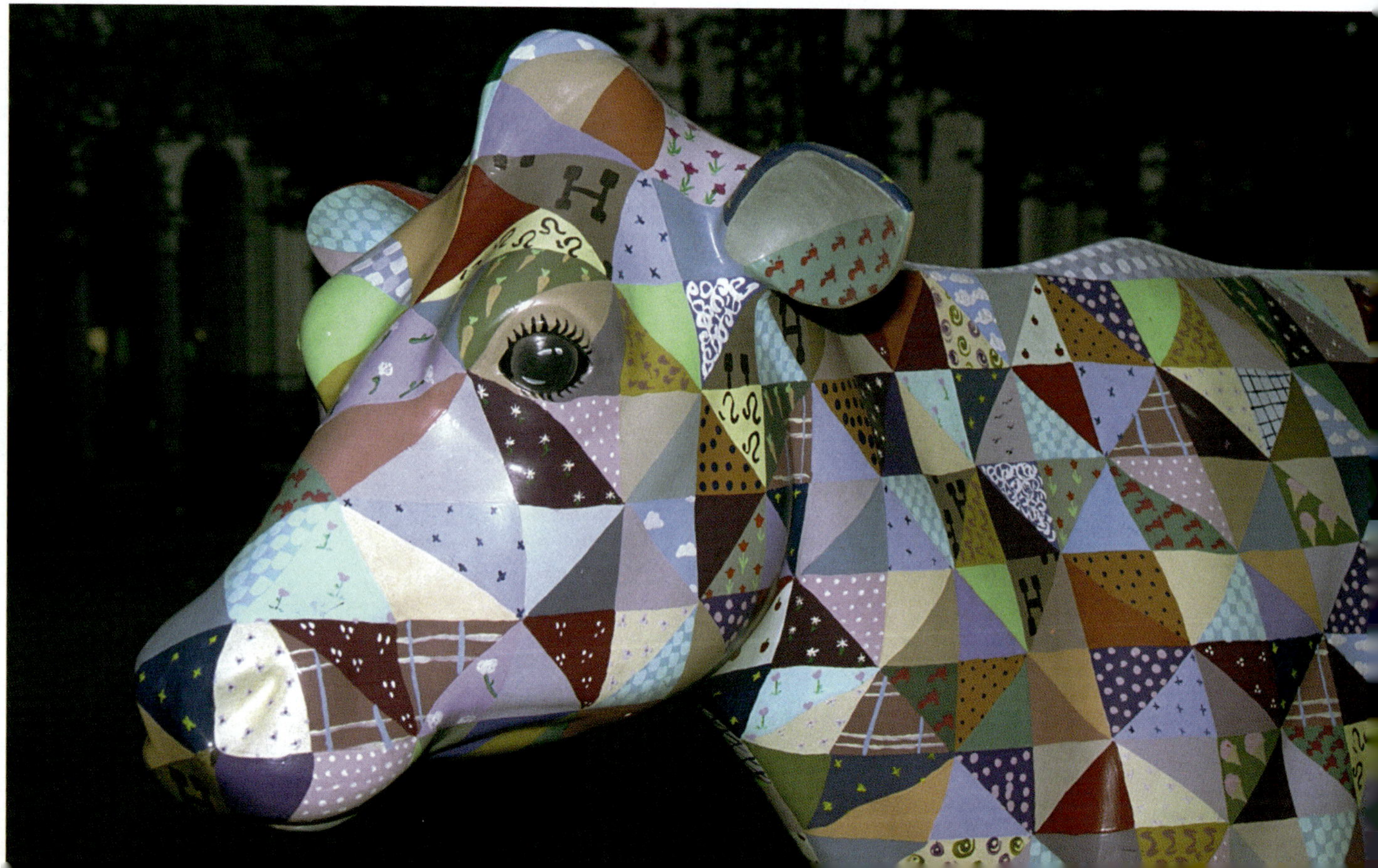

The Patient Bull

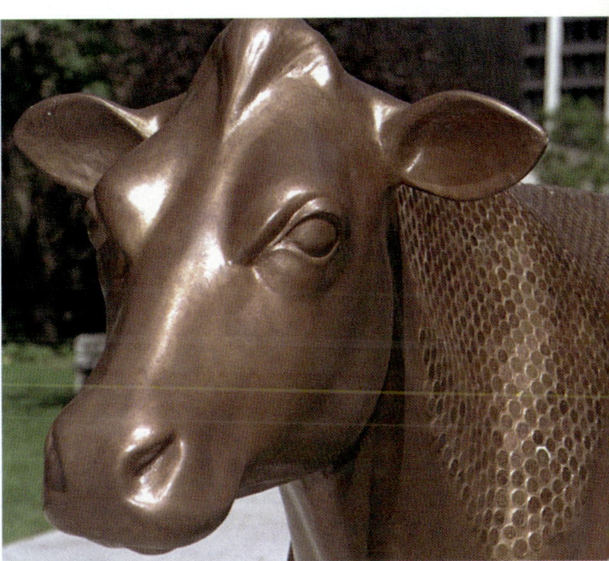

Artist: Bart Habermiller

Owner: Avenir Capital Corporation

Charity: National Sport Centre for Sydney-Bound Calgary Athletes

Every kid knows a penny saved is a penny earned. By that measure, Bart Habermiller's copper-coloured beauty has acquired enough cash to buy into a bull market.

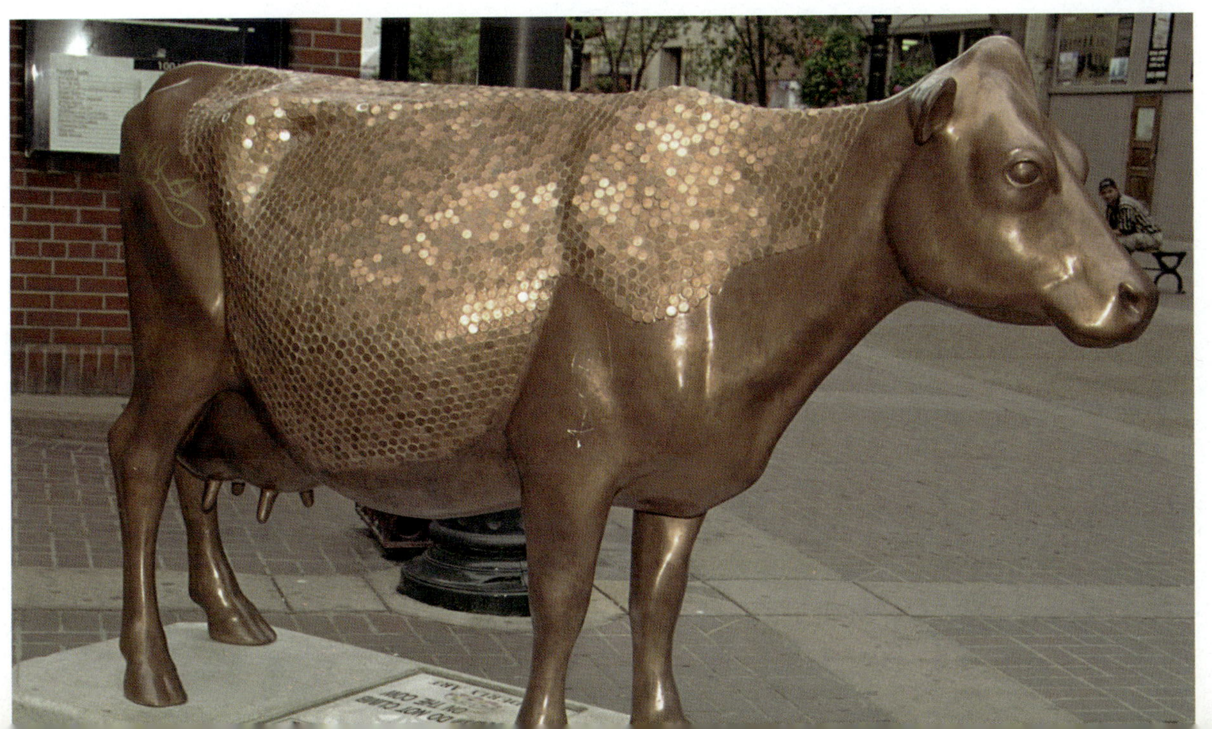

Peek-A-Moo

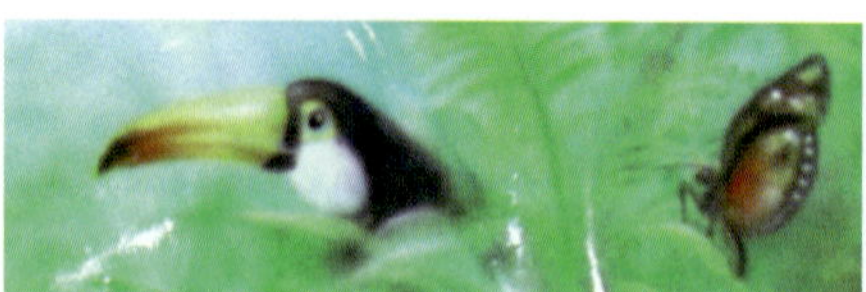

Artist: Rick Janzen

Owner: HTC Electric Alberta Ltd.

A soul-stirring vision of a mysterious rain forest, *Peek-A-Moo* is one of the superstars of the Udderly Art pantheon. Swathed in misty shades of deep green, Rick Janzen's vine-shrouded forest hides treasures—toucans, exotic butterflies and monkeys—which slowly reveal themselves to onlookers' gaze.

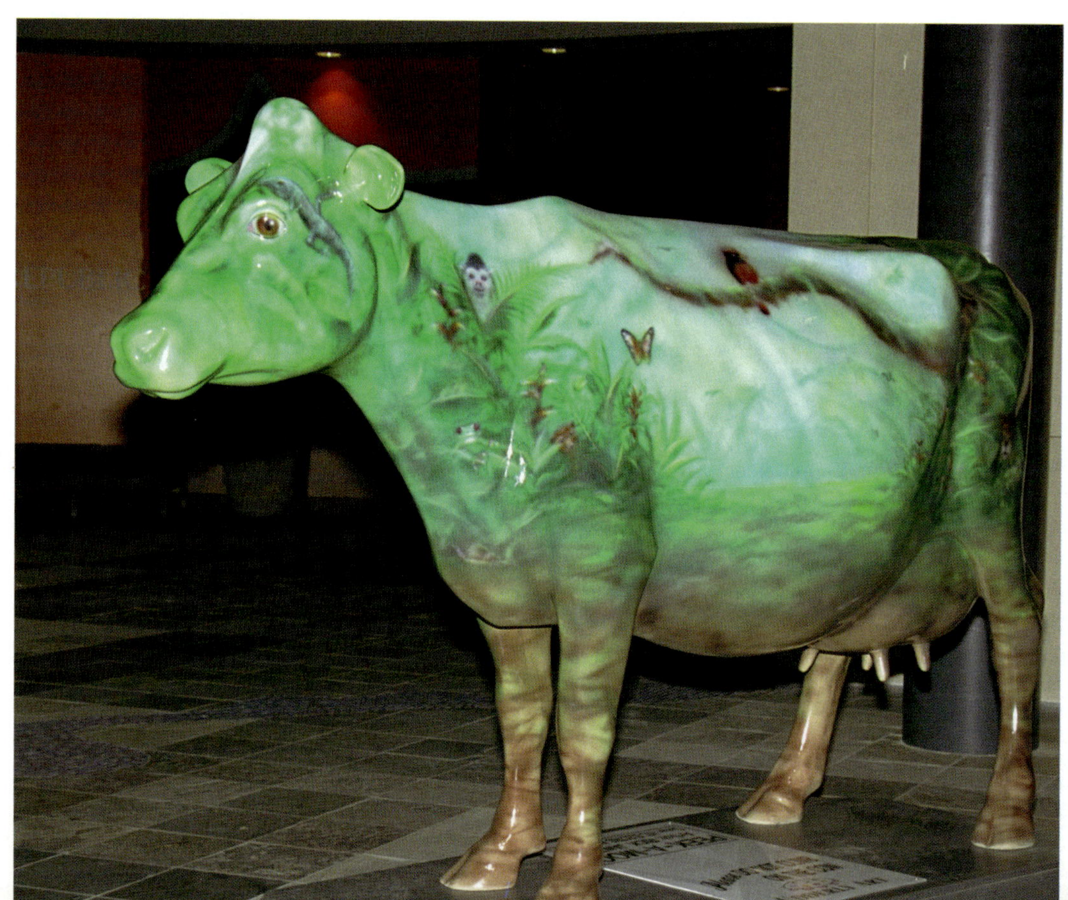

The Physics of Angels

Artist: Errol Lee Fullen

Owner: Ber-Mac Electrical & Instrumentation Ltd.

Charity: Alberta Children's Hospital Foundation

Angels are everywhere, including the head of the nearest pin. But Errol Lee Fullen has given us an astronomical representation of their traditional home: the heavens. Galaxies and novae wink down from the shimmering night sky containing even the occasional black hole.

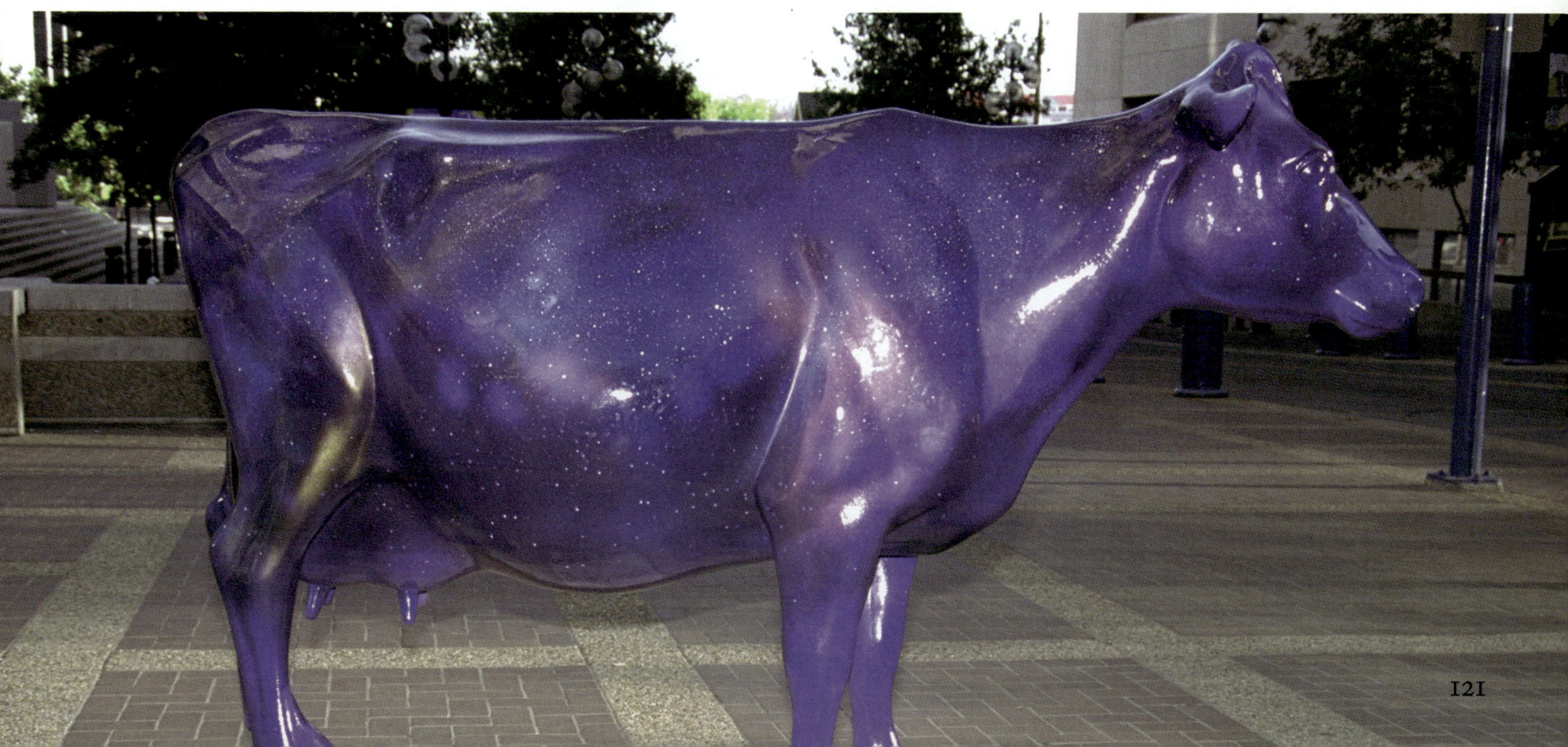

Perforated Cow

Artist: Chris Cran

Owner: River Cafe

Charity: Inn from the Cold

Udderly Art fans like to refer to Chris Cran's air-conditioned, water-cooled creation as the *Holy Cow.* Cute nickname. As to reasons, it's fairly obvious. In his undying quest for the original, Cran spent more than 36 hours meticulously drilling hundreds of holes in the fibreglass fundament of his quadruped canvas. Then Cran covered the hole-y hide with the same variety of metal-flaked, sparkling paint that his pal Bob Cowan, a local garage genius, once used to jazz up his beloved Corvette back in the mid-70s.

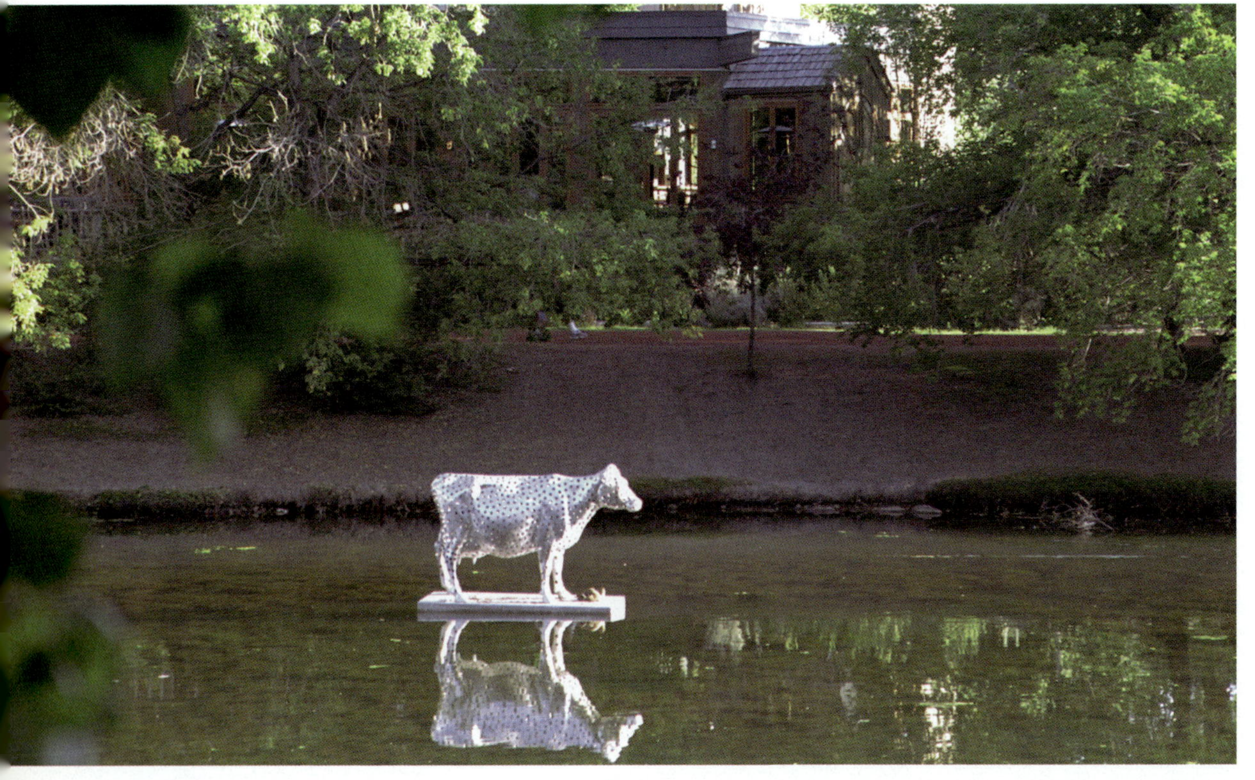

Originally, Cran had envisioned a chrome-plated cow boldly gleaming in the midday sun. Then he discovered that even a tiny bottle of the required undercoat would have set him back a cool $300. "And after that, I would've had to dip the cow in successive baths of copper, nickel and chrome," he moaned.

Suddenly, metal-flaked sparkles sounded like a heck of a good alternative, kind to both the eye and the pocketbook.

Chrome or no chrome, Cran ultimately produced a certified crowd-pleaser—particularly because of its eventual home, moored in the gentle, lapping waters south of Prince's Island. Joining an indigenous population of geese and ducks, the contented critter cooled its hole-y hooves in the soothing lagoon for the first several months of its existence.

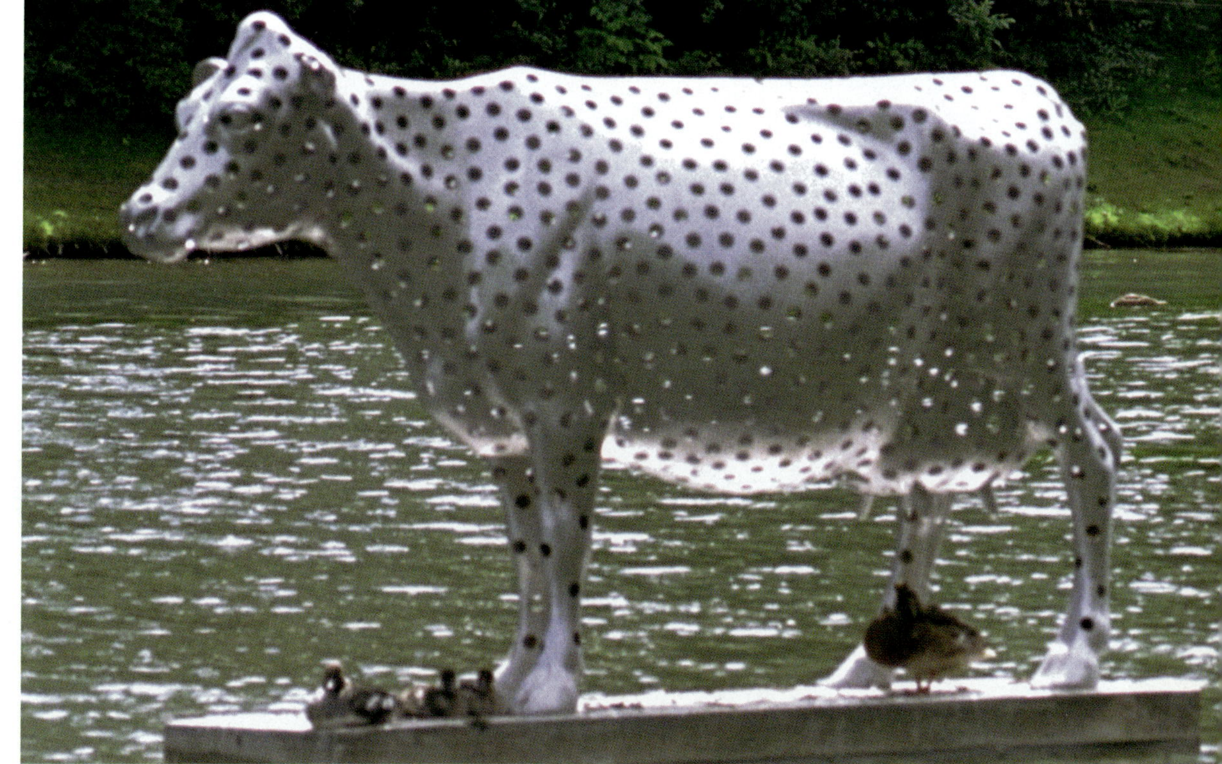

Pixel

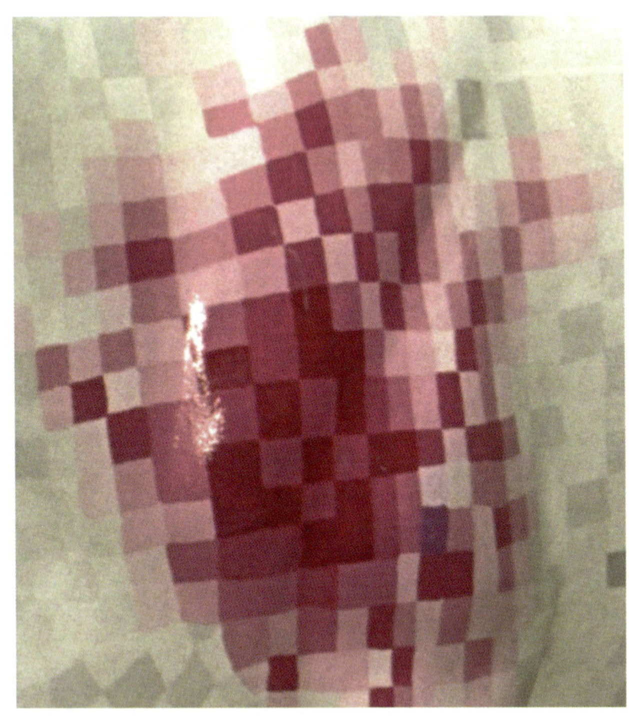

Artist: TAG Advertising (formerly The Agency Group)

Owner: University of Calgary Chancellor's Club (donated by Udderly Art)

Charity: University of Calgary Chancellor's Club Scholarships

The first Udderly Art cow to hit the streets, *Pixel* was a cooperative effort by TAG staff. In the world of graphic design, a pixel is a tiny square, and this cow's hide is composed of 7,760 one-inch squares, each hand-pencilled and hand-painted. Small wonder it took 14 volunteers about 400 hours to finish her.

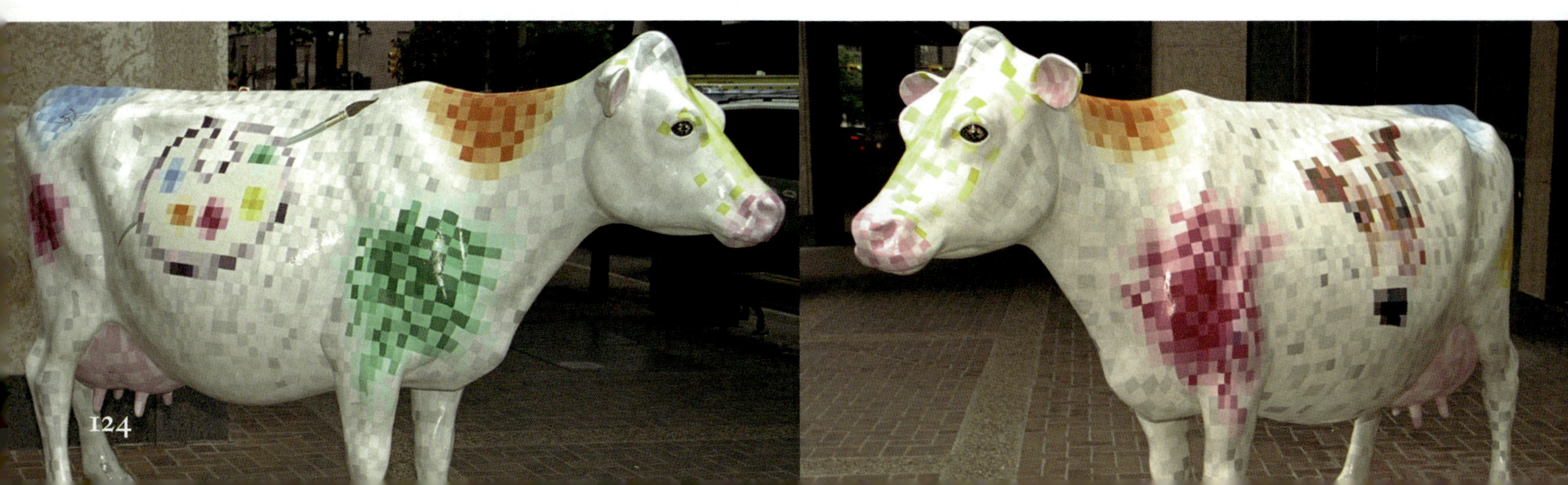

Prudy Piper

Artist: Dean Stanton

Owner: Prudential Steel Ltd.

Charity: Calgary Stampede Foundation

From the drafting table to the work site, *Prudy Piper* tells the story of the steel pipe business from A to Z. Boiled down to basics, the equation goes like this: Steel = strength = $$$ in the client's bank account.

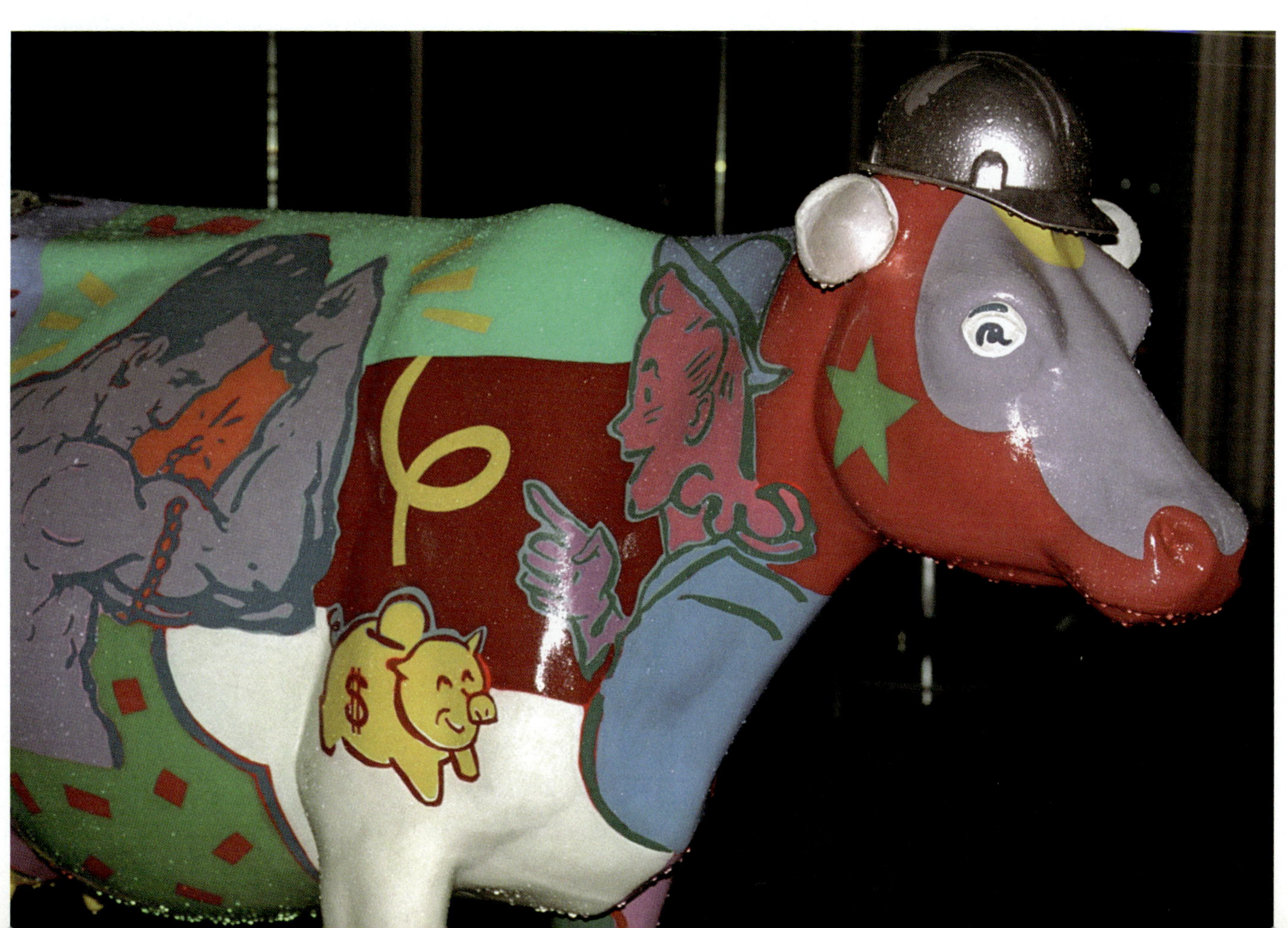

Pump Jackie

Artist: Dean Stanton

Owner: Alberta Energy Co. Ltd

Charity: Rockyview General Hospital Development Council

Every inch a lady, *Pump Jackie* is primly attired in a modest and feminine dress, complete with purse. But don't let the rouge and eye-shadow bamboozle you. She's a roughneck at heart. For proof, check the oil rigs and hardhats on her gown.

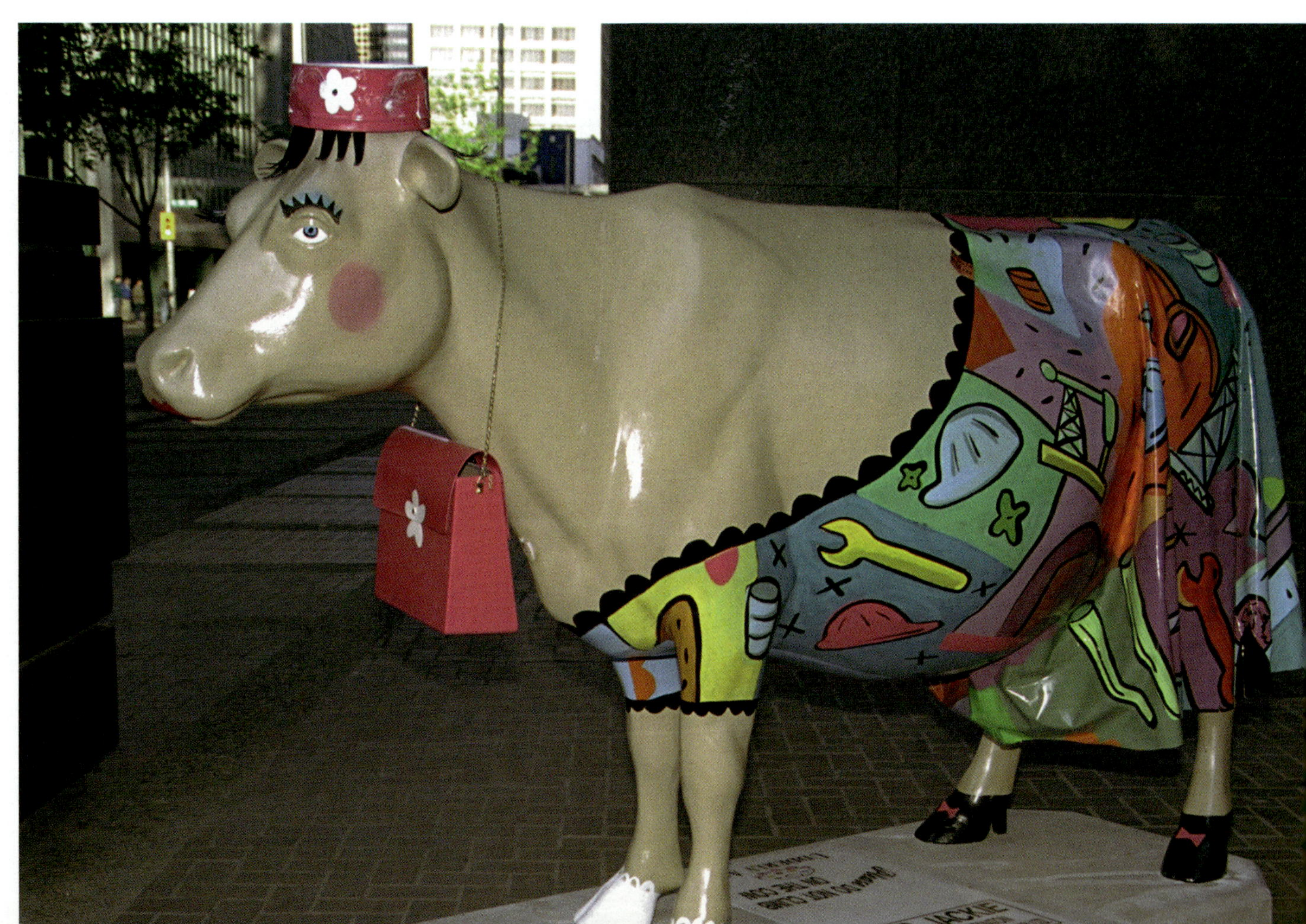

Quantum Cow

Artists: Kevin and Freya Olafson
Owner: Quantum Learning
Charity: Royal Winnipeg Ballet

An impressionistic cow-llage mingling chuckles and formidable math formulae, *Quantum Cow* gives 100 percent pure milk the Winnipeg artists insist. A closer look is rewarded by a glimpse of cows coming home under a harvest moon. Take another glance at the cow's south end heading north to see the "Friendly Manitoba" licence plate on her udder.

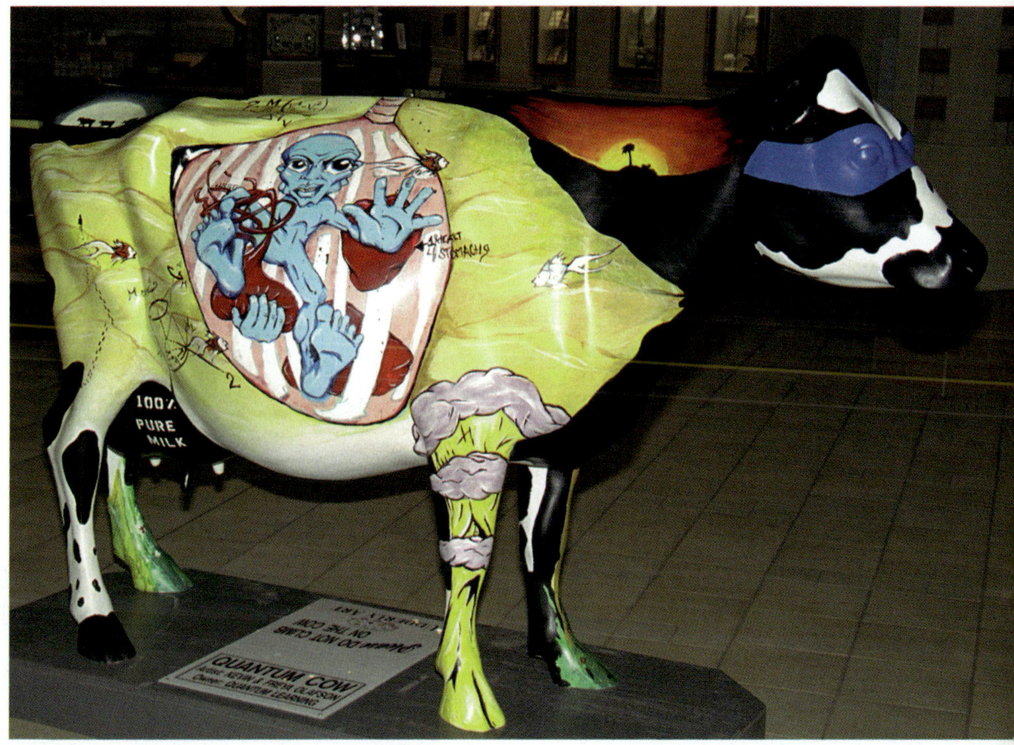

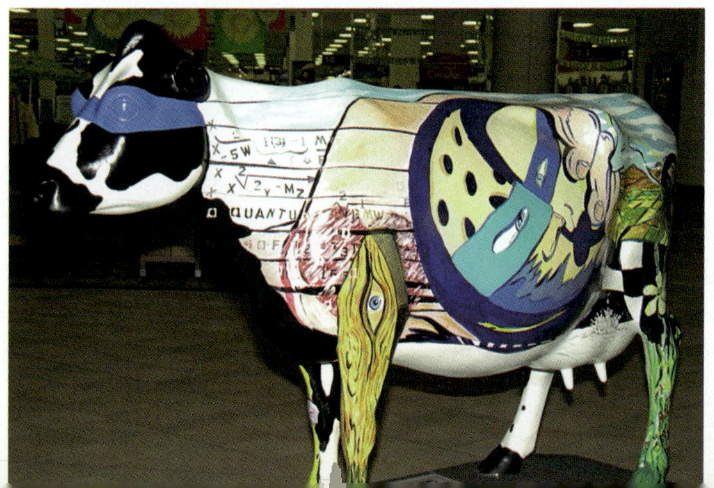

Reach for Your Rainbow

Artists: Students and Staff of Foothills Academy

Owner: Friends of Foothills Academy (donated by Parents of Foothills Students)

Charity: Foothills Academy Society

This was clearly a case of cooperative cow-llaboration at its finest.

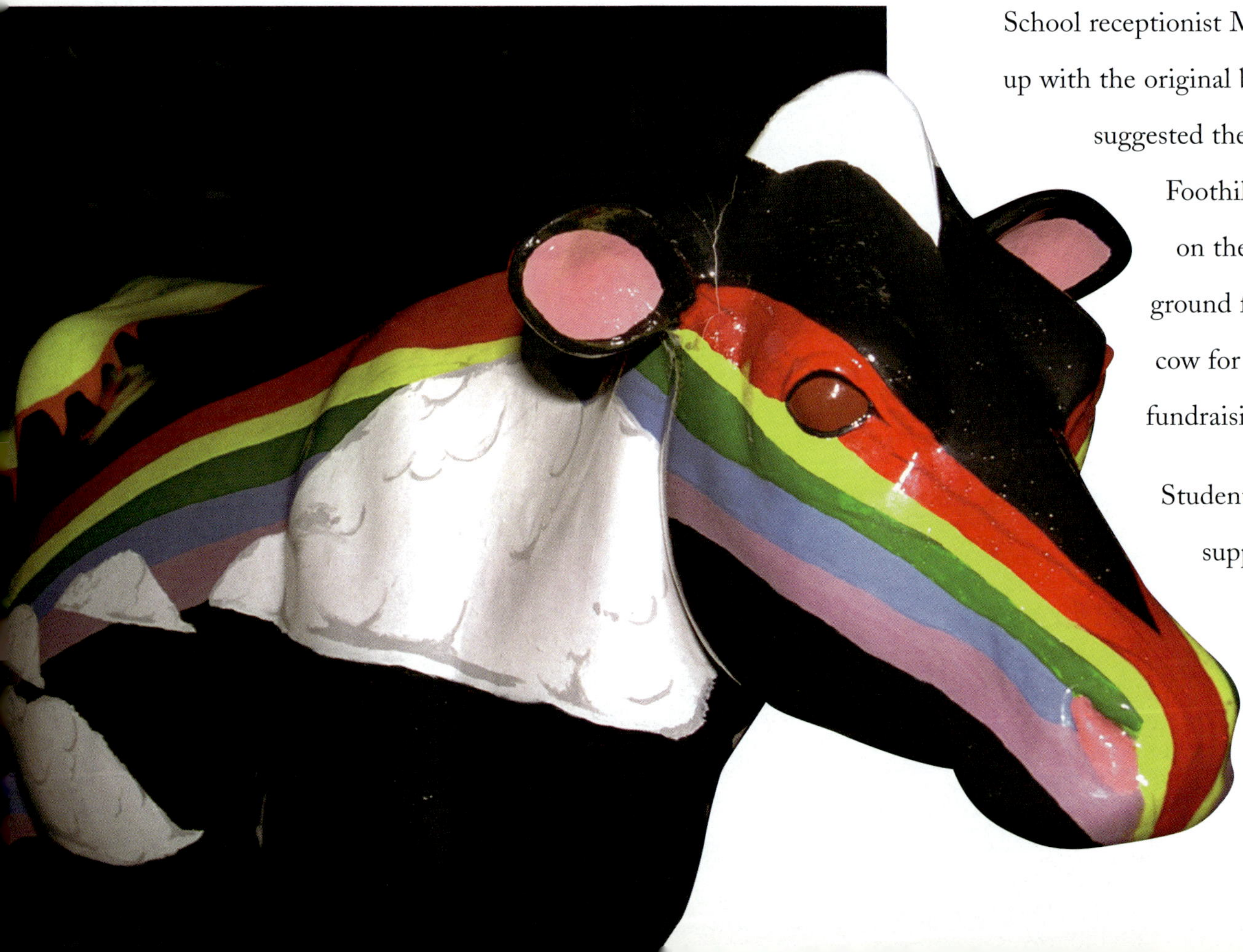

School receptionist Marlene Neale came up with the original brainstorm. She suggested the Friends of Foothills Academy get in on the Udderly Art ground floor by buying a cow for fun and fundraising.

Student Kim Sherwood supplied the artistic inspiration as well as the name. And a keen crowd of

Foothills Academy students pooled their considerable talents to create the finished product, their work overseen by language arts teacher Warren Paulovich.

This is not just an attractive work of art—it's a rainbow-splashed bovine billboard, offering an implicit message of hope for students, staff, friends and strangers alike.

Winner of the school's Design and Name the Cow Contest entered by 160 Academy students, Sherwood, a Foothills senior, put it eloquently in a memorable message of her own: "You're always going to have dark days in your life with dark clouds," Kim explained. "But there is always going to be a rainbow behind it with sunlight smiling through to let you follow your dreams . . . and reach for your rainbow."

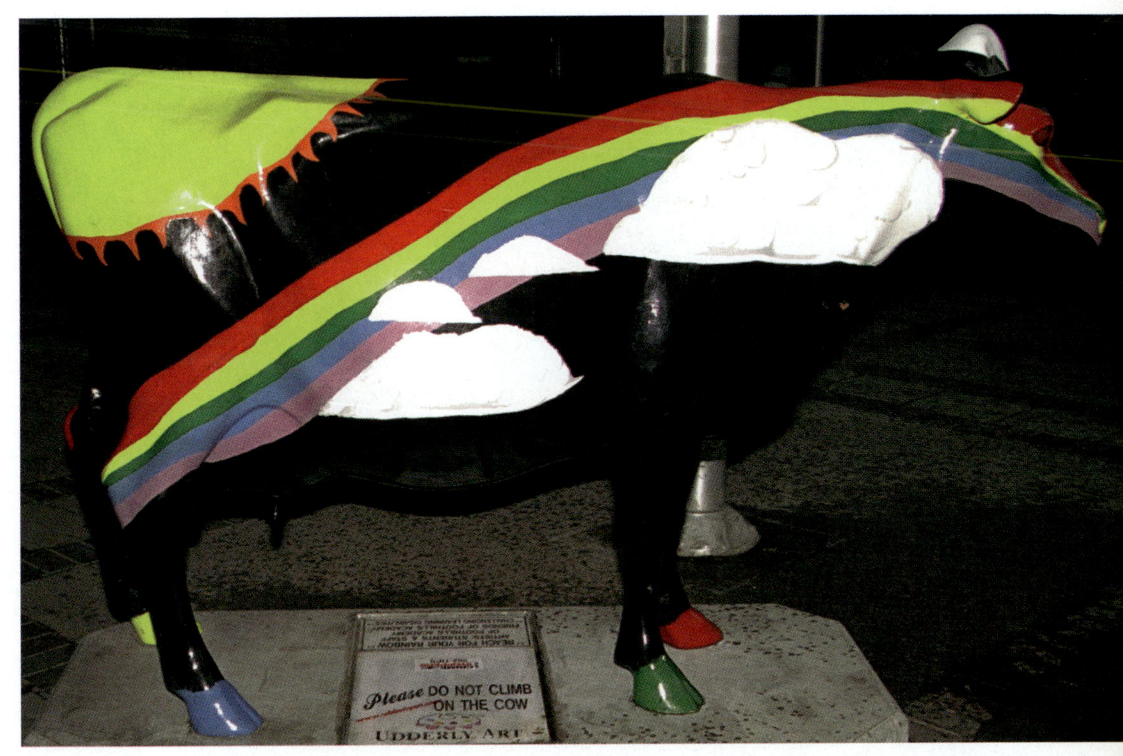

Roh-Cow

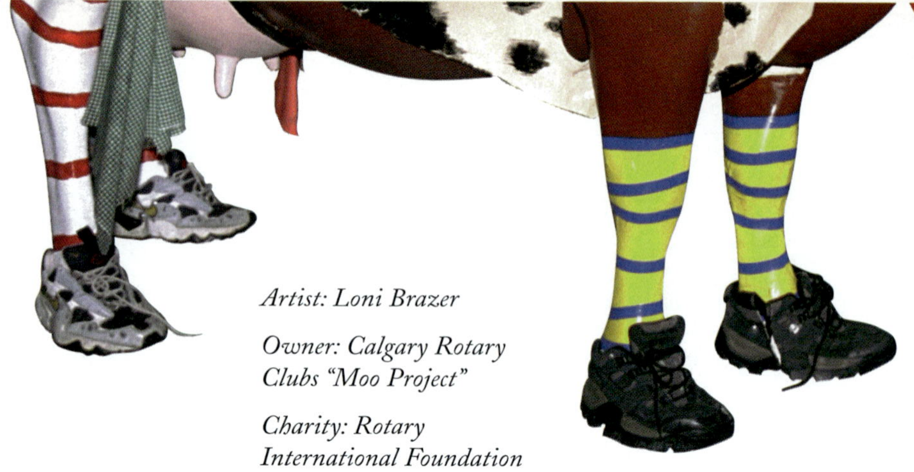

Artist: Loni Brazer

Owner: Calgary Rotary Clubs "Moo Project"

Charity: Rotary International Foundation

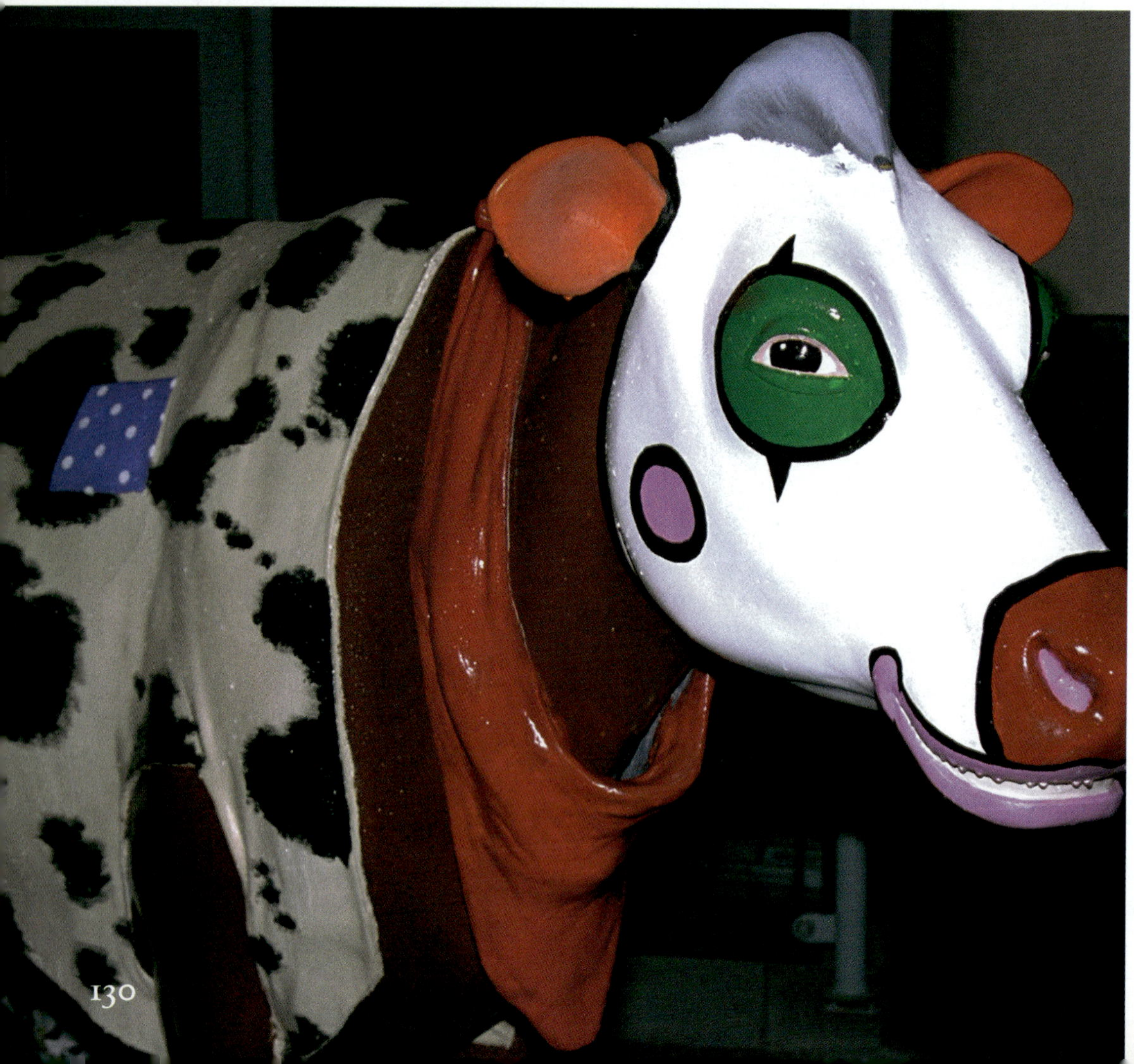

This is a remarkably accurate and entertaining take on the bullfighting rodeo clowns who risk their lives in the infield at Stampede time. Lori Brazer has every detail down cold, including the hoof-flattened Nikes and the l-o-o-o-ng gag kerchief. But wait—is that a calfskin vest the cow's wearing?

Sacred Cow

Artist: Dale Auger

Owner: City of Calgary

Charity: Calgary Special Olympics

Proud and handsome, *Sacred Cow* is a spirit wrestler with hooves and udder. The Bragg Creek artist capitalized on this opportunity to pay his respects to Native spiritual culture. Appropriately, *Sacred Cow* passed many tranquil months tethered in front of Calgary's historic old city hall.

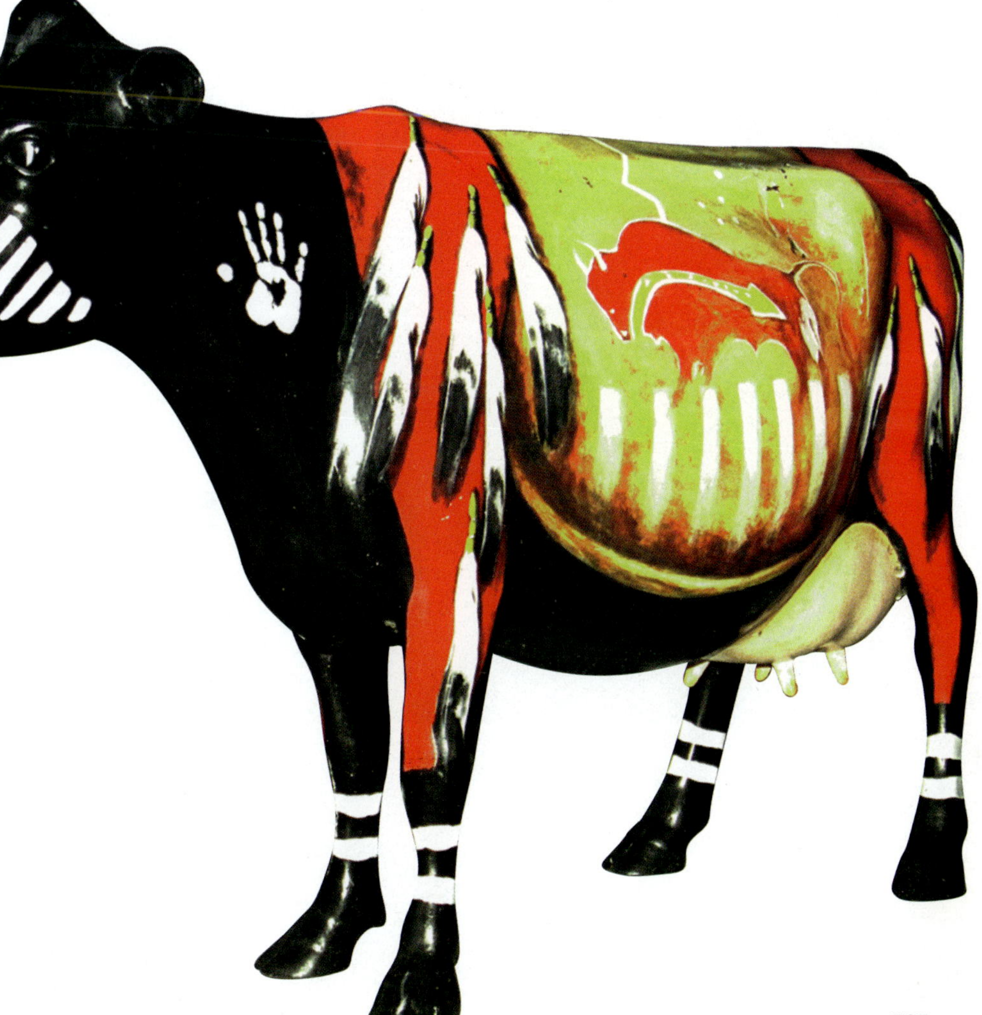

Saved by the Chinook

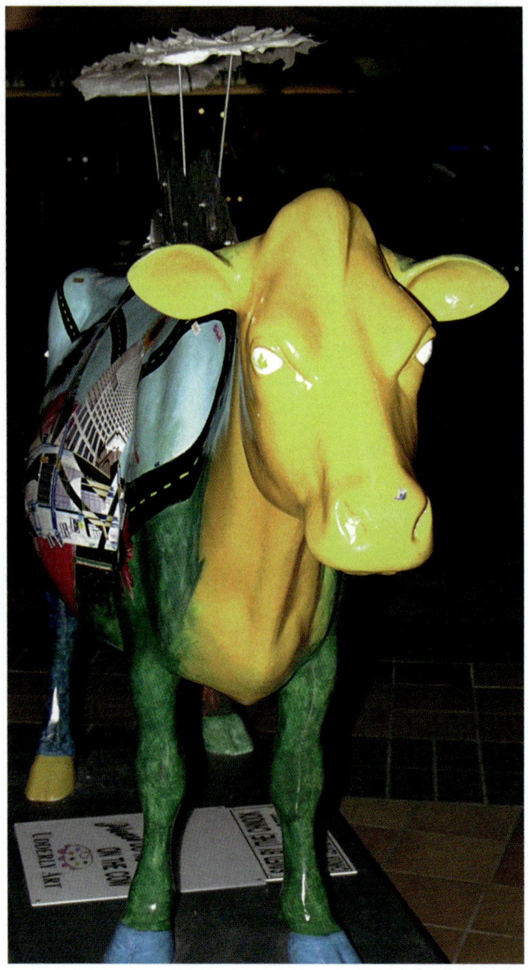

Artist: Petronella Overes

Owner: Chinook Centre Merchants' Association

Charity: Alberta Children's Hospital Foundation

Everybody in Southern Alberta knows the feeling of the midwinter blahs. It's why we welcome the arrival of the Chinook, even when it fosters a false spring and false hopes of an imminent end to the tyranny of ice and snow. This weather friendly creation is definitely something to smile about.

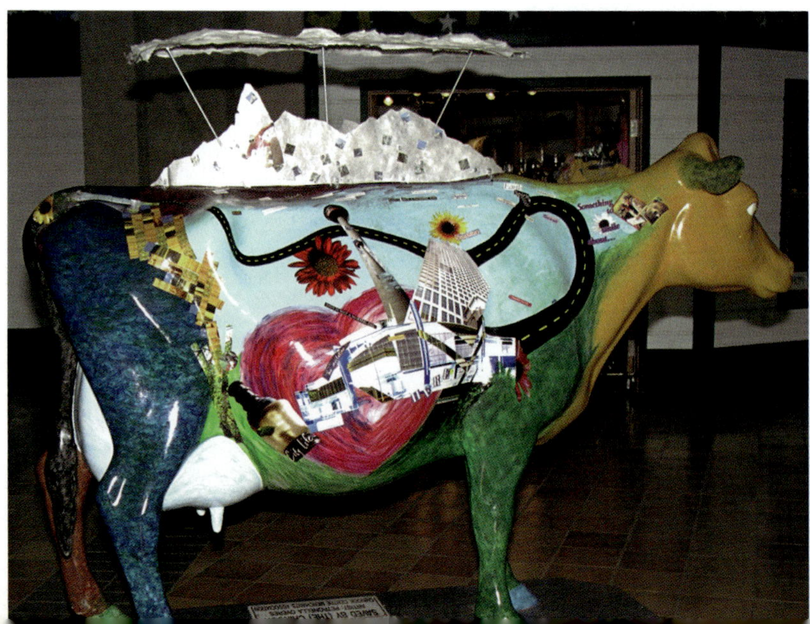

Simm-Bull

Artist: Lori Whiteside

Owner: Canadian Simmental Association

Charity: Street Teams

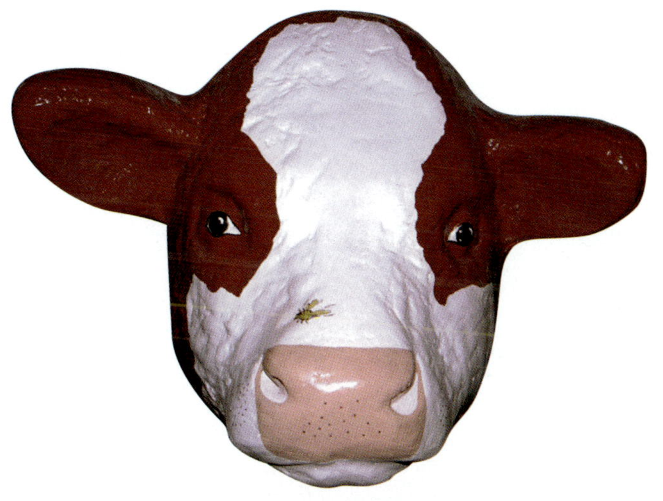

Everyone knows you can't have a herd of cows without a bull. So, after receiving an amused okay from Udderly Art, the Simmental folks used a mould purchased from a company in Manitoba, then donated it to the cause. The difference? That looks suspiciously like a wasps' nest where the udder should be.

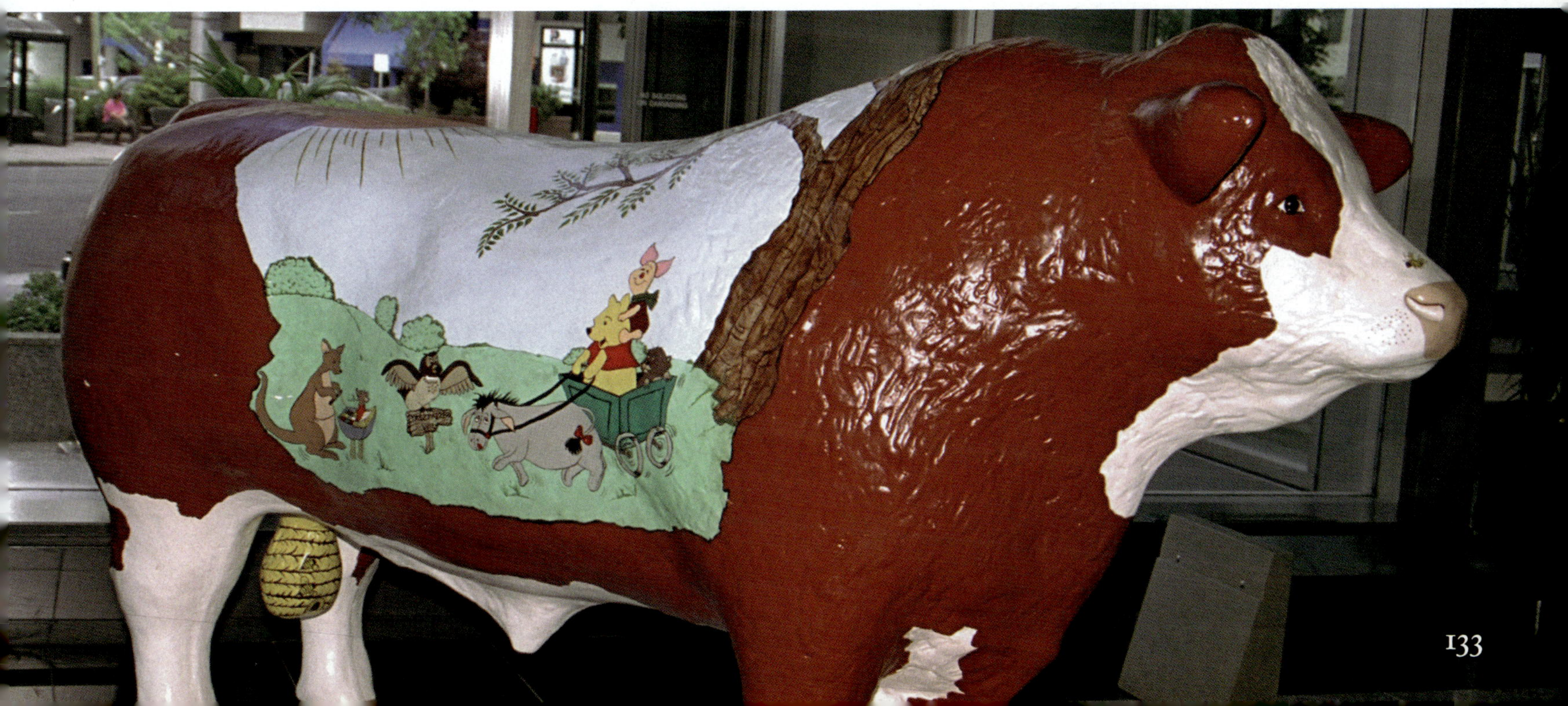

Serenity, AARC's Miracow of Recowvery

Artists: Karen MacKenzie-Brydon, Maria Seller-Huizing and Peri Best

Owner: Alberta Adolescent Recovery Centre (donated by Rob and Ruth Peters and Family)

Charity: Alberta Adolescent Recovery Centre

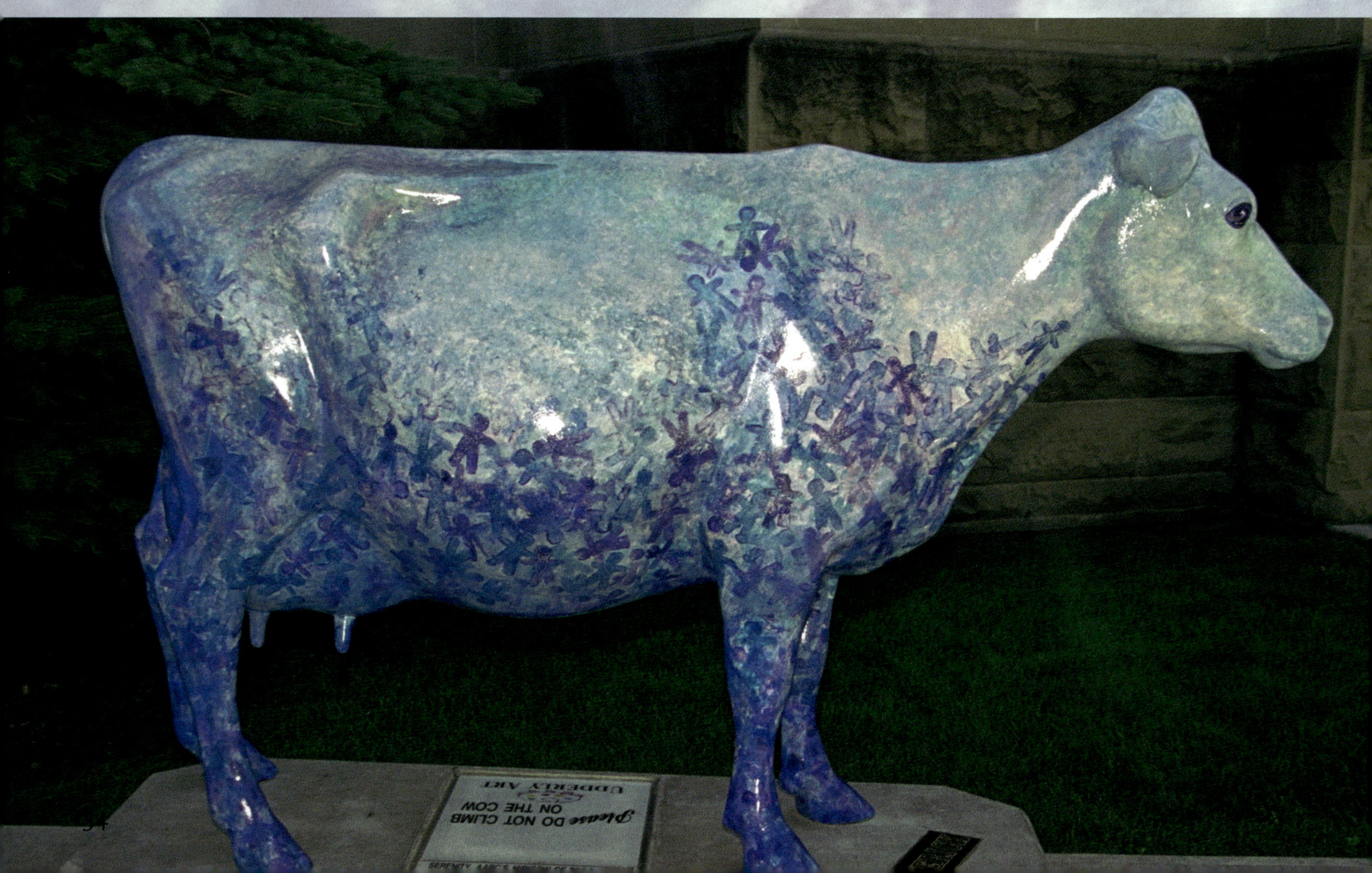

During the summer of 2000, artist Karen MacKenzie-Brydon spent as many hours as she could strolling Calgary streets, soaking up pleasure from Udderly Art's uplifting, mood-brightening panorama of dazzling cows.

"It was such a treat looking at cows—instead of my haunting, horrible search of the same streets in the summer of '98," MacKenzie-Brydon said, grateful for the contrast. Throughout that dark year, she had spent too many days and nights seeking her daughter, Elizabeth, then a 14-year-old habitual runaway with a severe drug problem.

Then one day Elizabeth's doctor pointed Karen toward the Alberta Adolescent Recovery Centre, an intensive, 12-step therapy that eventually helped free the youngster from her chains.

So naturally, when AARC approached Karen to apply her personal touch to its latest "pet"—the *Miracow of Recowvery*—she was thrilled.

She and her collaborators worked without brushes in acrylic paints. They chose blues, purples, pinks—the healing colours of sunrise and of a new morning for Elizabeth and her entire family.

"This cow was a celebration," said a smiling Karen, who placed tiny stars in each of Serenity's eyes. "I always relate stars to miracles."

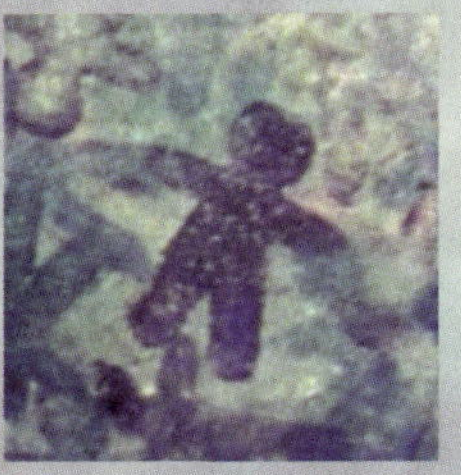

Some Enchanted Evening

Artist: Jennifer Garant

Owner: Sorrell Financial

Some enchanted evening, stroll back through time to the 1920s in Paris. With the help of this cud-dly cow, you may even meet Pablo Picasso, the revolutionary 20th century modernist painter. Jennifer Garant demonstrates amazing skill within many art styles, but *Some Enchanted Evening*'s eyes are definitely those of Picasso.

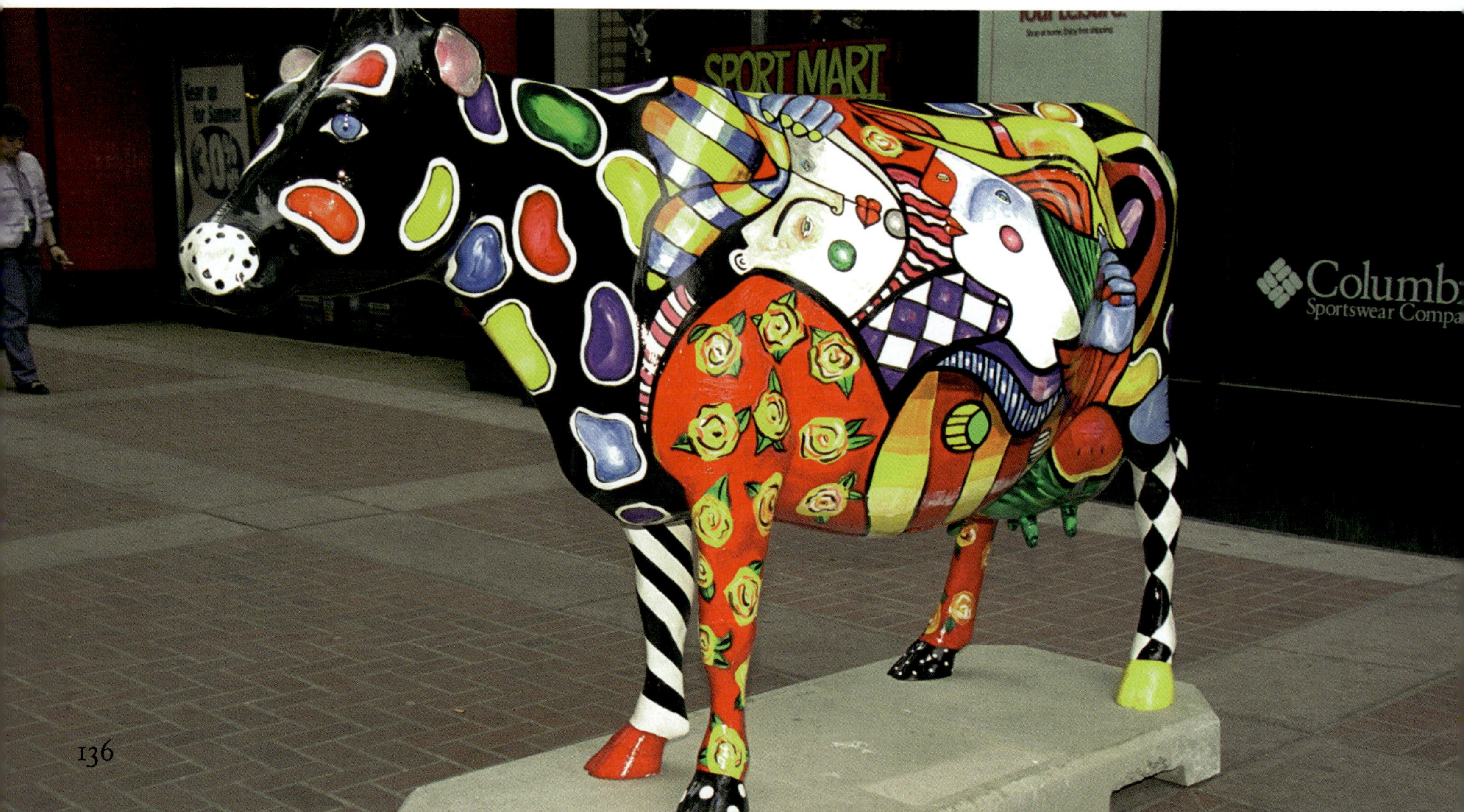

Stampede Princess

Artist: The Splinter Group

Owner: University of Calgary, Faculty of Fine Arts

Charity: University of Calgary, Fine Arts Program

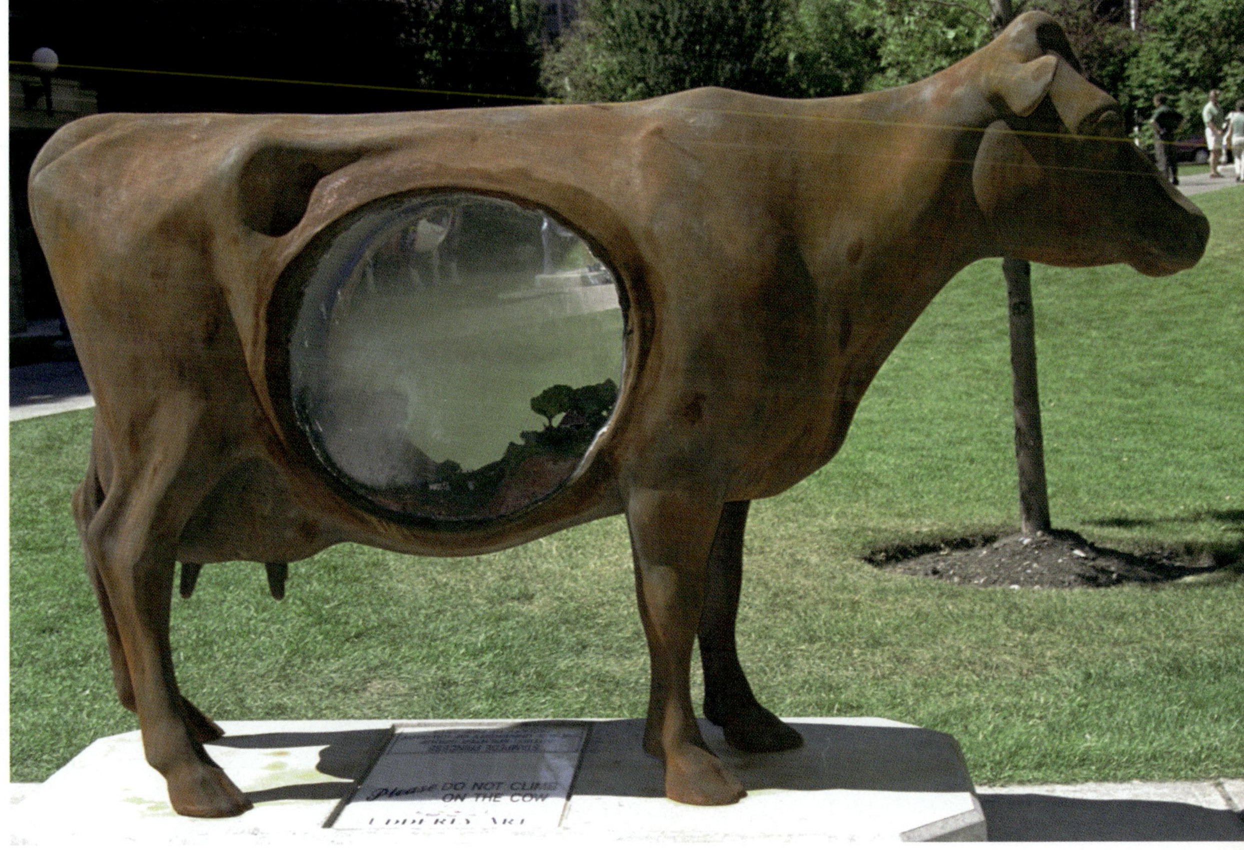

By building an idyllic world in the belly of the beast, The Splinter Group has taken a unique approach to the artistic task at hand. Cow fanciers are invited to gaze into a miniature, self-contained world. It's a valley where winter winds never howl, where the pasture's perpetually green and where the udders never go dry.

Sunflowers High as a Bovine's Eye

Artist: Audrey Mabee
Owner: Bell Intrigna
Charity: Children's Cottage

Something about a sunflower works wonders for the disposition. One of three Udderly Art cows decorated by the gifted Audrey Mabee, this cow's dazzling, golden sunflowers could brighten the mood of the most unrepentant sourpuss. Those glistening studs on the cow's scarlet sandals are a snappy touch, too.

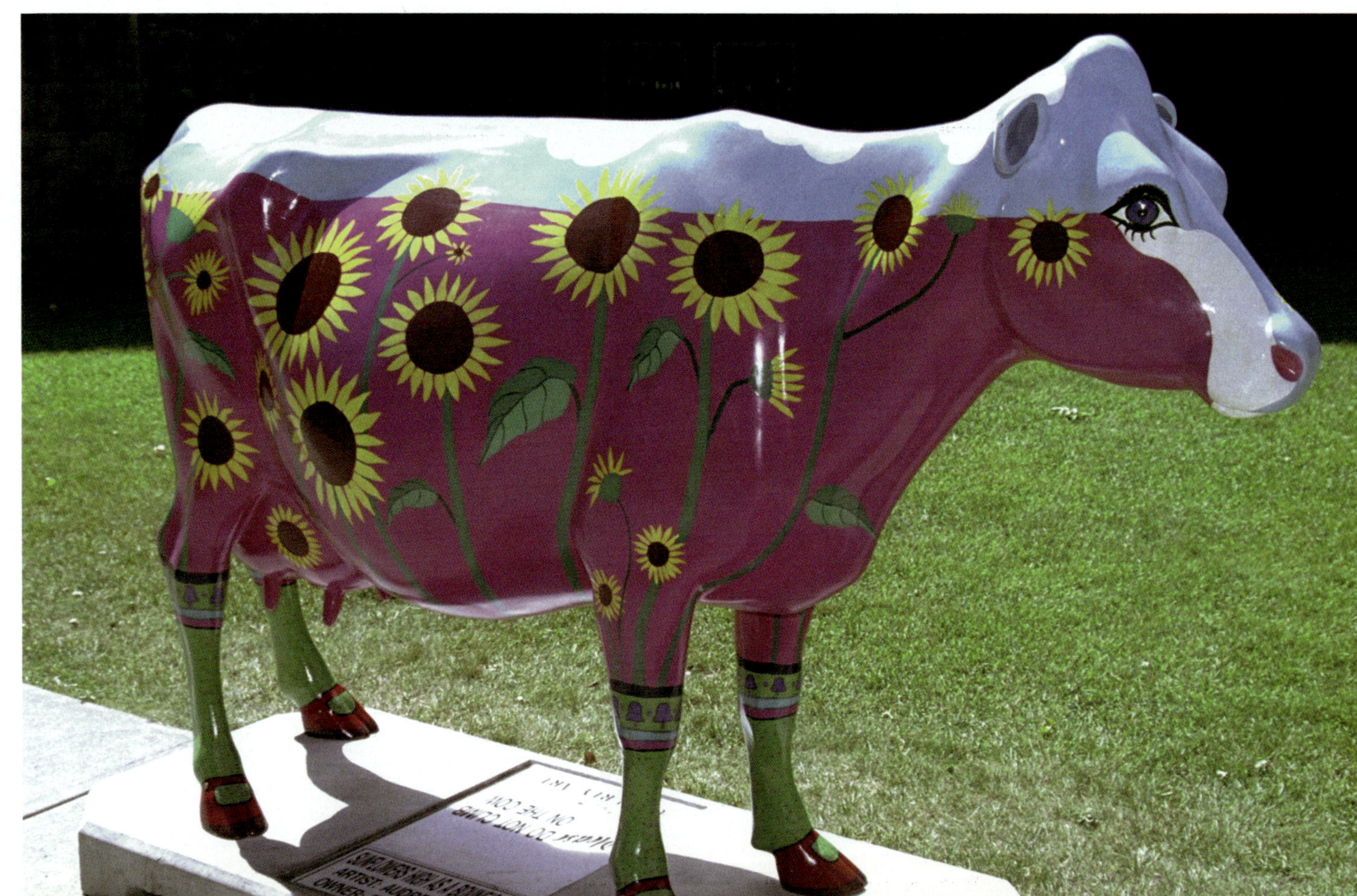

This Ain't No Bull

Artist: Esther Lill
Owner: Ross Smith Energy Group
Charity: Hospice Calgary Society

After one quick glance, nobody would dream of challenging Esther Lill's claim, which doubles as the name of this . . . er . . . cow. We're no experts in the various farmyard genealogies, but this . . . er . . . cow certainly bears a resemblance to the family's black sheep.

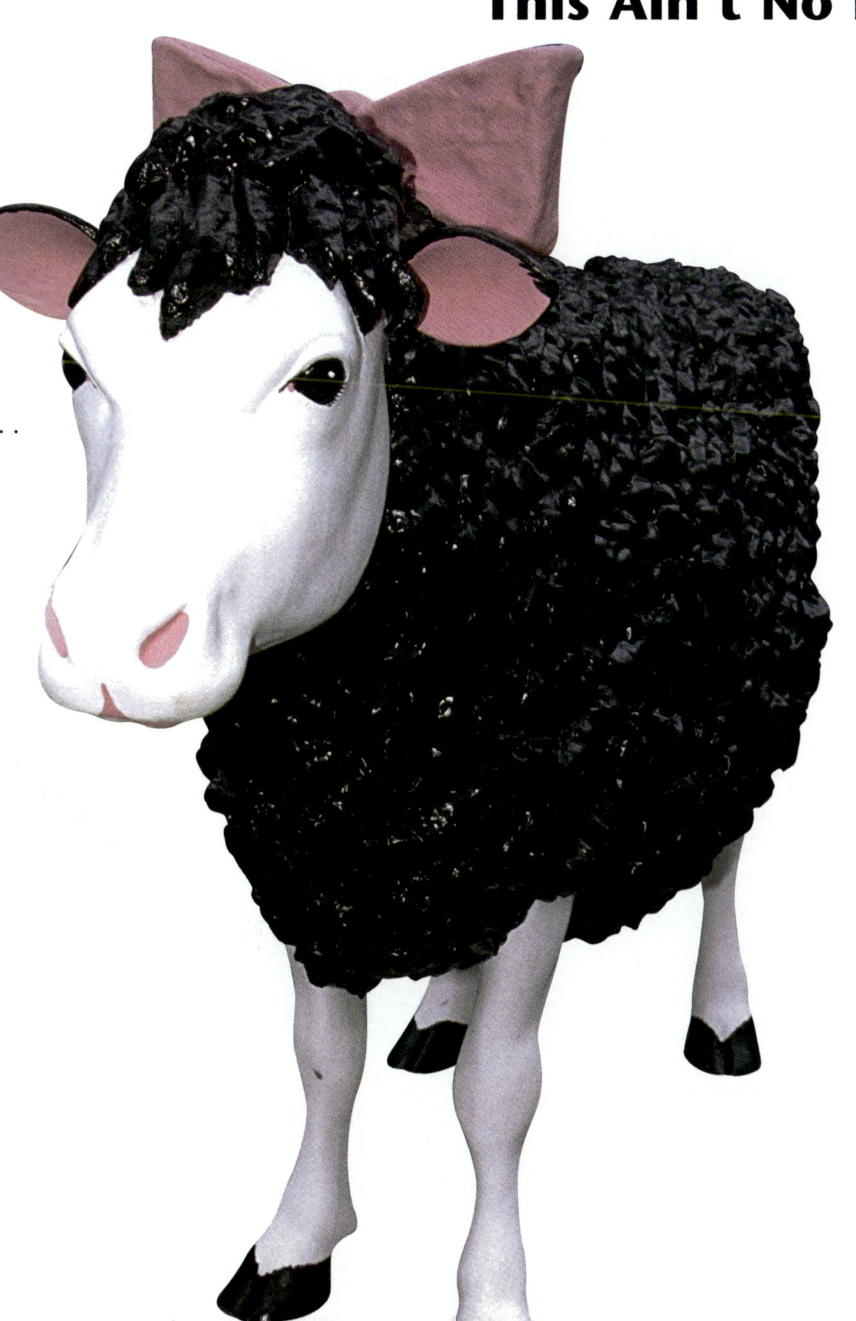

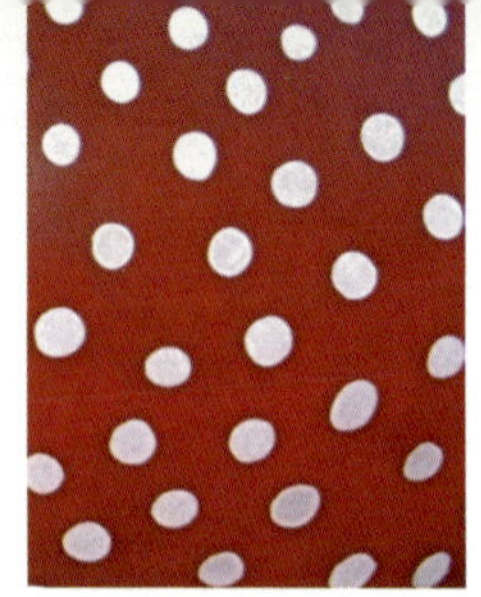

There's a Cow in My Kitchen

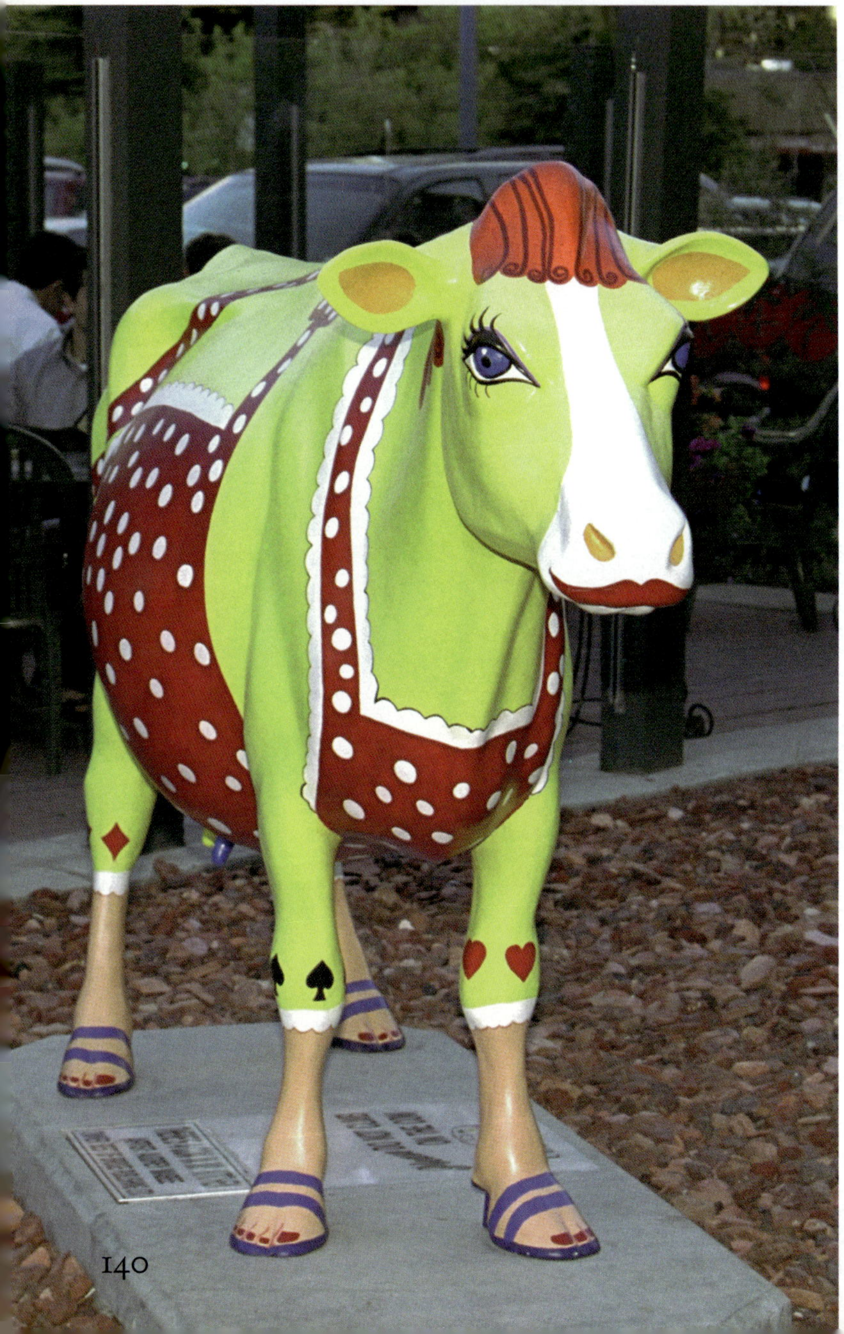

Artist: Audrey Mabee

Owner: Best of Bridge Publishing Ltd.

Charity: Women in Need Society

Officially, the aproned, cloven-hoofed moo . . . er . . . sous chef is known as *There's a Cow in my Kitchen.* But to her creator, Calgary artist Audrey Mabee, she'll always be *Bridget.*

Her reasons are obvious. This culinary cud-chomper was originally purchased by those fabulously successful authors Mary Halpin and the Best of Bridge Ladies (BOBL, for short), who commissioned Audrey to create the cow in their own image.

But this is no soulless business relationship. Mabee and the BOBL go back a long ways. Whenever the ladies—who have collectively coauthored half a dozen best-selling cookbooks—required pots or platters to illustrate their pages, they borrowed them from Audrey's studio.

And the BOBL were so pleased with the skill and wit Mabee brought to the finished product that they sent congratulatory flowers prior to her May 2000 exhibition at Harrison Galleries. They attended *en masse,* and two of the ladies bought Mabee originals that evening.

"Working with them has made me feel wonderful," enthused Mabee, who paid tribute to the BOBL by adding personal touches to *Bridget*'s fibreglass bod. Notice those painted spades, hearts, diamonds and clubs? They're a reminder that the Best of Bridge Ladies always deal a winning hand.

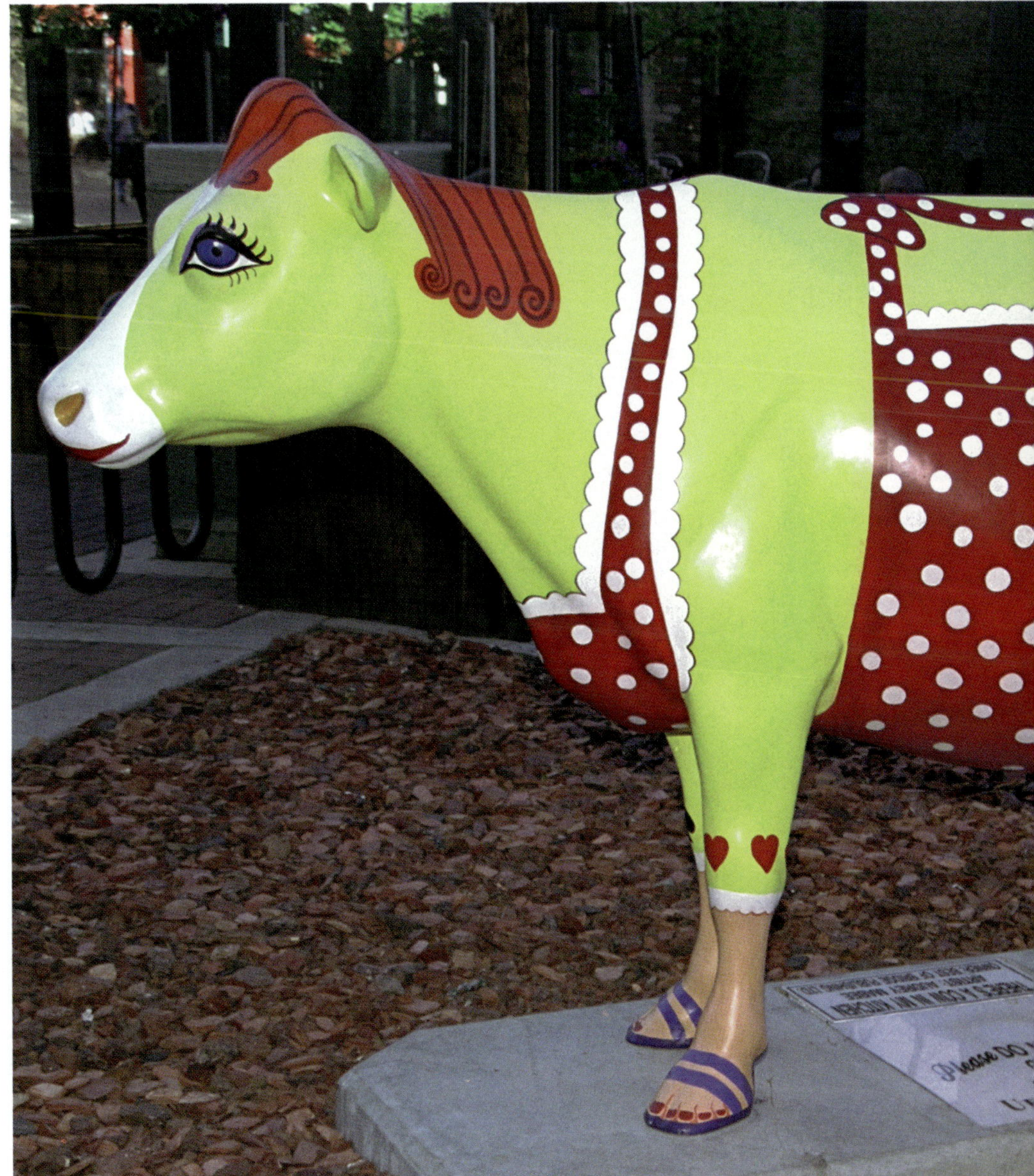

Tom Tom

Artist: Madelene Dollar

Owner: Thomas Navarro

Charity: Kids Cancer Care Foundation

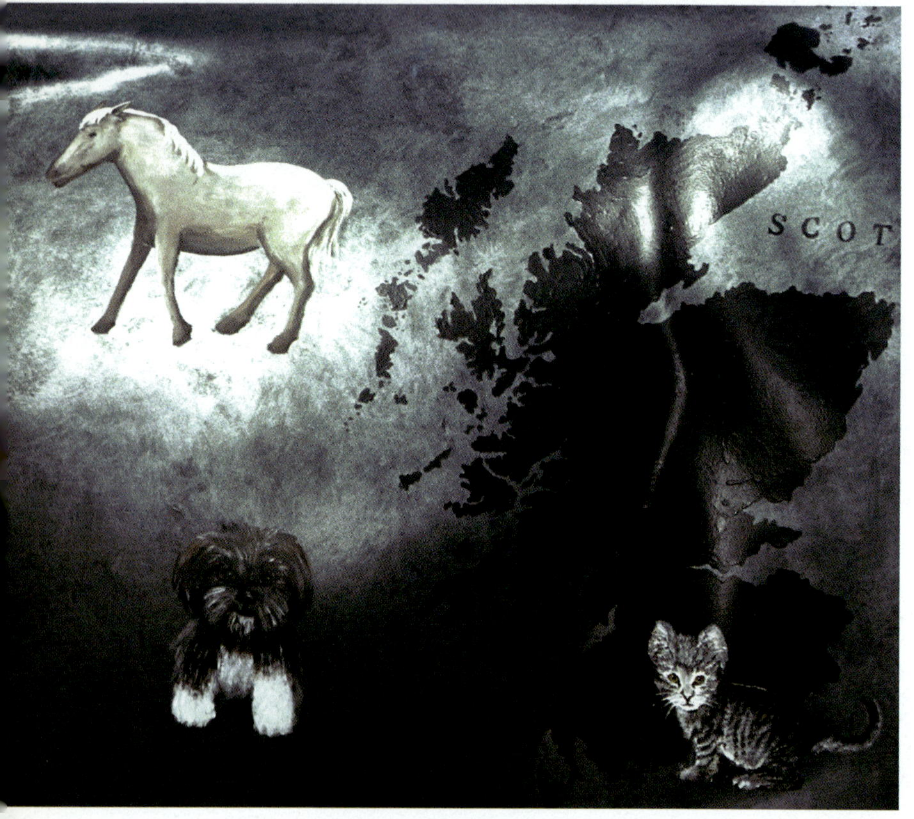

This is the last cow welcomed to the herd. And its story is poignant. She was created as a tribute to young Thomas Navarro, who died of cancer during the summer of 2000. A good-humoured, smiling young man, his last days were greatly enhanced by his appreciation of the playful Udderly Art cows. And when his grieving father, Marlito, told the story of Thomas in public, donations poured in, far exceeding the cost of a brand new cow. *Thomas* will stand forever as a memorial to a brave boy who loved to laugh.

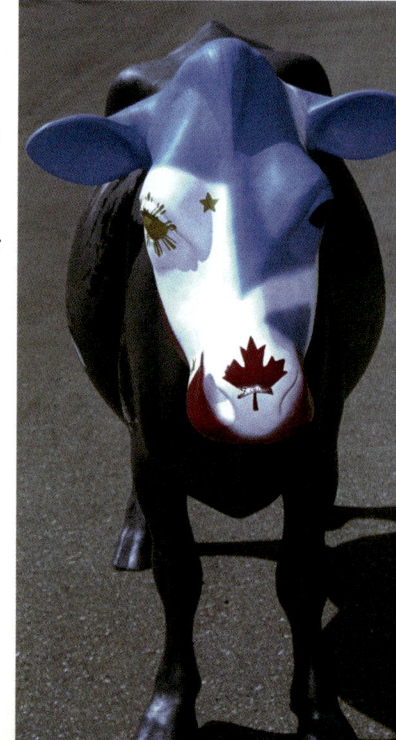

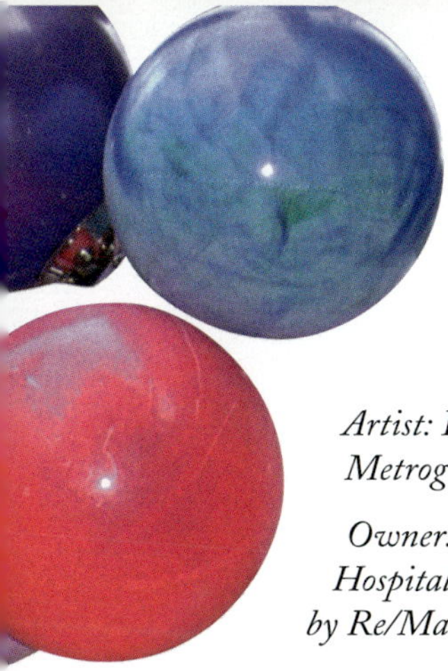

'Til the Kids Come Home

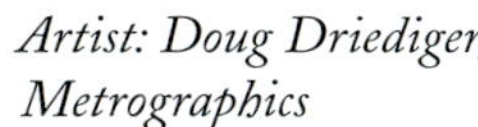

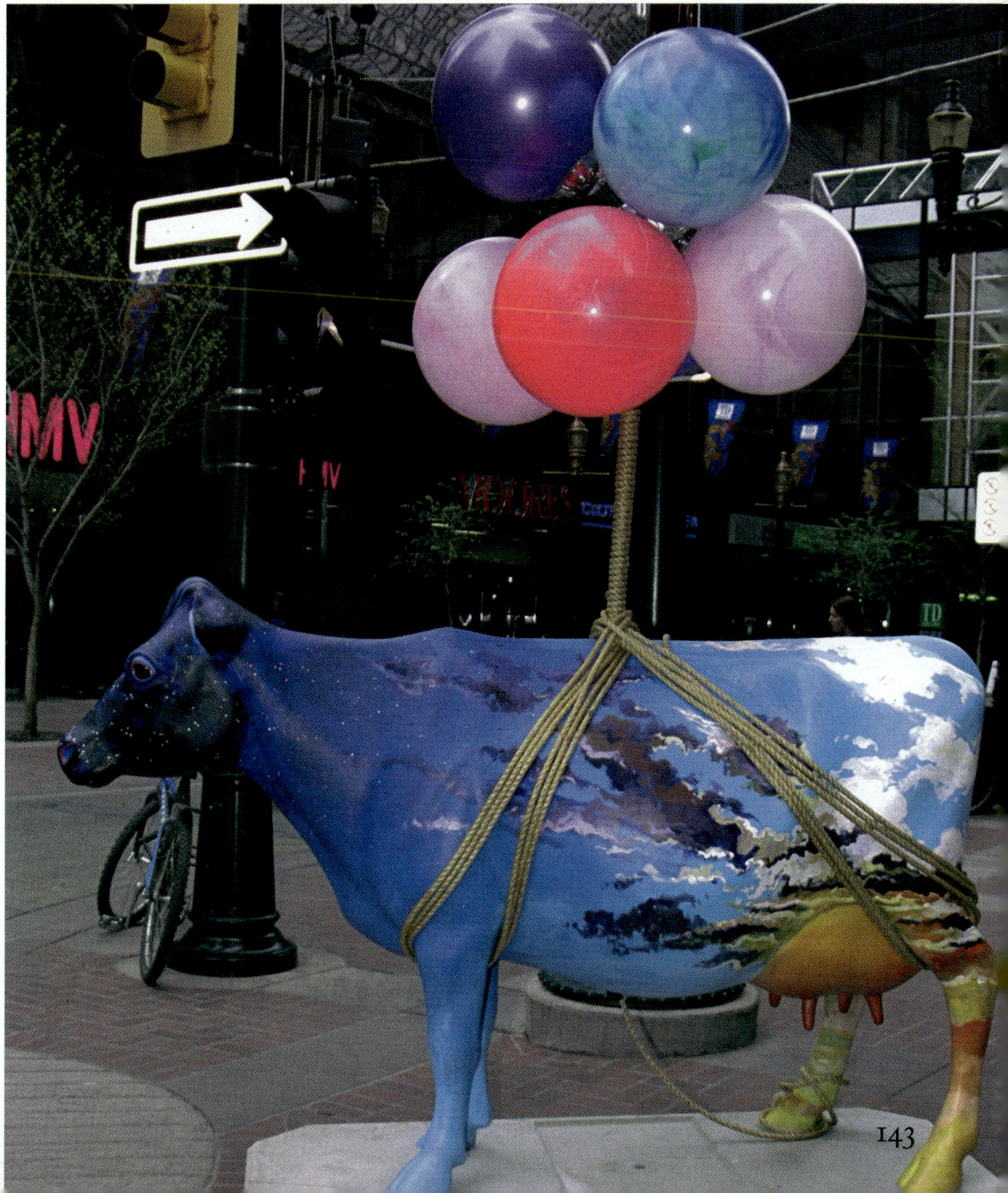

Artist: Doug Driediger, Metrographics

Owner: Alberta Children's Hospital Foundation (donated by Re/Max)

Charity: Alberta Children's Hospital Foundation

Winnie the Pooh and six sturdy balloons—with an approach like this, artist Doug Driediger couldn't fail to pull in an attentive and appreciative audience of kids. Better still, the Alberta Children's Hospital Foundation is the direct beneficiary of the cow's sale at auction.

Tutu Moo Moo

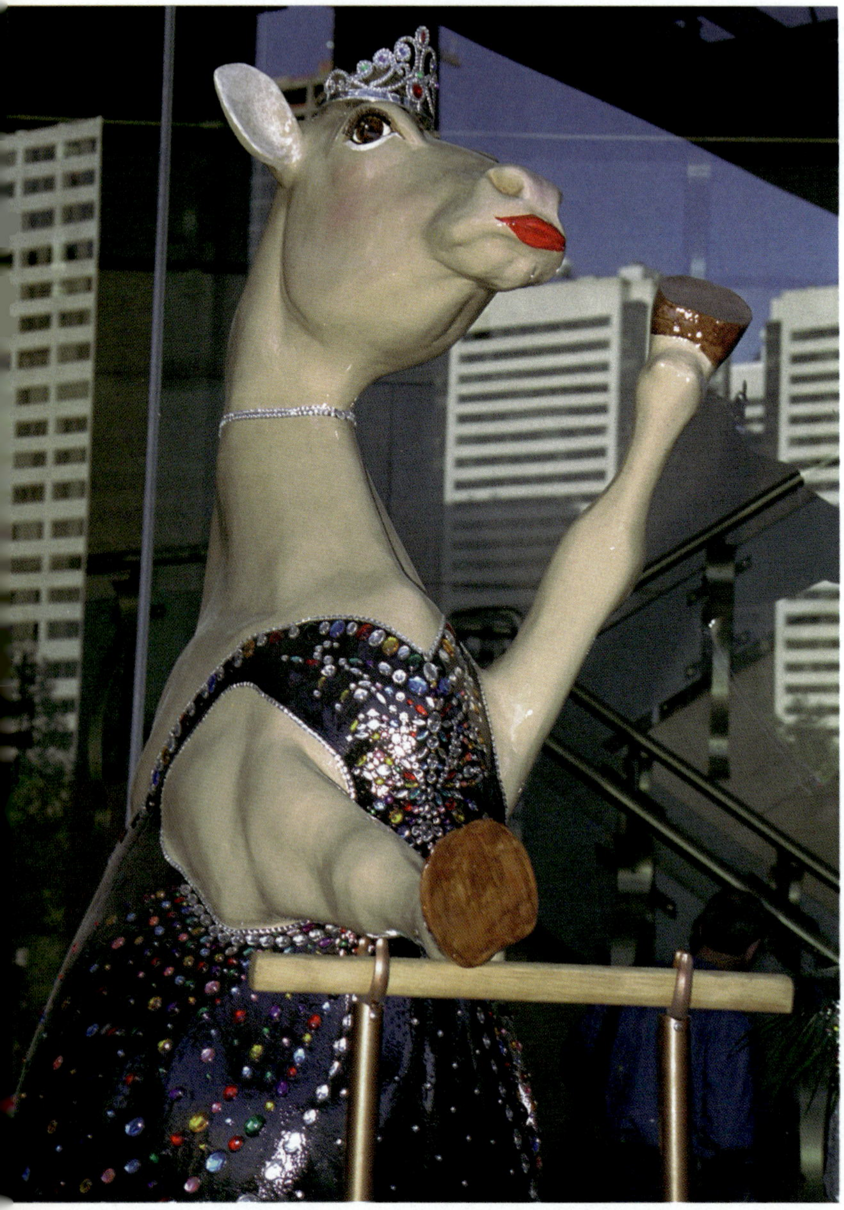

Artist: Bonnie Laycock

Owner: Calgary Humane Society (donated by Bonnie Laycock)

Charity: Calgary Humane Society

For sheer wit of execution and design, few artworks can match Bonnie Laycock's pouting, tiara-topped ballerina. And we're not just dispensing praise because Laycock is board chairperson (and all-around godmother) of Udderly Art. *Tutu Moo Moo,* one hoof laid cow-quettishly on the bar, does her stretching in a black spangled tutu, taking her warm-up very seriously indeed.

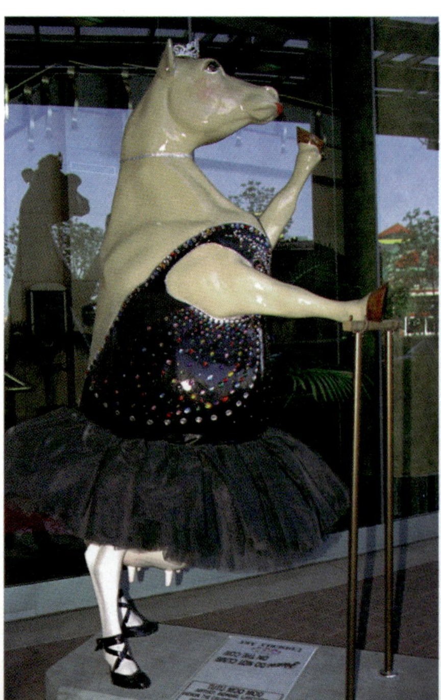

The Udder Shuttle

Artist: Kathy Barnson

Owner: Park & Jet

This sleek shuttle is packed with happy passengers grinning from their window seats. Their destination: Greener Pastures. They're bound to make it because the unit is all tuned up and gassed up by means of the fuel tank installed in the cow's udder.

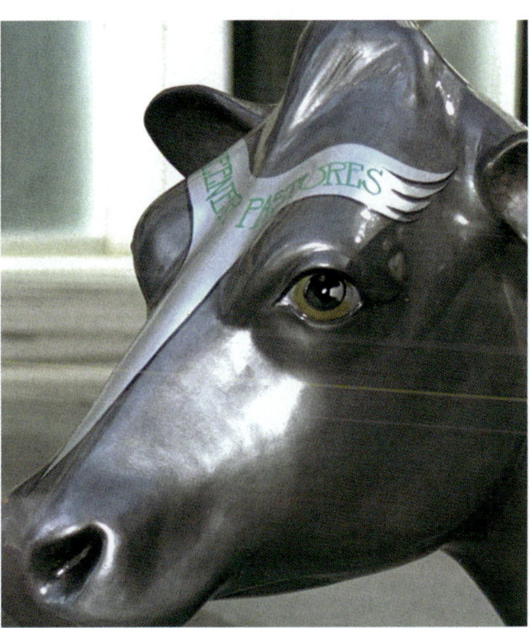

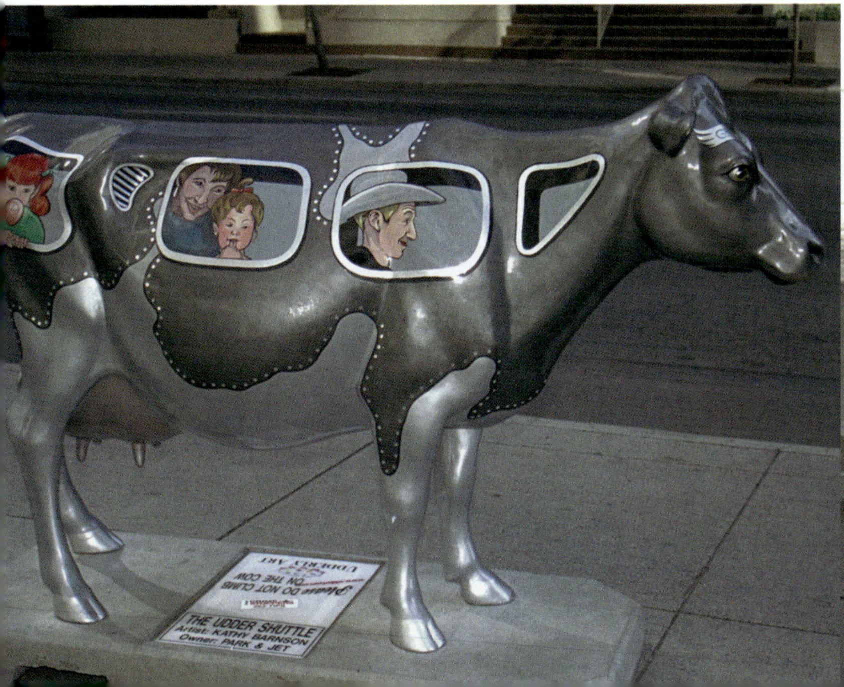

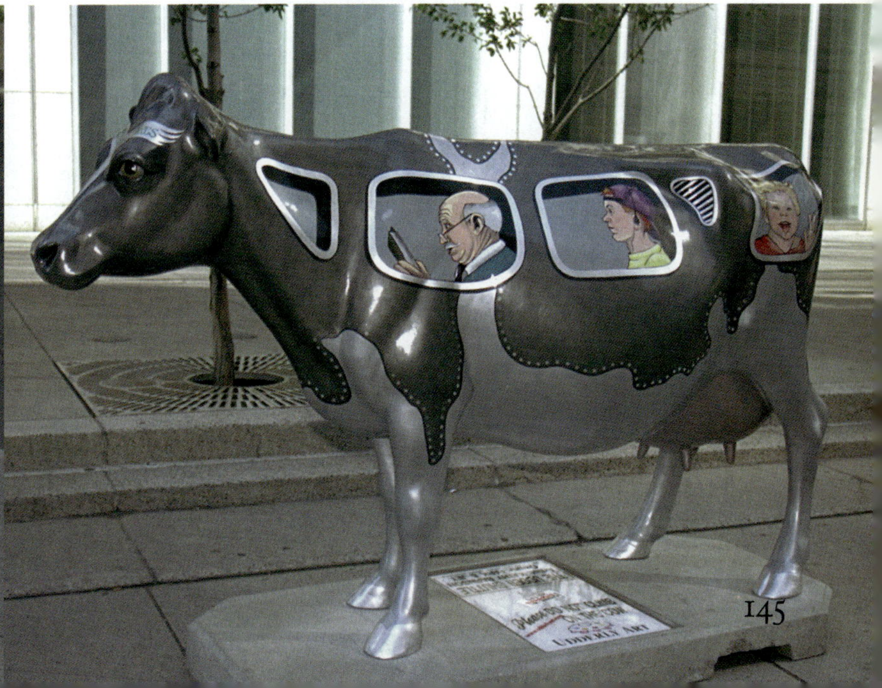

Udderly Content

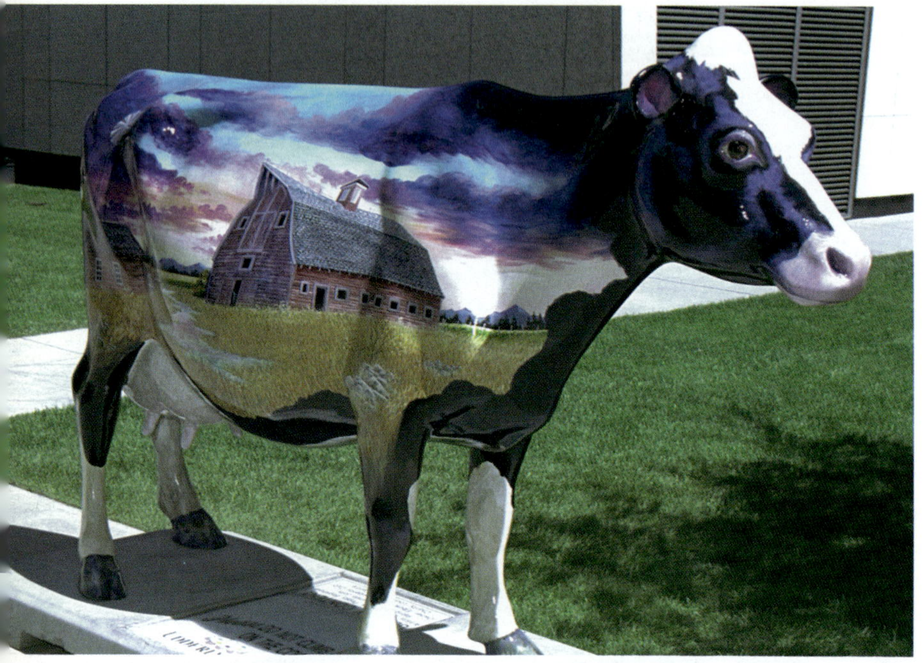

Artists: Jon Williams, Peggy Bagshaw, Patricia Lortie and Lynda Gilcrist

Owner: Elbow Valley Residents Club

Charity: Louise Dean Centre

Udderly content? What cow wouldn't be when dressed up with a realistic western scene this irresistible? A brilliant bluebird rests on a fencepost and draws the eye of the viewer into a captivating cow canvas offering a potpourri of rural symbols from stooks to windmills to the familiar red barn.

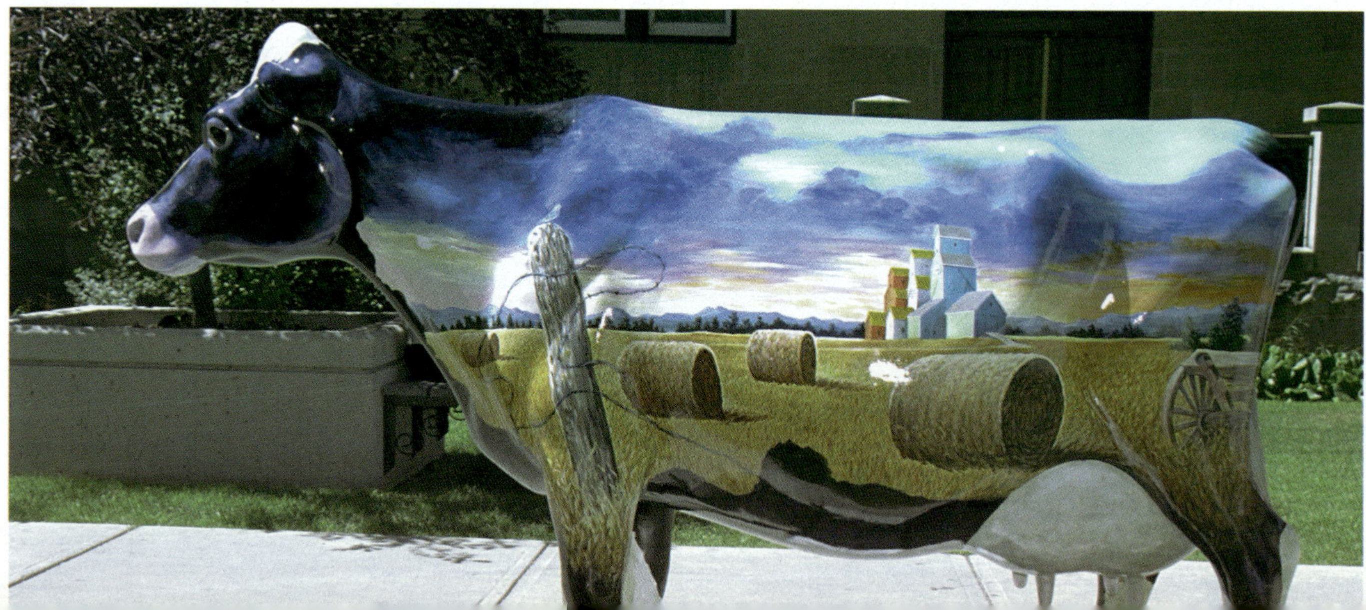

Vacca Azzurra

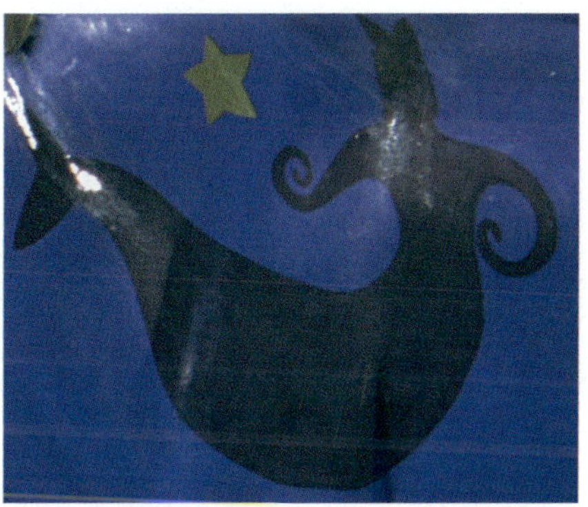

Artist: Carroll Taylor-Lindoe

Owner: Teatro

Charity: Hospice Calgary

You guessed it, the name means “blue cow,” and Taylor-Lindoe’s creation lives right up to it. A vigilant sentinel in front of Teatro, the downtown restaurant, *Vacca Azzura* evokes an indigo evening sky festooned with yellow stars and eerie dark shapes of barren branches.

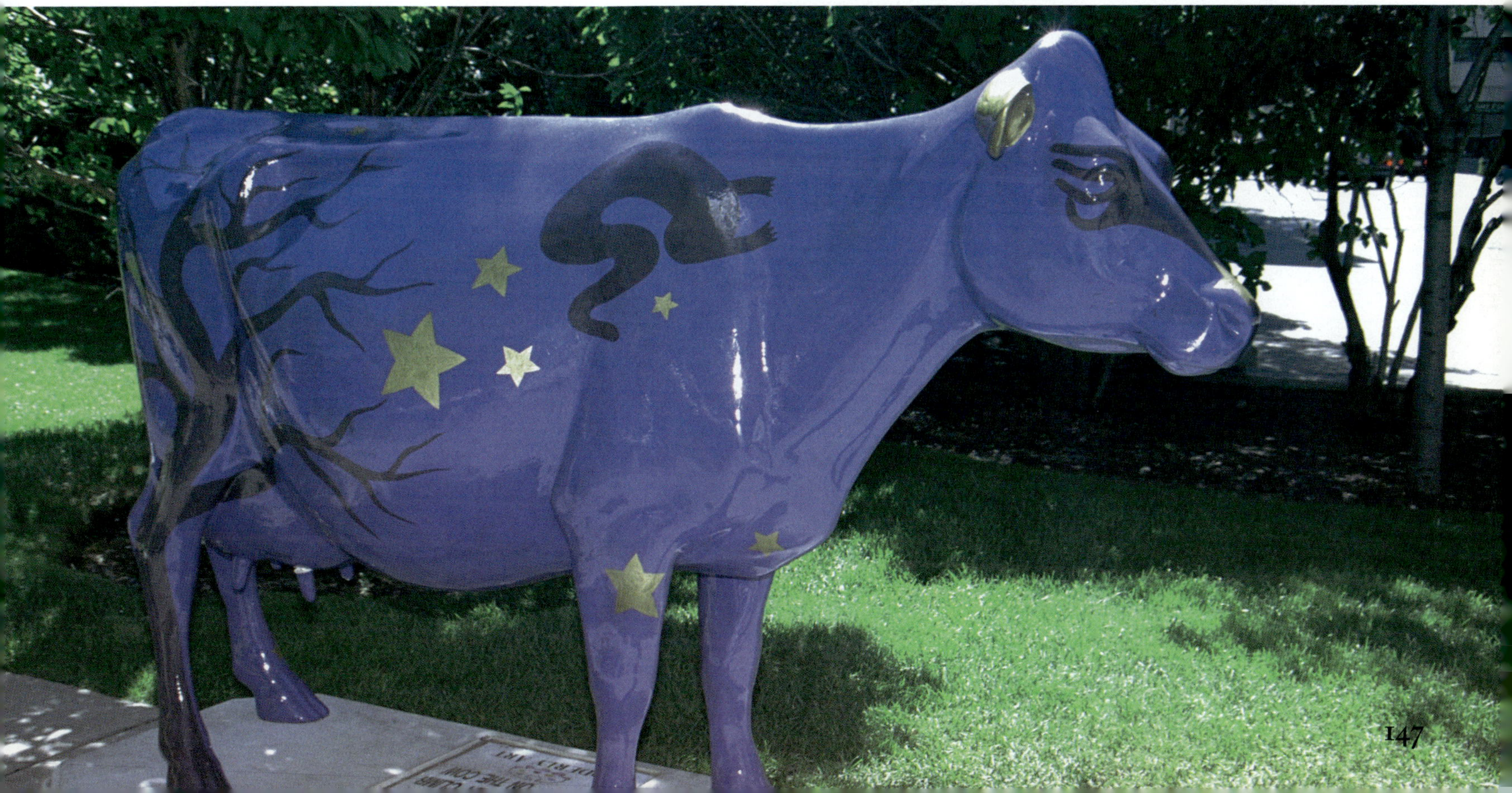

Vacca Quaerens

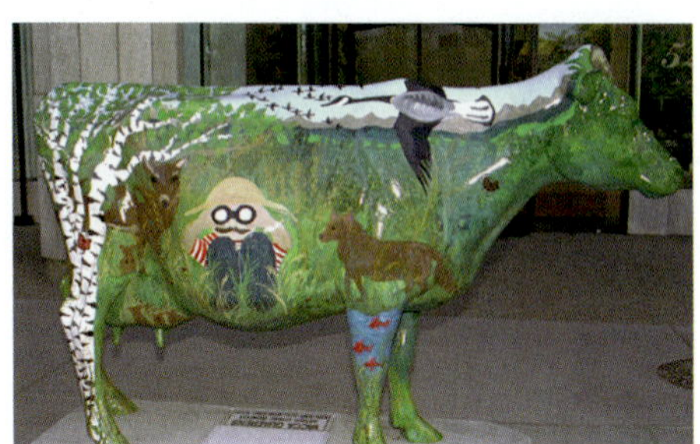

Artist: Lynnie Wonfor

Owner: Korn Ferry O'Callaghan Honey McKay

Charity: Calgary Zoo

Vacca what? *Vacca Quaerens.* It means "searching cow," which would explain the goggle-eyed peeper Lynnie Wonfor posted on each side of the fibreglass rib cage. Peering through binoculars, the searcher ignores Wonfor's butterflies, deer and coyotes. Instead, he, she or it is watching . . . you.

Visual CowMooNICATIONS

Artist: Renata Liwska. Digital Imaging: Maranda Reprographics

Owner: Smith & Associates

Charity: Hull Child & Family Services

She's a veritable cow-nucopia of warm childhood memories evoked by a stunning series of characters from fables and rhymes. Included on the roster: jack-in-the-box, the little star of "Twinkle, Twinkle" fame and a more nimble Jack, leaping over the candlestick.

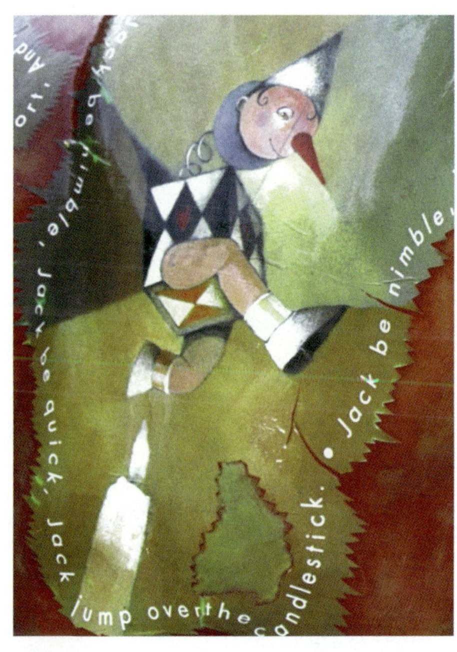

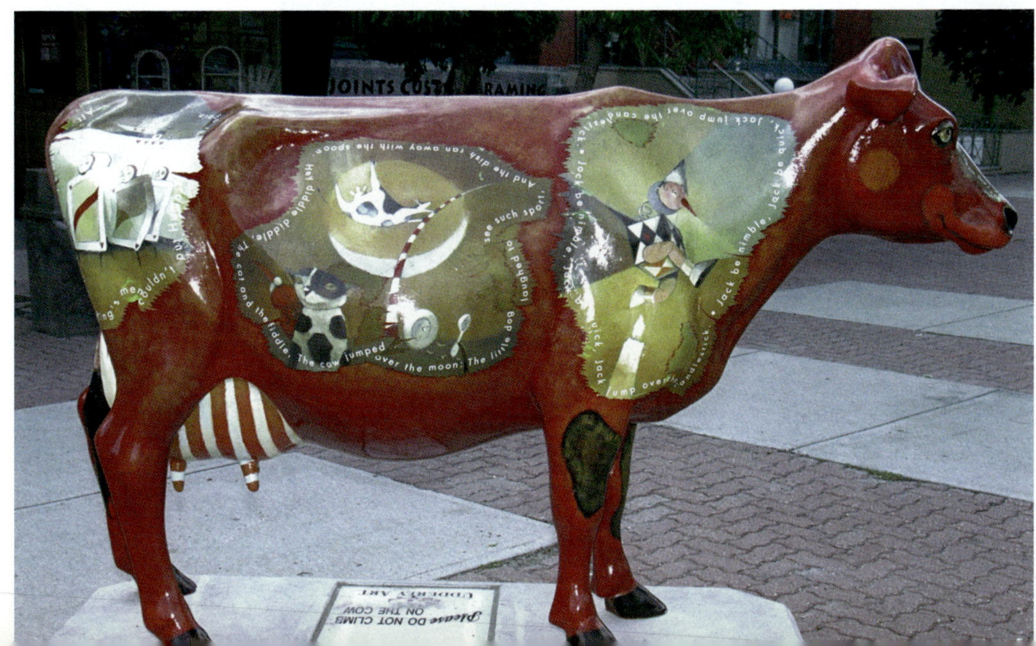

What Now "e" Cow

Artist: Green Fools Physical Theatre

Owner: Eatons, a division of Sears Canada Inc.

Hint: the "e" stands for Eatons. Crafted by a member of the Green Fools, this cow's purple and red circus getup reflects the troupe's current revue. Known as the *Great Western Canadian B & E Circus,* the show spent a month performing at Fort Calgary in summer 2000 before appearing at the Edmonton Fringe.

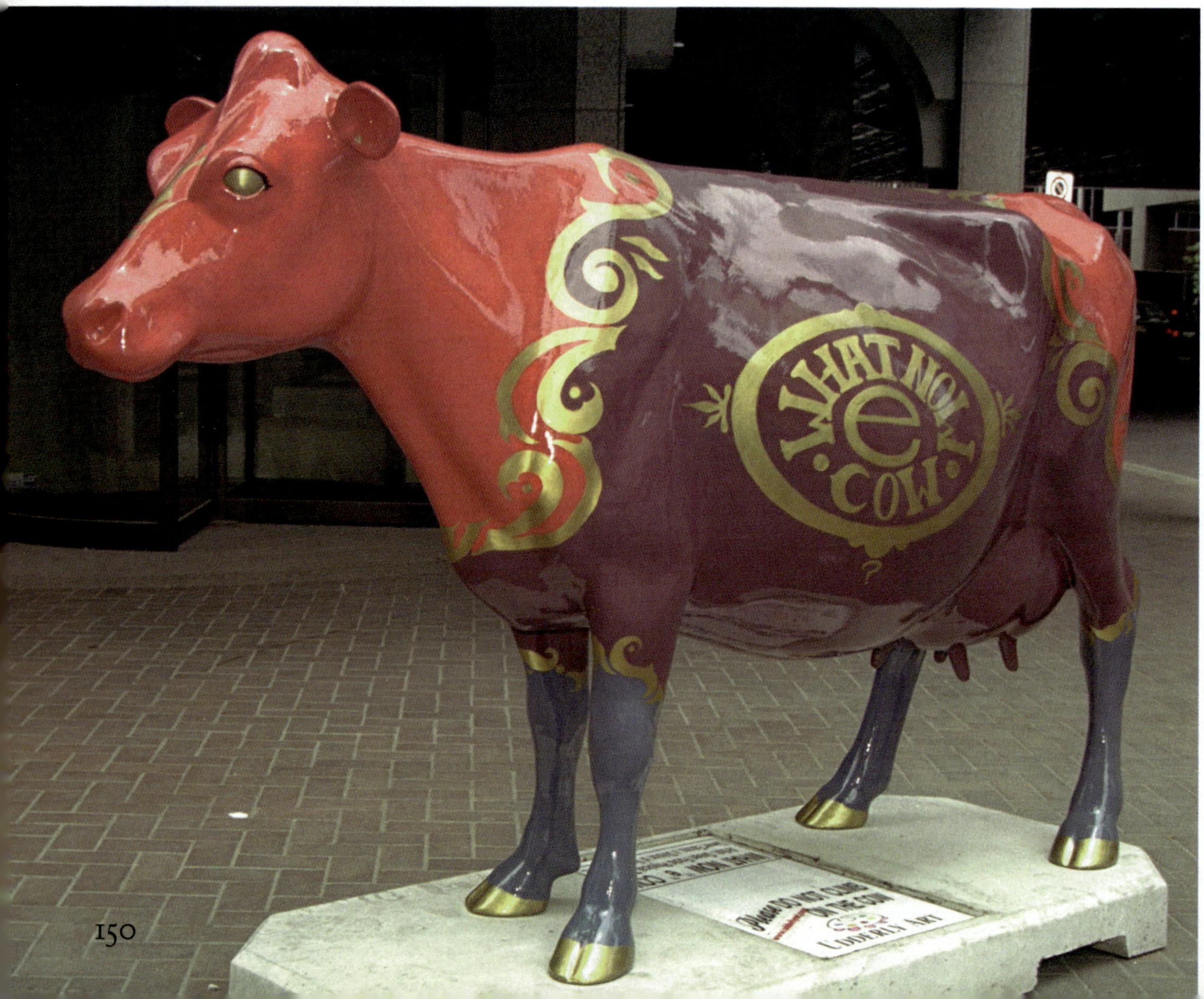

Wild Rose

Artist: Madelene Dollar

Owner: Alberta Treasury Branches

A bovine flower of the wide prairie, *Wild Rose* is a big-eyed, big-eared picture postcard. Madelene Dollar hasn't missed a trick in representing the foothills country—including yellow wheatfields, green hills and snowcapped mountains—spread beneath a cloudless sky.

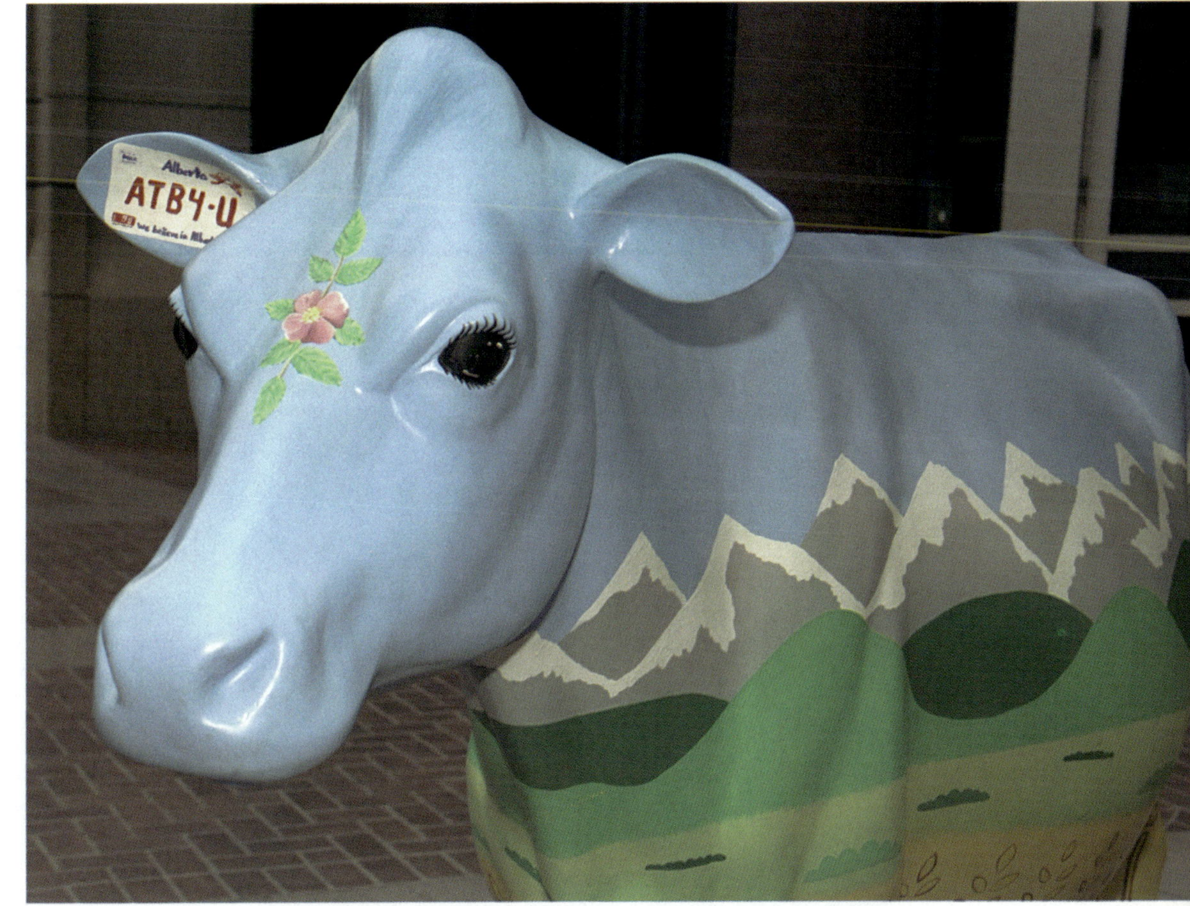

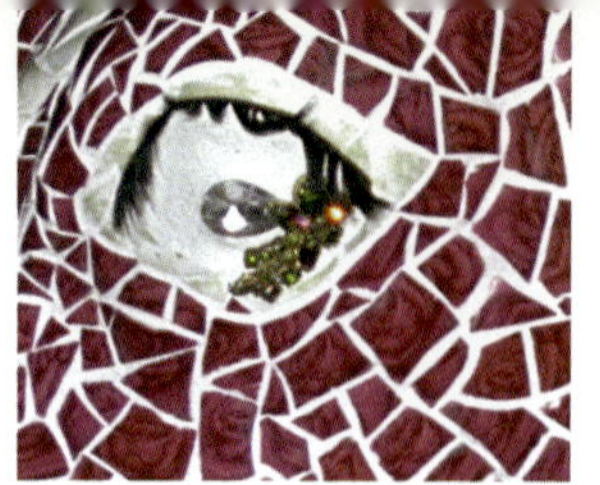

Wild Rosie

Artist: Leeanne Stringer
Owner: Sprint Canada Inc.
Charity: PREP Program

Fernie, British Columbia, artist Leeanne Stringer created an intricate mosaic, applying thousands of small pieces of hand-cut china to *Wild Rosie*'s exterior. Each piece holds a single minuscule rose. Proceeds from the auction sale of *Wild Rosie* go to a resource and learning centre for children with Down's syndrome.

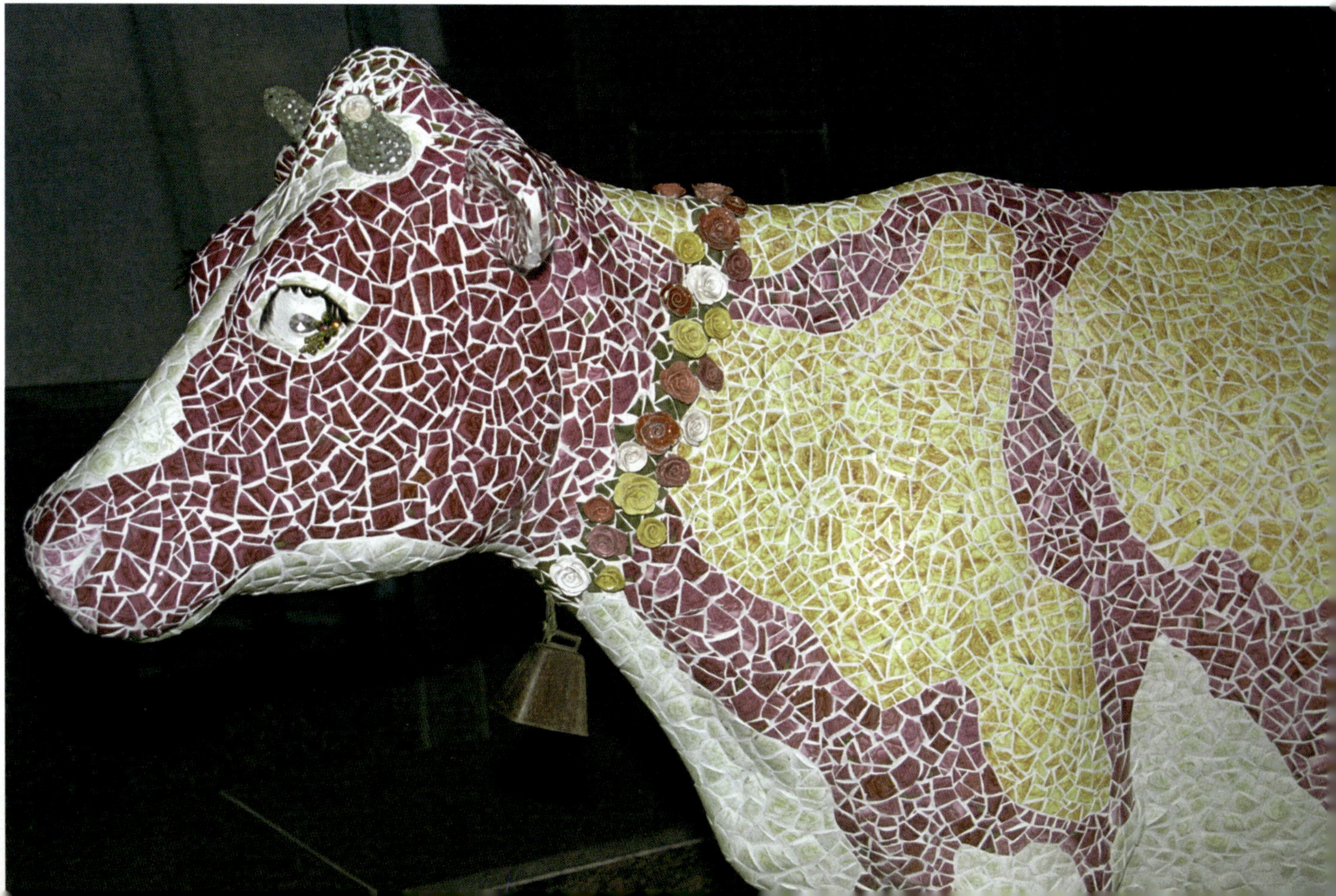

Wilma Dearing

Artist: Jeff de Boer

Owner: Enmax Corporation

Charity: Kids Cancer Care Foundation

The Kids Cancer Care Foundation couldn't have found a more appealing poster cow than Wilma, a high-flying, white-scarfed rocket girl with her goggled eyes on the big prize. Jeff de Boer's amusing piece is a winner with big ideas—an ideal symbol for a nonprofit group determined to create a healthier world for sick children.

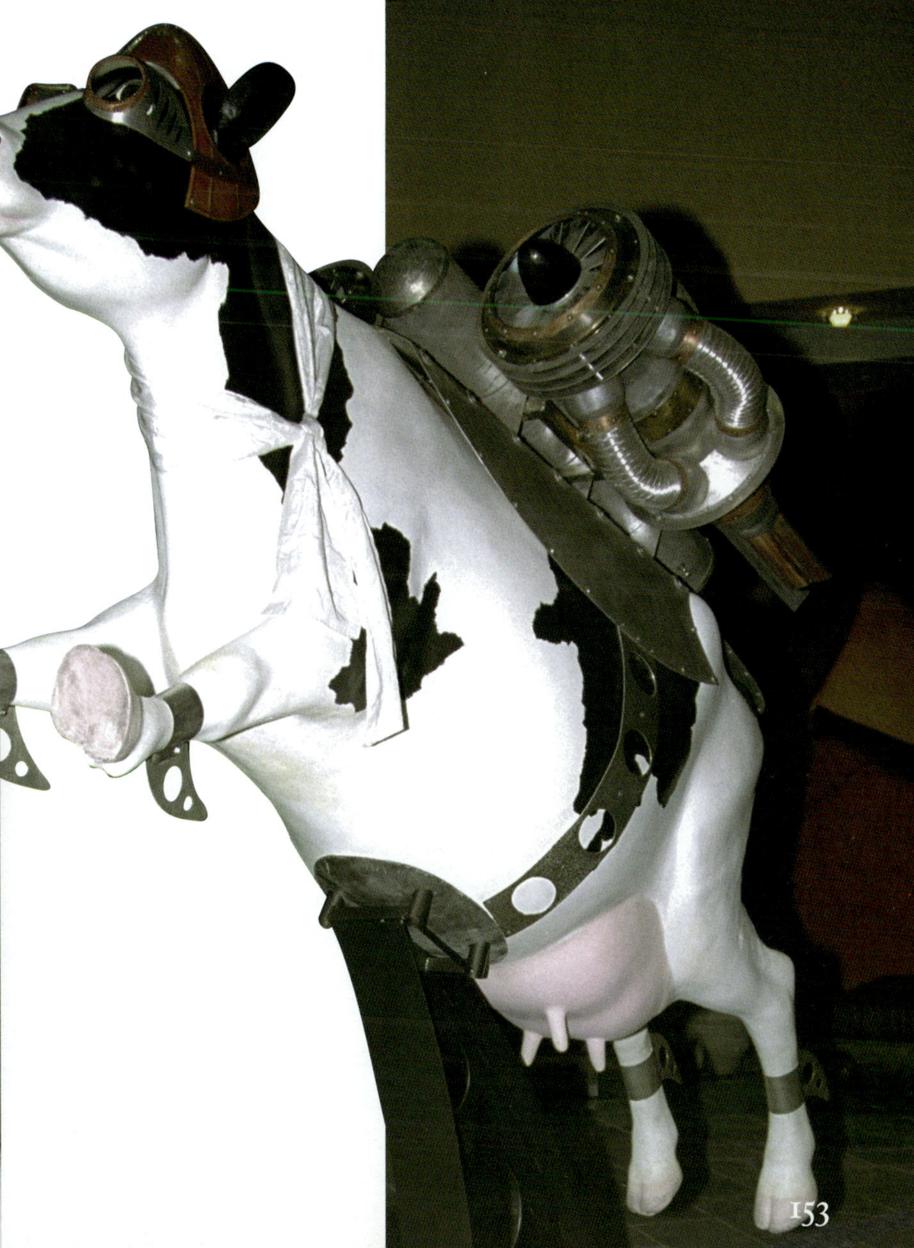

Wrapping Up Alberta

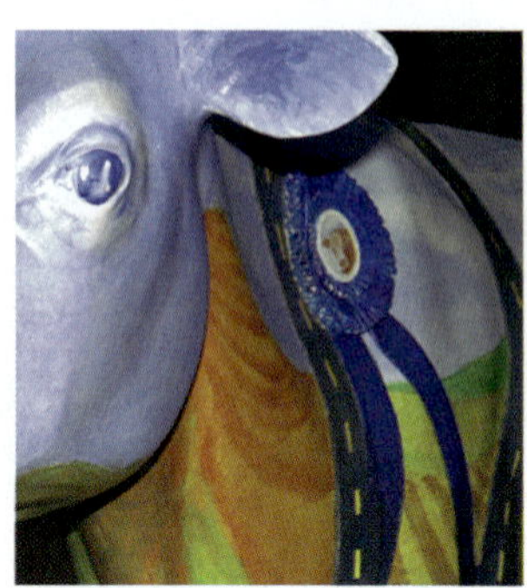

Artist: Noni Boyle

Owner: Alsa Road Construction Ltd.

Charity: Kids Cancer Care Foundation

Any doubts that this is a blue-chip artwork will be dispelled by a glance at the blue ribbon "pinned" to the cow's left front shoulder. Noni Boyle paid homage to her province by gift wrapping the yellow-green prairies in a network of blue-gray rural highways. Always an optimist, Boyle left nary a pothole in sight.

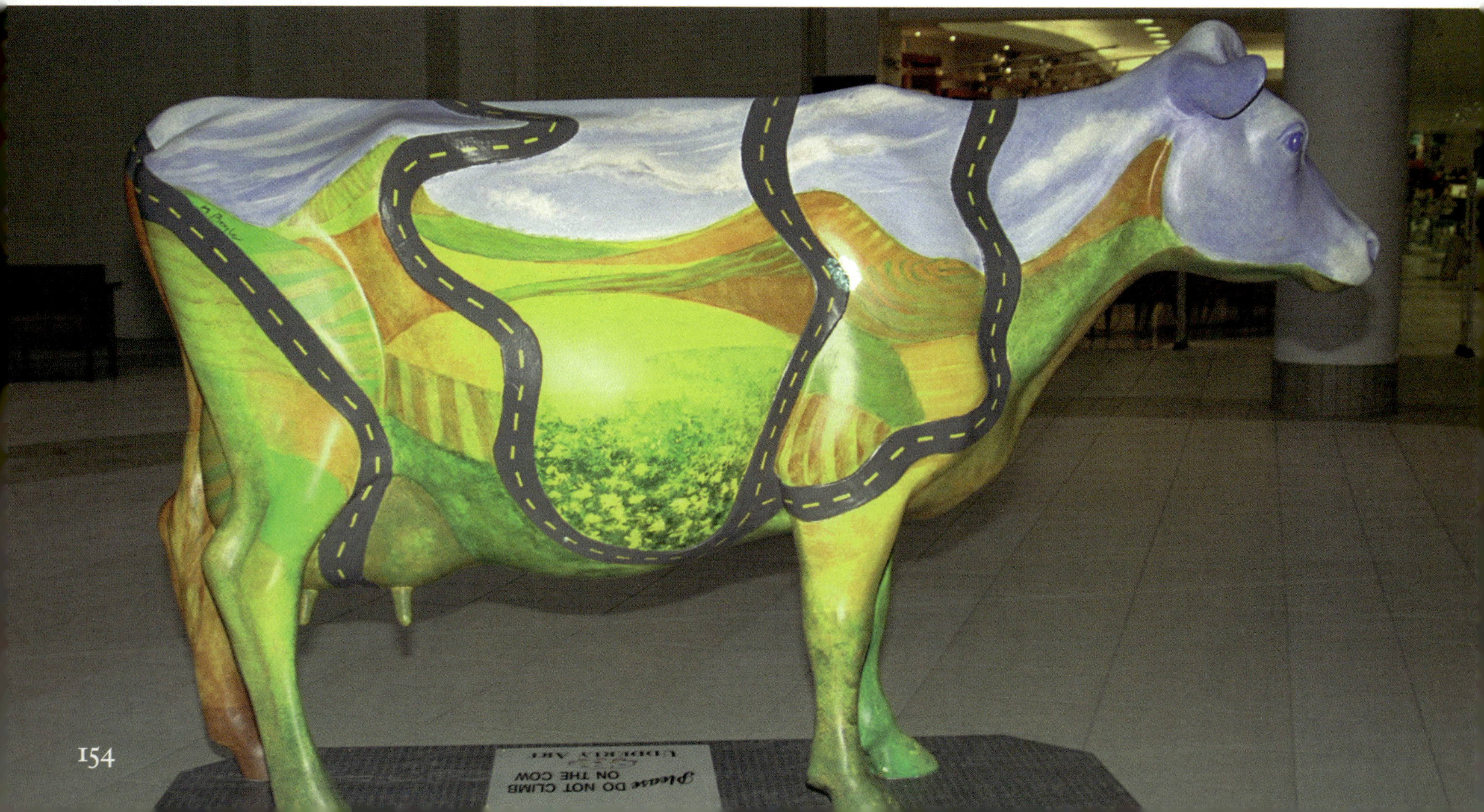

Yippee Yi Yay Cow Pattern

Artist: Steven Mack

Owner: Haskayne & Partners

Precise and clean as a pure woollen Scottish plaid, Steven Mack's cow (and its name) were clearly inspired by a comic hit song from a few years back. But there's nothing laughable about this Maverick's décor—"woven" lines as crisp and sweet as any artist could fashion them.

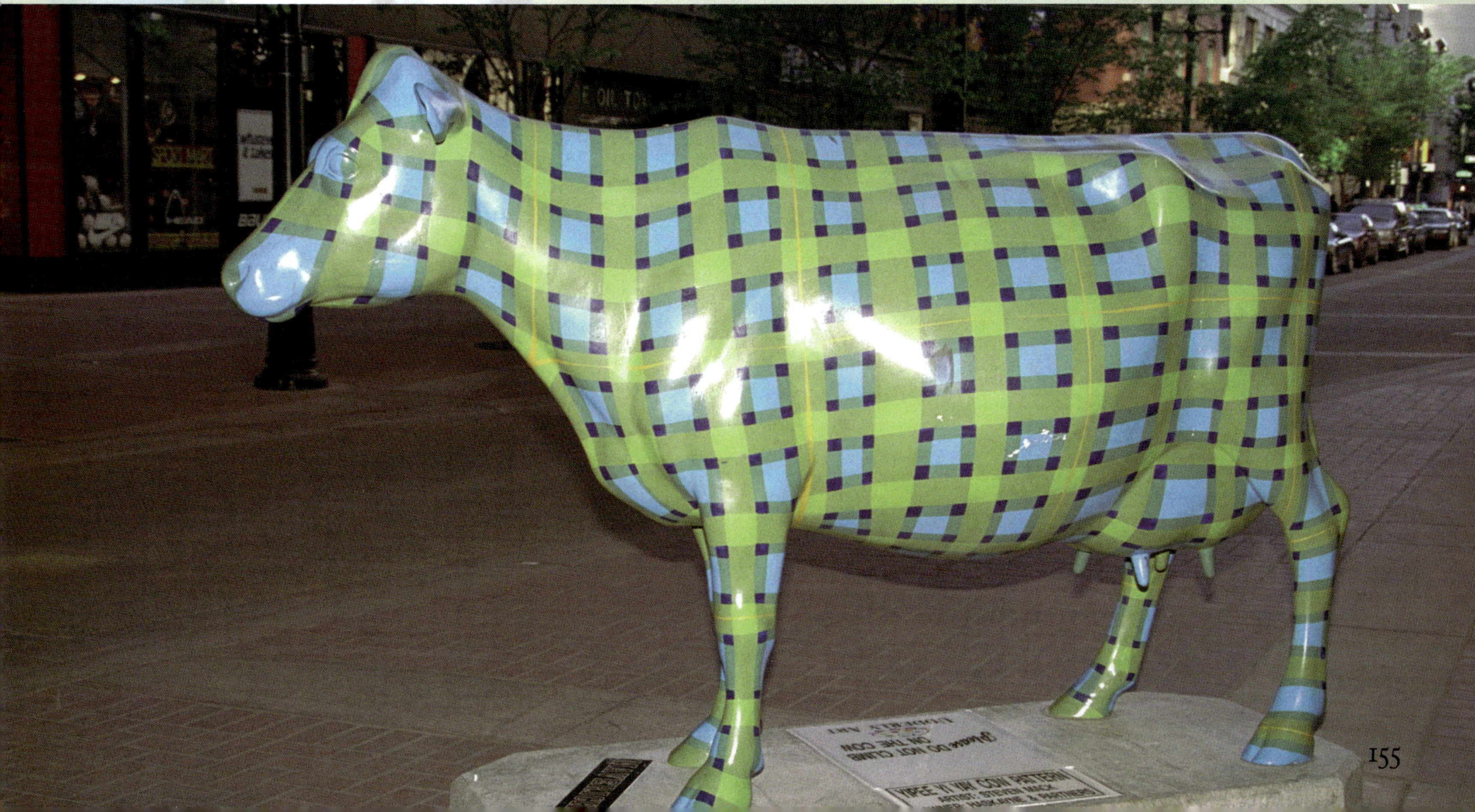

Ze Cow

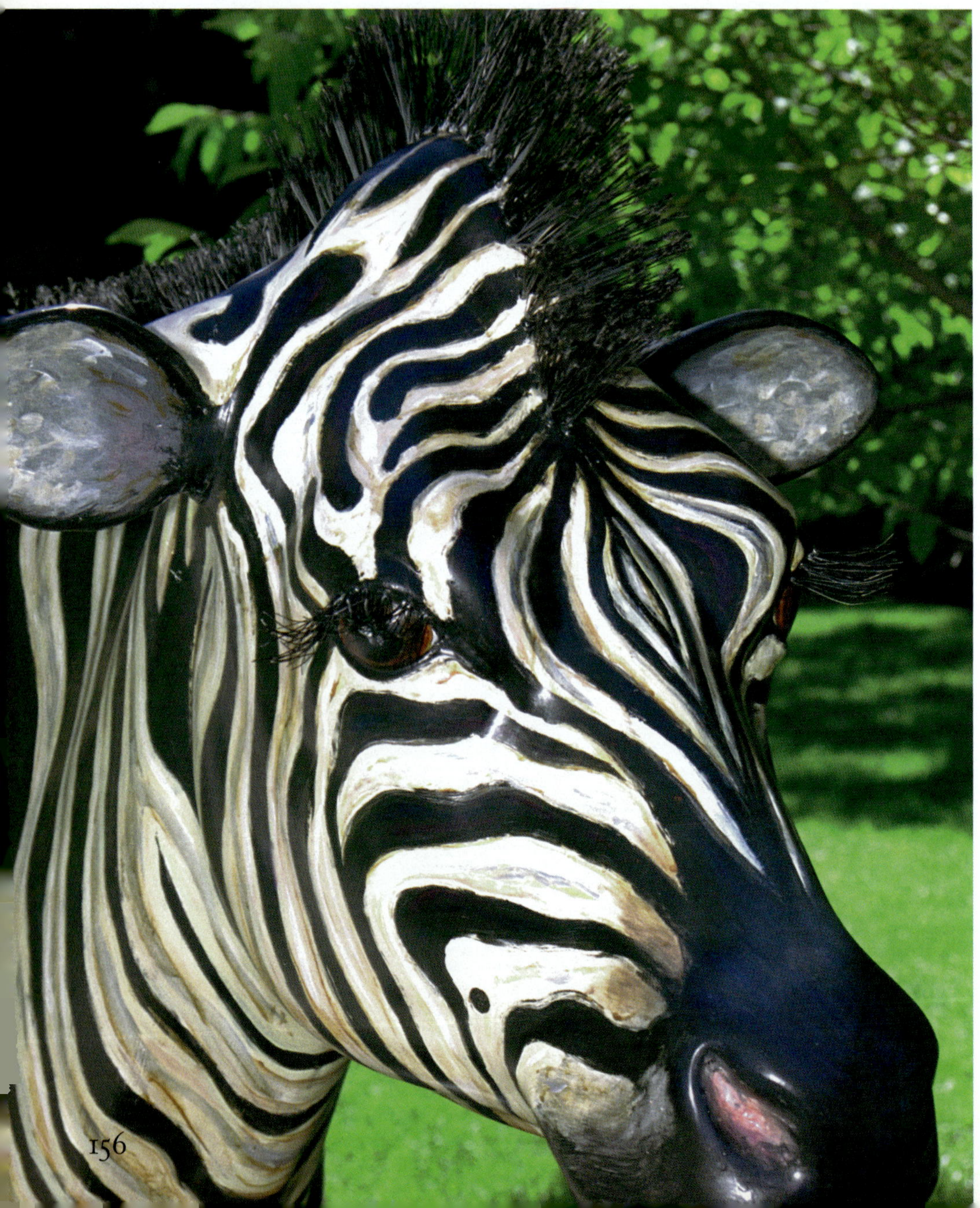

Artist: Judy Sproule

Owner: Half Brand Ranch

Charity: Calgary Stampede Foundation

Nothing against the noble milk producer, but Calgary artist Judy Sproule couldn't help believing that inside every cow there's a horse dying to break free.

The cow is a symbol of nurturing motherhood, which everyone agrees is an extremely good thing. But even devoted moms enjoy kicking up their heels once in a while.

So Sproule thought she'd give her cow a taste of range-roaming freedom. But her artist's eye quickly told her a horse may not be the way to go.

"The size and the dimensions weren't right," she said. "Then I thought of a zebra—big belly, short legs. A zebra's physique is much more in tune with a cow's."

Hence, *Ze Cow,* a gloriously striped hybrid. Sproule's artistic vision created a costume any party-loving cow might choose to celebrate a Halloween moo-squerade.

Any creative challenges? Only material for the zebra mane, which Sproule finally tracked down at a Calgary broom manufacturer.

The result was a picturesque piece of art that has brought joy to thousands of Calgarians—Sproule in particular.

"I got very attached to her," the artist confessed. "Before I was finished, I ended up talking to her."

Their topics of conversation remain a well-guarded secret between creator and cow.

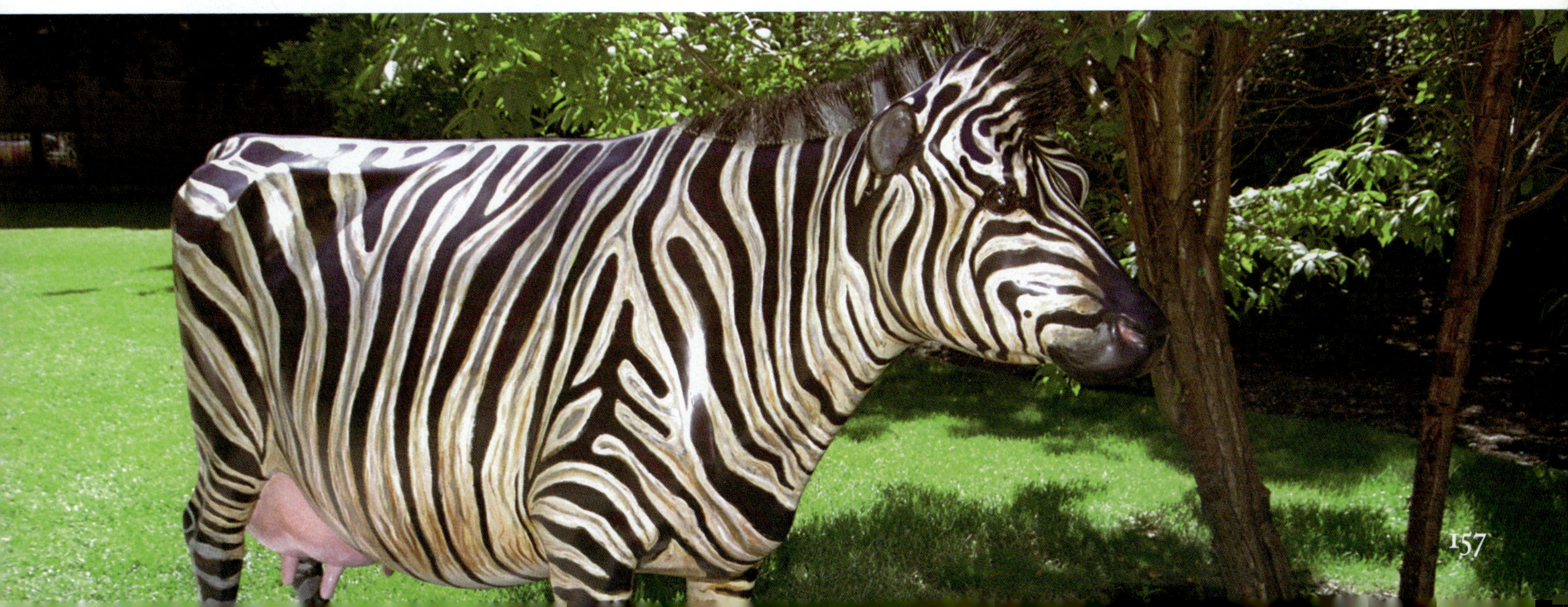

Zoocow

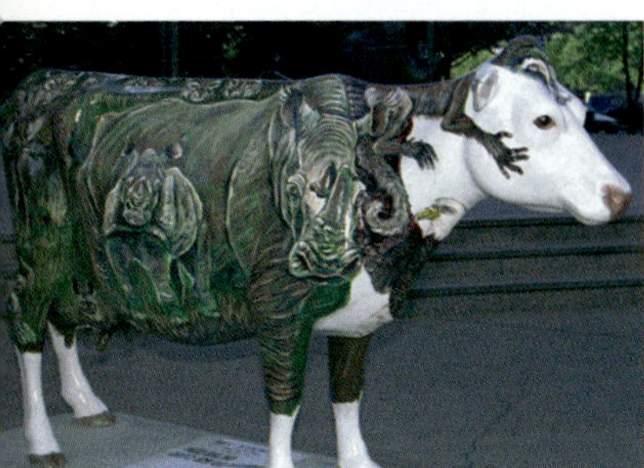

Artist: Gwen Hughes

Owner: McCrum's Office Furnishings

If you can't spare the shoe leather to circumnavigate Calgary's Zoo, stop by *Zoocow* for a more condensed, inanimate version. Gwen Hughes has tucked water buffalo, boars, rhinos, apes, lions and hippos into a swirl of veldt, jungle and river scenes. A particularly deft touch is the leopard's paw dangling languidly in a running stream.

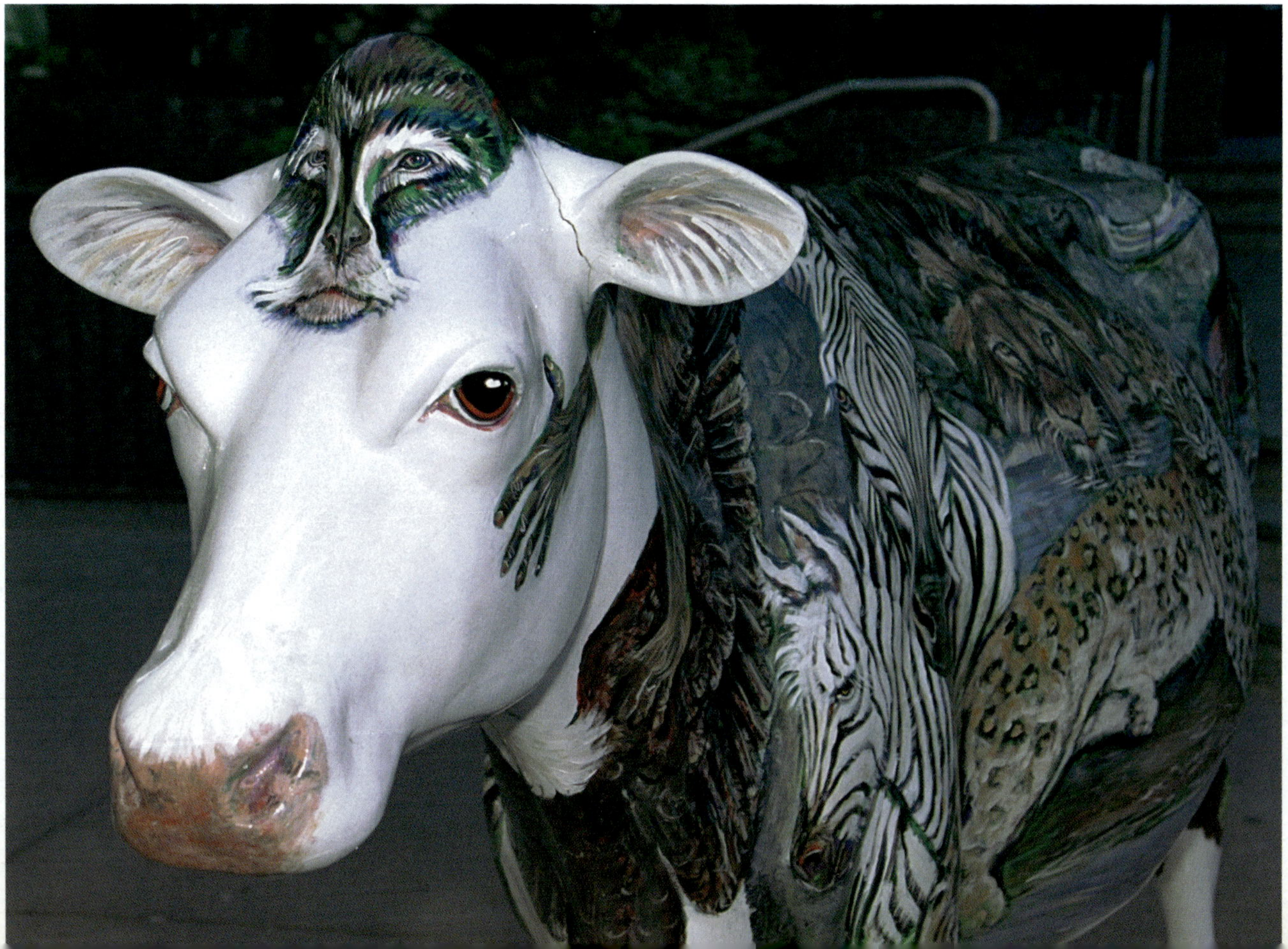

Zoomoo2000.cow

Artist: Herb Sellin

Owner: Calgary Zoo (donated by the Royal Bank Financial Group Foundation)

Charity: Calgary Zoological Society

Zoomoo2000.cow is an impressionistic, highly ambitious heifer fashioned by Herb Sellin, who studded his metallic-based beast with 30,000 glass gems in 52 colours.

More than 80 exotic animals, including a cobra cow's tail, peer out from the glittering surface. An enthusiastic fan of the Genome Project, Herb points out that we're all built from the same stuff—cows and humans alike.

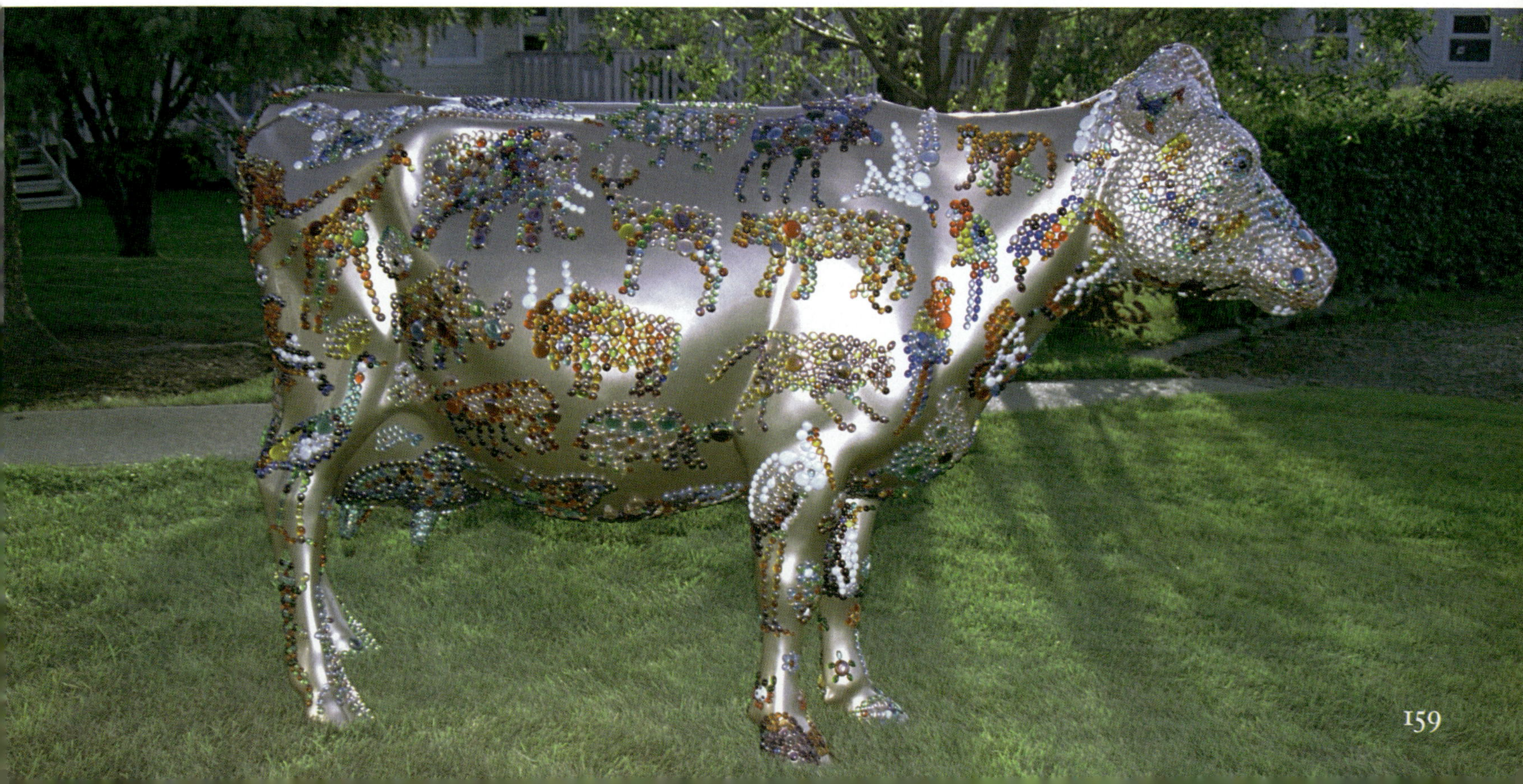

Udderly Art Volunteers

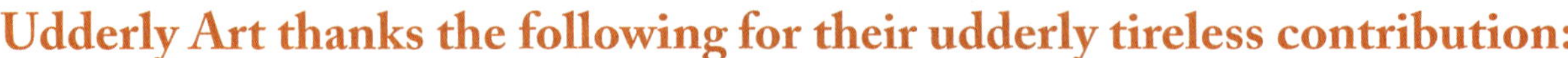

Udderly Art thanks the following for their udderly tireless contribution:

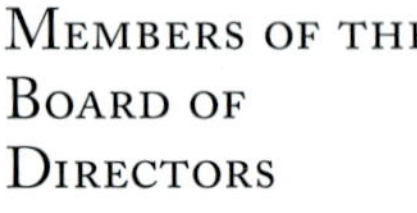

Members of the Board of Directors

Bonnie Laycock
Jim McCartney
Terry Koch
Ann MacDiarmid
Ken Matheson
Jack Perraton
Marcella Szel

Volunteers

Bissett, David
Bissett, Leslie
Boyd, Steve
Brookman, George
Brown, Bob
Brown, Laura
Brown, Nancy
Bury, Anne
Carbury, Joe
Cavill, Pat
Chalack, Dr. David
Chyz, Donna
Clark, Paul
Collins, Peter
Copithorne, Danny
Crawford, Anne
Dinning, Georgia
Fache, Gord
Fehr, Dianne
Gallagher, Ashley
Gebraad, Melissa
Goresht, Sam
Grandan, Donna
Guthrath Siebens, Sharon
Healey, Mary Lynn
Healey, Maureen
Holemans, Dyan
Hughes, Jimmy
Hunt, Judy
Hutchinson, Keesa
Ingles, Claire
Irwin, Will
Jepson, Harold
Kaplar, Clayton
Karr, Avril
Keshavjee, Mo
Kinash, Peter
Koch, Terry
Kuhn, Paul
Laycock, Bonnie
Laycock, Jonathan
Laycock, Keith
MacCaulder, Brenda
MacDiarmid, Ann
Mack, Cam
Marrington, Keith
Mastin, Colleayn
Matheson, Ken
Mayell, Megan
McCartney, Jim
McConnell, Penny
McDonald, Frannie
Napper, Terry
Olecko, Dave
Osler, Jock
Pattillo, Sue
Perraton, Q.C., Jack
Peters, Nancy
Reardon, Jay
Rokosh, Pat
Rose, Alison
Rutherford, Dave
Sanofsky, Pamela
Shapka, Guy
Slade, Don
Smith Angel, Susan
Smith, Hope
Snyder, Cody,
Solvbjerg, Greg
Sparks, Linda
Spencer, Julie
Steen, Jack
Stewart, Don
Strueby, Earl
Szel, Q.C., Marcella
Taylor, Alistair
Timmer, Andrea
Tukkimaki, V.J.
Valentine, Fred
Wagner, Colin
Watts, Linda
Weddell, Peggy
White, Richard
Whitney, Drake
Wiggan, Maryanne
Wissner, Corinne
Wotherspoon, Eileen
Yalholnitsky, Willa
Young, Claire

Ah, yes, I wrote the "Purple Cow"—
I'm sorry, now, I wrote it!
But I can tell you, anyhow,
I'll kill you if you quote it.

Gelett Burgess [1914]